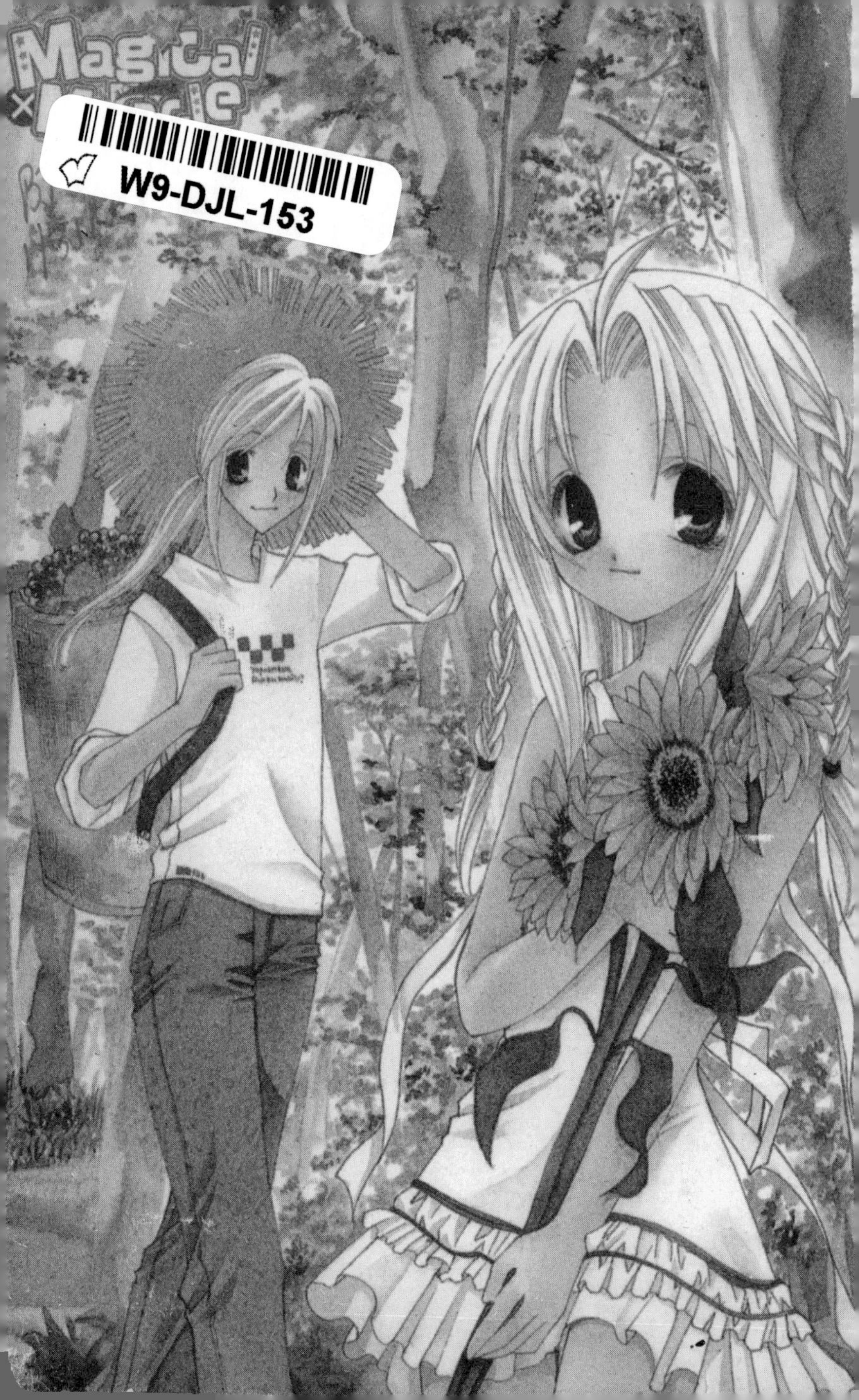
Magical
W9-DJL-153

Welcome!!

CONTENTS

MAGICAL MIRACLE

Magical × Miracle

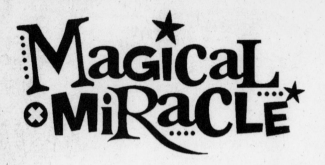

Volume 2

By
Yuzu Mizutani

TOKYOPOP®

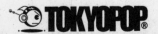

HAMBURG // LONDON // LOS ANGELES // TOKYO

Magical x Miracle Vol.2
Created by Yuzu Mizutani

Translation - Yoohae Yang
English Adaptation - Mark Ilvedson
Associate Editor - Hope Donovan
Retouch and Lettering - Corey Whitfield and Jihye Hong
Production Artist - Fawn Lau
Cover Design - James Lee

Editor - Paul Morrisey
Digital Imaging Manager - Chris Buford
Production Manager - Elisabeth Brizzi
Managing Editor - Sheldon Drzka
VP of Production - Ron Klamert
Editor-in-Chief - Rob Tokar
Publisher - Mike Kiley
President and C.O.O. - John Parker
C.E.O. and Chief Creative Officer - Stuart Levy

A  Manga

TOKYOPOP Inc.
5900 Wilshire Blvd. Suite 2000
Los Angeles, CA 90036

E-mail: info@TOKYOPOP.com
Come visit us online at www.TOKYOPOP.com

ISBN: 1-59816-329-9

First TOKYOPOP printing: August 2006
10 9 8 7 6 5 4 3 2 1
Printed in the USA

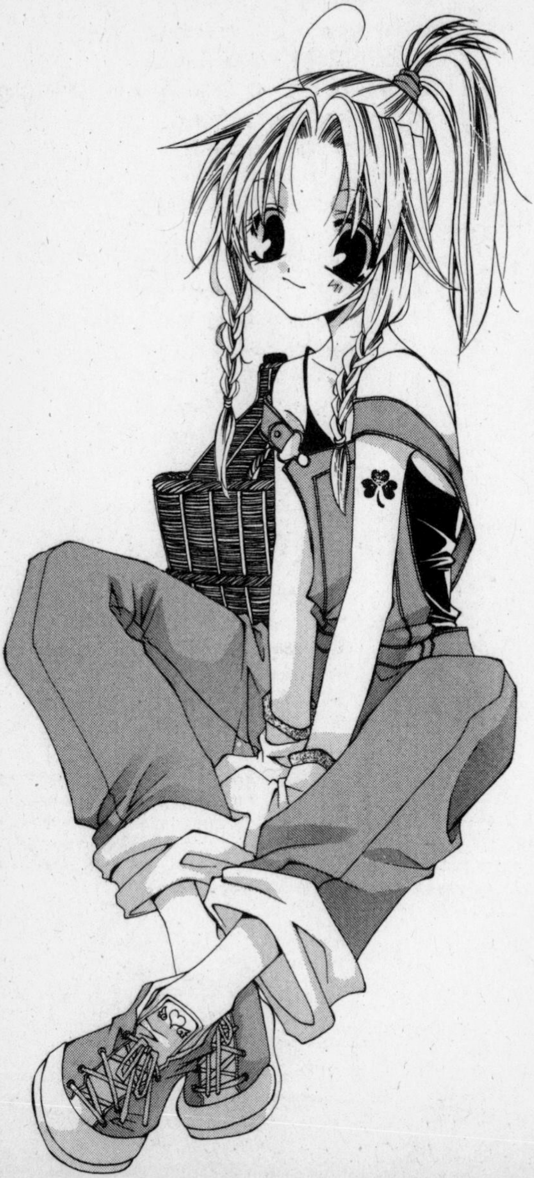

Story So Far...

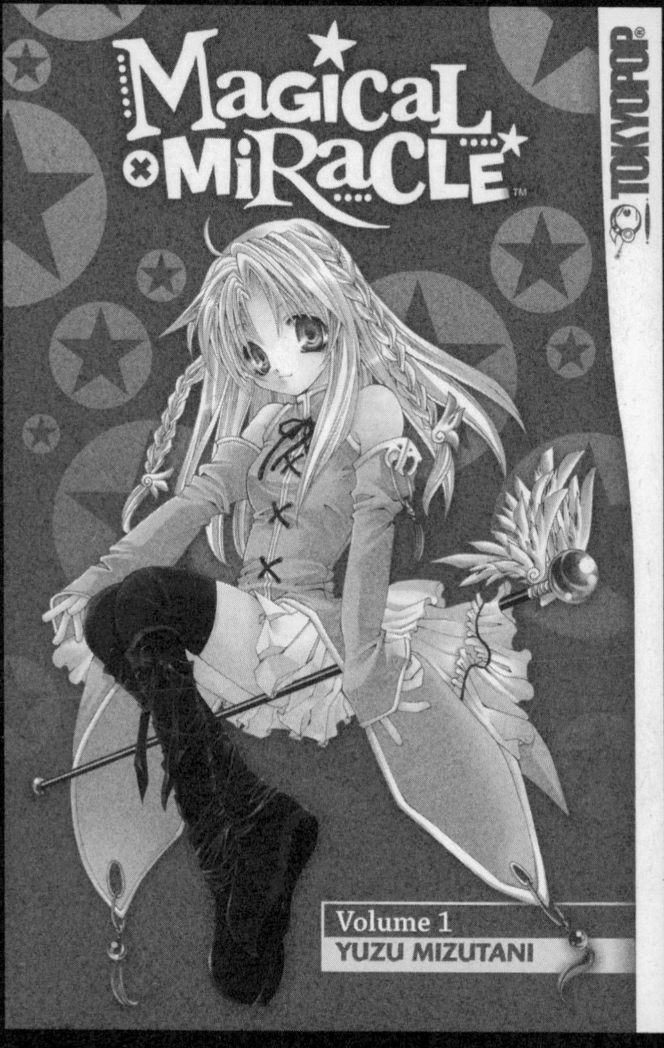
MAGICAL MIRACLE
TOKYOPOP
Volume 1
YUZU MIZUTANI

IT'S A TALE OF MAGIC, MYSTERY, AND MISTAKEN IDENTITY! MERLEAWE HAS JUST ARRIVED IN VIEGALD, WHERE SHE HOPES TO STUDY MAGIC AT ONE OF THE BEST SCHOOLS IN THE KINGDOM. BUT SHORTLY AFTER SHE ARRIVES, THE GREAT MAGICIAN SYLTHFARN--THE MASTER WIZARD OF VIEGALD--GOES MISSING. WITH PANIC SETTING IN AND A COUNTRY IN NEED, THE FOLLOWERS OF SYLTHFARN DISCOVER THAT MERLEAWE LOOKS REMARKABLY LIKE THE GREAT MAGICIAN. WITH THE RIGHT TRAINING AND GUIDANCE, SHE JUST MIGHT PASS AS SYLTHFARN. BUT IS MERLEAWE "MAN" ENOUGH TO BRING PEACE TO THE KINGDOM?

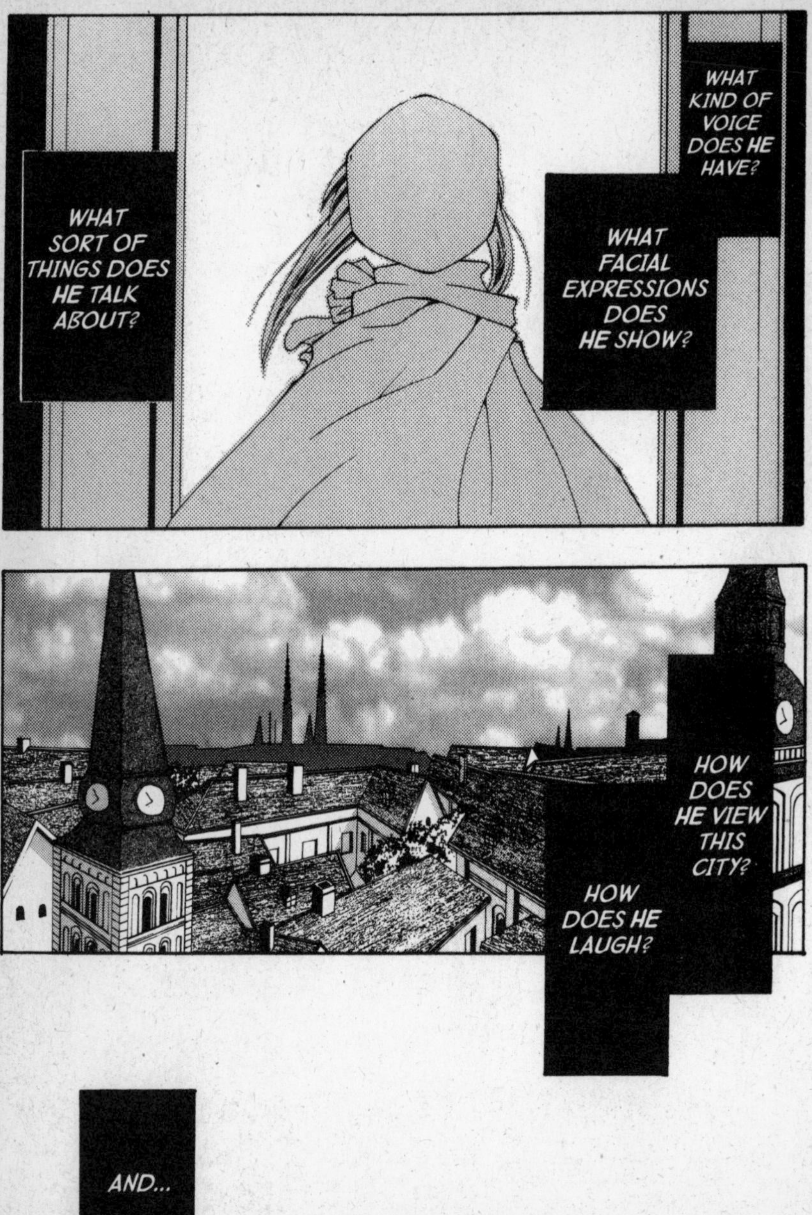
WHAT KIND OF VOICE DOES HE HAVE?
WHAT FACIAL EXPRESSIONS DOES HE SHOW?
WHAT SORT OF THINGS DOES HE TALK ABOUT?
HOW DOES HE VIEW THIS CITY?
HOW DOES HE LAUGH?
AND...

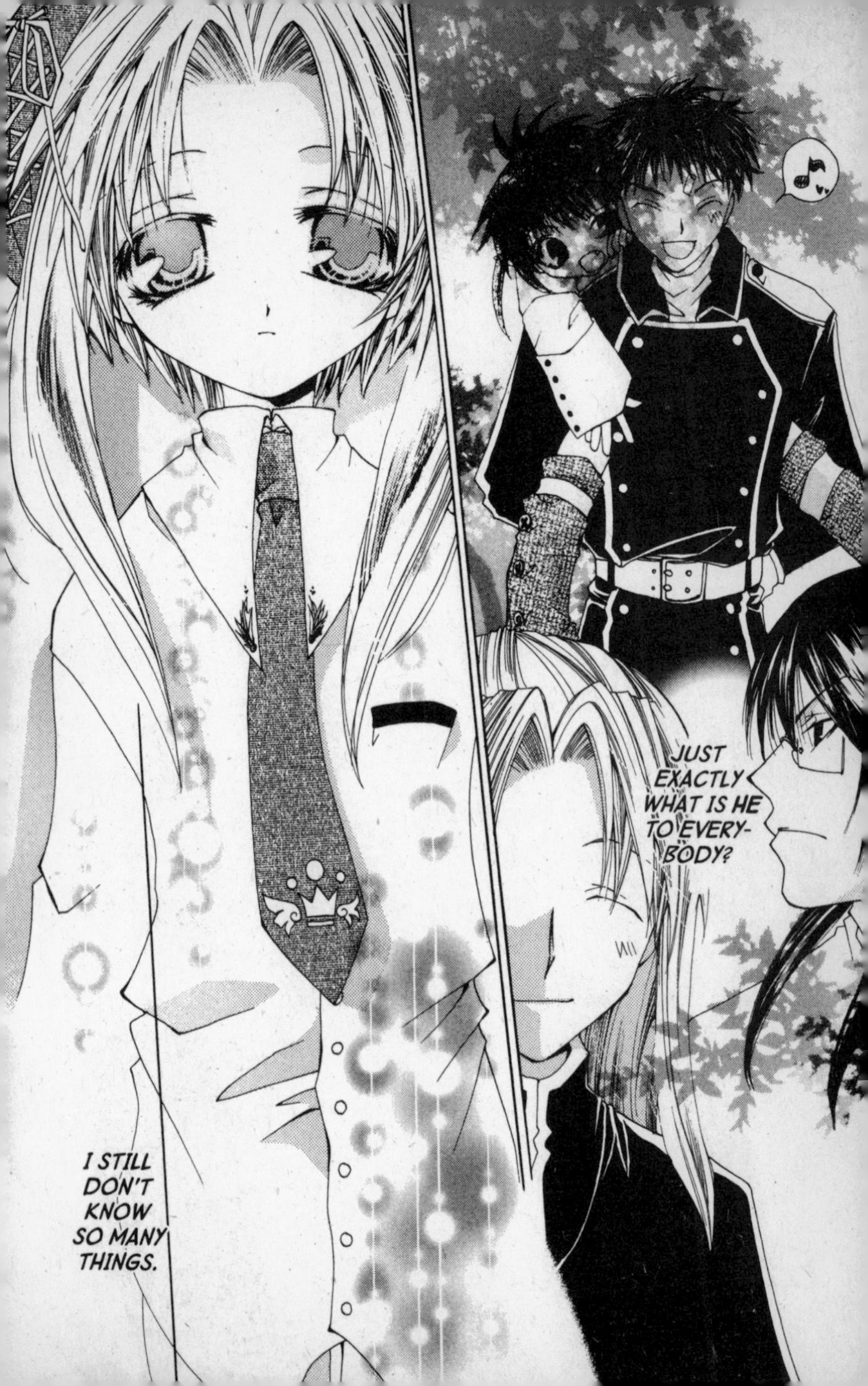
JUST EXACTLY WHAT IS HE TO EVERY-BODY?
I STILL DON'T KNOW SO MANY THINGS.

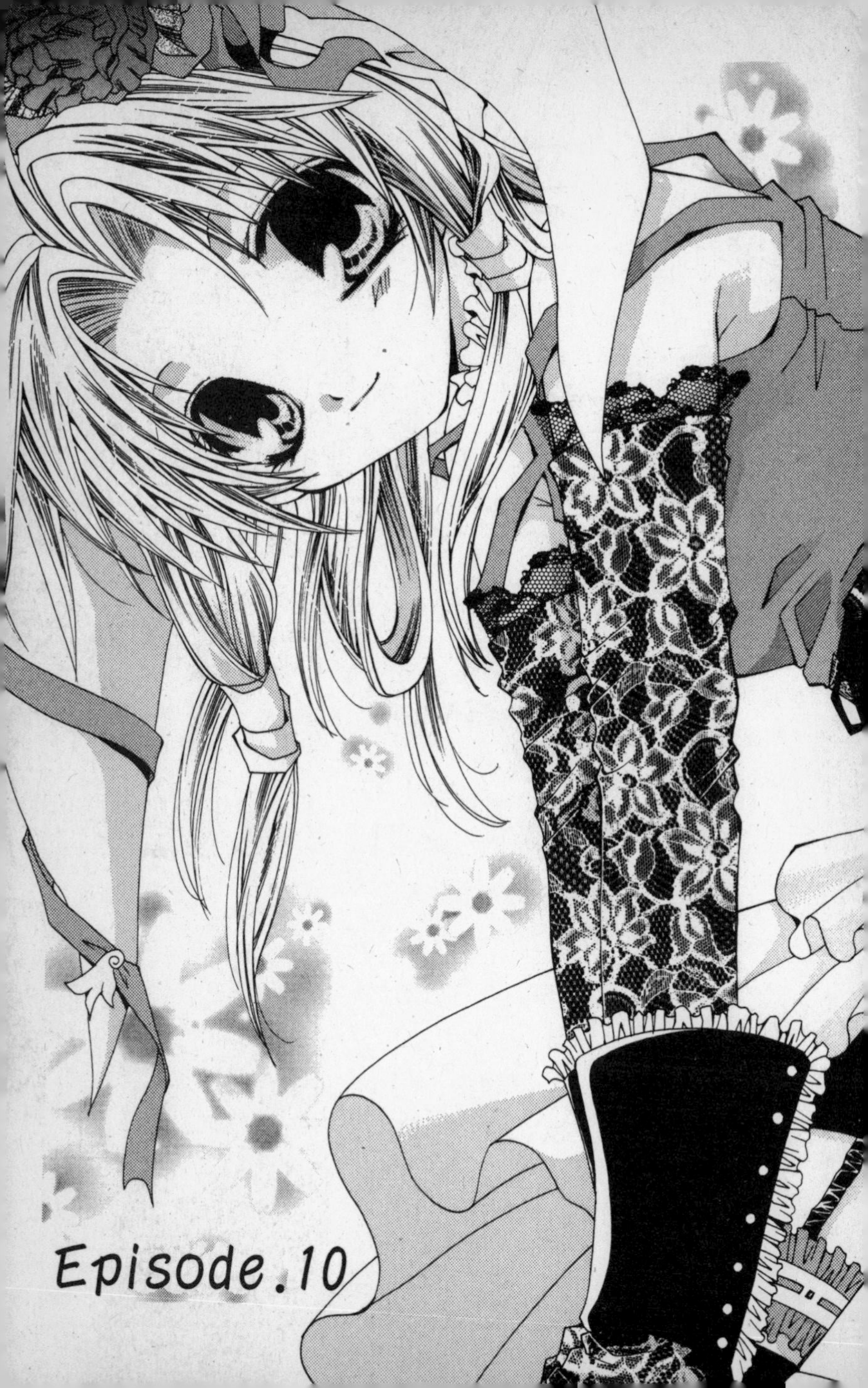
Episode.10

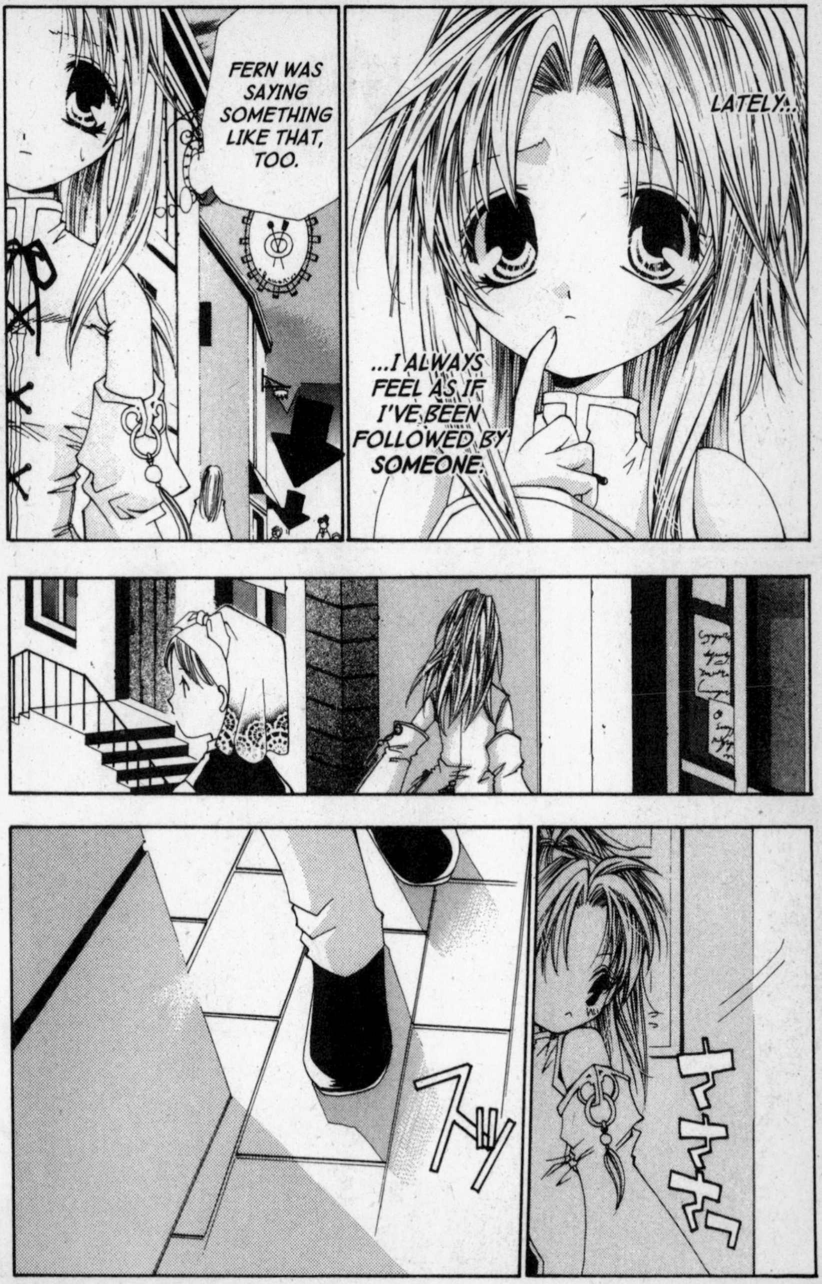
LATELY...
...I ALWAYS FEEL AS IF I'VE BEEN FOLLOWED BY SOMEONE.
FERN WAS SAYING SOMETHING LIKE THAT, TOO.

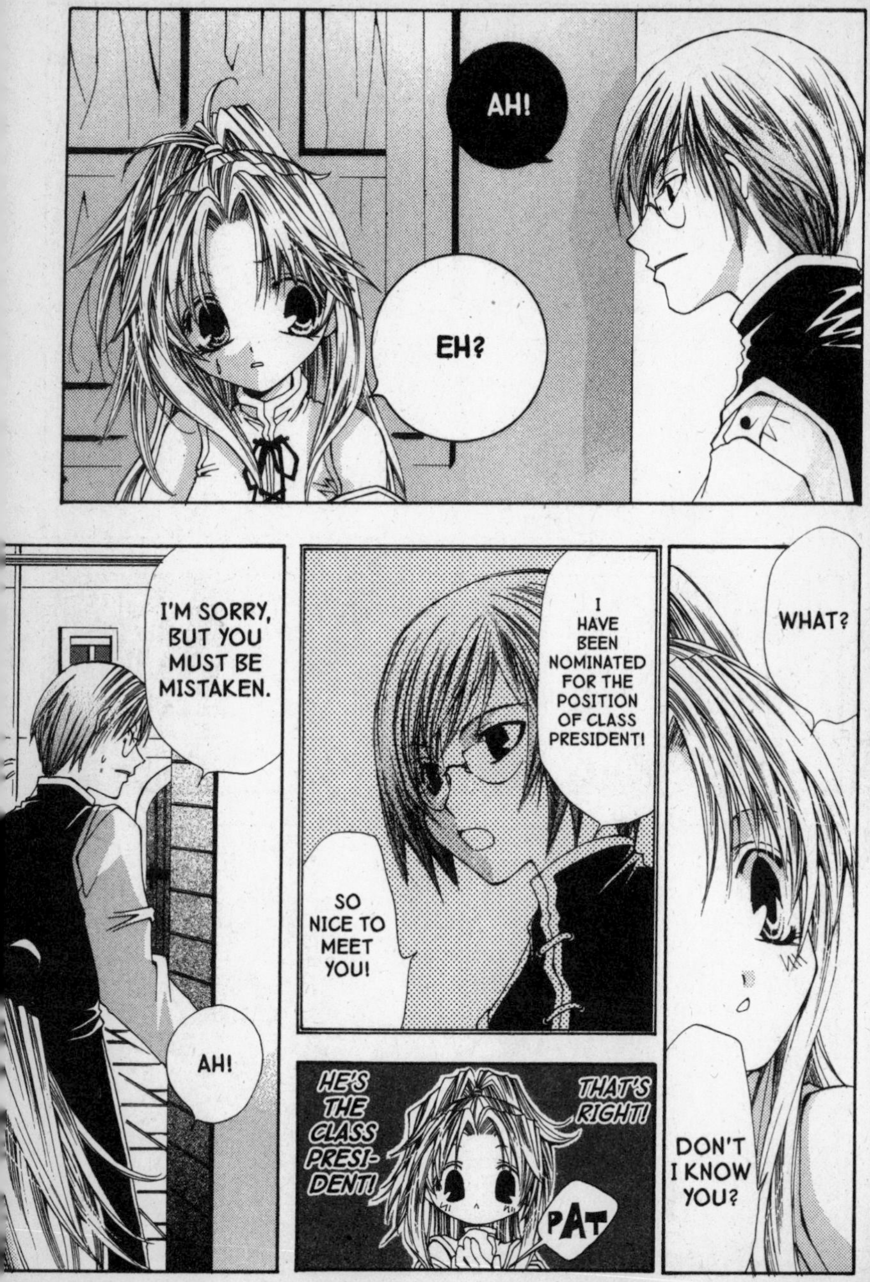
AH!
EH?
WHAT?
DON'T I KNOW YOU?
I HAVE BEEN NOMINATED FOR THE POSITION OF CLASS PRESIDENT!
SO NICE TO MEET YOU!
THAT'S RIGHT!
HE'S THE CLASS PRESI-DENT!
PAT
I'M SORRY, BUT YOU MUST BE MISTAKEN.
AH!

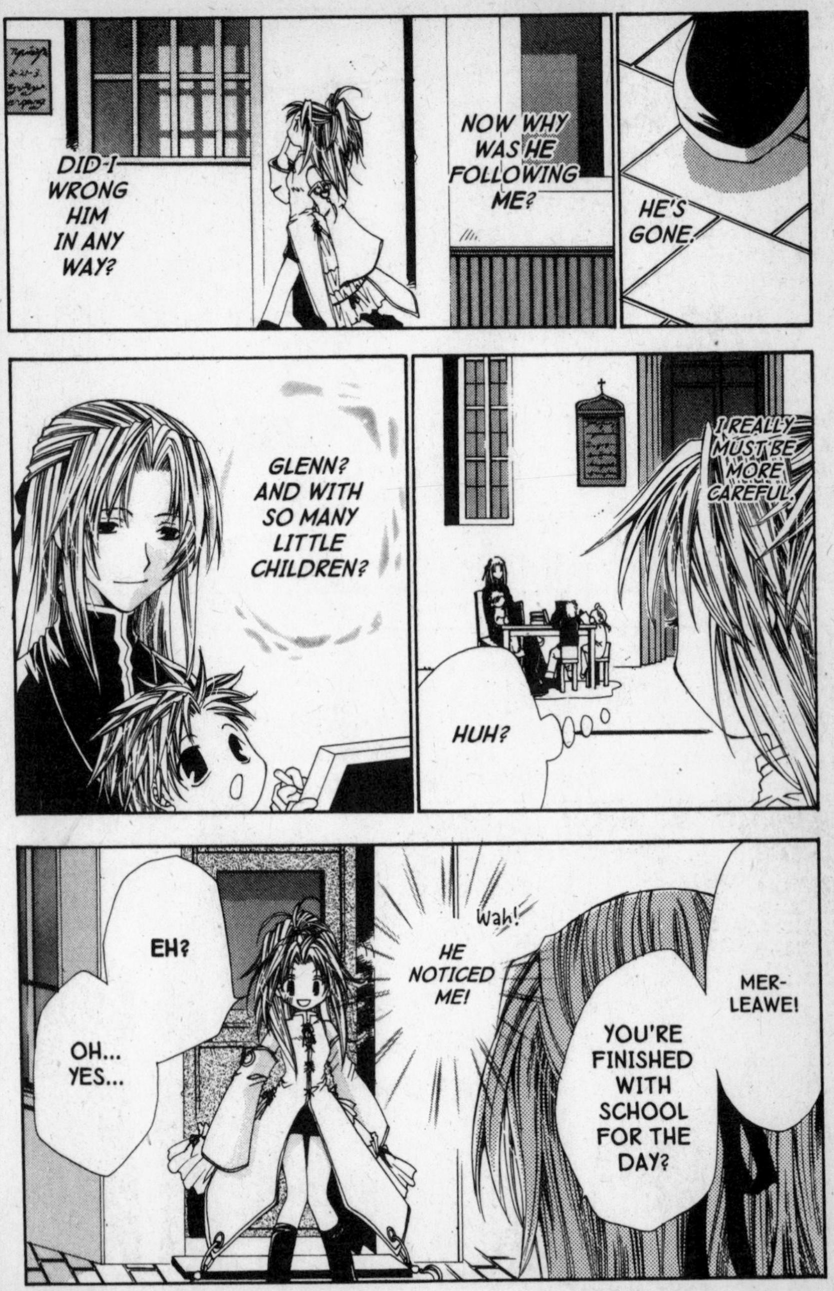
HE'S GONE.
NOW WHY WAS HE FOLLOWING ME?
DID I WRONG HIM IN ANY WAY?
I REALLY MUST BE MORE CAREFUL.
HUH?
GLENN? AND WITH SO MANY LITTLE CHILDREN?
MER-LEAWE!
YOU'RE FINISHED WITH SCHOOL FOR THE DAY?
Wah!
HE NOTICED ME!
EH?
OH... YES...

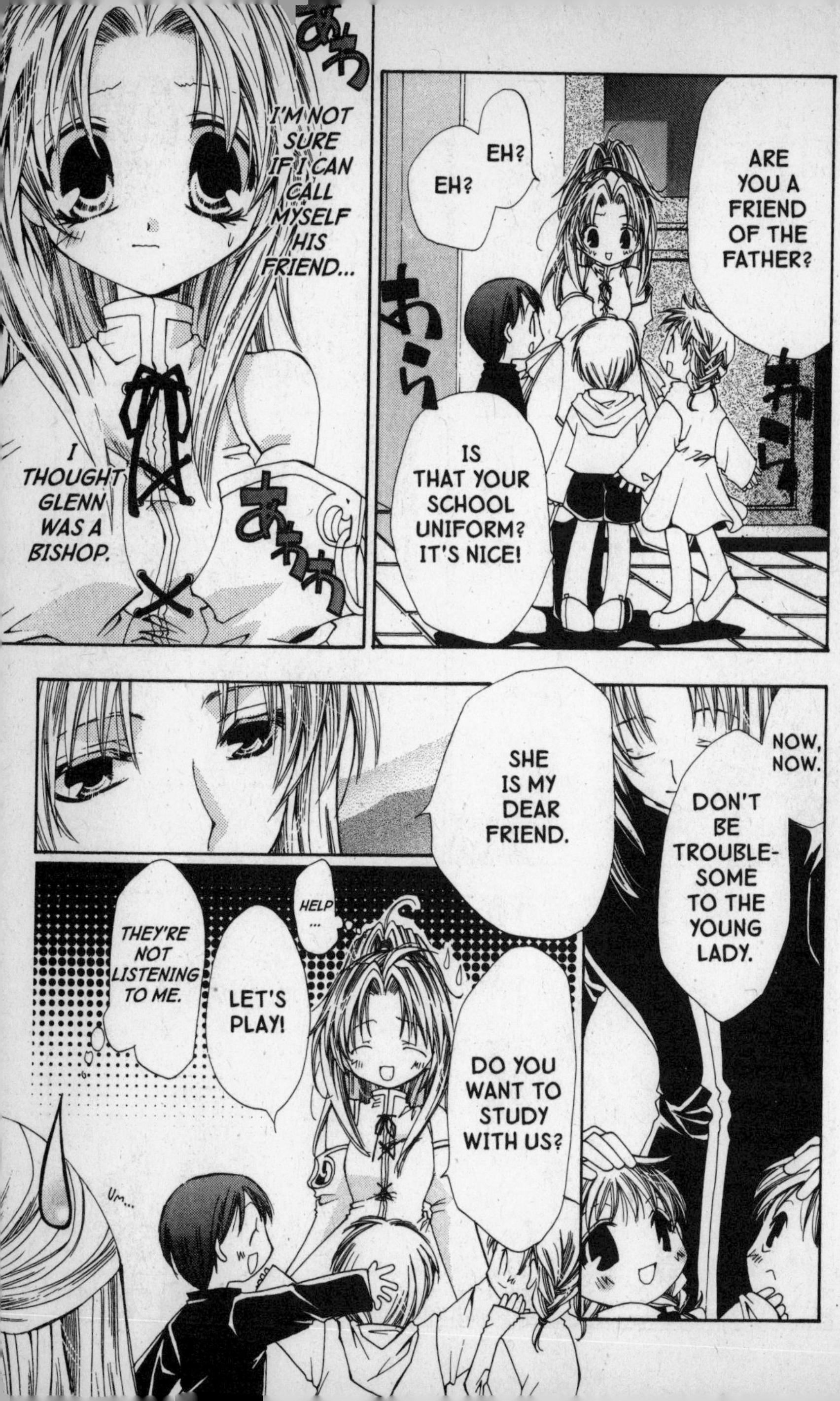

ARE YOU A FRIEND OF THE FATHER?
あら
EH?
EH?
あら
IS THAT YOUR SCHOOL UNIFORM? IT'S NICE!
あわ
I'M NOT SURE IF I CAN CALL MYSELF HIS FRIEND...
あわわ
I THOUGHT GLENN WAS A BISHOP.
NOW, NOW.
DON'T BE TROUBLESOME TO THE YOUNG LADY.
SHE IS MY DEAR FRIEND.
DO YOU WANT TO STUDY WITH US?
HELP...
LET'S PLAY!
THEY'RE NOT LISTENING TO ME.
UM...

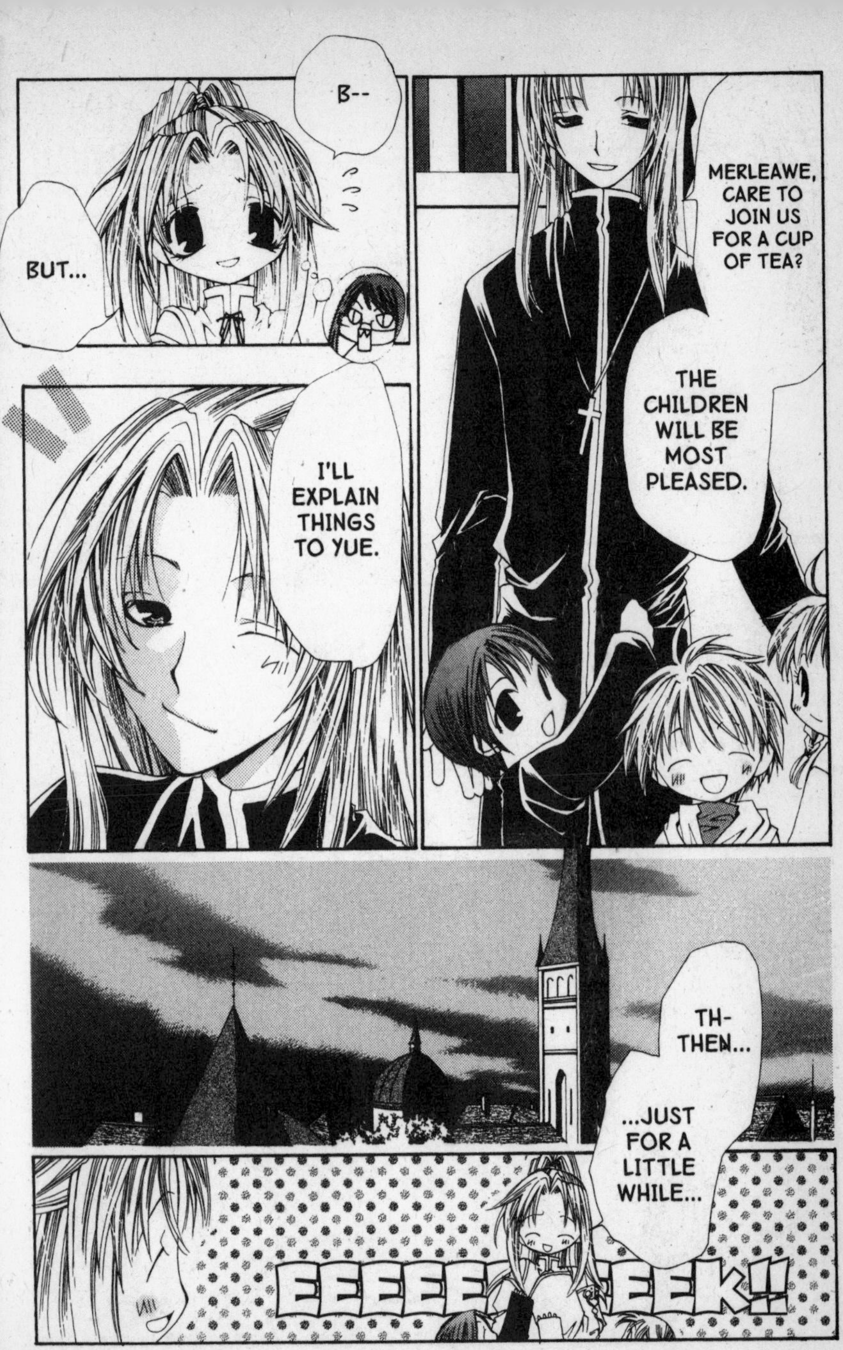
MERLEAWE, CARE TO JOIN US FOR A CUP OF TEA?
THE CHILDREN WILL BE MOST PLEASED.
B--
BUT...
I'LL EXPLAIN THINGS TO YUE.
TH- THEN...
...JUST FOR A LITTLE WHILE...
EEEEE EEEK!!

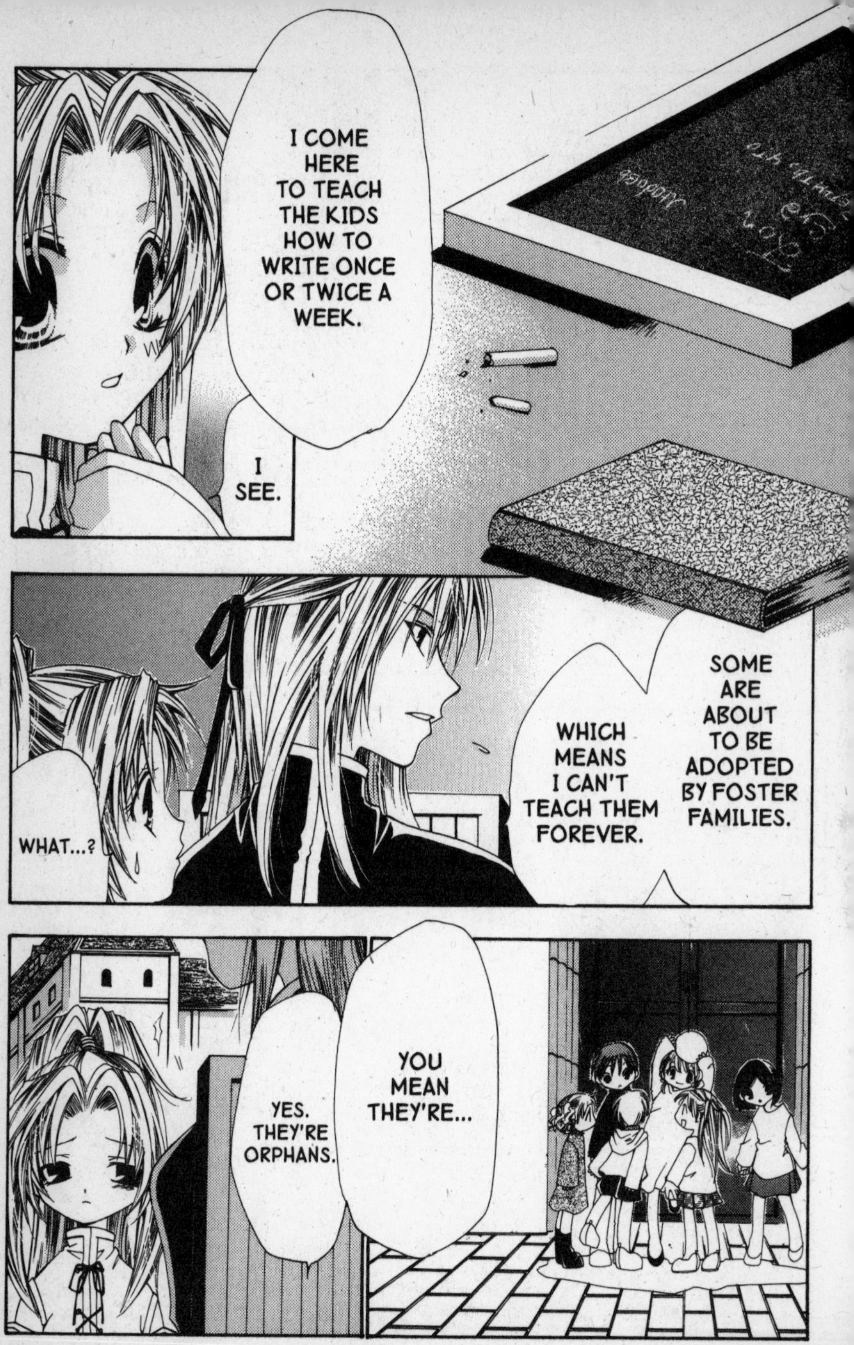

I COME HERE TO TEACH THE KIDS HOW TO WRITE ONCE OR TWICE A WEEK.
I SEE.
SOME ARE ABOUT TO BE ADOPTED BY FOSTER FAMILIES.
WHICH MEANS I CAN'T TEACH THEM FOREVER.
WHAT...?
YOU MEAN THEY'RE...
YES. THEY'RE ORPHANS.

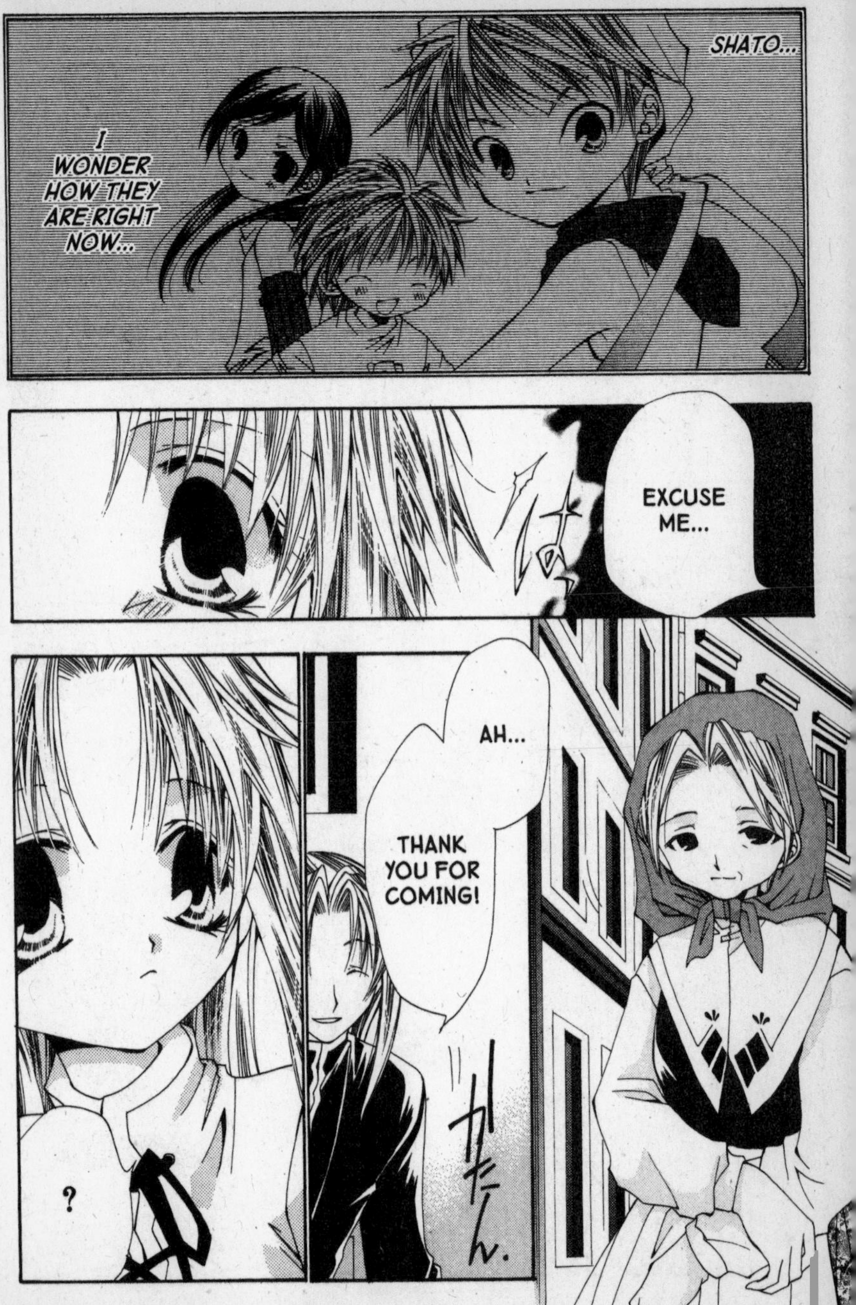
SHATO...
I WONDER HOW THEY ARE RIGHT NOW...
EXCUSE ME...
AH...
THANK YOU FOR COMING!
?

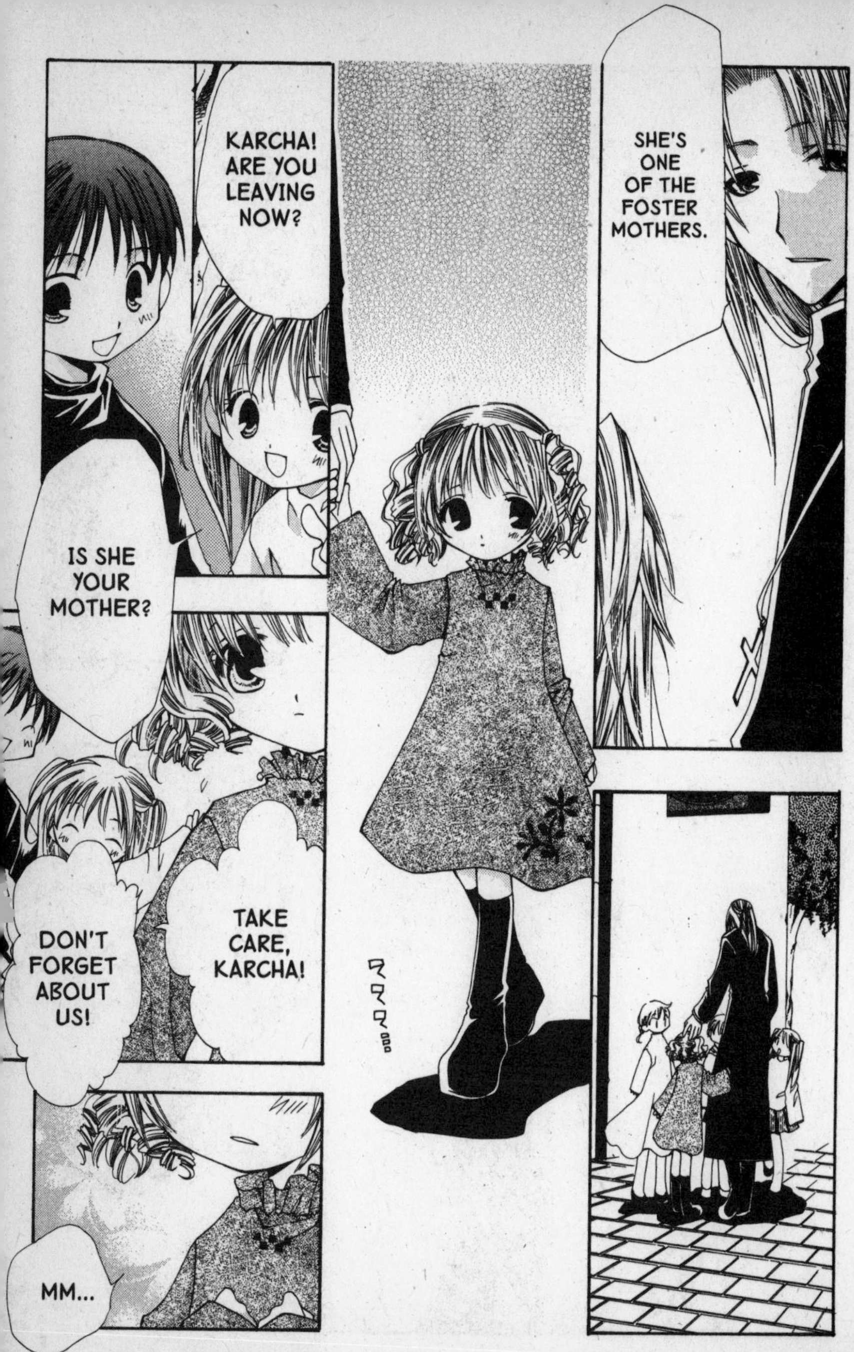

SHE'S ONE OF THE FOSTER MOTHERS.
KARCHA! ARE YOU LEAVING NOW?
IS SHE YOUR MOTHER?
TAKE CARE, KARCHA!
DON'T FORGET ABOUT US!
MM...

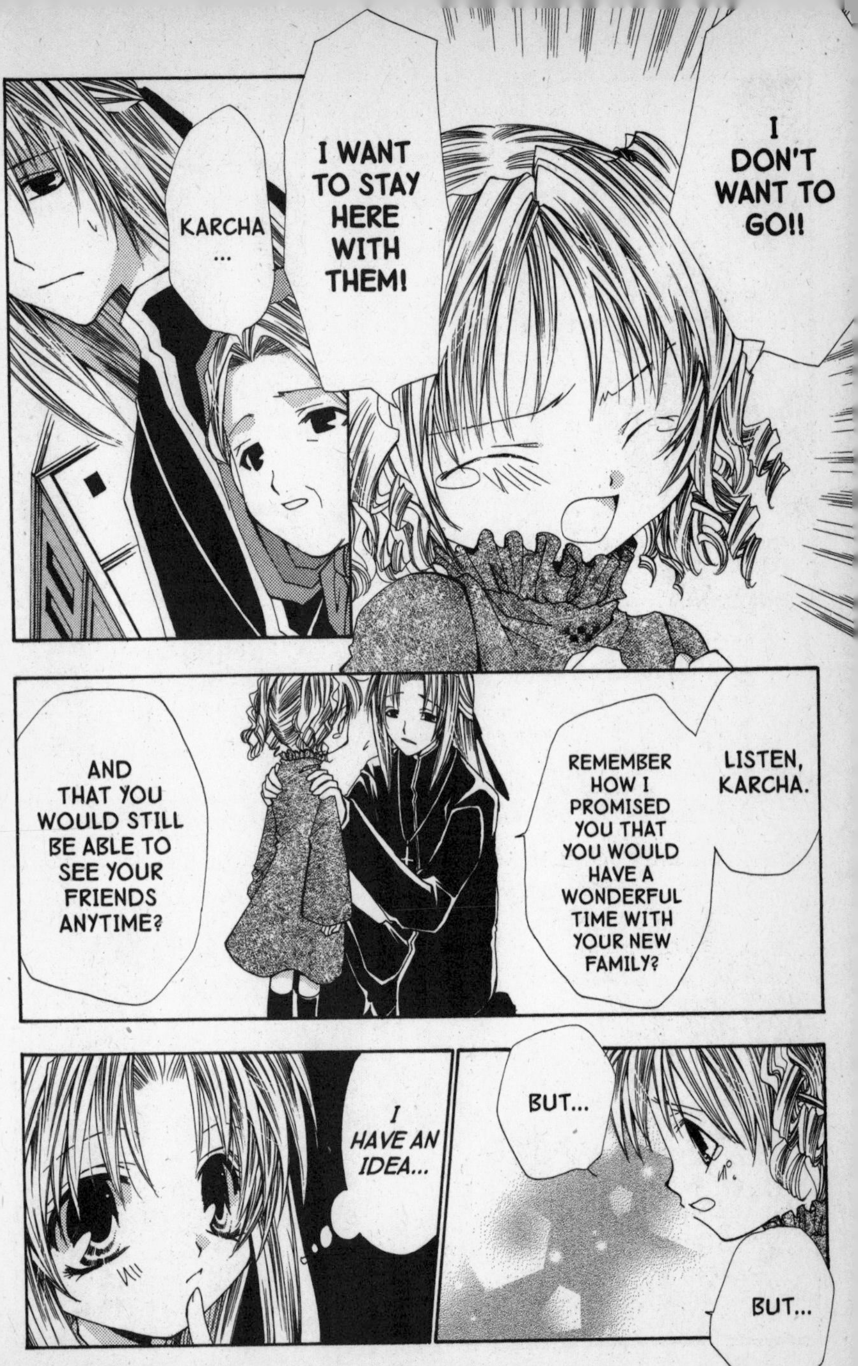
I DON'T WANT TO GO!!
I WANT TO STAY HERE WITH THEM!
KARCHA ...
LISTEN, KARCHA.
REMEMBER HOW I PROMISED YOU THAT YOU WOULD HAVE A WONDERFUL TIME WITH YOUR NEW FAMILY?
AND THAT YOU WOULD STILL BE ABLE TO SEE YOUR FRIENDS ANYTIME?
BUT...
BUT...
I HAVE AN IDEA...

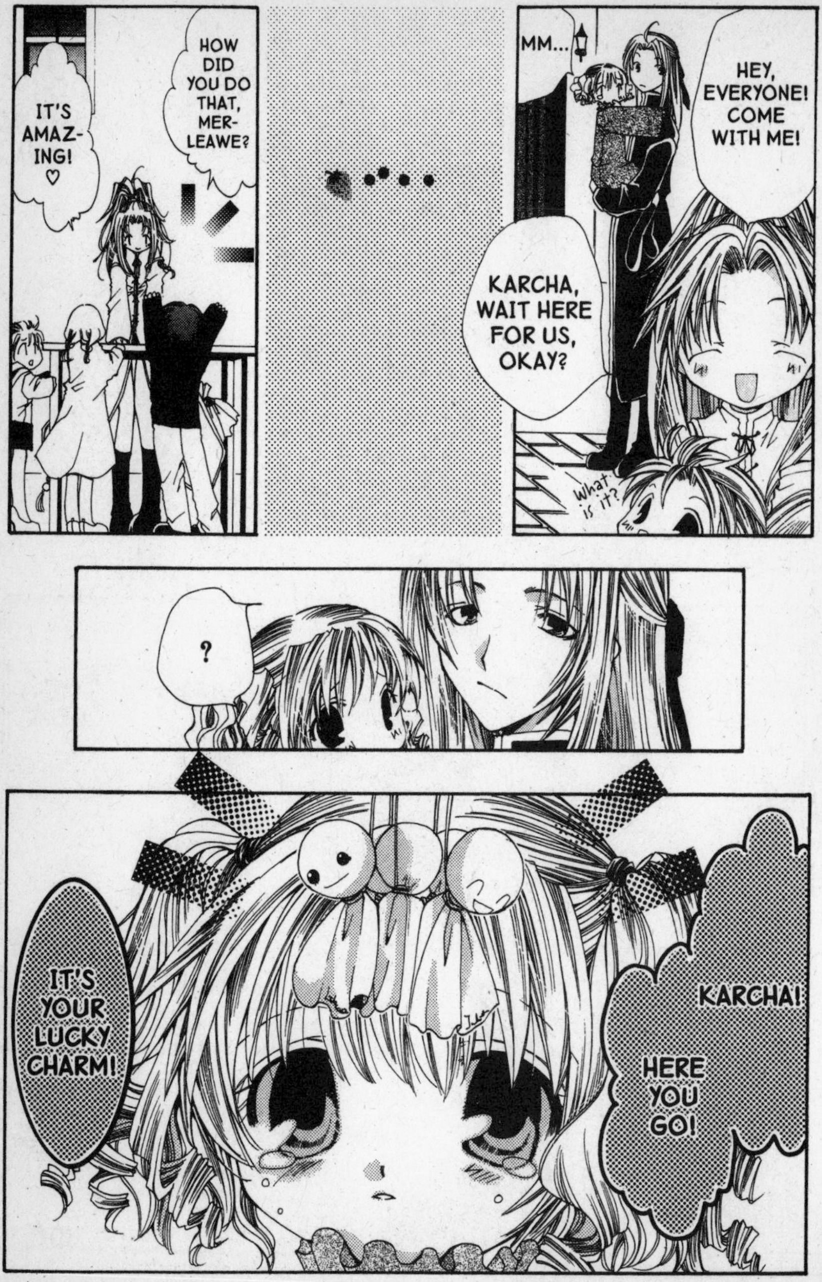
HEY, EVERYONE! COME WITH ME!
MM...
KARCHA, WAIT HERE FOR US, OKAY?
What is it?
....
HOW DID YOU DO THAT, MER-LEAWE?
IT'S AMAZ-ING! ♡
?
KARCHA!
HERE YOU GO!
IT'S YOUR LUCKY CHARM!

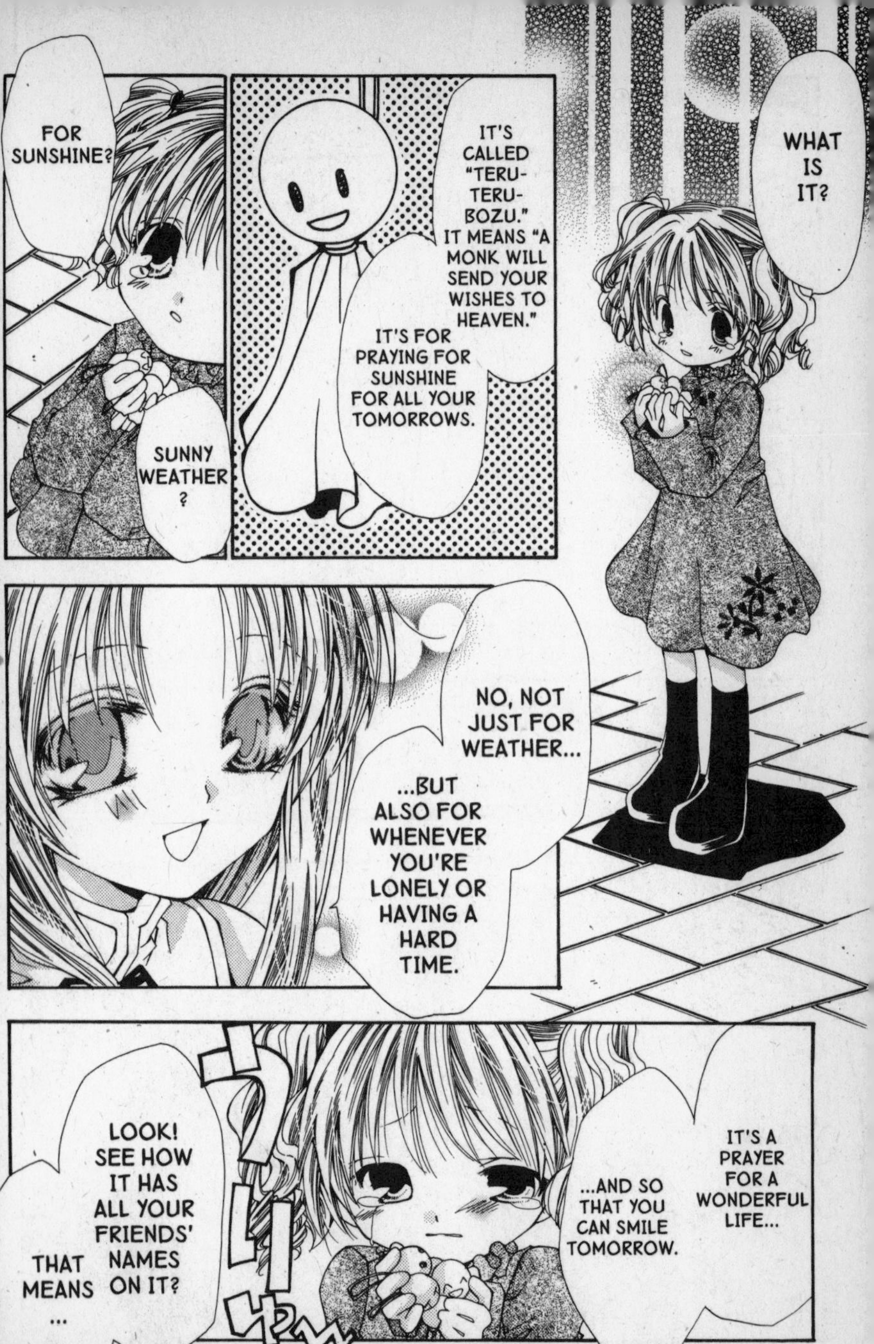
WHAT IS IT?
IT'S CALLED "TERU-TERU-BOZU." IT MEANS "A MONK WILL SEND YOUR WISHES TO HEAVEN."
IT'S FOR PRAYING FOR SUNSHINE FOR ALL YOUR TOMORROWS.
FOR SUNSHINE?
SUNNY WEATHER ?
NO, NOT JUST FOR WEATHER...
...BUT ALSO FOR WHENEVER YOU'RE LONELY OR HAVING A HARD TIME.
IT'S A PRAYER FOR A WONDERFUL LIFE...
...AND SO THAT YOU CAN SMILE TOMORROW.
LOOK! SEE HOW IT HAS ALL YOUR FRIENDS' NAMES ON IT?
THAT MEANS ...

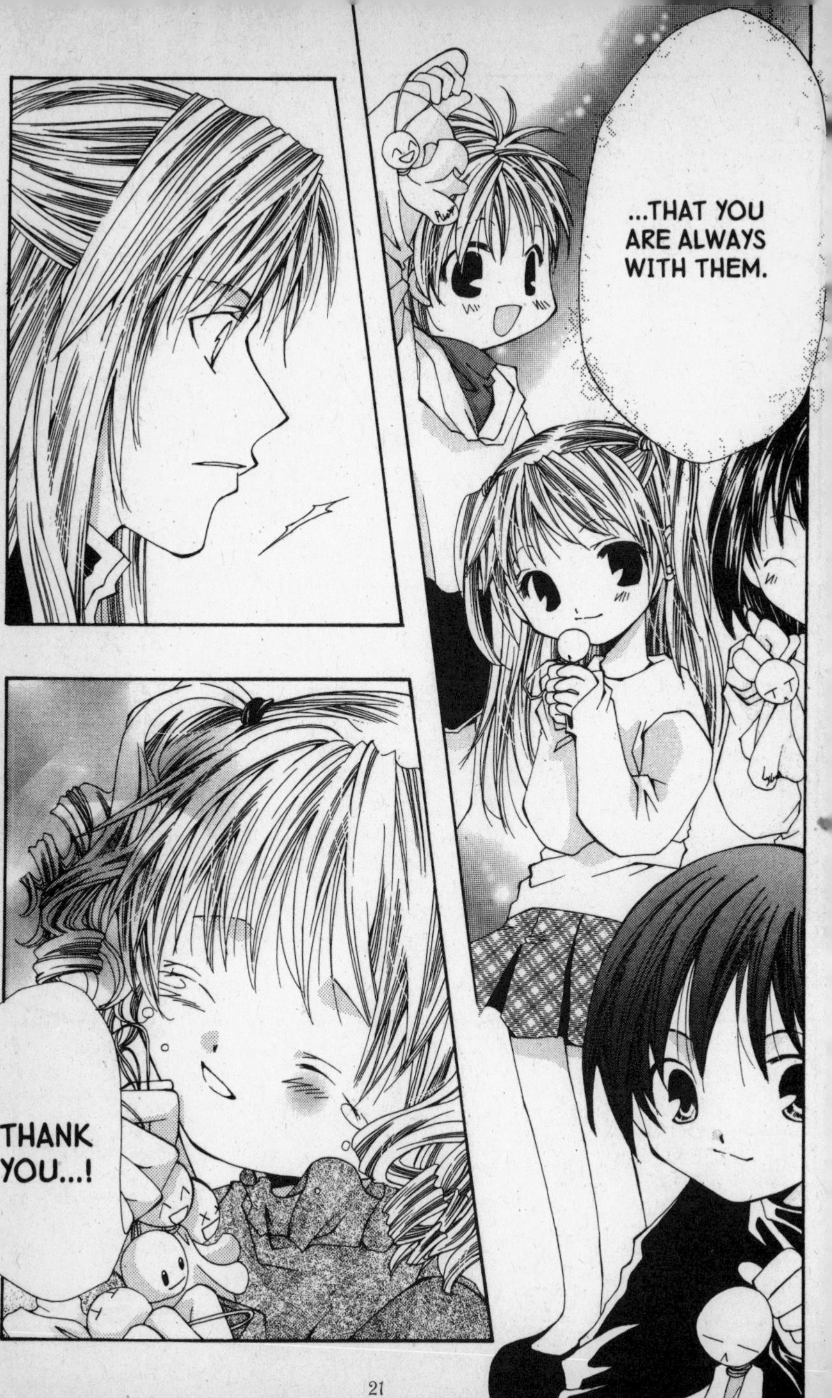
...THAT YOU ARE ALWAYS WITH THEM.
THANK YOU...!

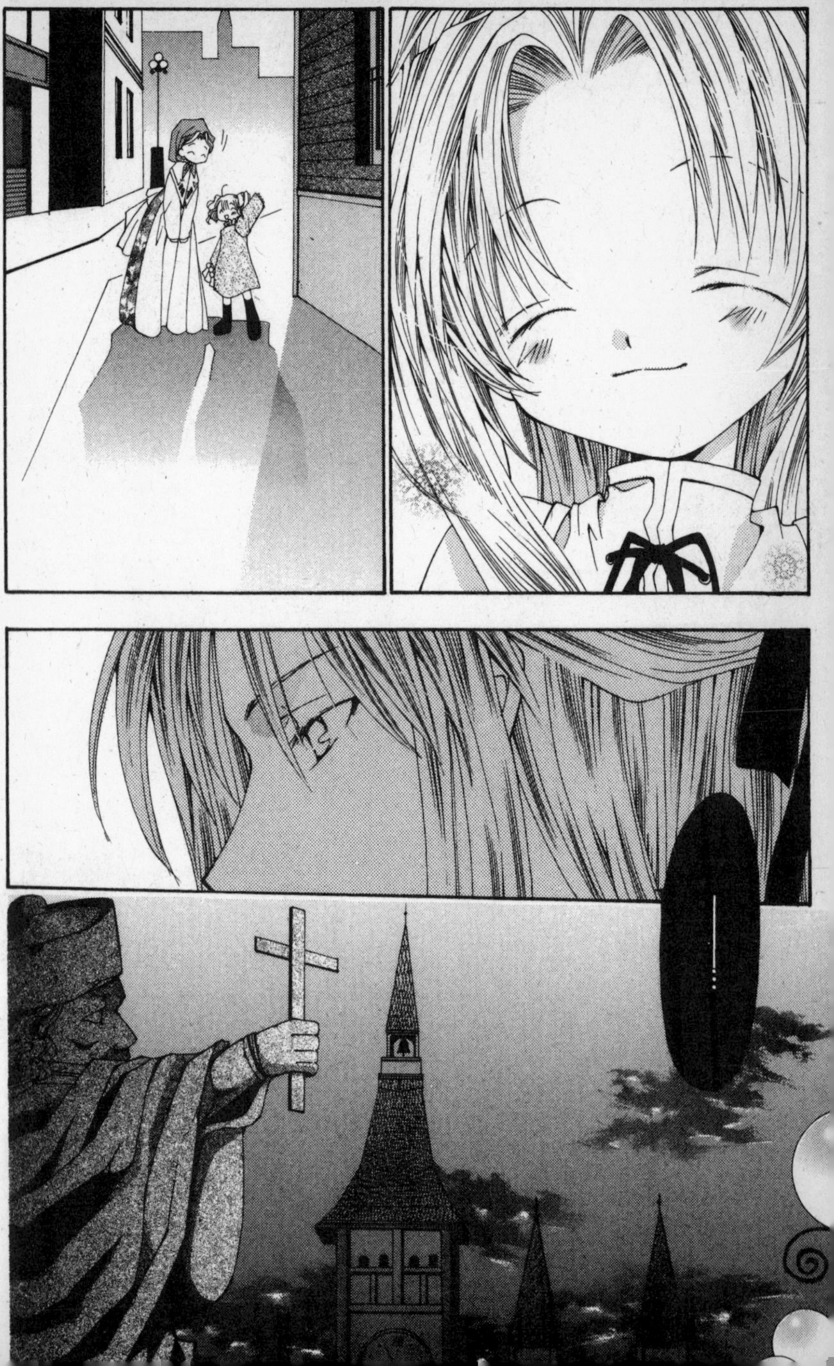
……

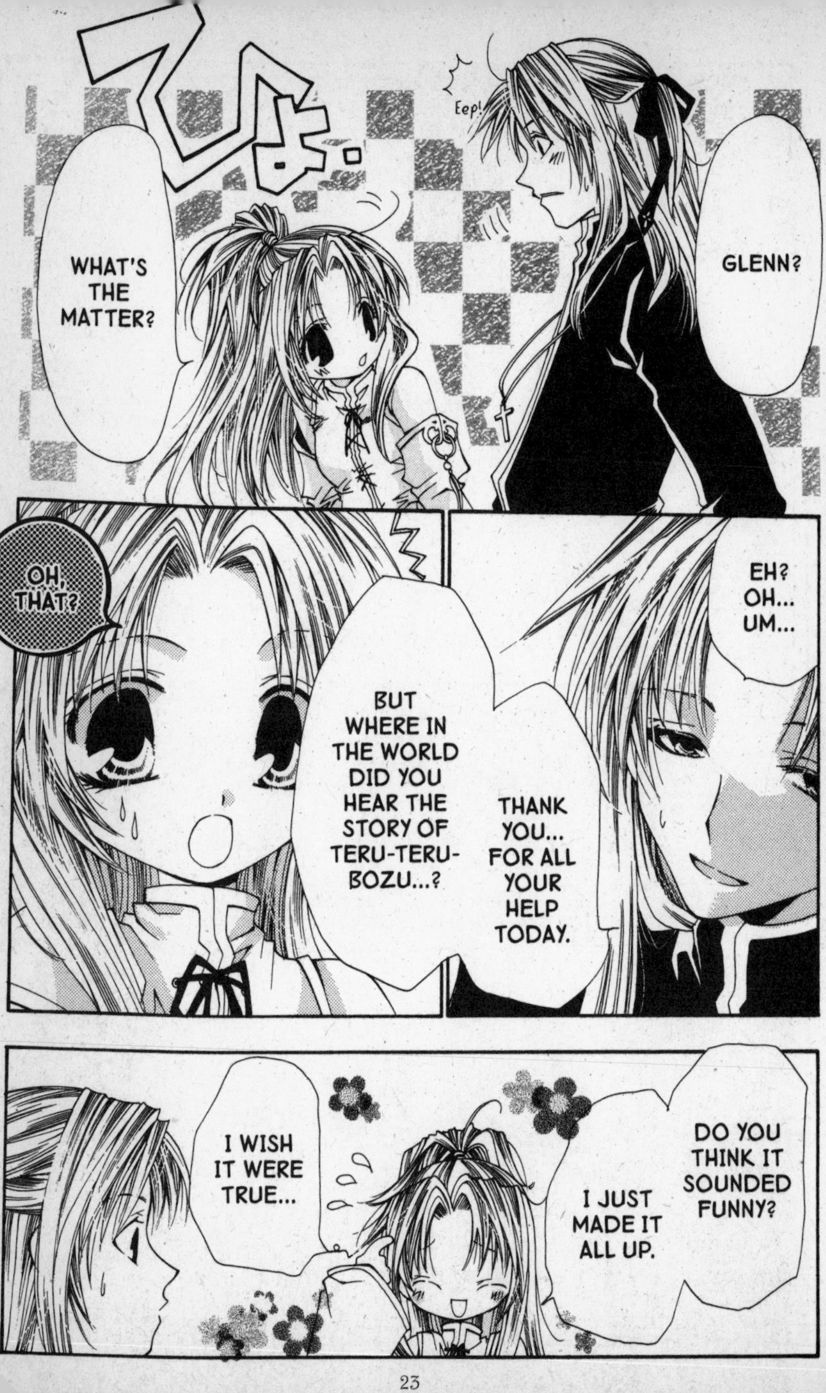
GLENN?
Eep!
WHAT'S THE MATTER?
EH? OH... UM...
THANK YOU... FOR ALL YOUR HELP TODAY.
BUT WHERE IN THE WORLD DID YOU HEAR THE STORY OF TERU-TERU-BOZU...?
OH, THAT?
DO YOU THINK IT SOUNDED FUNNY?
I JUST MADE IT ALL UP.
I WISH IT WERE TRUE...

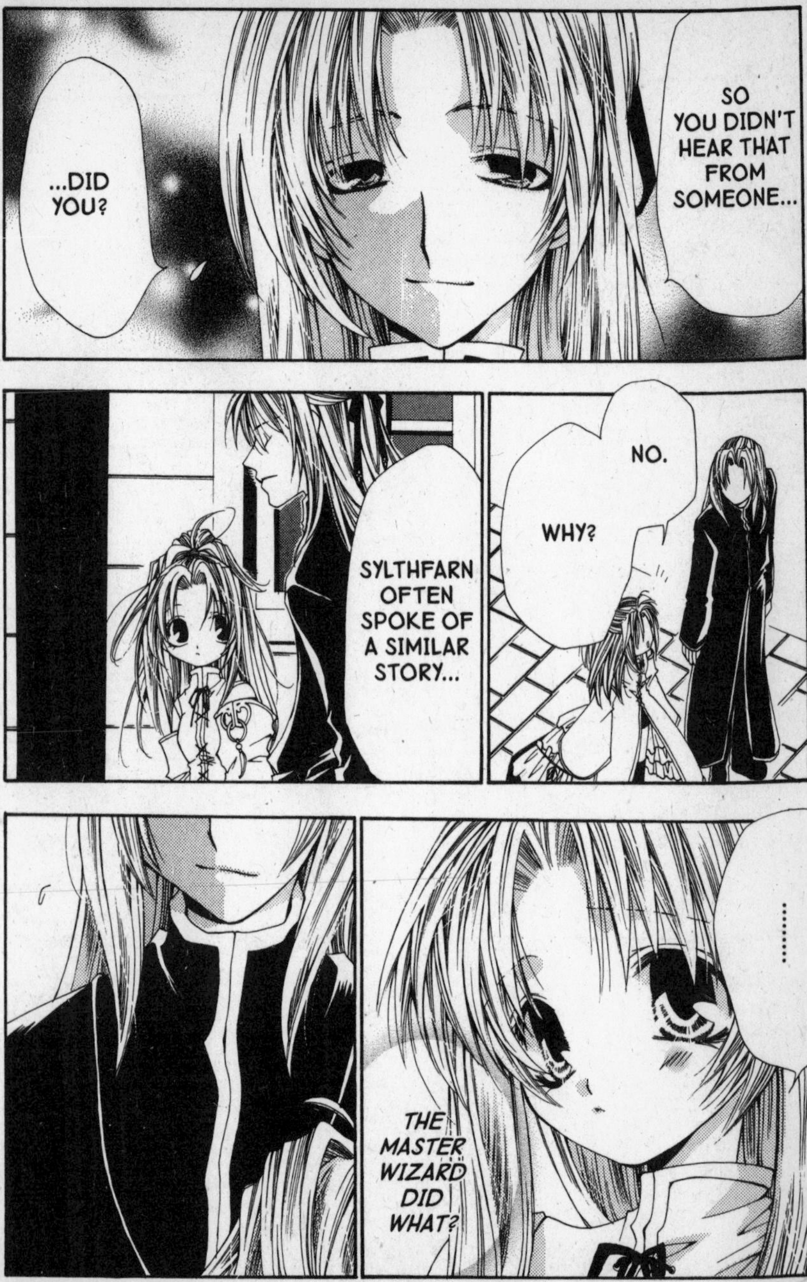
SO YOU DIDN'T HEAR THAT FROM SOMEONE...
...DID YOU?
NO.
WHY?
SYLTHFARN OFTEN SPOKE OF A SIMILAR STORY...
......
THE MASTER WIZARD DID WHAT?

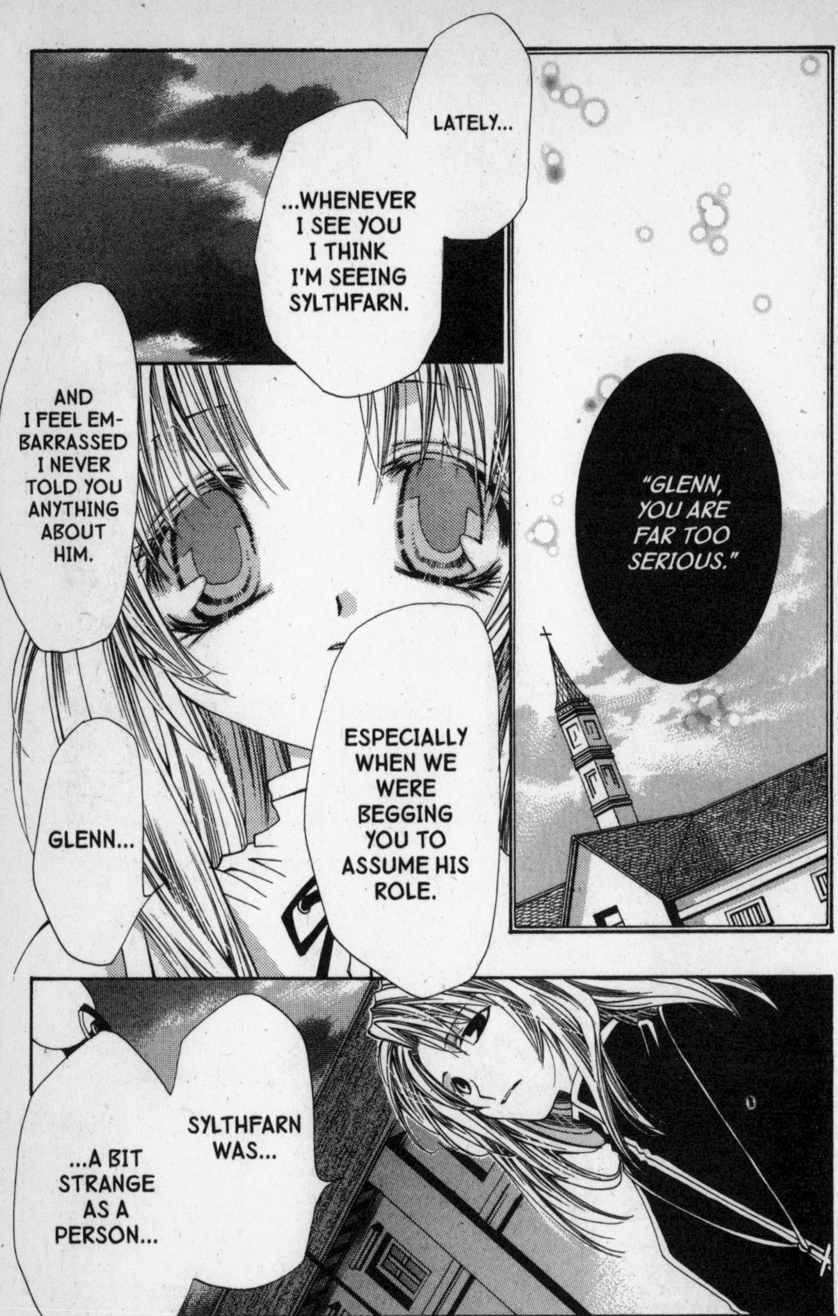
"GLENN, YOU ARE FAR TOO SERIOUS."
LATELY...
...WHENEVER I SEE YOU I THINK I'M SEEING SYLTHFARN.
AND I FEEL EM-BARRASSED I NEVER TOLD YOU ANYTHING ABOUT HIM.
ESPECIALLY WHEN WE WERE BEGGING YOU TO ASSUME HIS ROLE.
GLENN...
SYLTHFARN WAS...
...A BIT STRANGE AS A PERSON...

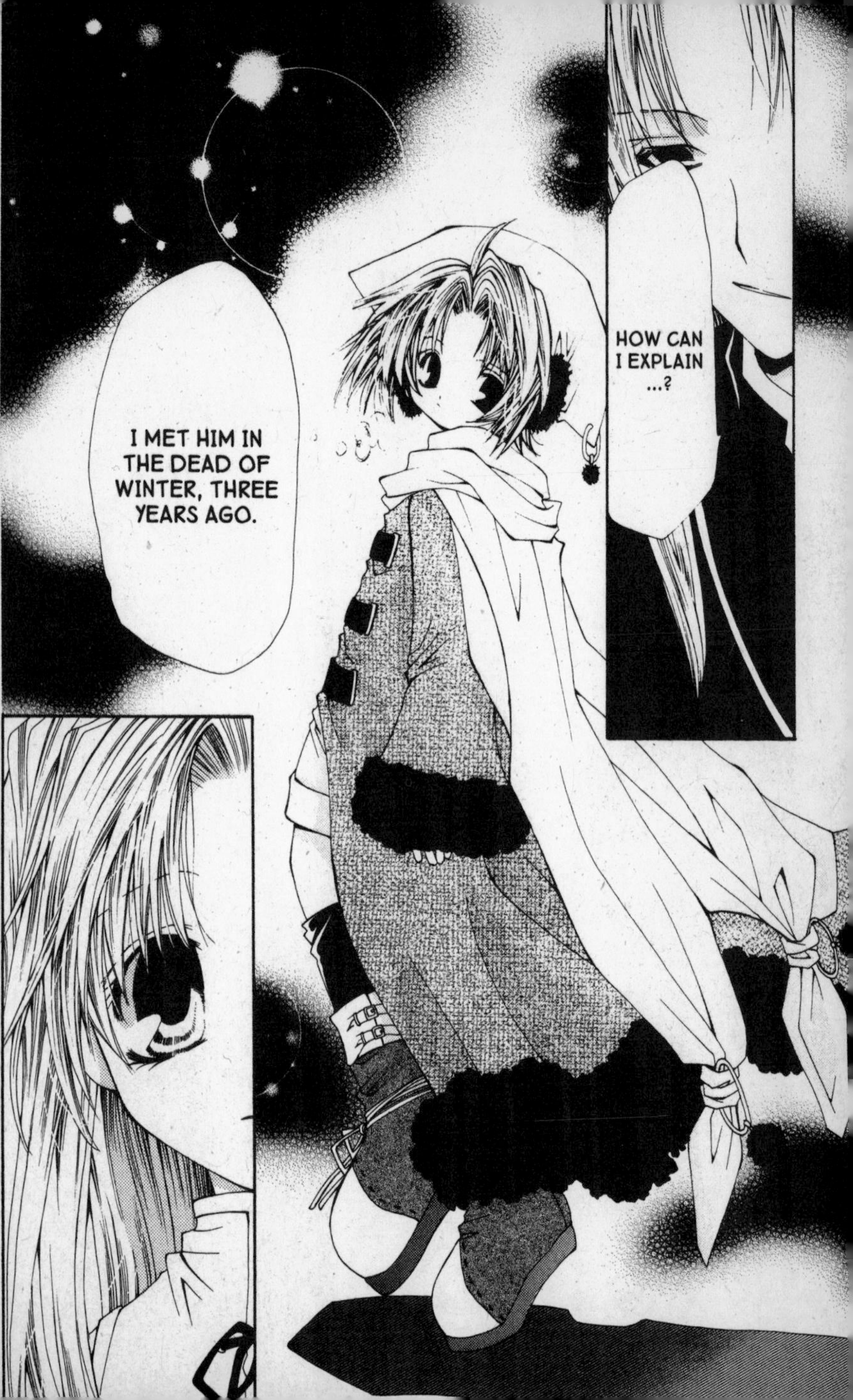
HOW CAN I EXPLAIN ...?
I MET HIM IN THE DEAD OF WINTER, THREE YEARS AGO.

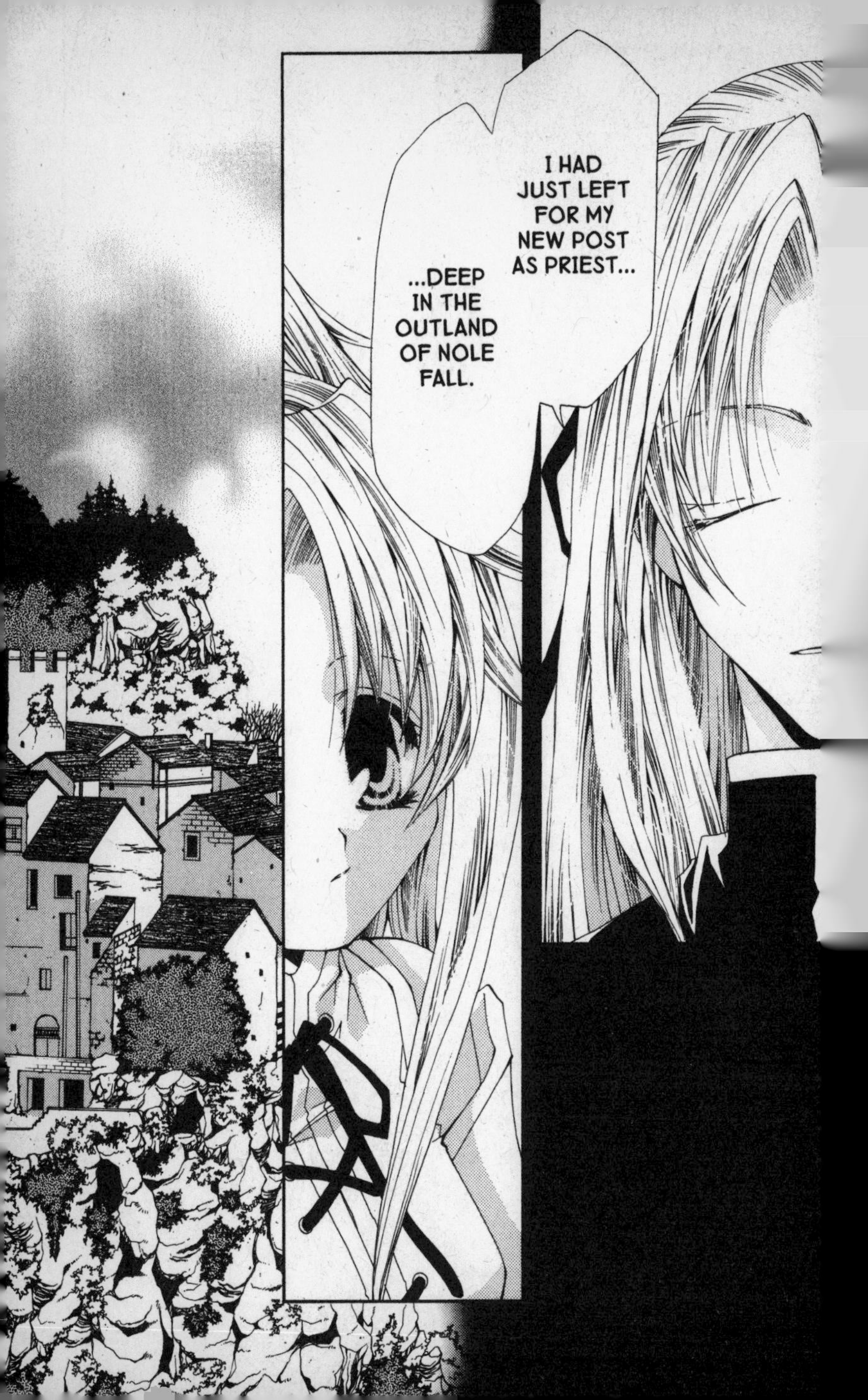
I HAD JUST LEFT FOR MY NEW POST AS PRIEST...
...DEEP IN THE OUTLAND OF NOLE FALL.

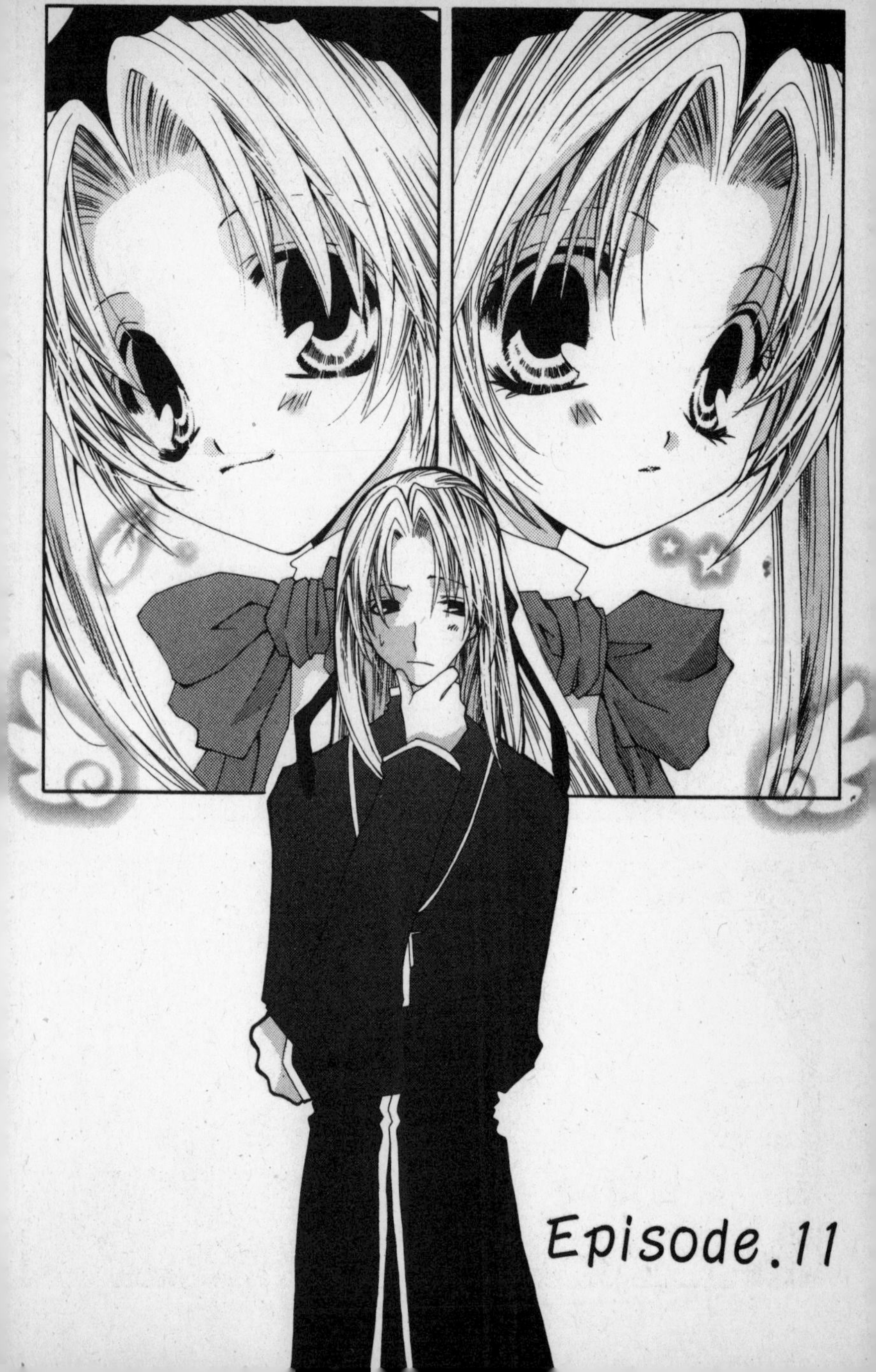
Episode.11

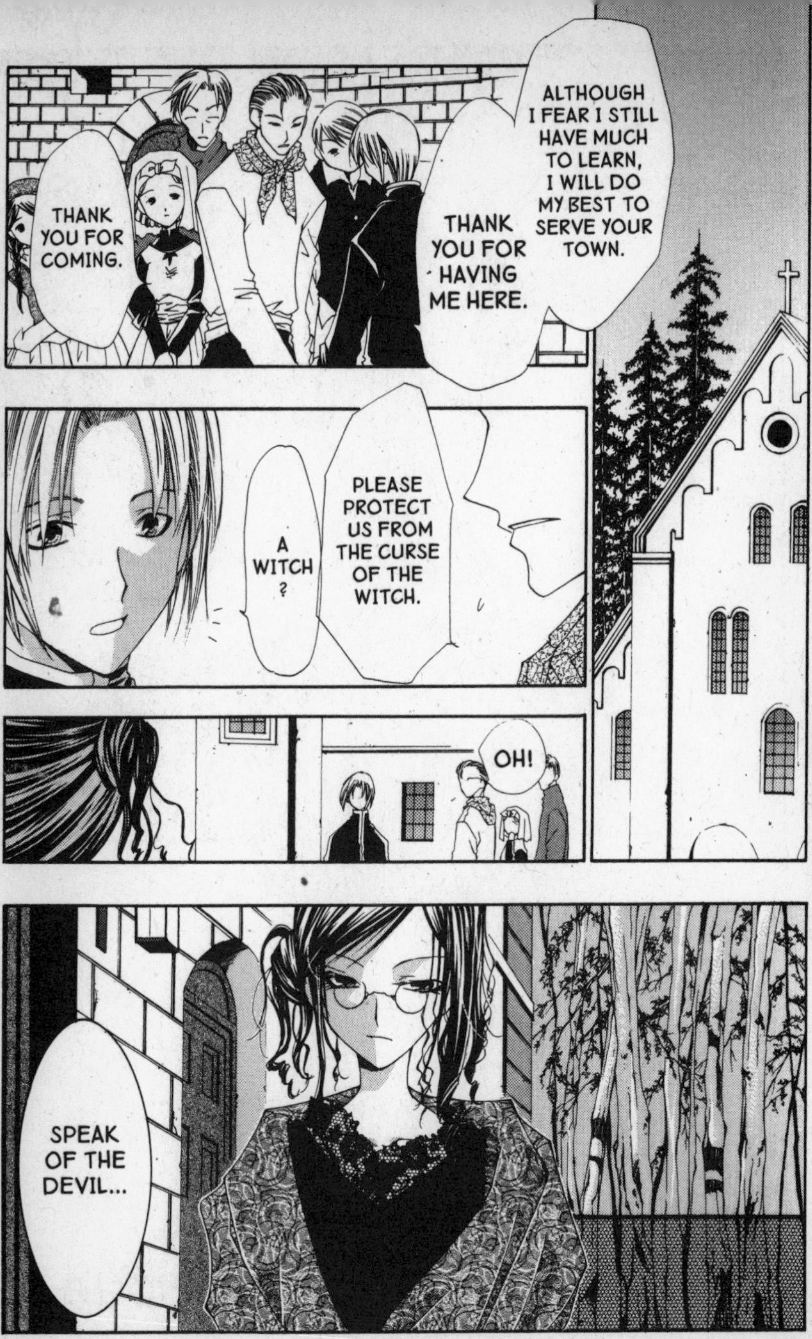
ALTHOUGH I FEAR I STILL HAVE MUCH TO LEARN, I WILL DO MY BEST TO SERVE YOUR TOWN.
THANK YOU FOR HAVING ME HERE.
THANK YOU FOR COMING.
PLEASE PROTECT US FROM THE CURSE OF THE WITCH.
A WITCH?
OH!
SPEAK OF THE DEVIL...

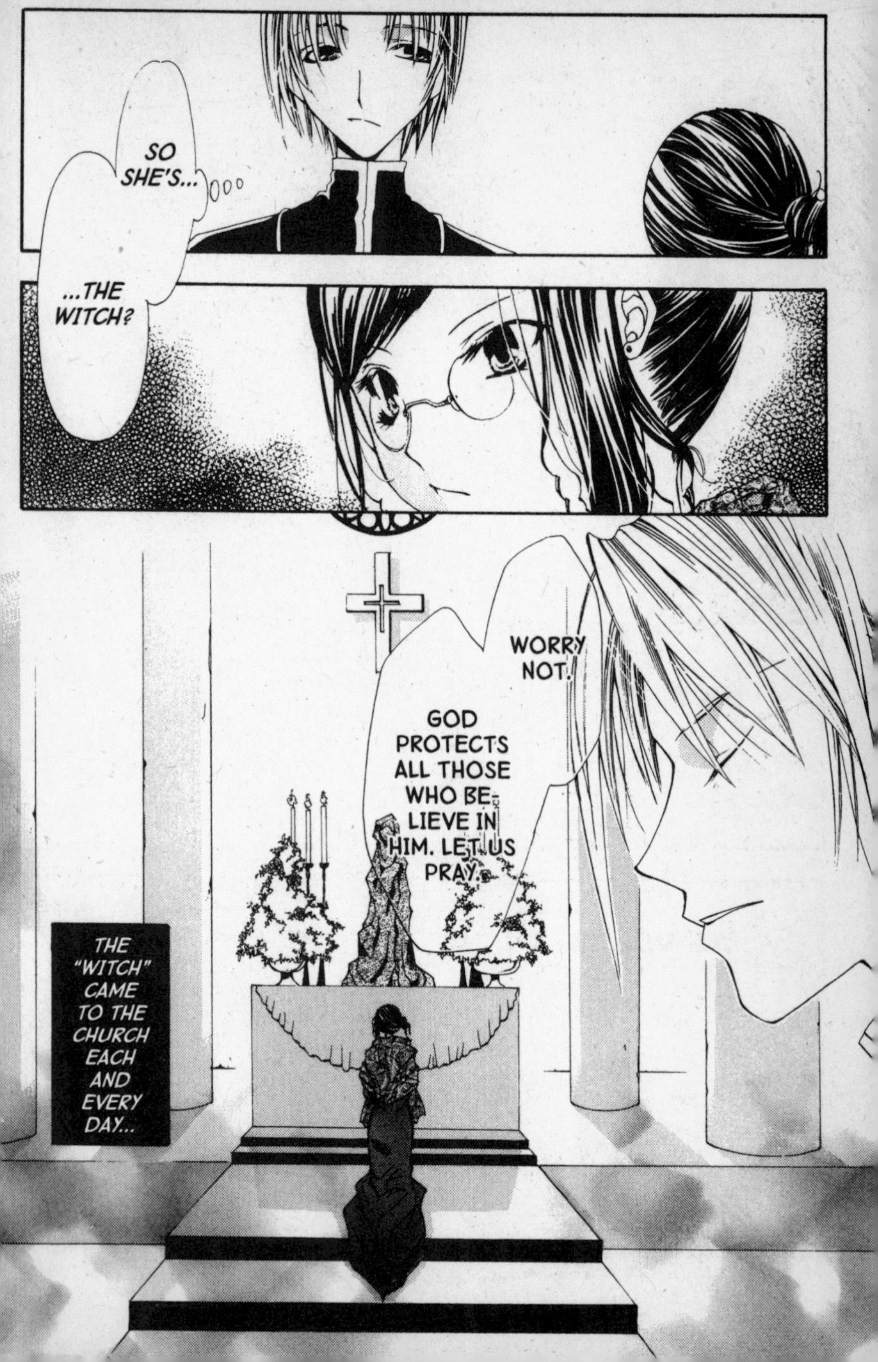
SO SHE'S...
...THE WITCH?
WORRY NOT.
GOD PROTECTS ALL THOSE WHO BE-LIEVE IN HIM. LET US PRAY.
THE "WITCH" CAME TO THE CHURCH EACH AND EVERY DAY...

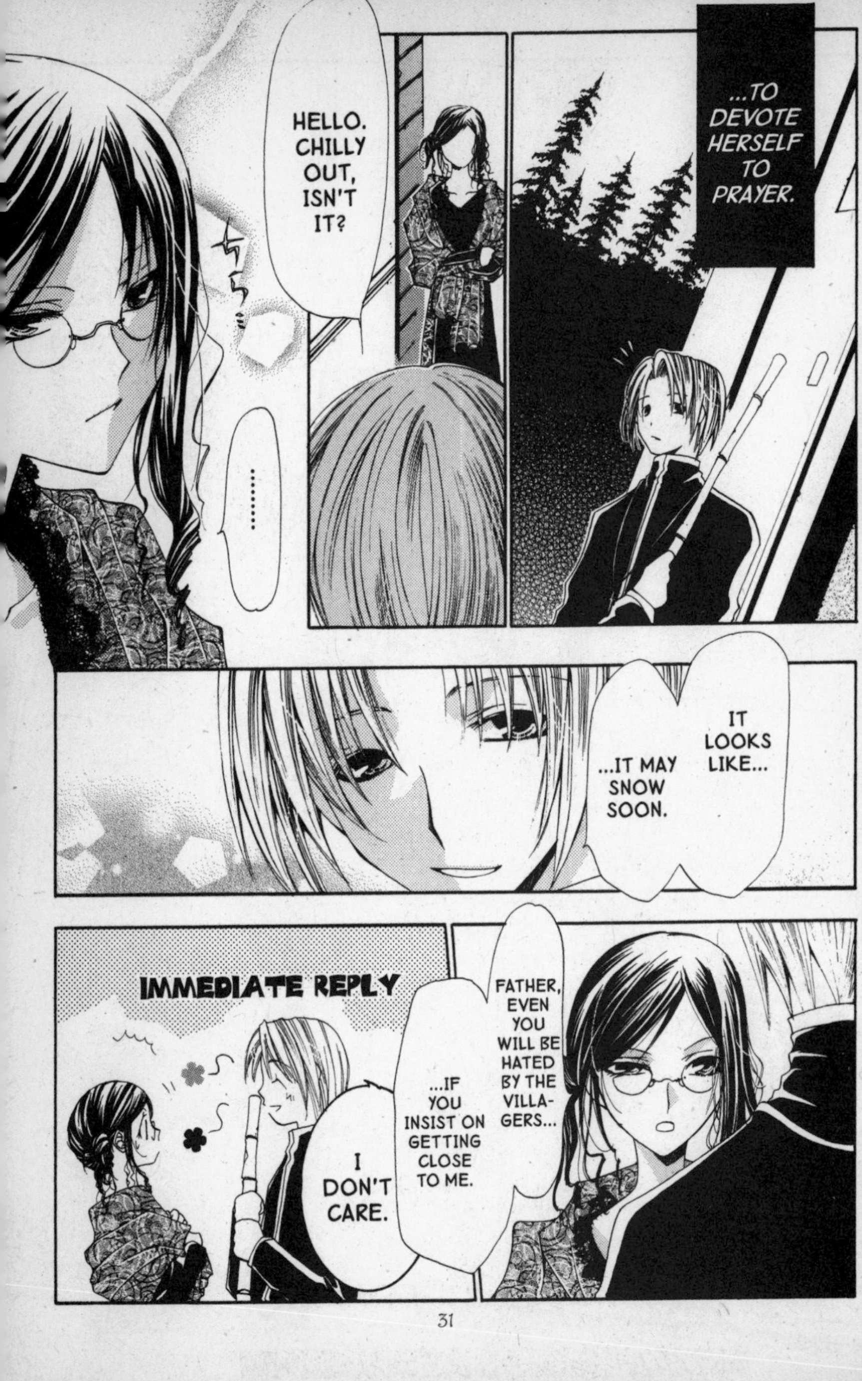
...TO DEVOTE HERSELF TO PRAYER.
HELLO. CHILLY OUT, ISN'T IT?
....
IT LOOKS LIKE...
...IT MAY SNOW SOON.
FATHER, EVEN YOU WILL BE HATED BY THE VILLA-GERS...
...IF YOU INSIST ON GETTING CLOSE TO ME.
IMMEDIATE REPLY
I DON'T CARE.

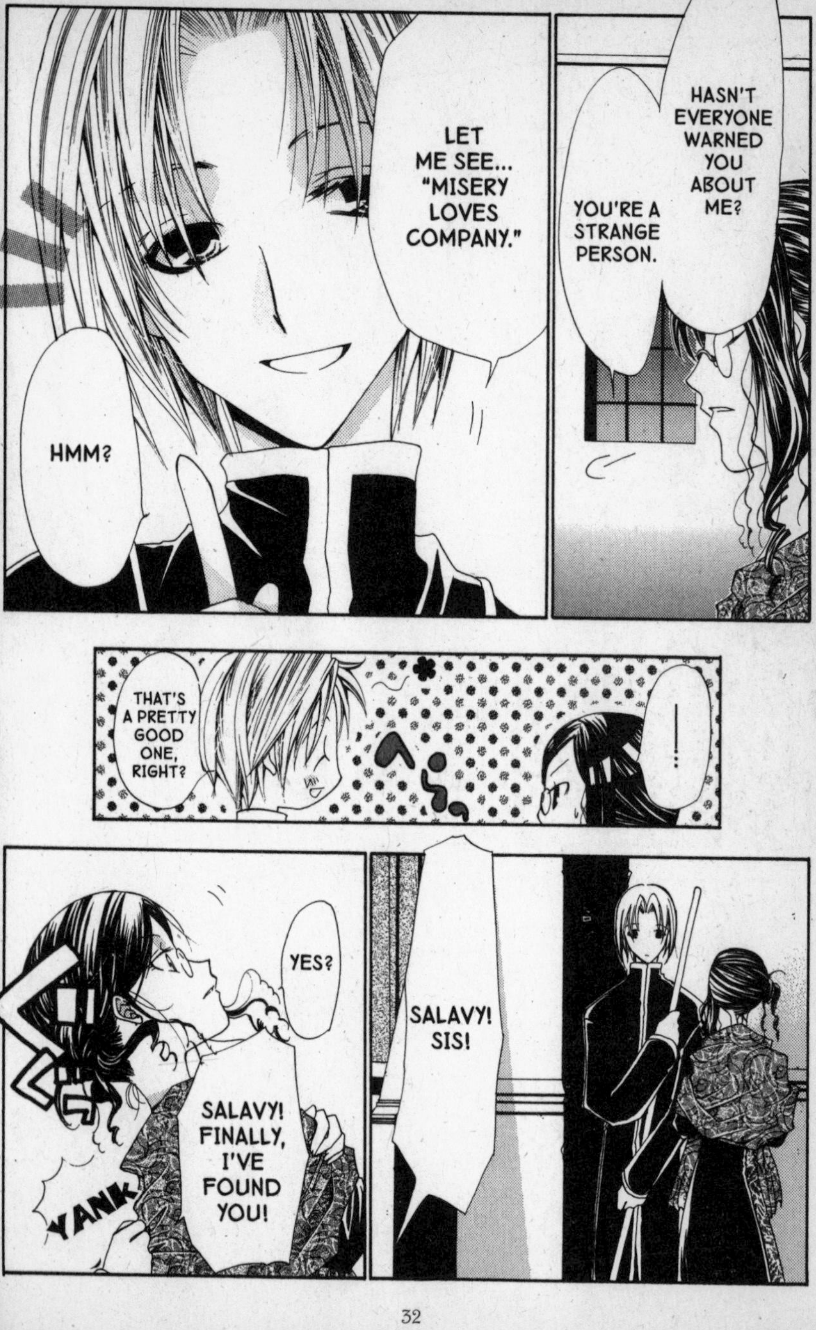
HASN'T EVERYONE WARNED YOU ABOUT ME?
YOU'RE A STRANGE PERSON.
LET ME SEE... "MISERY LOVES COMPANY."
HMM?
!
THAT'S A PRETTY GOOD ONE, RIGHT?
SALAVY! SIS!
YES?
SALAVY! FINALLY, I'VE FOUND YOU!
YANK

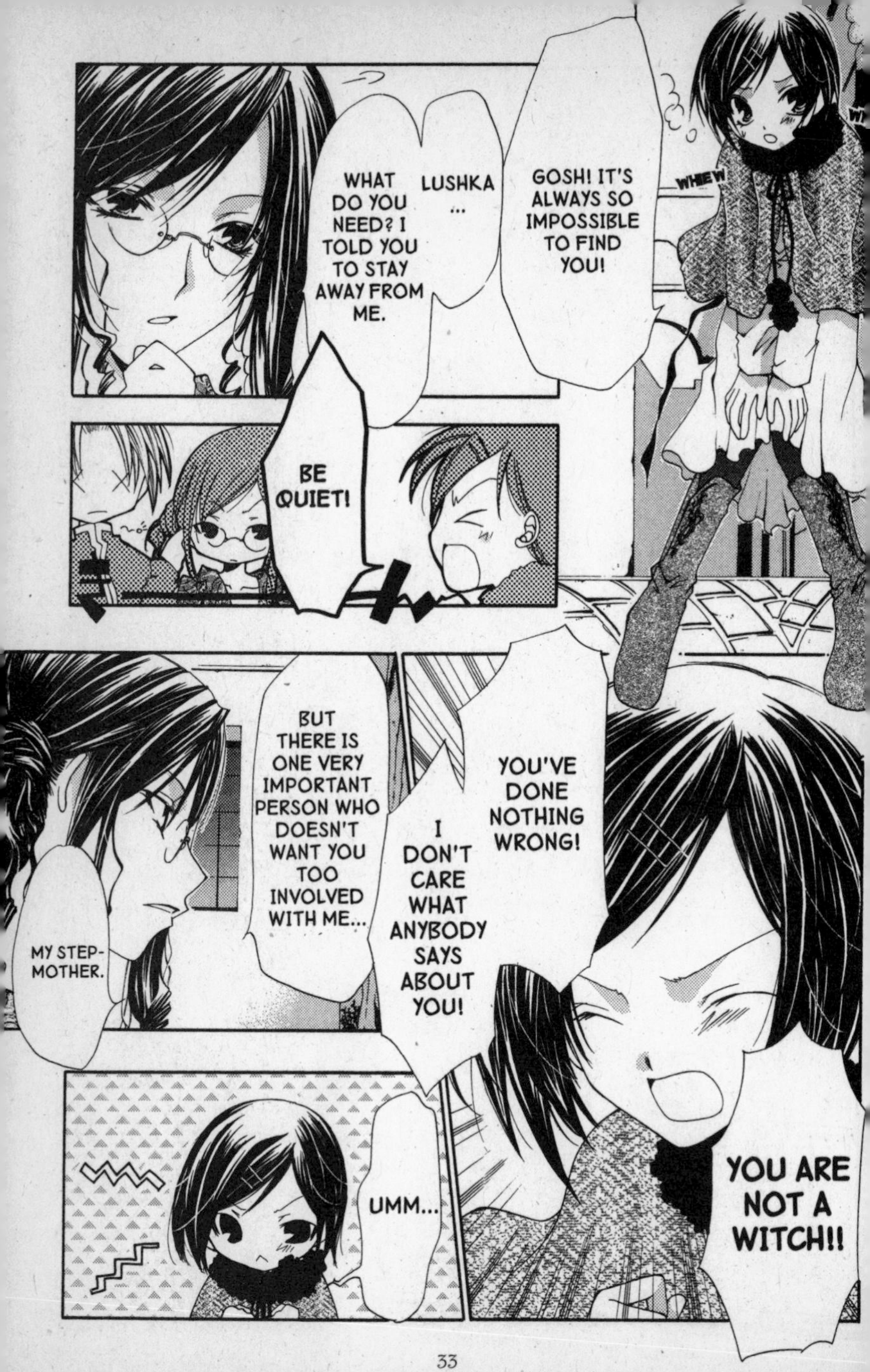
WHIEW
GOSH! IT'S ALWAYS SO IMPOSSIBLE TO FIND YOU!
LUSHKA ...
WHAT DO YOU NEED? I TOLD YOU TO STAY AWAY FROM ME.
BE QUIET!
YOU'VE DONE NOTHING WRONG!
I DON'T CARE WHAT ANYBODY SAYS ABOUT YOU!
YOU ARE NOT A WITCH!!
BUT THERE IS ONE VERY IMPORTANT PERSON WHO DOESN'T WANT YOU TOO INVOLVED WITH ME...
MY STEP-MOTHER.
UMM...

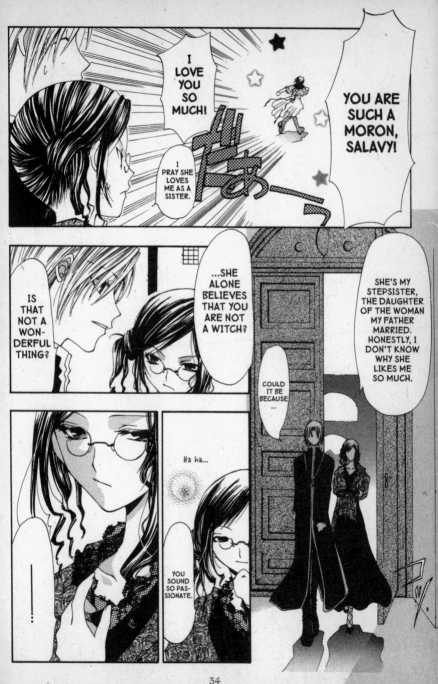

YOU ARE SUCH A MORON, SALAVY!
I LOVE YOU SO MUCH!
I PRAY SHE LOVES ME AS A SISTER.
SHE'S MY STEPSISTER, THE DAUGHTER OF THE WOMAN MY FATHER MARRIED. HONESTLY, I DON'T KNOW WHY SHE LIKES ME SO MUCH.
COULD IT BE BECAUSE ...
...SHE ALONE BELIEVES THAT YOU ARE NOT A WITCH?
IS THAT NOT A WONDERFUL THING?
Ha ha...
YOU SOUND SO PASSIONATE.
......

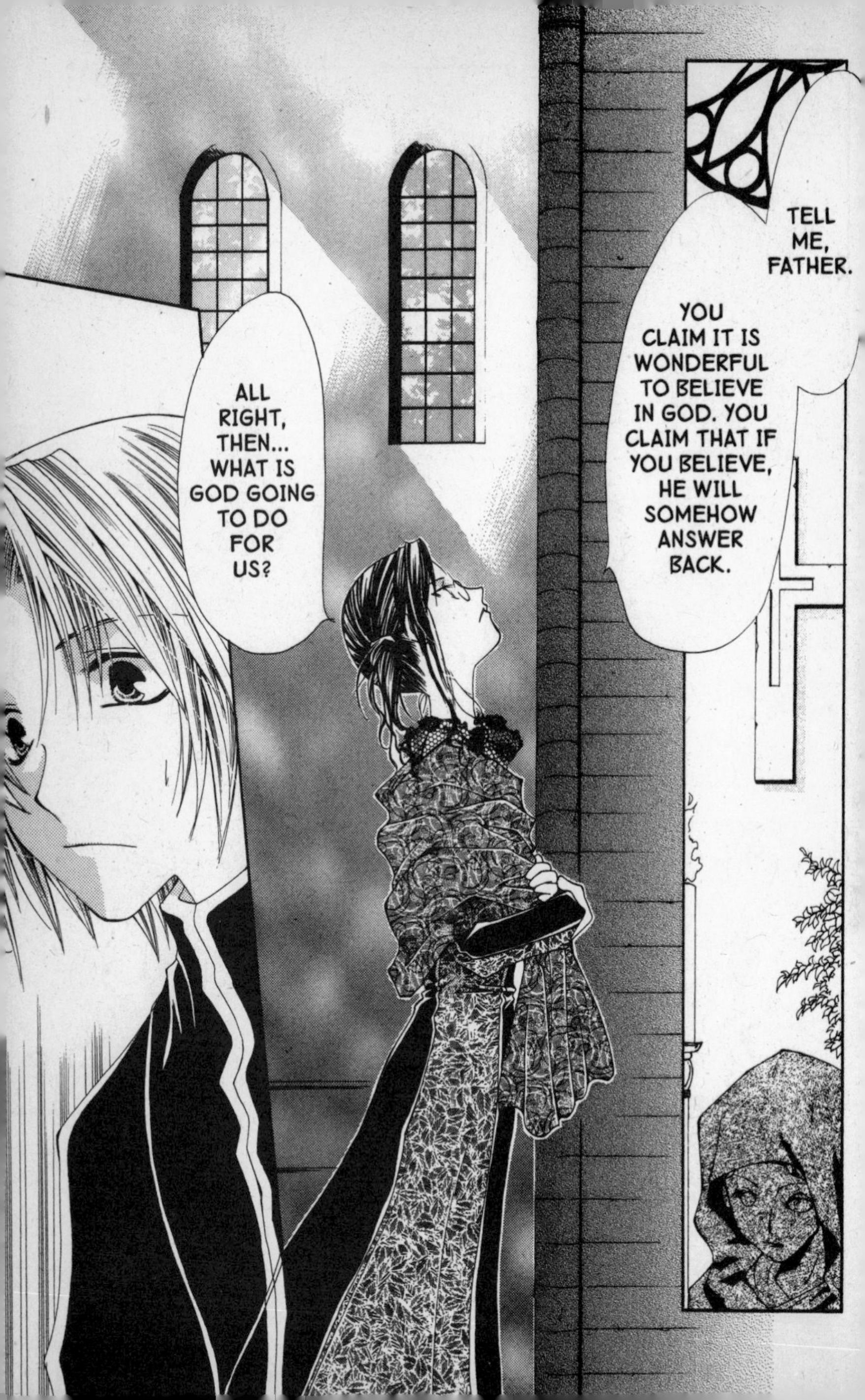
TELL ME, FATHER.
YOU CLAIM IT IS WONDERFUL TO BELIEVE IN GOD. YOU CLAIM THAT IF YOU BELIEVE, HE WILL SOMEHOW ANSWER BACK.
ALL RIGHT, THEN... WHAT IS GOD GOING TO DO FOR US?

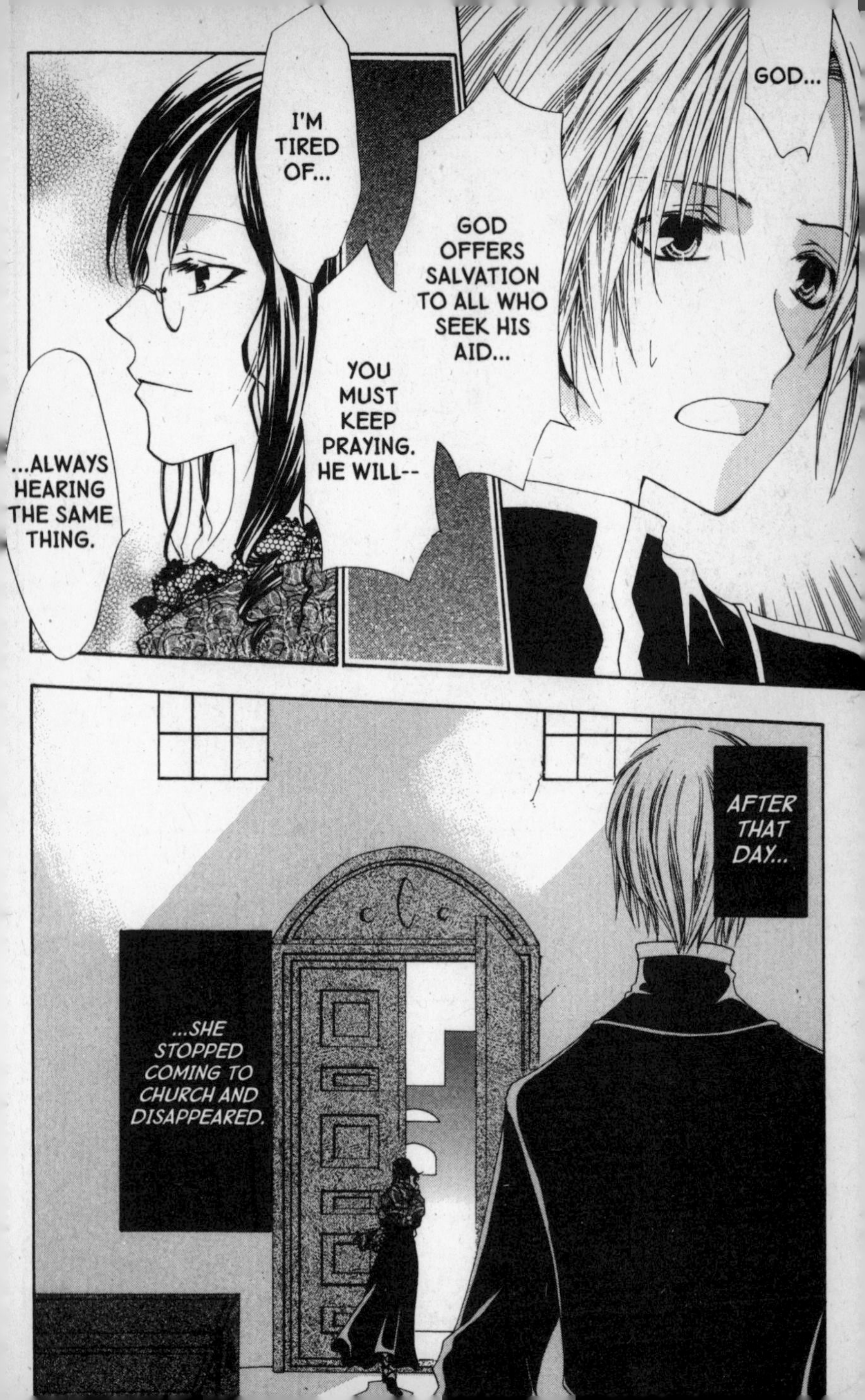
GOD...
GOD OFFERS SALVATION TO ALL WHO SEEK HIS AID...
YOU MUST KEEP PRAYING. HE WILL--
I'M TIRED OF...
...ALWAYS HEARING THE SAME THING.
AFTER THAT DAY...
...SHE STOPPED COMING TO CHURCH AND DISAPPEARED.

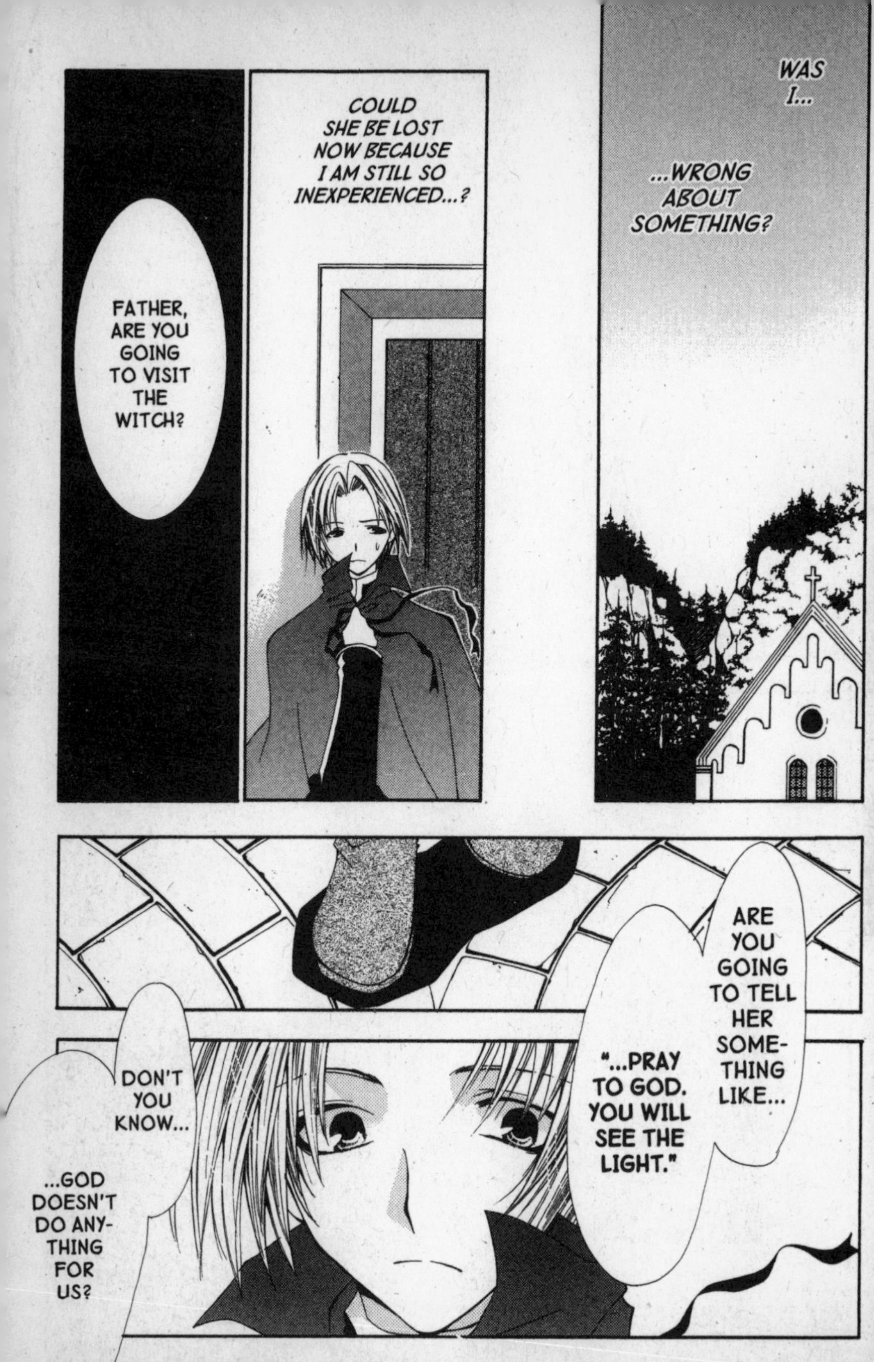
WAS I...
...WRONG ABOUT SOMETHING?
COULD SHE BE LOST NOW BECAUSE I AM STILL SO INEXPERIENCED...?
FATHER, ARE YOU GOING TO VISIT THE WITCH?
ARE YOU GOING TO TELL HER SOME-THING LIKE...
"...PRAY TO GOD. YOU WILL SEE THE LIGHT."
DON'T YOU KNOW...
...GOD DOESN'T DO ANY-THING FOR US?

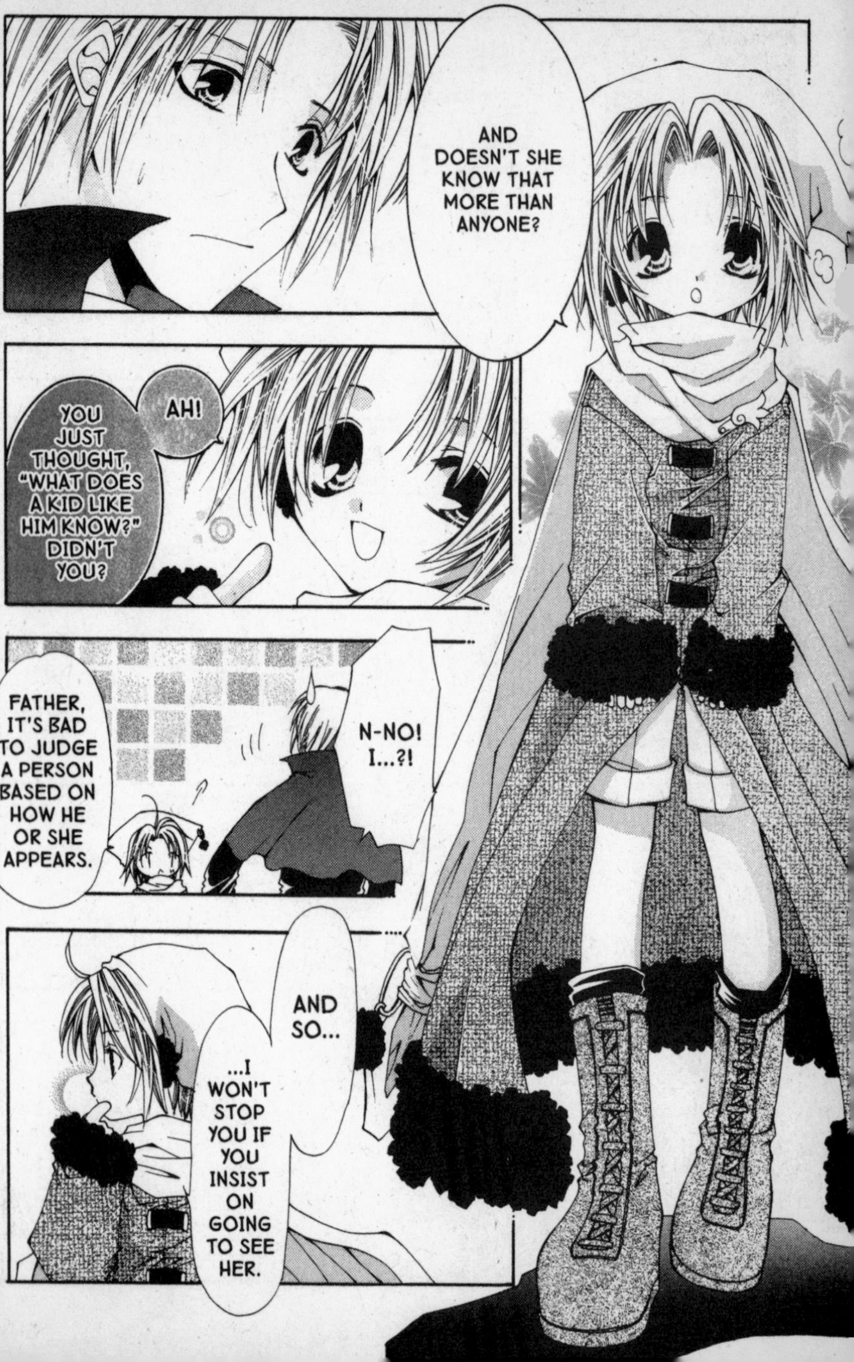
AND DOESN'T SHE KNOW THAT MORE THAN ANYONE?
AH!
YOU JUST THOUGHT, "WHAT DOES A KID LIKE HIM KNOW?" DIDN'T YOU?
N-NO! I...?!
FATHER, IT'S BAD TO JUDGE A PERSON BASED ON HOW HE OR SHE APPEARS.
AND SO...
...I WON'T STOP YOU IF YOU INSIST ON GOING TO SEE HER.

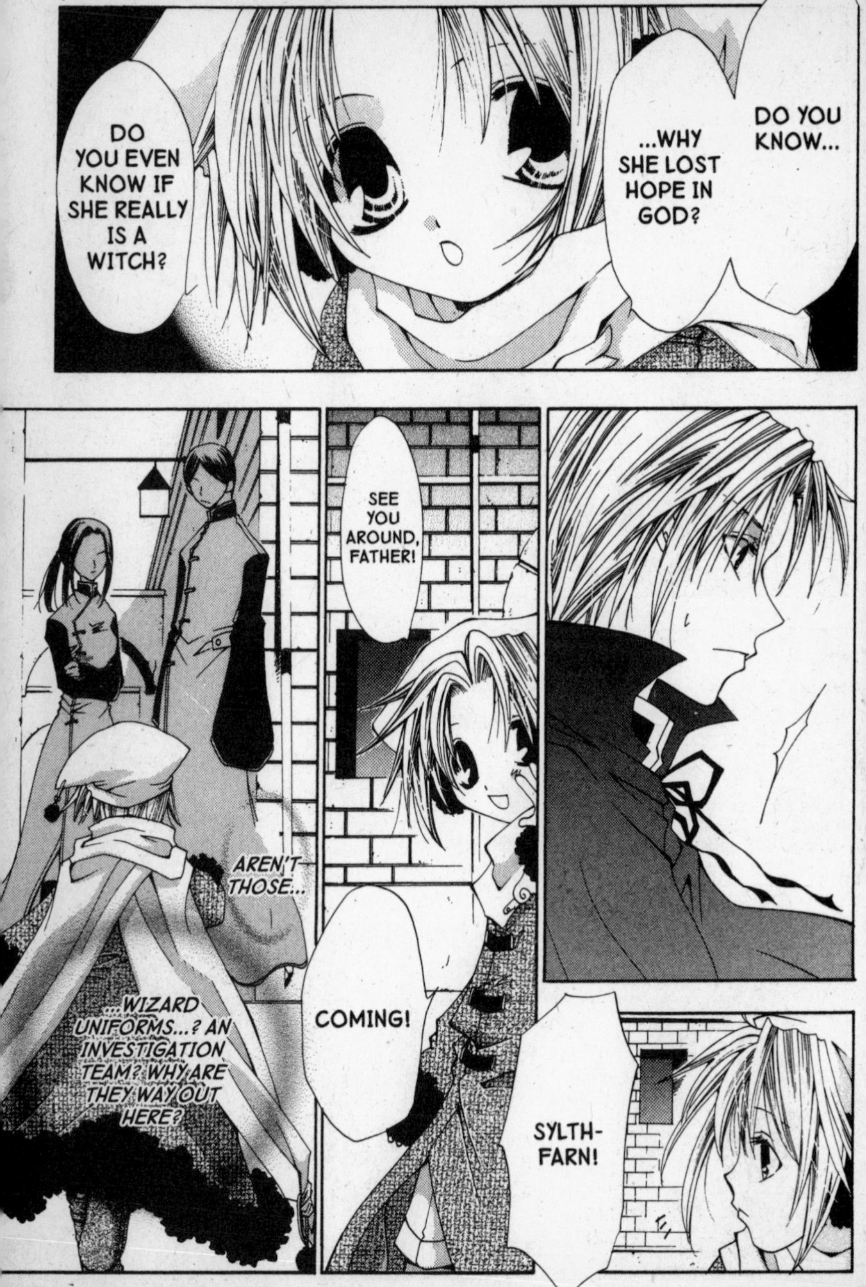
DO YOU KNOW...
...WHY SHE LOST HOPE IN GOD?
DO YOU EVEN KNOW IF SHE REALLY IS A WITCH?
SYLTH-FARN!
SEE YOU AROUND, FATHER!
COMING!
AREN'T THOSE...
...WIZARD UNIFORMS...? AN INVESTIGATION TEAM? WHY ARE THEY WAY OUT HERE?

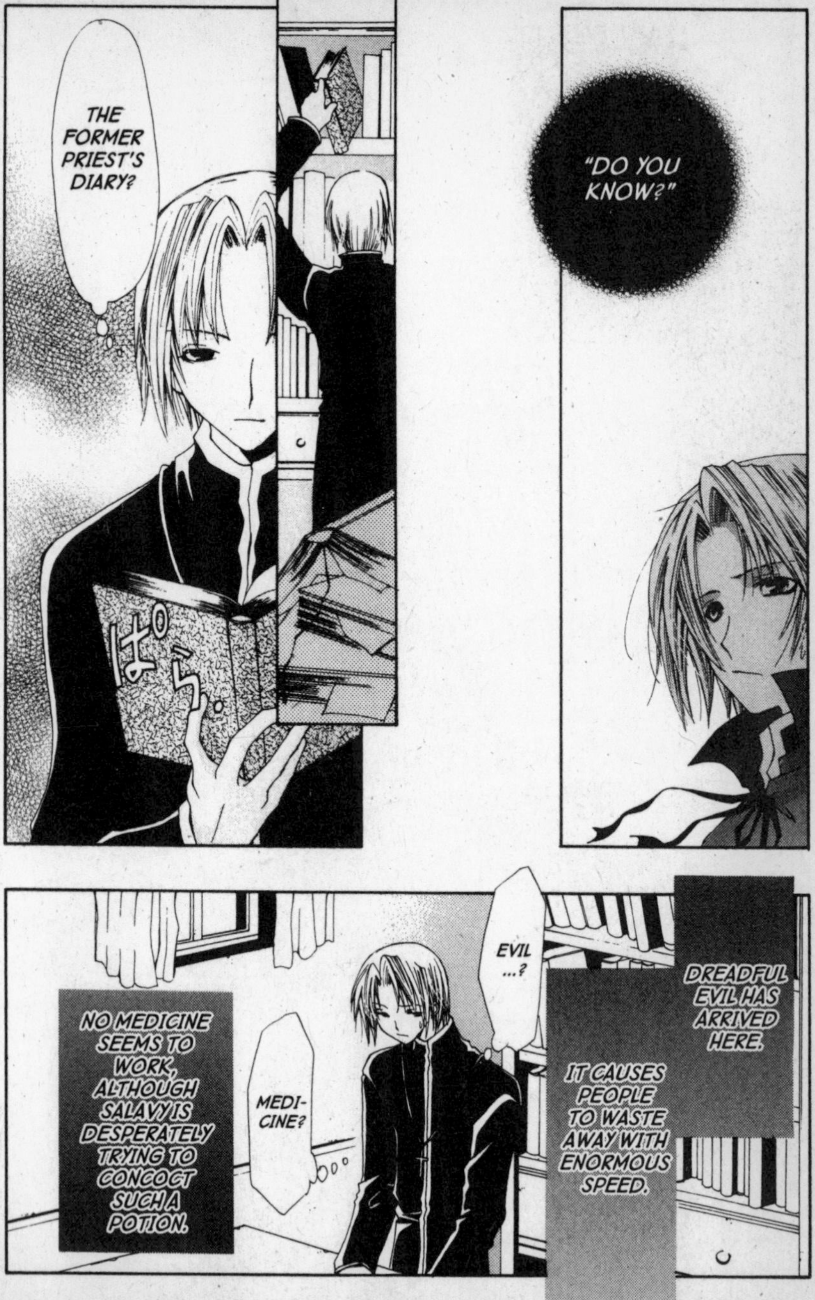
"DO YOU KNOW?"
THE FORMER PRIEST'S DIARY?
ぱら。
DREADFUL EVIL HAS ARRIVED HERE.
IT CAUSES PEOPLE TO WASTE AWAY WITH ENORMOUS SPEED.
EVIL ...?
NO MEDICINE SEEMS TO WORK, ALTHOUGH SALAVY IS DESPERATELY TRYING TO CONCOCT SUCH A POTION.
MEDI-CINE?

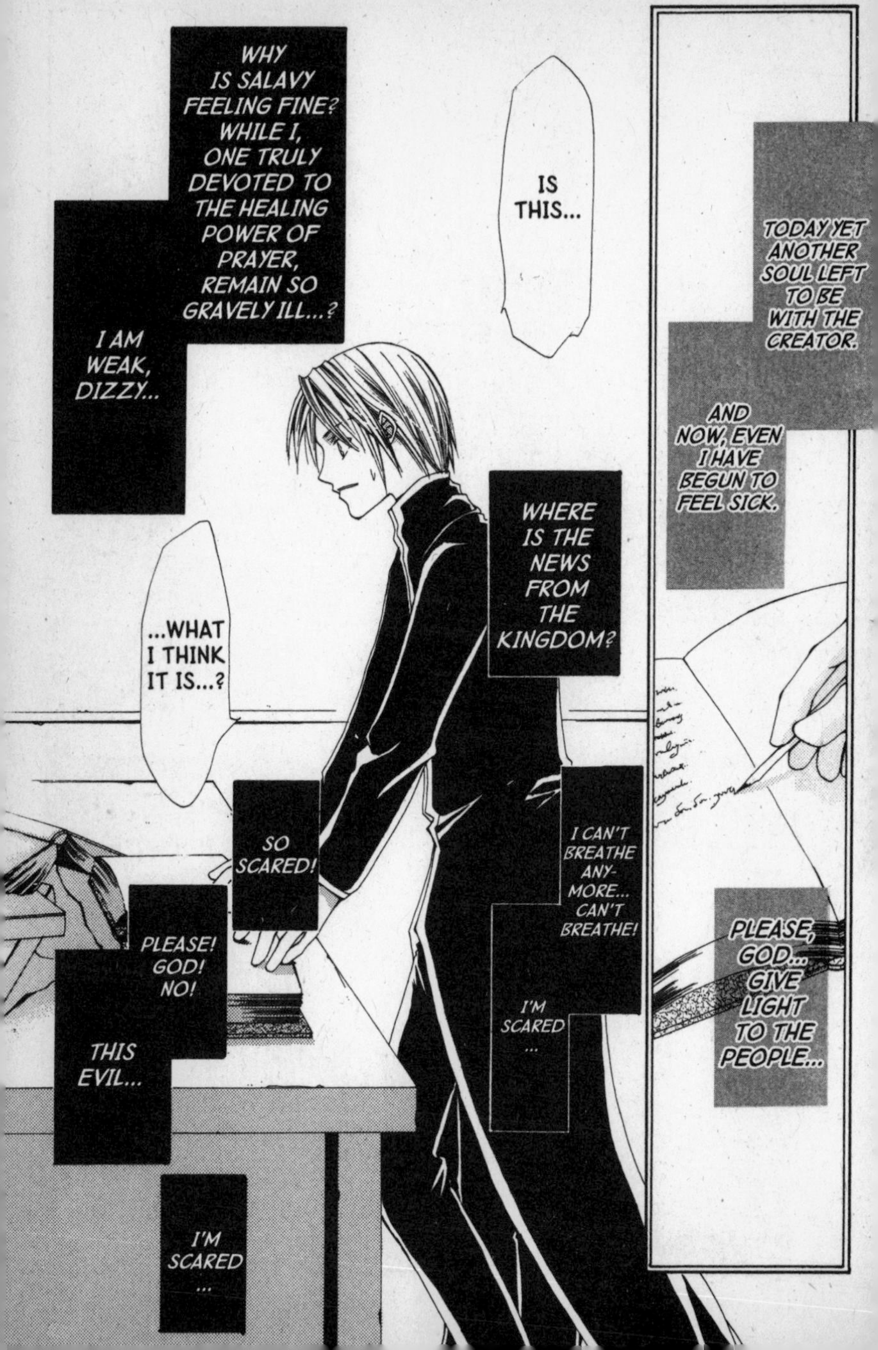
TODAY YET ANOTHER SOUL LEFT TO BE WITH THE CREATOR.
AND NOW, EVEN I HAVE BEGUN TO FEEL SICK.
PLEASE, GOD... GIVE LIGHT TO THE PEOPLE...
IS THIS...
WHY IS SALAVY FEELING FINE? WHILE I, ONE TRULY DEVOTED TO THE HEALING POWER OF PRAYER, REMAIN SO GRAVELY ILL...?
I AM WEAK, DIZZY...
WHERE IS THE NEWS FROM THE KINGDOM?
...WHAT I THINK IT IS...?
I CAN'T BREATHE ANY-MORE... CAN'T BREATHE!
I'M SCARED...
SO SCARED!
PLEASE! GOD! NO!
THIS EVIL...
I'M SCARED...

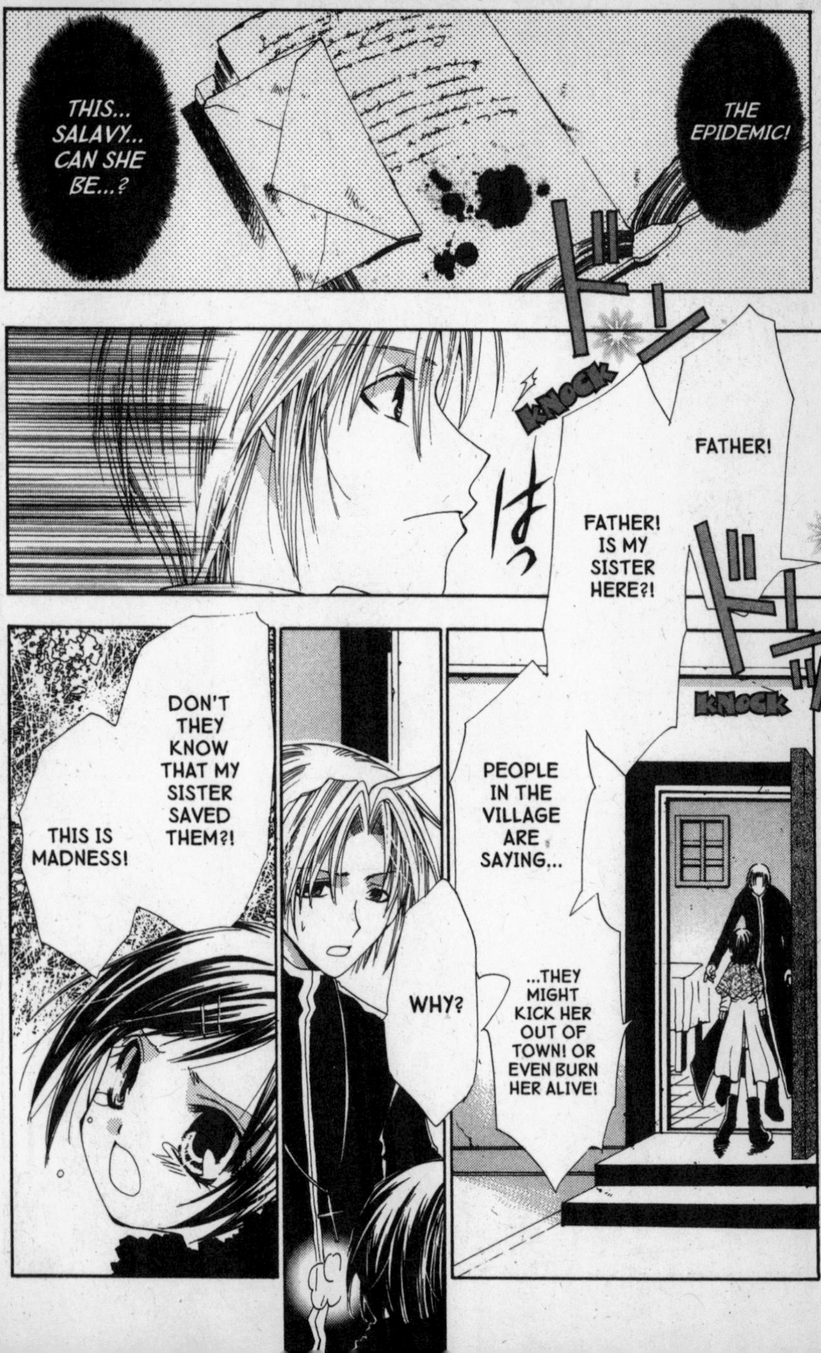
THE EPIDEMIC!
THIS... SALAVY... CAN SHE BE...?
KNOCK
FATHER!
FATHER! IS MY SISTER HERE?!
はっ
KNOCK
PEOPLE IN THE VILLAGE ARE SAYING...
...THEY MIGHT KICK HER OUT OF TOWN! OR EVEN BURN HER ALIVE!
WHY?
DON'T THEY KNOW THAT MY SISTER SAVED THEM?!
THIS IS MADNESS!

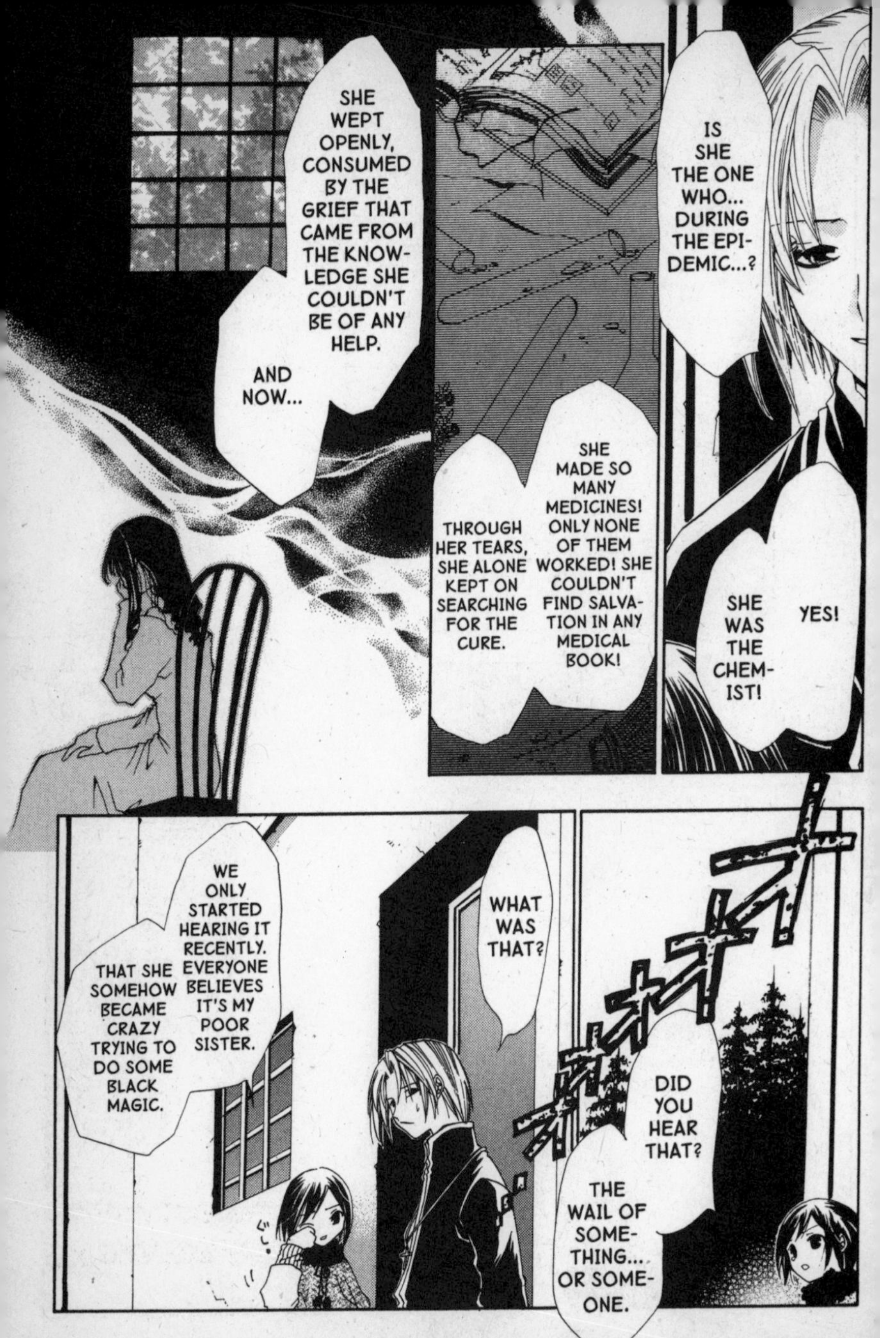
IS SHE THE ONE WHO... DURING THE EPI-DEMIC...?
YES!
SHE WAS THE CHEM-IST!
SHE MADE SO MANY MEDICINES! ONLY NONE OF THEM WORKED! SHE COULDN'T FIND SALVA-TION IN ANY MEDICAL BOOK!
THROUGH HER TEARS, SHE ALONE KEPT ON SEARCHING FOR THE CURE.
SHE WEPT OPENLY, CONSUMED BY THE GRIEF THAT CAME FROM THE KNOW-LEDGE SHE COULDN'T BE OF ANY HELP.
AND NOW...
DID YOU HEAR THAT?
THE WAIL OF SOME-THING... OR SOME-ONE.
WHAT WAS THAT?
WE ONLY STARTED HEARING IT RECENTLY. EVERYONE BELIEVES IT'S MY POOR SISTER.
THAT SHE SOMEHOW BECAME CRAZY TRYING TO DO SOME BLACK MAGIC.

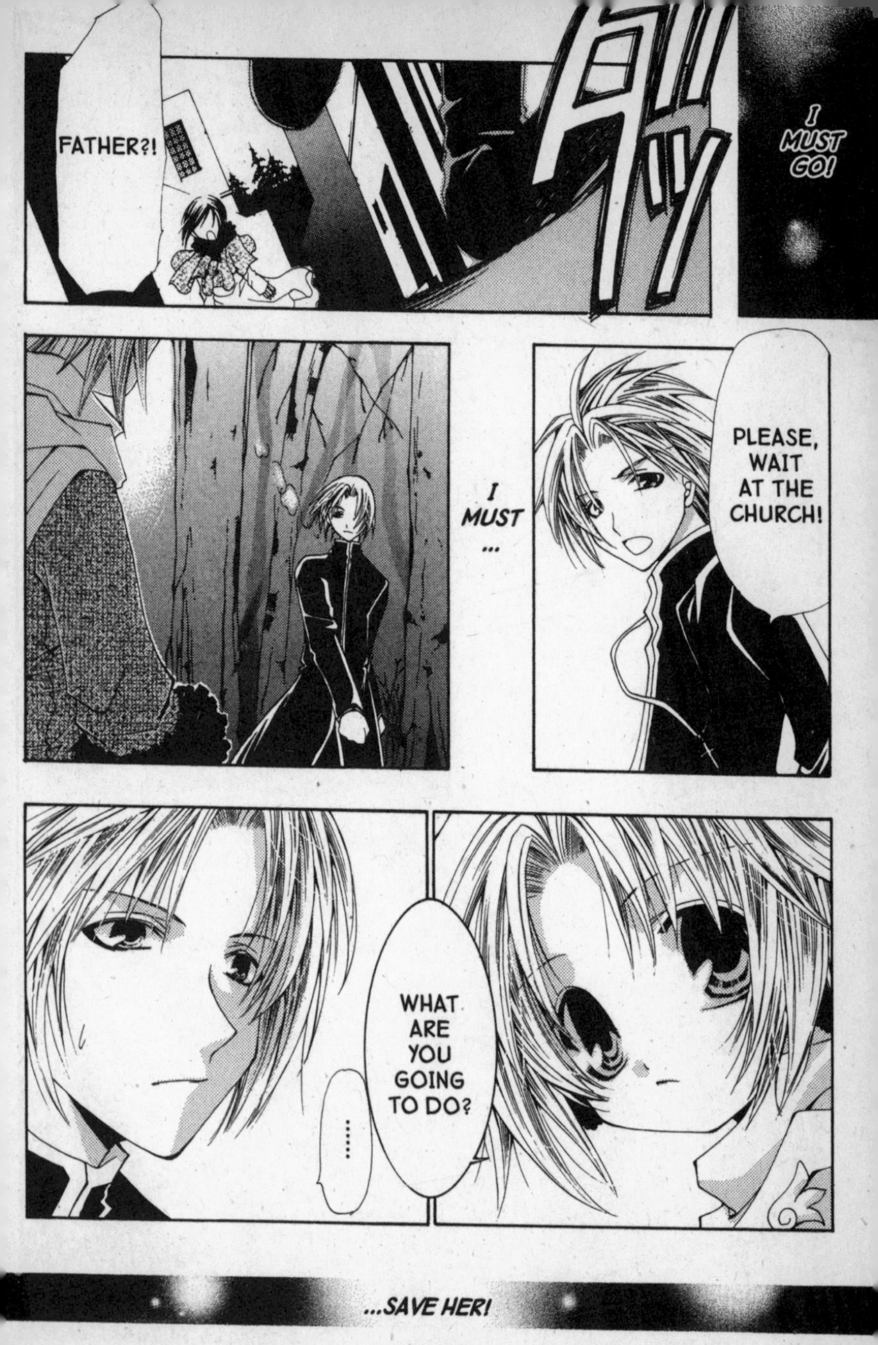
I MUST GO!
FATHER?!
PLEASE, WAIT AT THE CHURCH!
I MUST ...
WHAT ARE YOU GOING TO DO?
......
...SAVE HER!

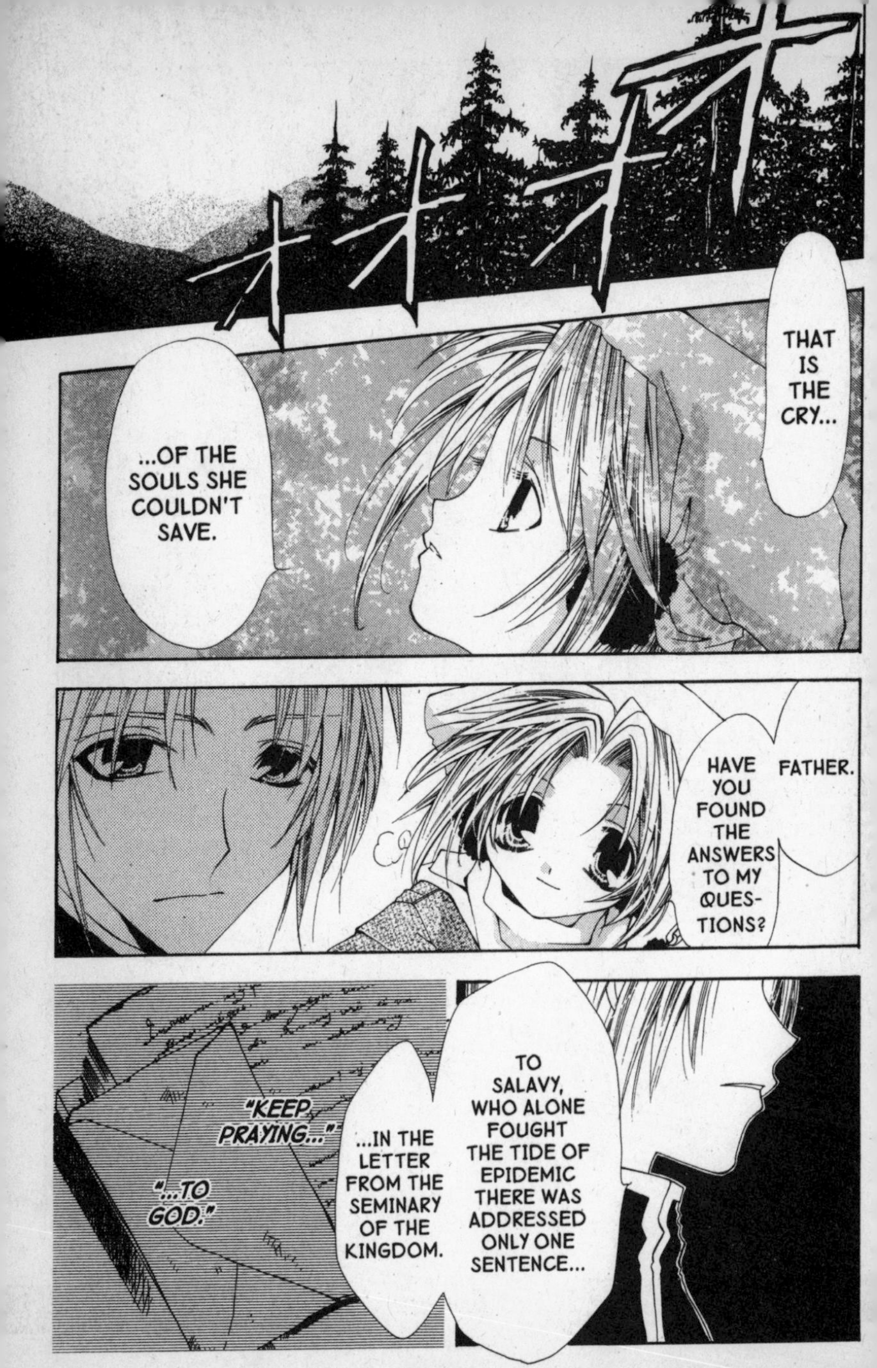
THAT IS THE CRY...
...OF THE SOULS SHE COULDN'T SAVE.
FATHER.
HAVE YOU FOUND THE ANSWERS TO MY QUES-TIONS?
TO SALAVY, WHO ALONE FOUGHT THE TIDE OF EPIDEMIC THERE WAS ADDRESSED ONLY ONE SENTENCE...
...IN THE LETTER FROM THE SEMINARY OF THE KINGDOM.
"KEEP PRAYING..."
"...TO GOD."

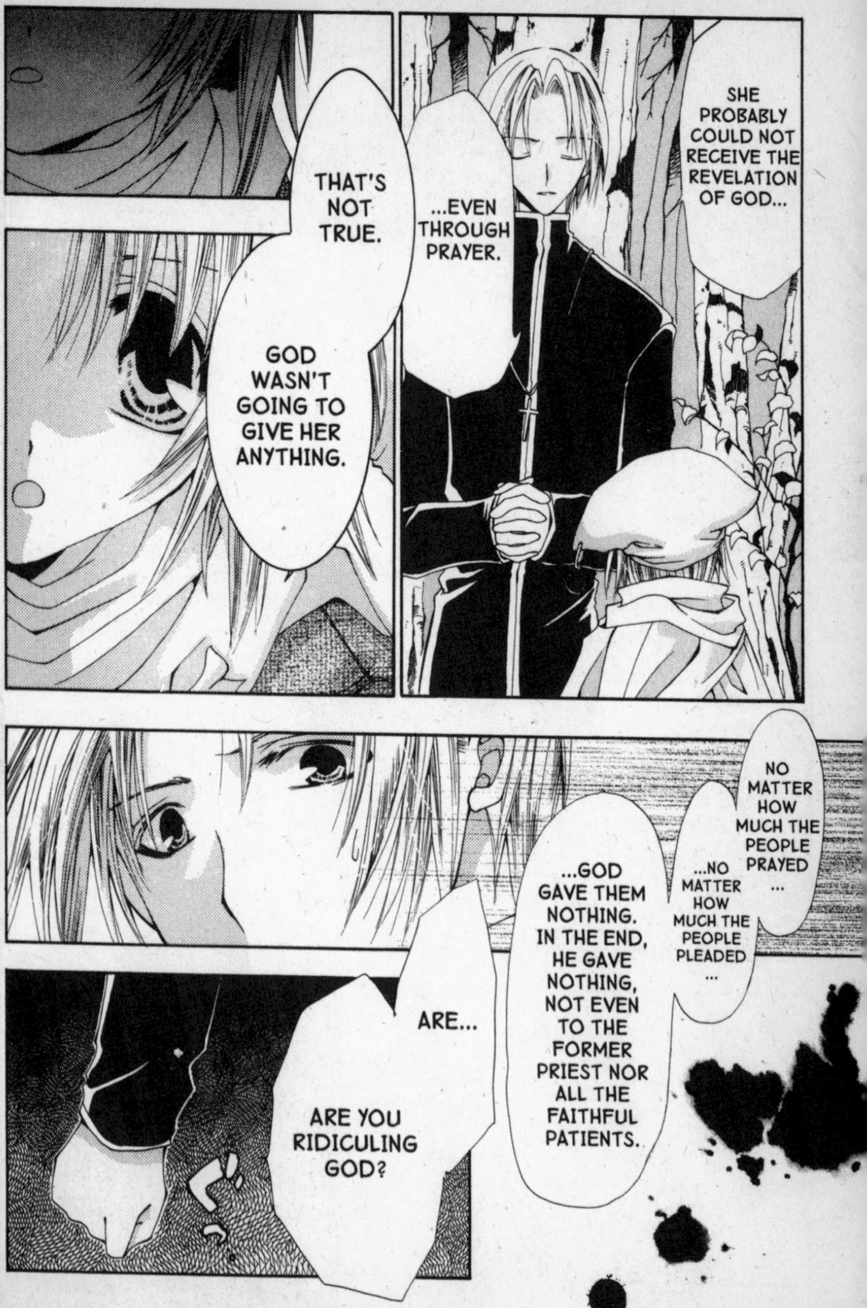
SHE PROBABLY COULD NOT RECEIVE THE REVELATION OF GOD...
...EVEN THROUGH PRAYER.
THAT'S NOT TRUE.
GOD WASN'T GOING TO GIVE HER ANYTHING.
NO MATTER HOW MUCH THE PEOPLE PRAYED ...
...NO MATTER HOW MUCH THE PEOPLE PLEADED ...
...GOD GAVE THEM NOTHING. IN THE END, HE GAVE NOTHING, NOT EVEN TO THE FORMER PRIEST NOR ALL THE FAITHFUL PATIENTS.
ARE...
ARE YOU RIDICULING GOD?

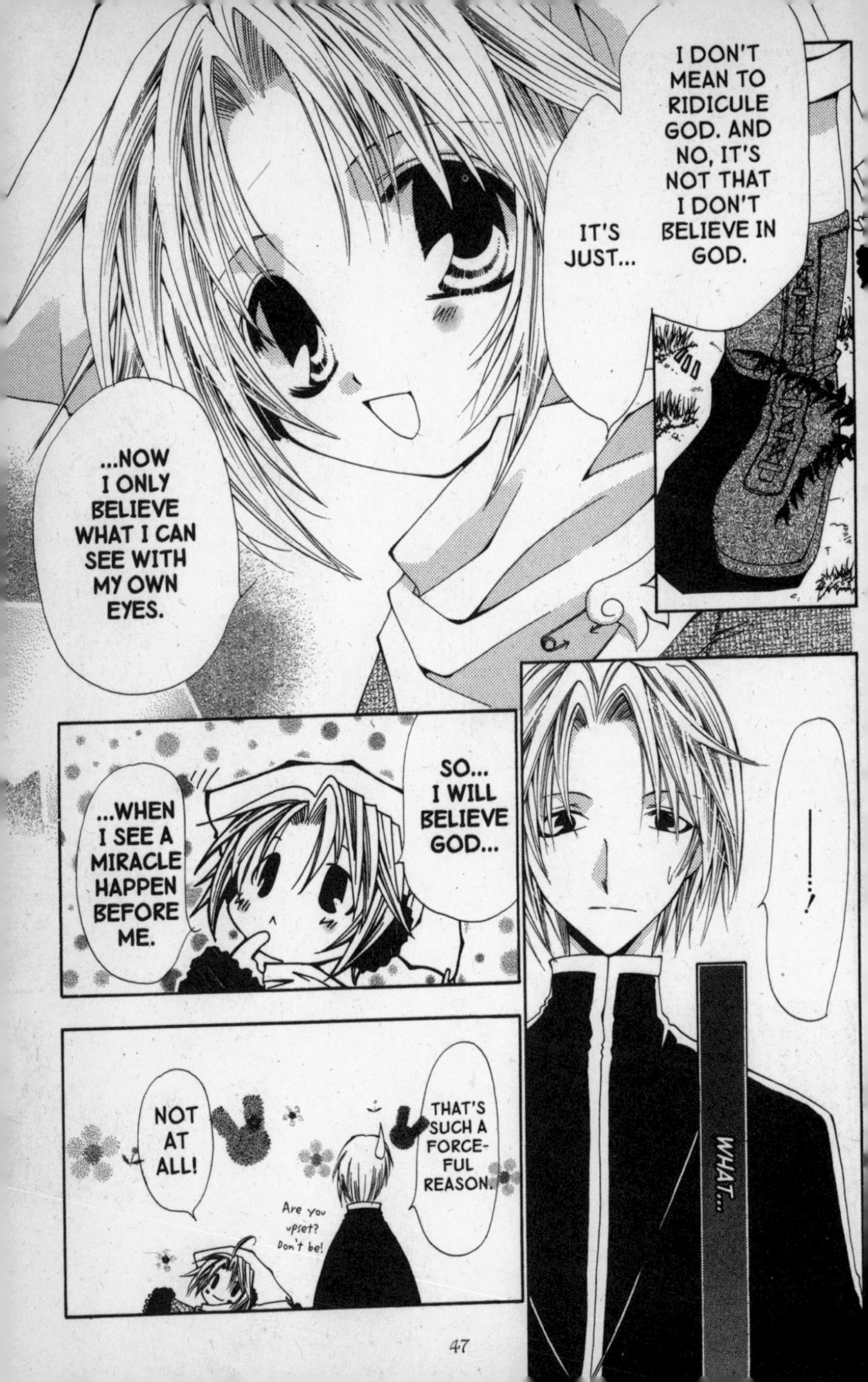
I DON'T MEAN TO RIDICULE GOD. AND NO, IT'S NOT THAT I DON'T BELIEVE IN GOD.
IT'S JUST...
...NOW I ONLY BELIEVE WHAT I CAN SEE WITH MY OWN EYES.
...!
WHAT...
SO... I WILL BELIEVE GOD...
...WHEN I SEE A MIRACLE HAPPEN BEFORE ME.
THAT'S SUCH A FORCE-FUL REASON.
NOT AT ALL!
Are you upset? Don't be!

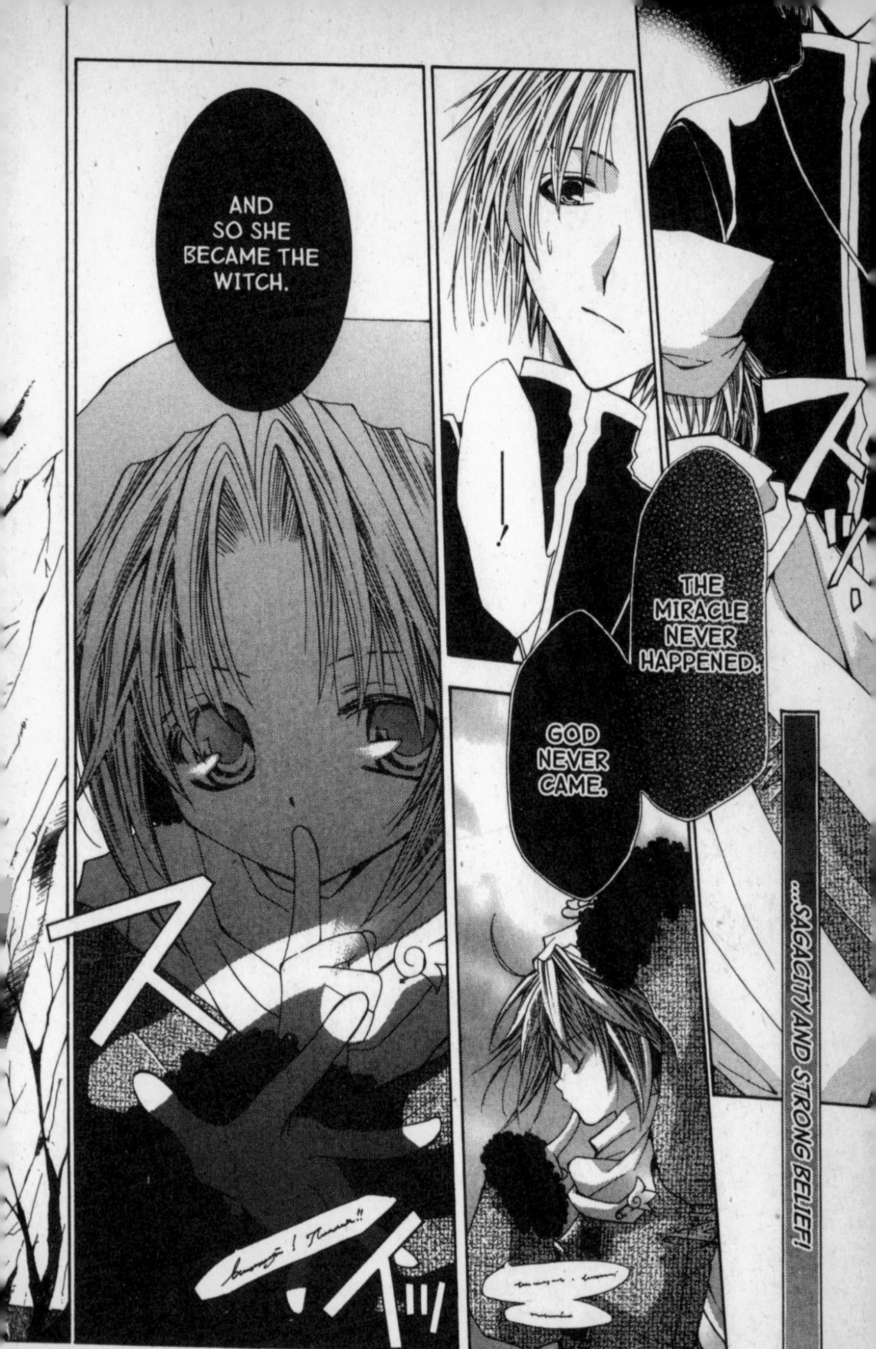
THE MIRACLE NEVER HAPPENED.
GOD NEVER CAME.
...SAGACITY AND STRONG BELIEF!
AND SO SHE BECAME THE WITCH.

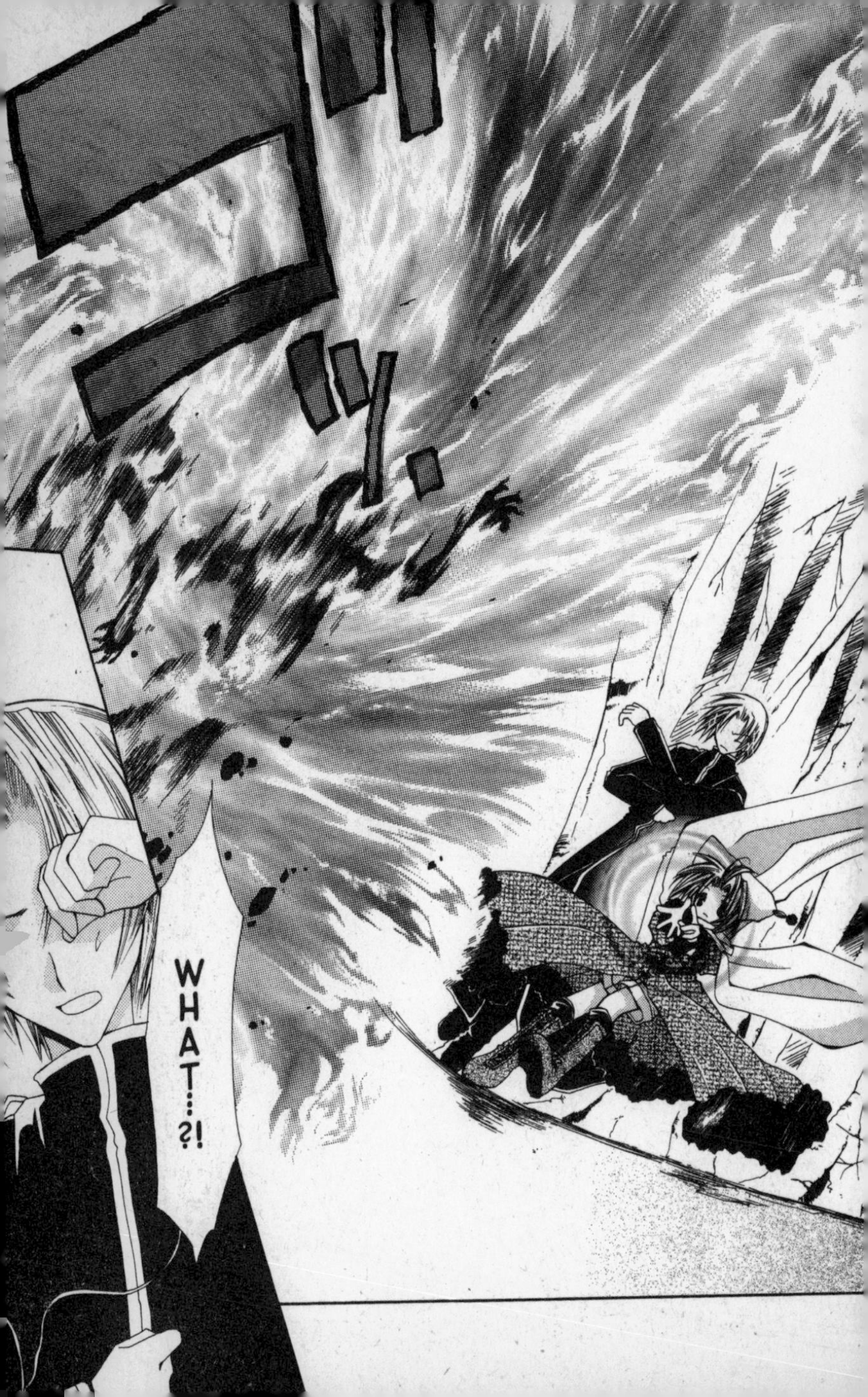
WHAT...?!

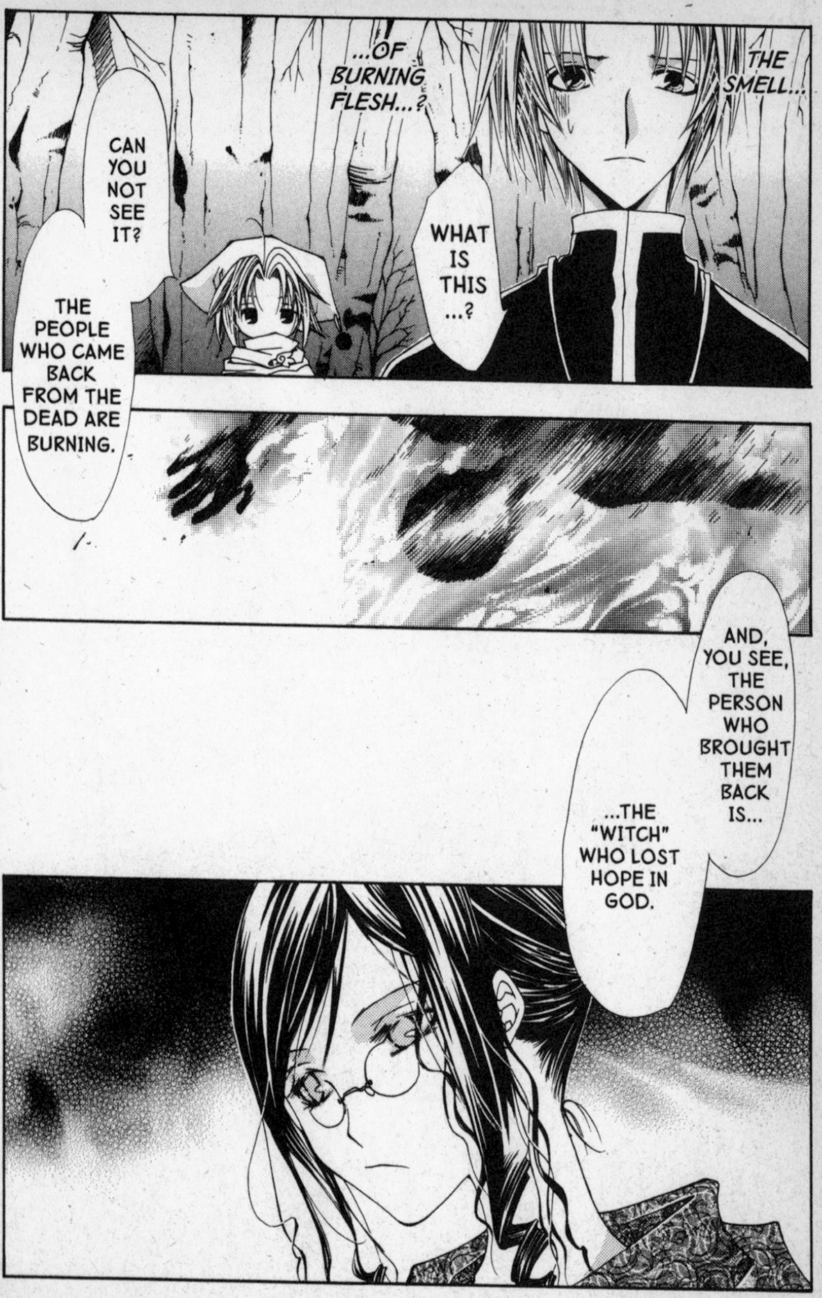
THE SMELL...
...OF BURNING FLESH...?
WHAT IS THIS ...?
CAN YOU NOT SEE IT?
THE PEOPLE WHO CAME BACK FROM THE DEAD ARE BURNING.
AND, YOU SEE, THE PERSON WHO BROUGHT THEM BACK IS...
...THE "WITCH" WHO LOST HOPE IN GOD.

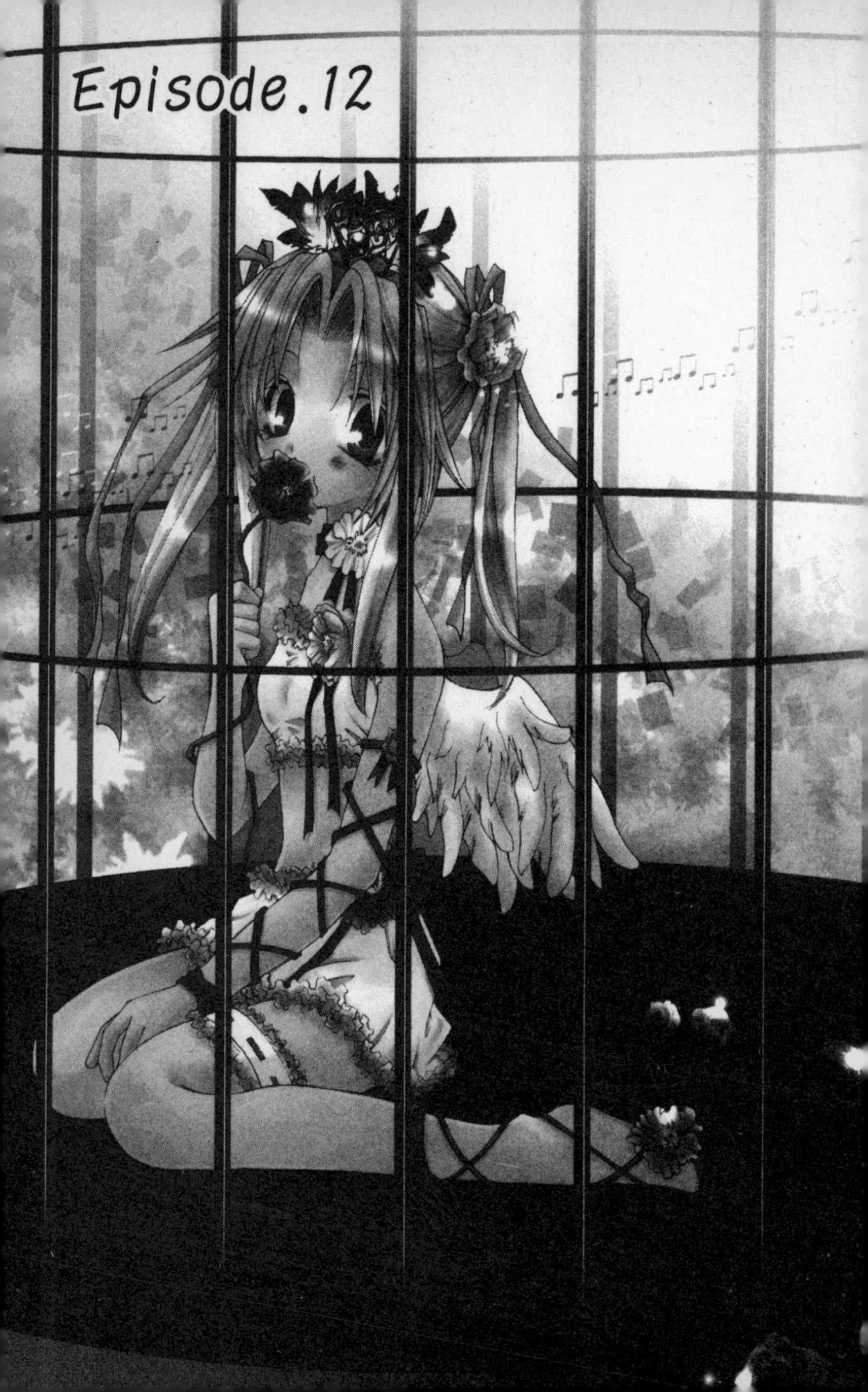
Episode.12

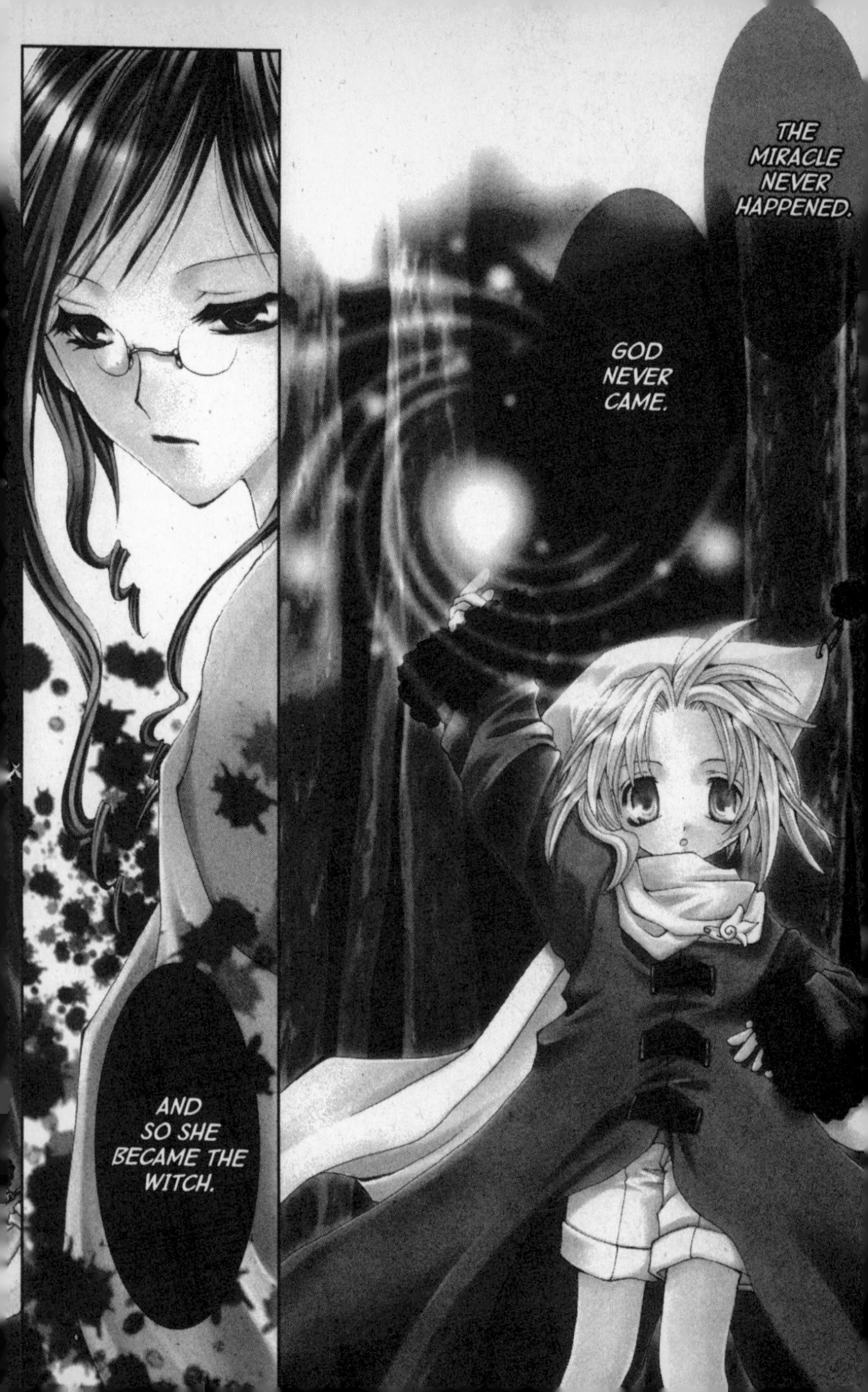
THE MIRACLE NEVER HAPPENED.
GOD NEVER CAME.
AND SO SHE BECAME THE WITCH.

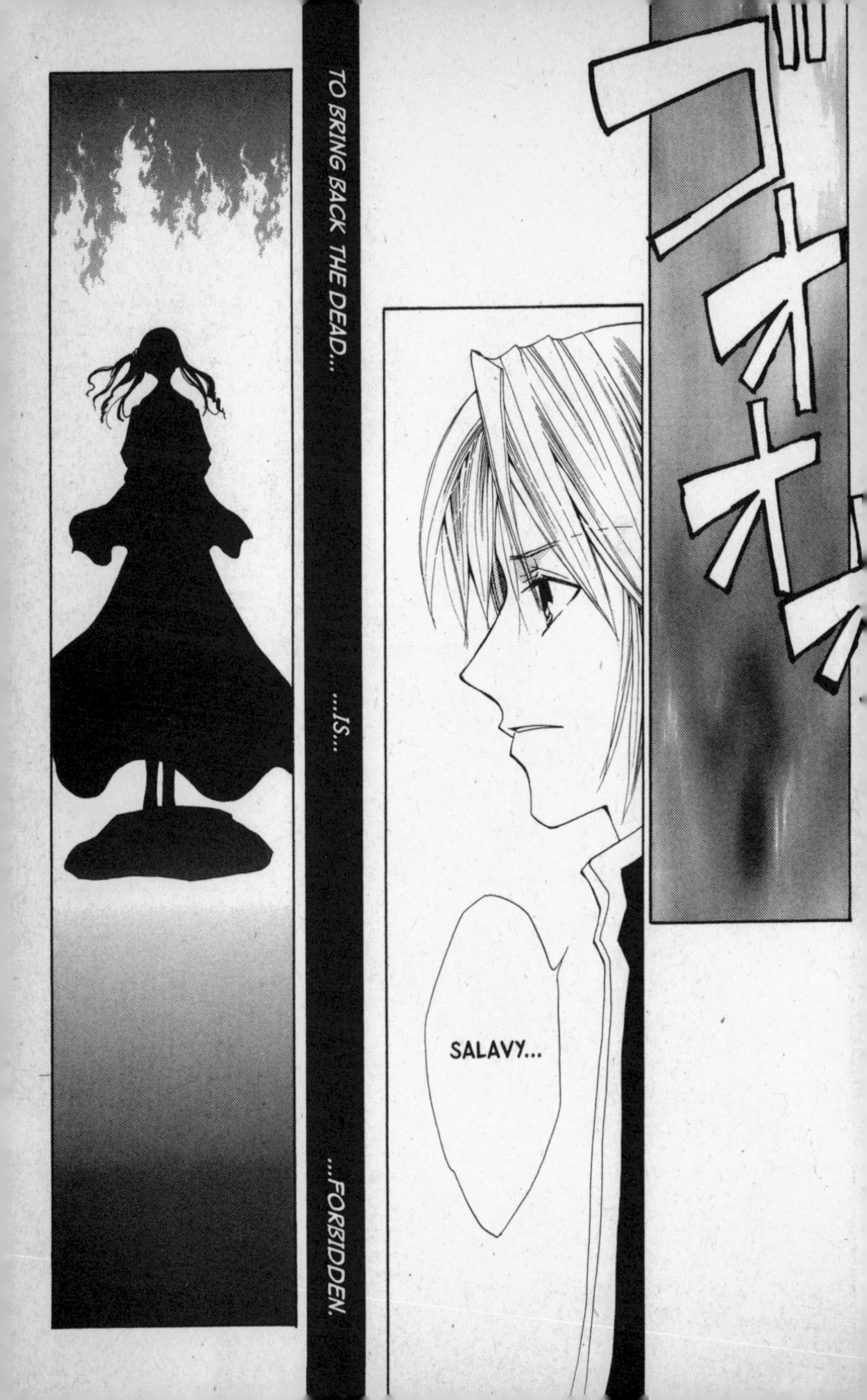
SALAVY...
TO BRING BACK THE DEAD...
...IS...
...FORBIDDEN.

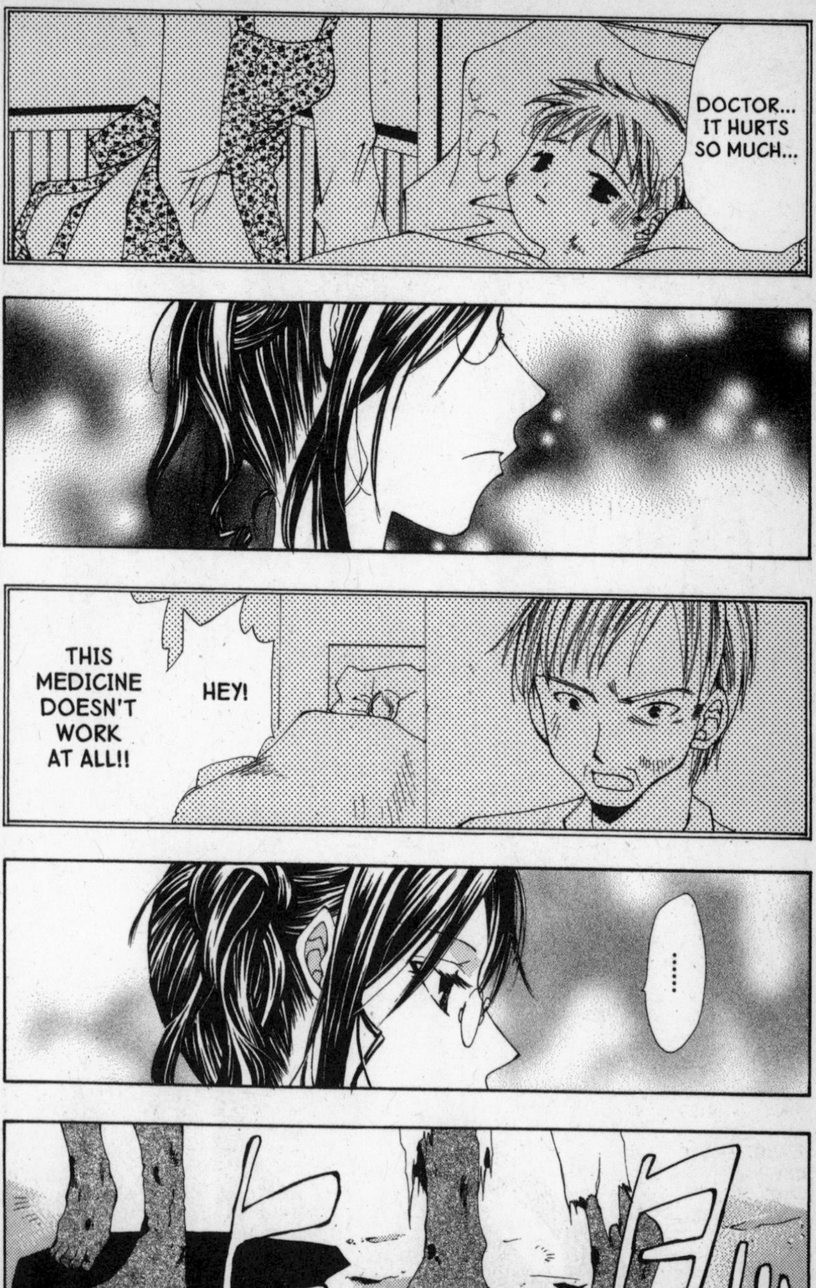
DOCTOR... IT HURTS SO MUCH...
HEY!
THIS MEDICINE DOESN'T WORK AT ALL!!
......

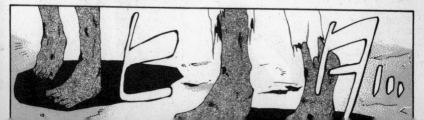

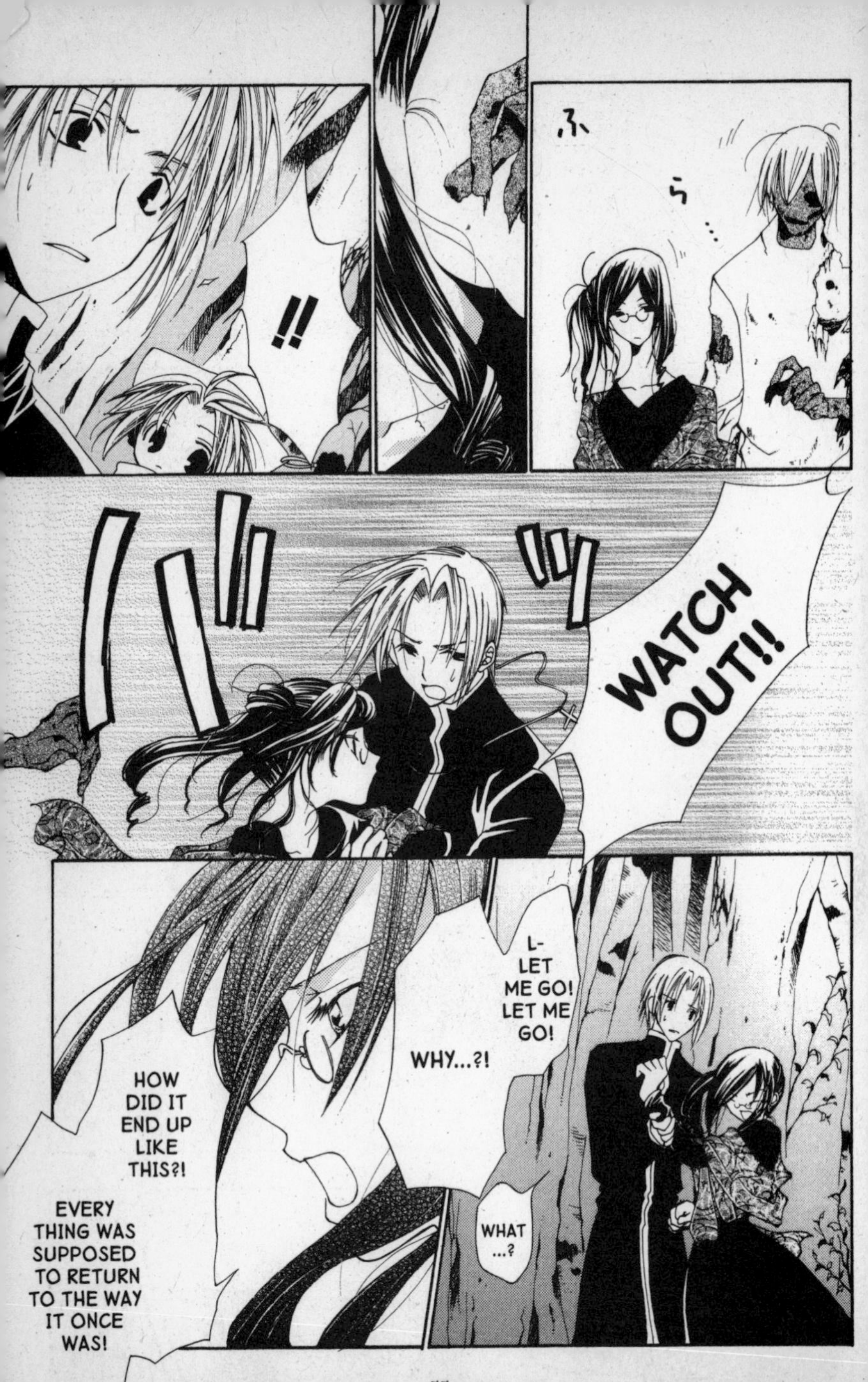
ふら…
!!
WATCH OUT!!
L- LET ME GO! LET ME GO!
WHAT ...?
WHY...?!
HOW DID IT END UP LIKE THIS?!
EVERY THING WAS SUPPOSED TO RETURN TO THE WAY IT ONCE WAS!

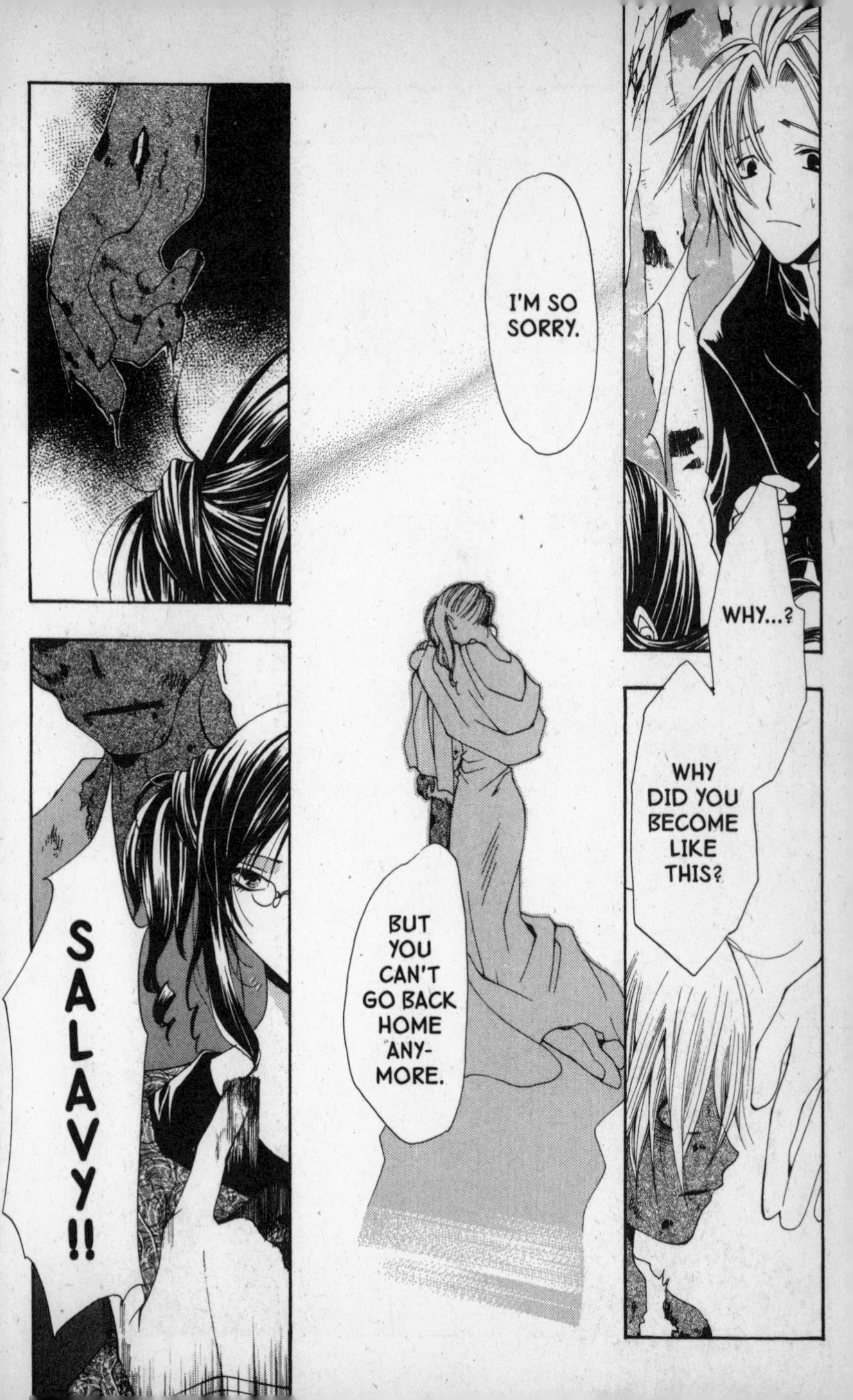
WHY...?
WHY DID YOU BECOME LIKE THIS?
I'M SO SORRY.
BUT YOU CAN'T GO BACK HOME ANY-MORE.
SALAVY!!

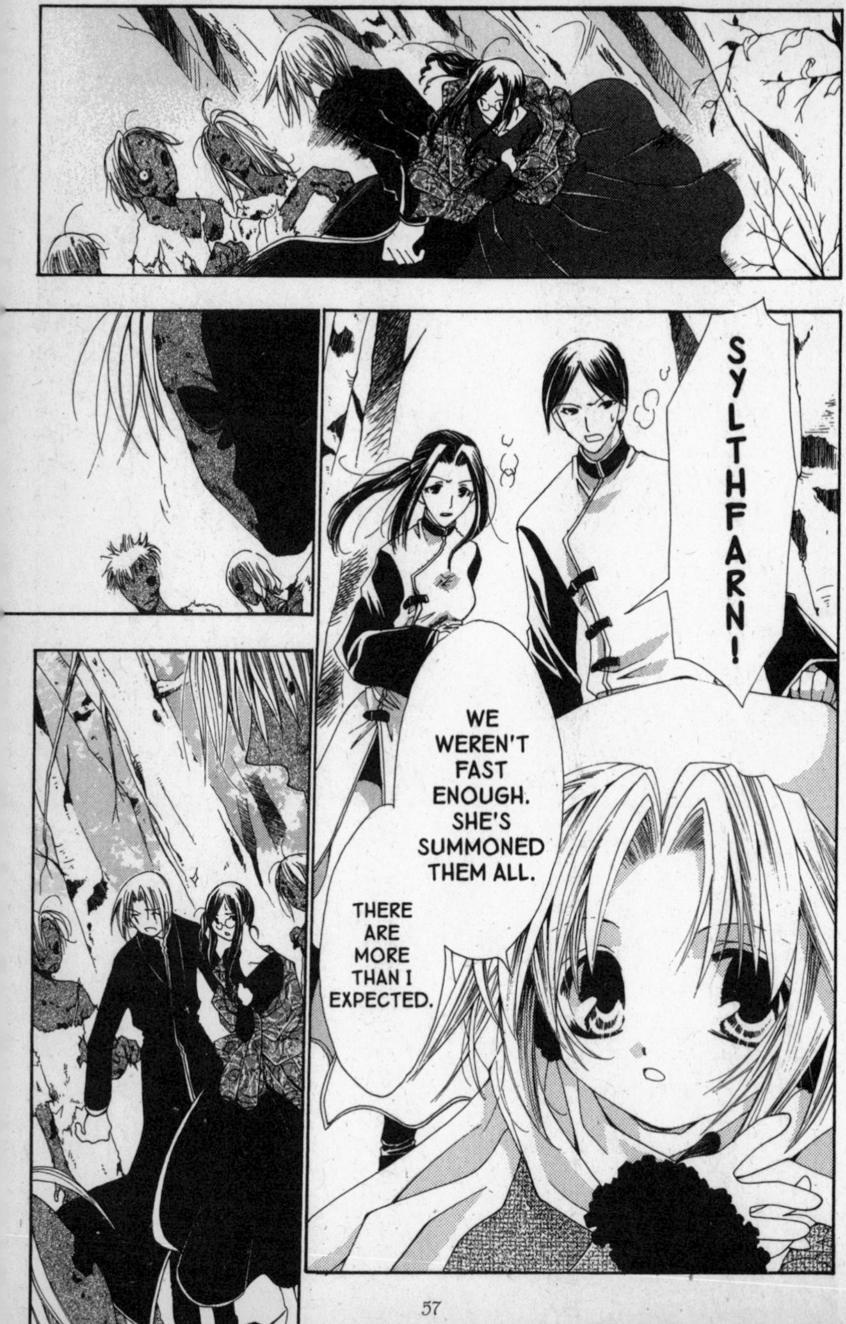
SYLTHFARN!
WE WEREN'T FAST ENOUGH. SHE'S SUMMONED THEM ALL.
THERE ARE MORE THAN I EXPECTED.

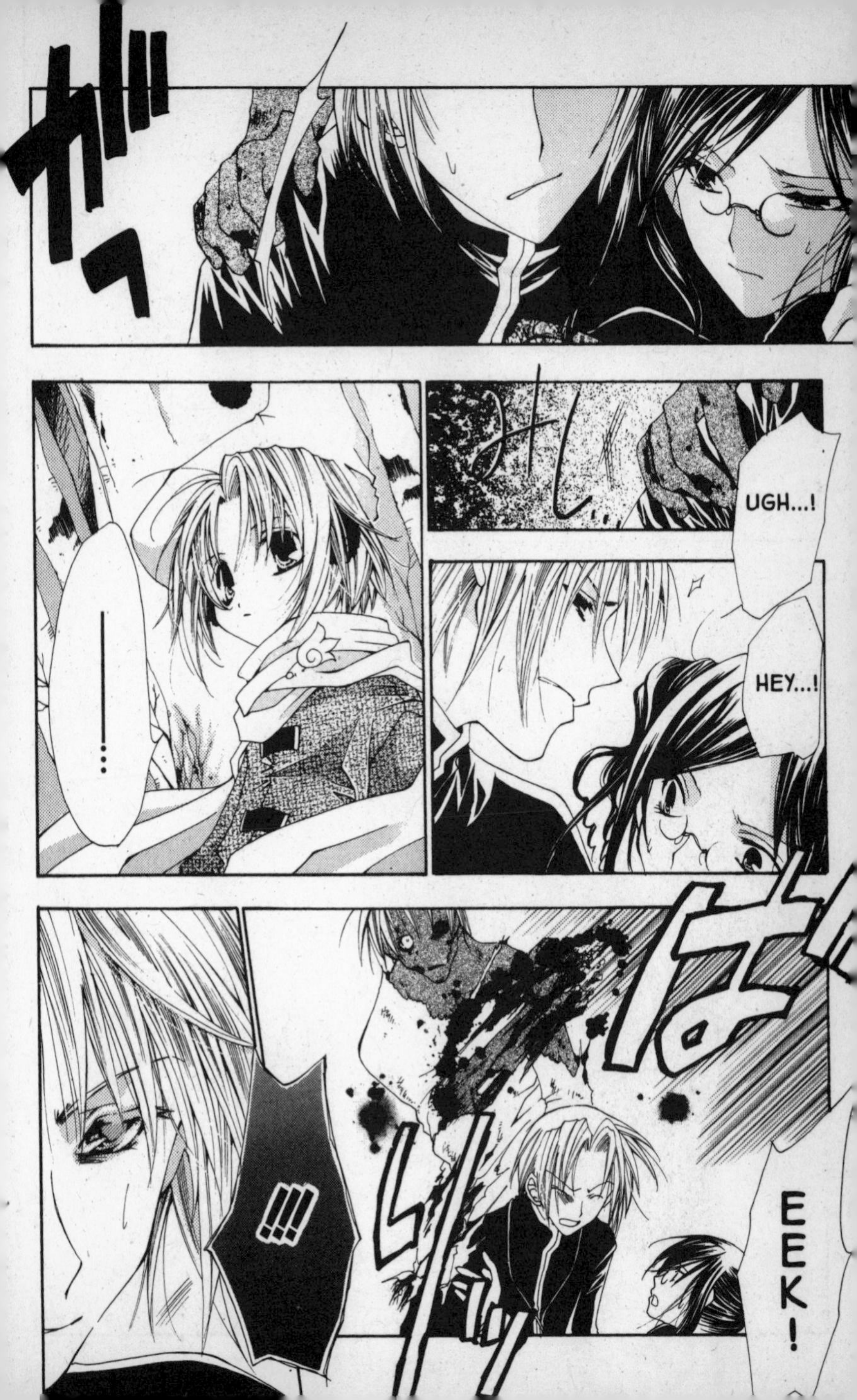
UGH...!
HEY...!
—......
EEK!
!!!

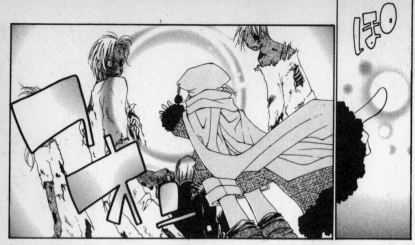

EVEN IN SUCH A TIME OF NEED...

...WILL GOD NOT SAVE US?

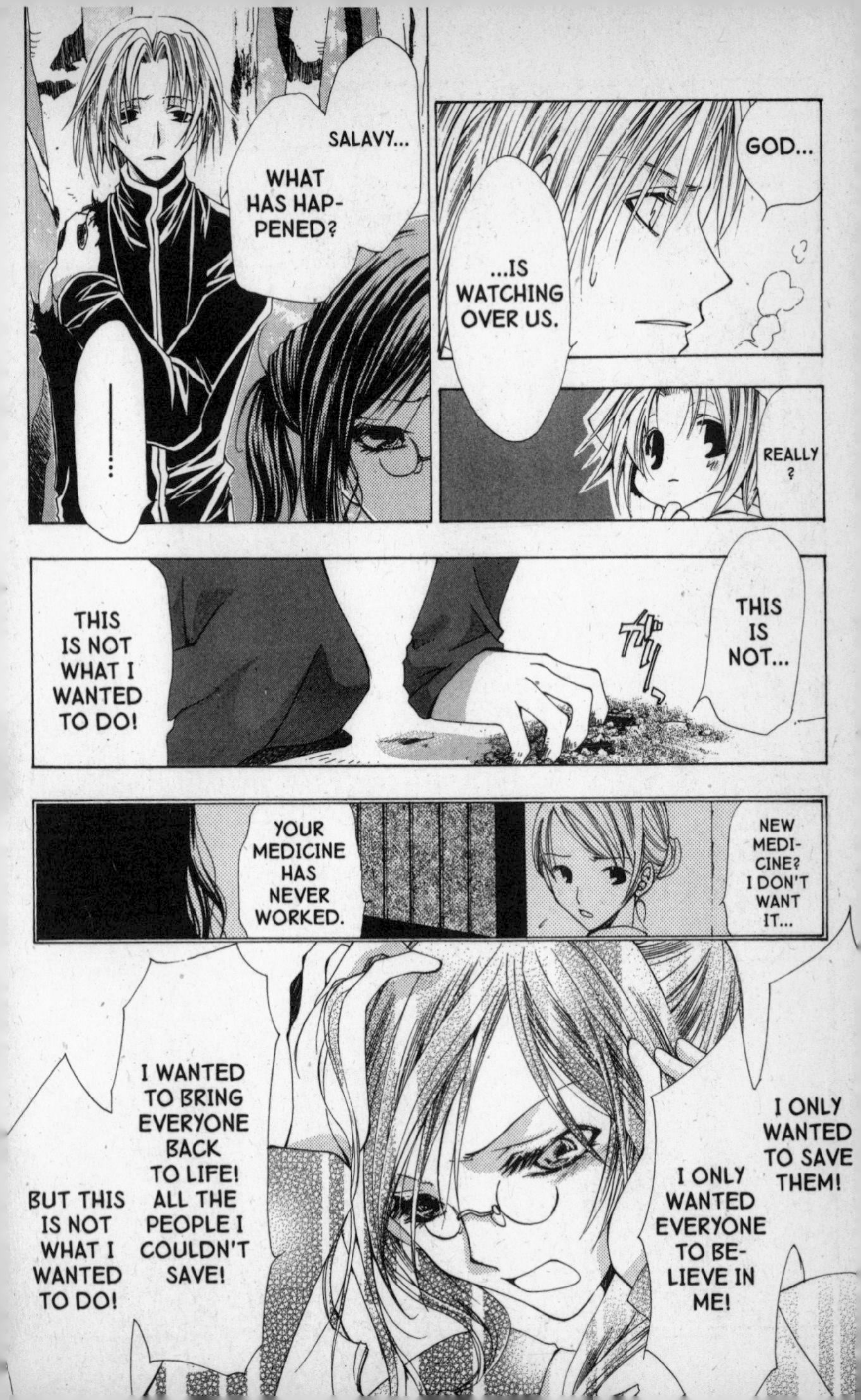
GOD...
...IS WATCHING OVER US.
REALLY?
SALAVY... WHAT HAS HAPPENED?
...!
THIS IS NOT...
THIS IS NOT WHAT I WANTED TO DO!
NEW MEDICINE? I DON'T WANT IT...
YOUR MEDICINE HAS NEVER WORKED.
I ONLY WANTED TO SAVE THEM!
I ONLY WANTED EVERYONE TO BELIEVE IN ME!
I WANTED TO BRING EVERYONE BACK TO LIFE! ALL THE PEOPLE I COULDN'T SAVE!
BUT THIS IS NOT WHAT I WANTED TO DO!

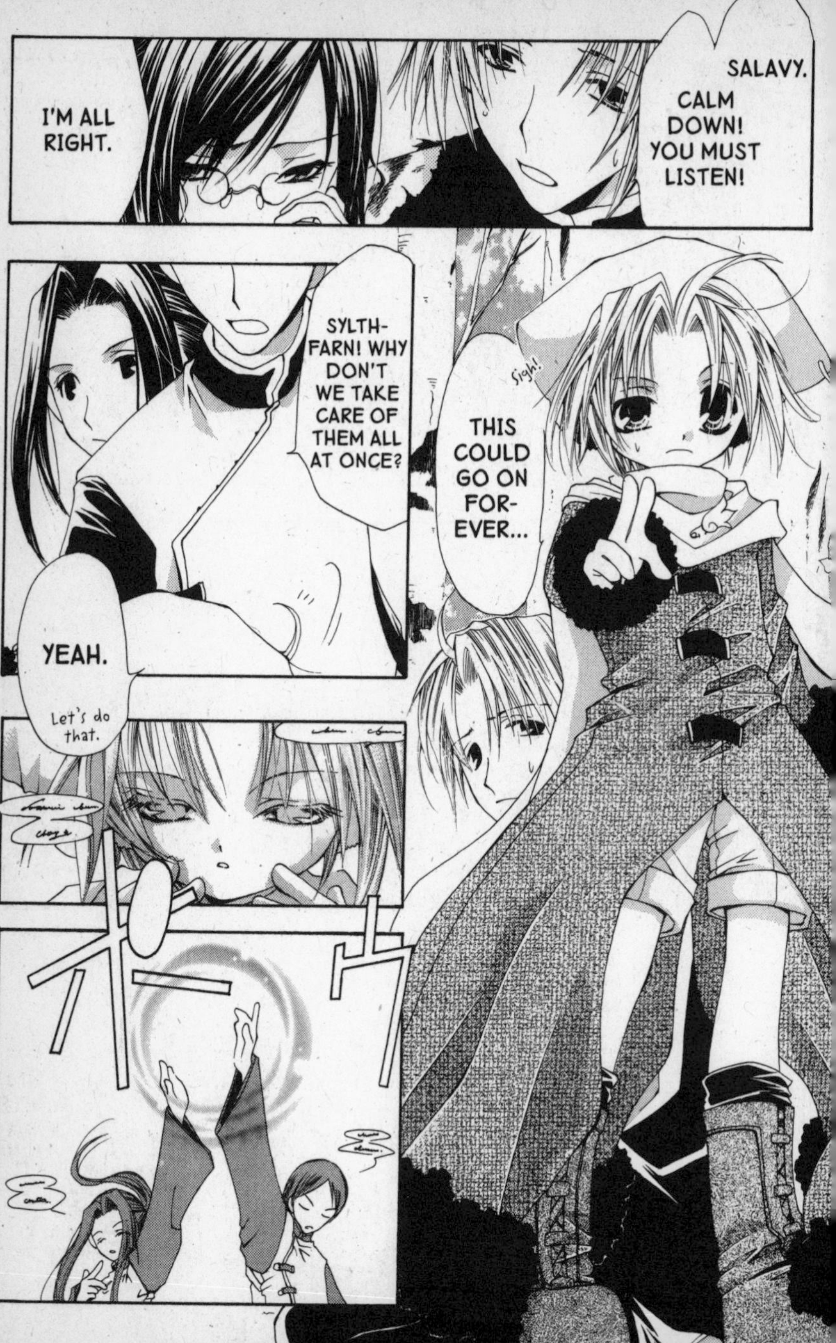
SALAVY.
CALM DOWN! YOU MUST LISTEN!
I'M ALL RIGHT.
Sigh!
THIS COULD GO ON FOR-EVER...
SYLTH-FARN! WHY DON'T WE TAKE CARE OF THEM ALL AT ONCE?
YEAH.
Let's do that.

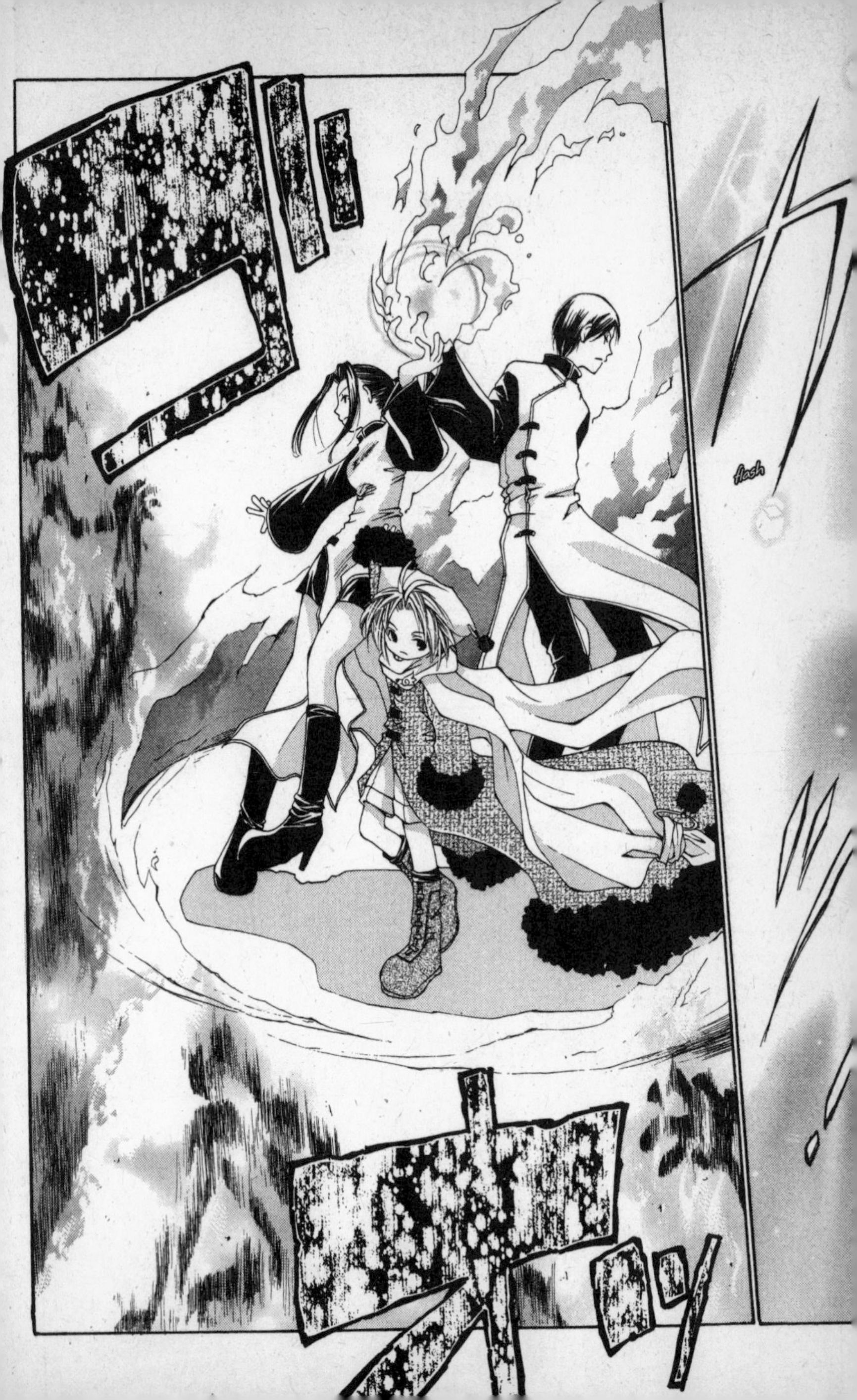
flash

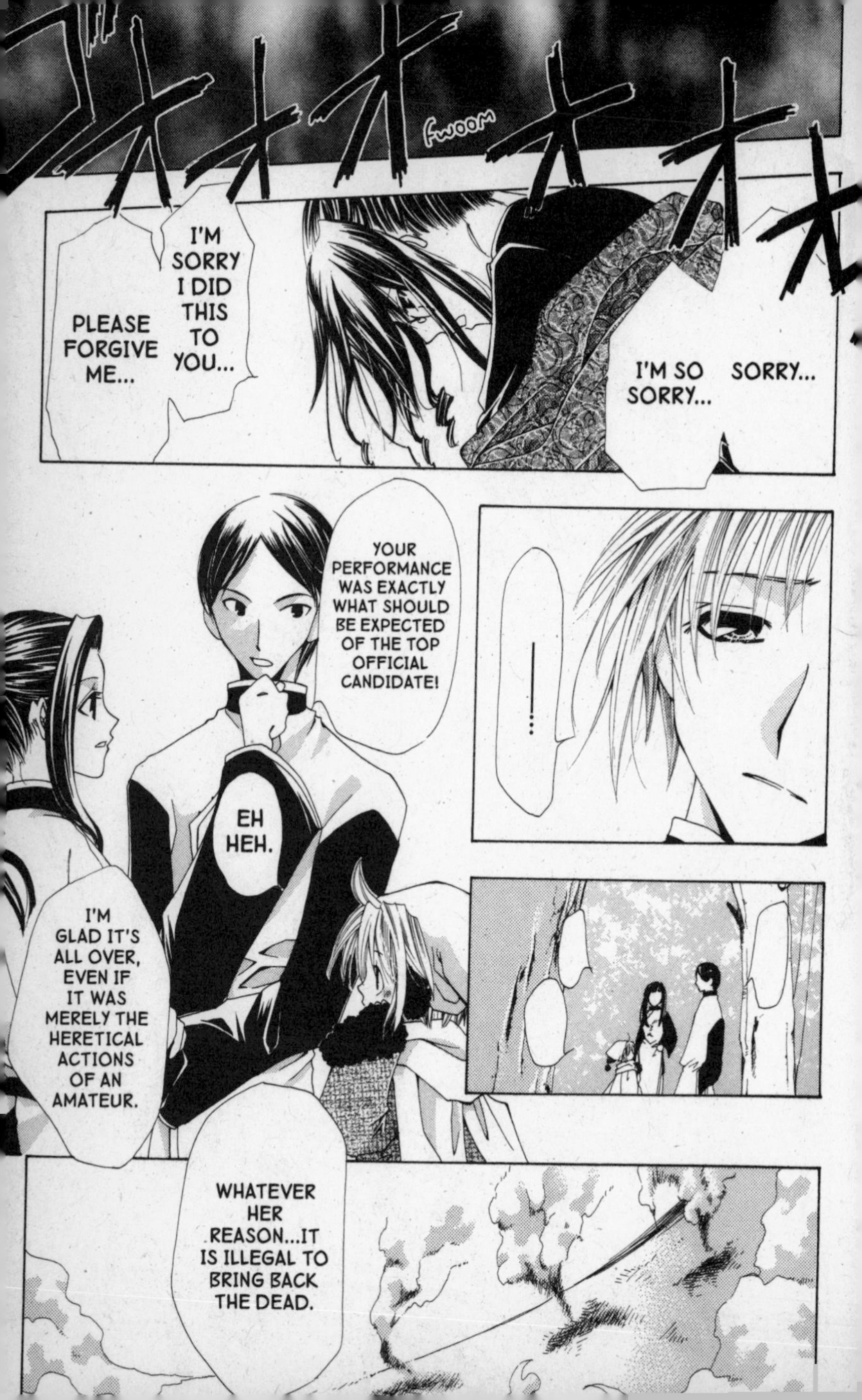
fwoom
I'M SO SORRY... SORRY...
I'M SORRY I DID THIS TO YOU...
PLEASE FORGIVE ME...
......
YOUR PERFORMANCE WAS EXACTLY WHAT SHOULD BE EXPECTED OF THE TOP OFFICIAL CANDIDATE!
EH HEH.
I'M GLAD IT'S ALL OVER, EVEN IF IT WAS MERELY THE HERETICAL ACTIONS OF AN AMATEUR.
WHATEVER HER REASON...IT IS ILLEGAL TO BRING BACK THE DEAD.

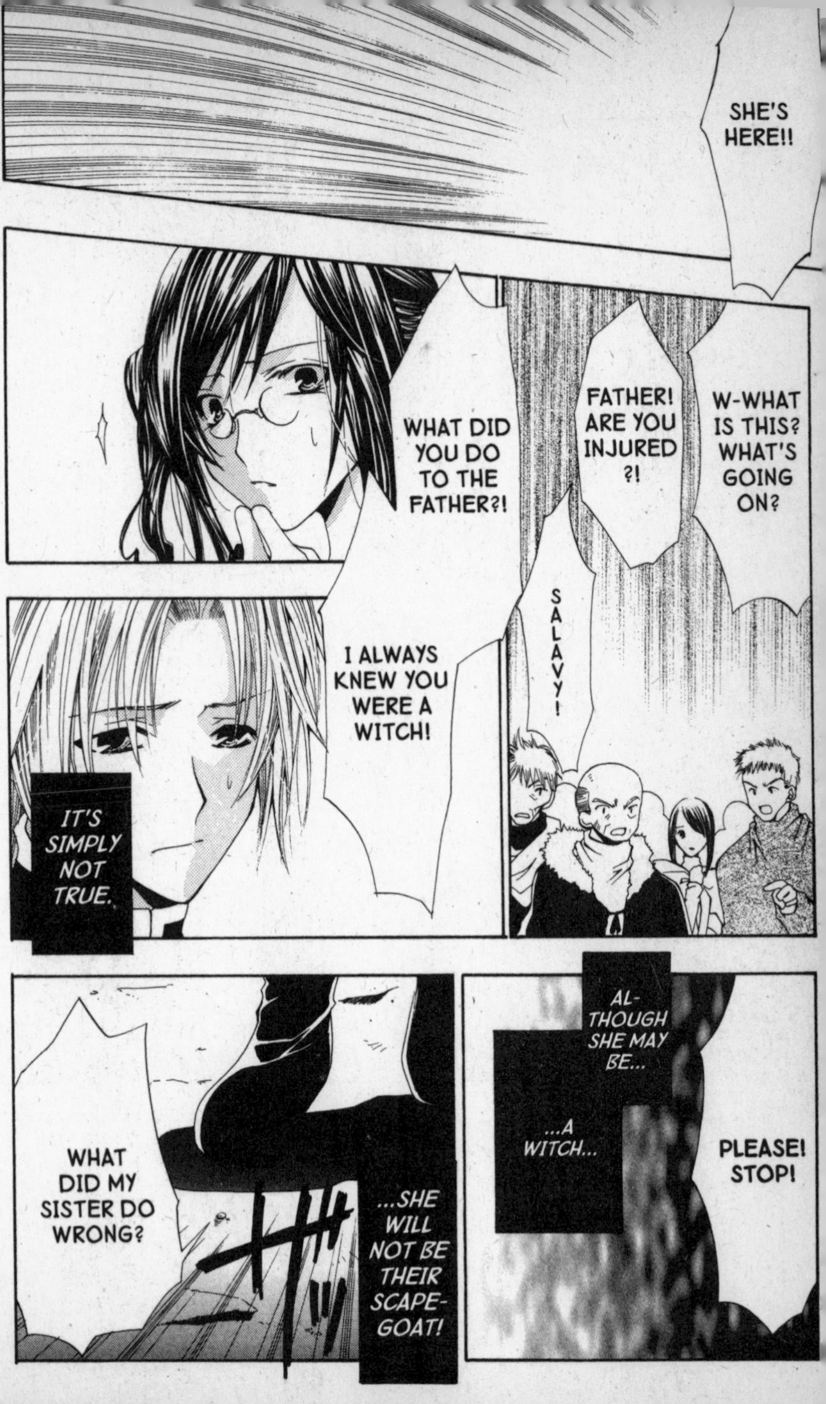
SHE'S HERE!!
W-WHAT IS THIS? WHAT'S GOING ON?
FATHER! ARE YOU INJURED?!
SALAVY!
WHAT DID YOU DO TO THE FATHER?!
I ALWAYS KNEW YOU WERE A WITCH!
IT'S SIMPLY NOT TRUE.
PLEASE! STOP!
AL-THOUGH SHE MAY BE...
...A WITCH...
...SHE WILL NOT BE THEIR SCAPE-GOAT!
WHAT DID MY SISTER DO WRONG?

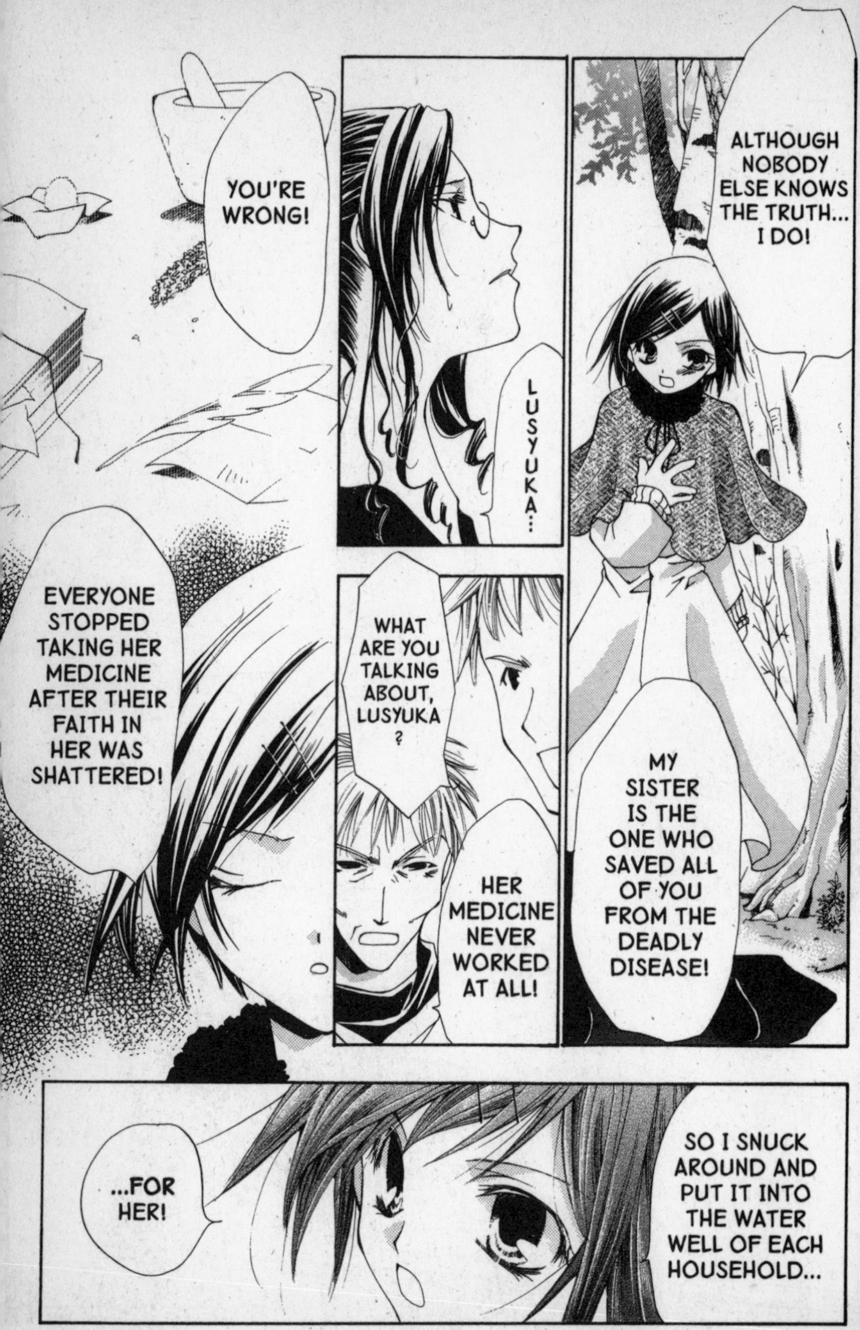
ALTHOUGH NOBODY ELSE KNOWS THE TRUTH... I DO!
MY SISTER IS THE ONE WHO SAVED ALL OF YOU FROM THE DEADLY DISEASE!
LUSYUKA...
WHAT ARE YOU TALKING ABOUT, LUSYUKA?
HER MEDICINE NEVER WORKED AT ALL!
YOU'RE WRONG!
EVERYONE STOPPED TAKING HER MEDICINE AFTER THEIR FAITH IN HER WAS SHATTERED!
SO I SNUCK AROUND AND PUT IT INTO THE WATER WELL OF EACH HOUSEHOLD...
...FOR HER!

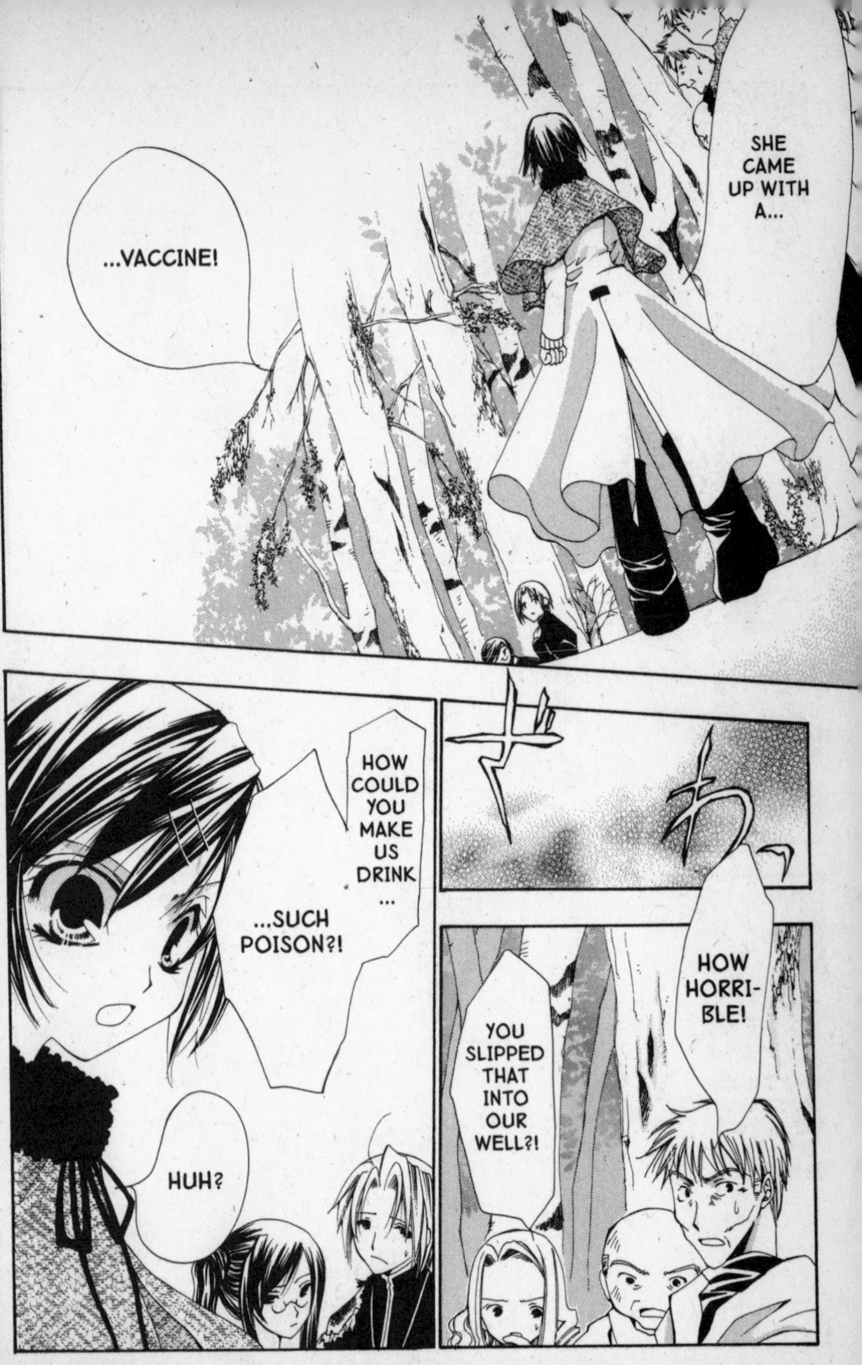
SHE CAME UP WITH A...
...VACCINE!
HOW HORRI-BLE!
YOU SLIPPED THAT INTO OUR WELL?!
HOW COULD YOU MAKE US DRINK ...
...SUCH POISON?!
HUH?

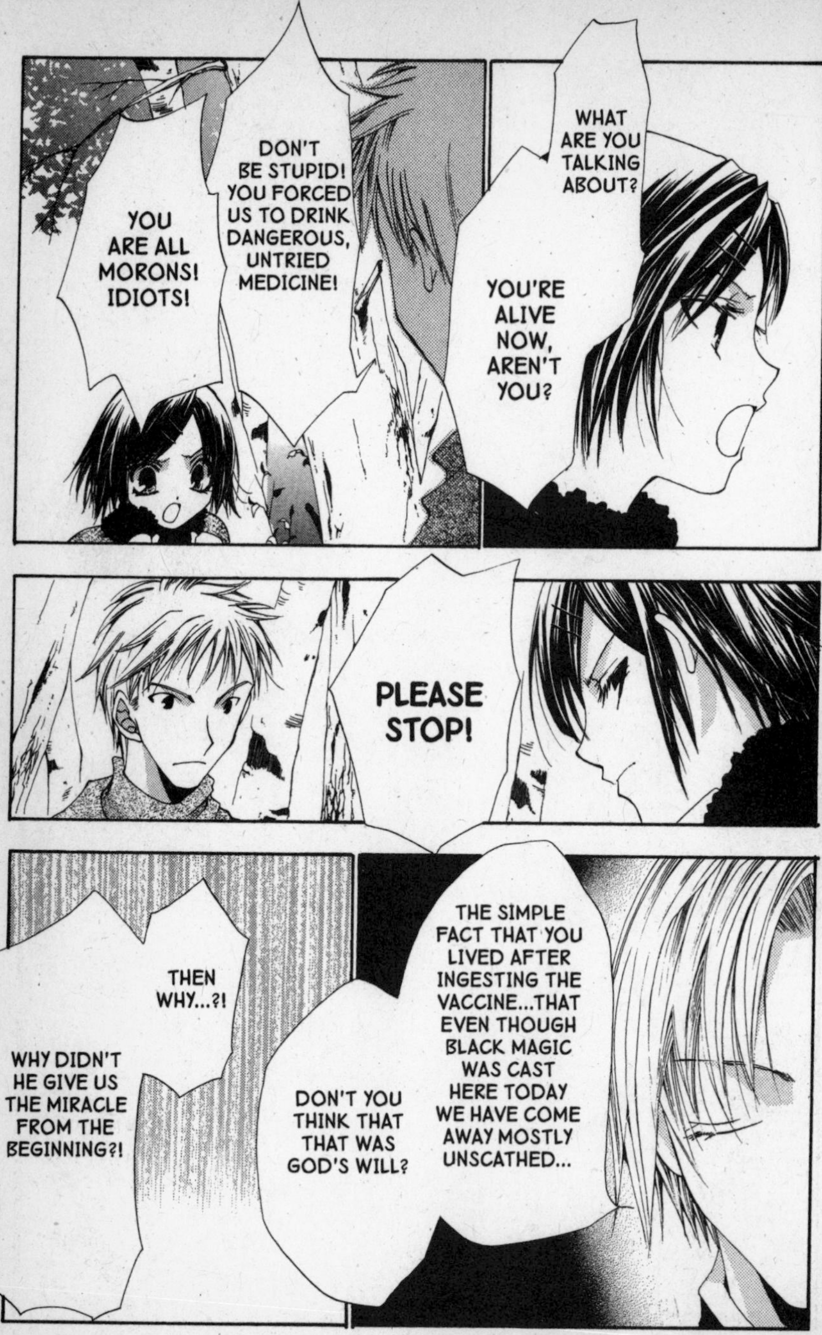
WHAT ARE YOU TALKING ABOUT?
YOU'RE ALIVE NOW, AREN'T YOU?
DON'T BE STUPID! YOU FORCED US TO DRINK DANGEROUS, UNTRIED MEDICINE!
YOU ARE ALL MORONS! IDIOTS!
PLEASE STOP!
THE SIMPLE FACT THAT YOU LIVED AFTER INGESTING THE VACCINE...THAT EVEN THOUGH BLACK MAGIC WAS CAST HERE TODAY WE HAVE COME AWAY MOSTLY UNSCATHED...
DON'T YOU THINK THAT THAT WAS GOD'S WILL?
THEN WHY...?!
WHY DIDN'T HE GIVE US THE MIRACLE FROM THE BEGINNING?!

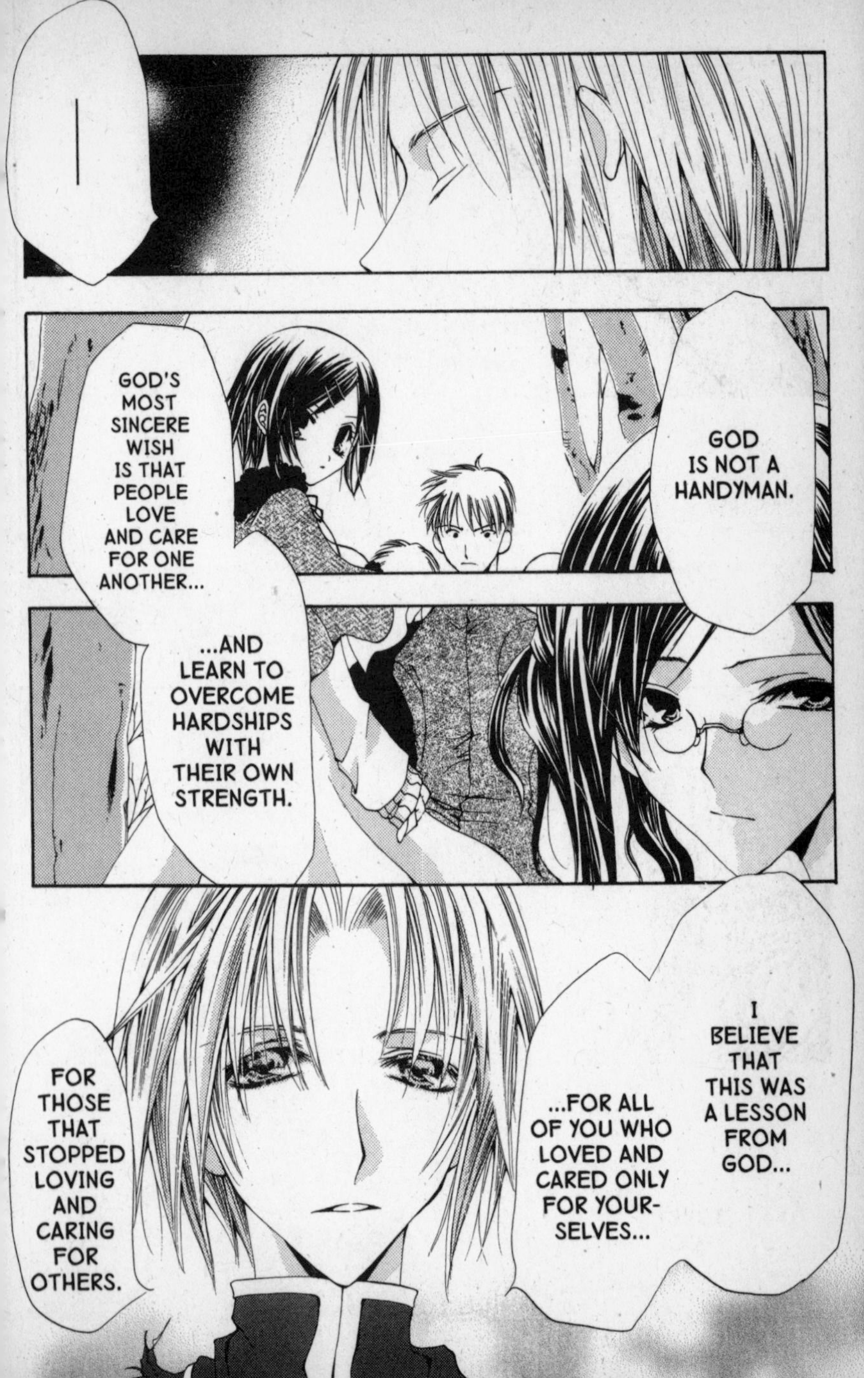
—
GOD IS NOT A HANDYMAN.
GOD'S MOST SINCERE WISH IS THAT PEOPLE LOVE AND CARE FOR ONE ANOTHER...
...AND LEARN TO OVERCOME HARDSHIPS WITH THEIR OWN STRENGTH.
I BELIEVE THAT THIS WAS A LESSON FROM GOD...
...FOR ALL OF YOU WHO LOVED AND CARED ONLY FOR YOUR-SELVES...
FOR THOSE THAT STOPPED LOVING AND CARING FOR OTHERS.

......

WE'RE SORRY...

I'M SORRY, TOO.

IT'S ALL RIGHT.

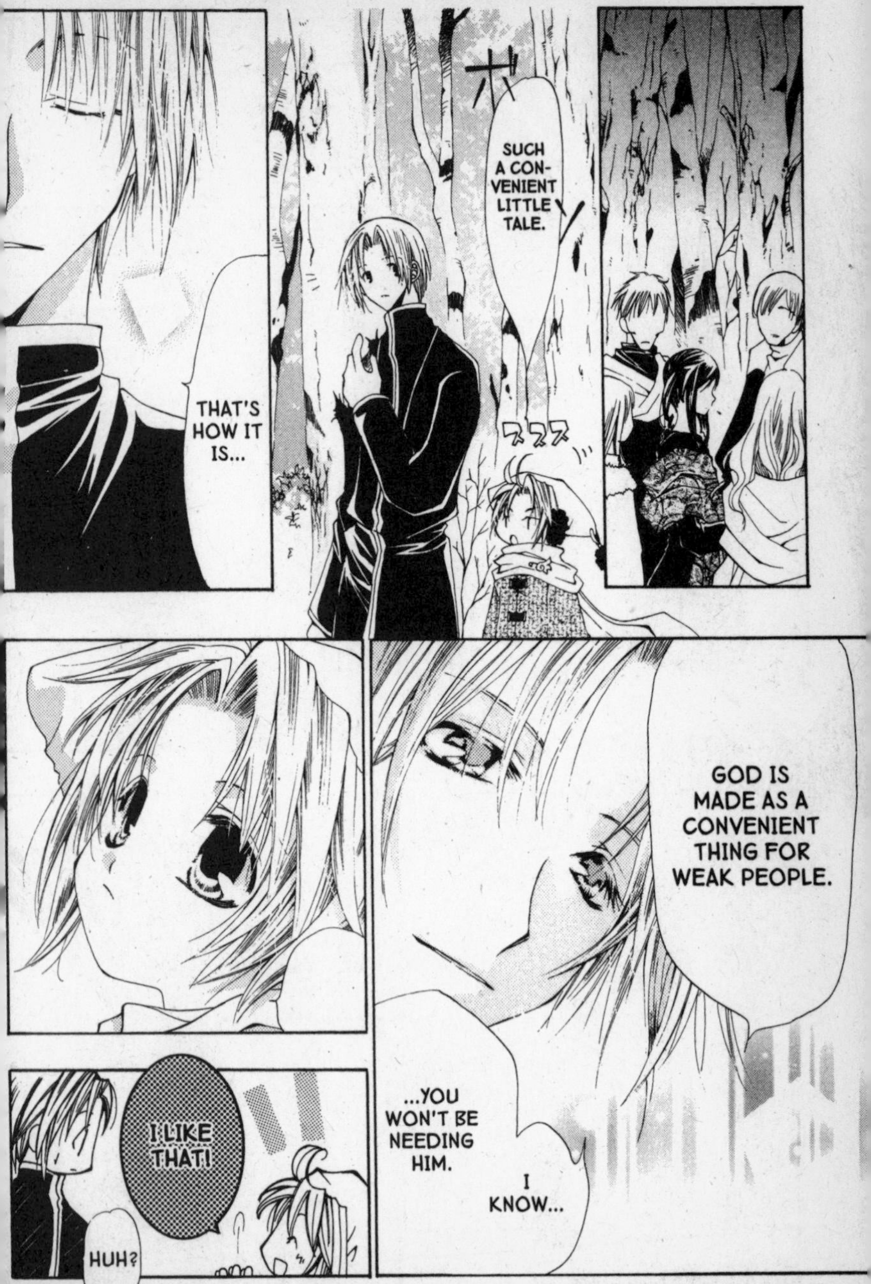
SUCH A CON-VENIENT LITTLE TALE.
THAT'S HOW IT IS...
GOD IS MADE AS A CONVENIENT THING FOR WEAK PEOPLE.
...YOU WON'T BE NEEDING HIM.
I KNOW...
I LIKE THAT!
HUH?

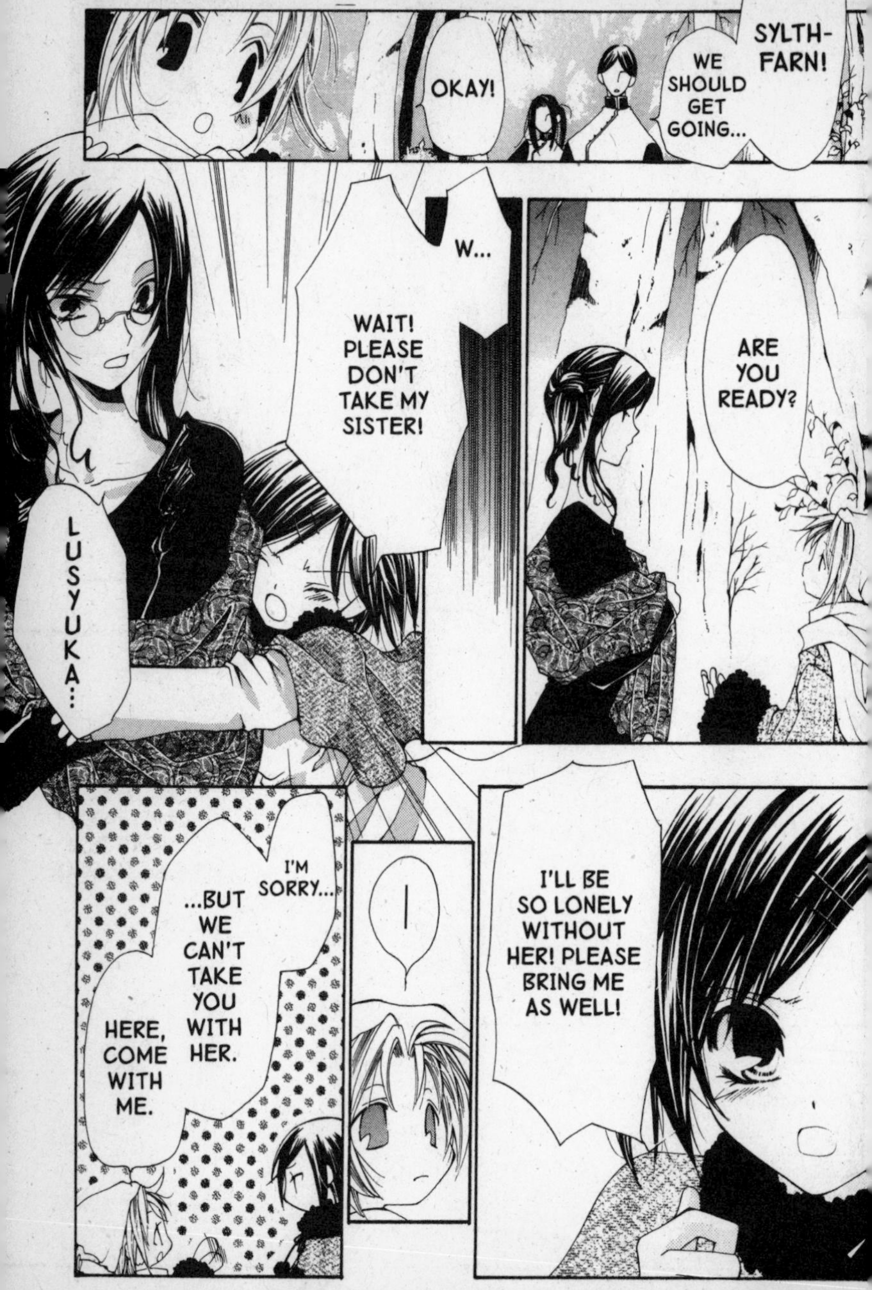
SYLTH-FARN!
WE SHOULD GET GOING...
OKAY!
ARE YOU READY?
W...
WAIT! PLEASE DON'T TAKE MY SISTER!
LUSYUKA...
I'LL BE SO LONELY WITHOUT HER! PLEASE BRING ME AS WELL!
I
I'M SORRY...
...BUT WE CAN'T TAKE YOU WITH HER.
HERE, COME WITH ME.

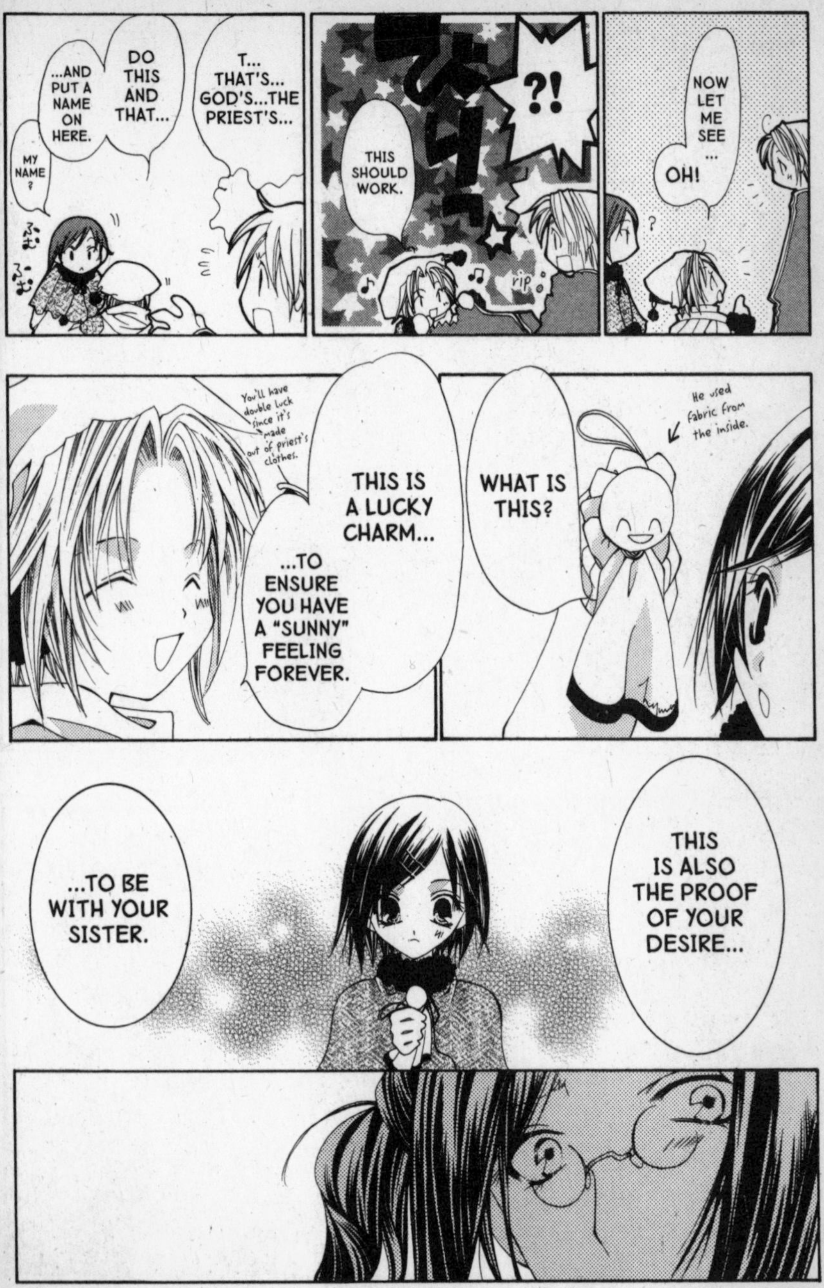
NOW LET ME SEE ... OH!
?!
THIS SHOULD WORK.
rip
T... THAT'S... GOD'S...THE PRIEST'S...
DO THIS AND THAT...
...AND PUT A NAME ON HERE.
MY NAME?
ふむふむ
WHAT IS THIS?
He used fabric from the inside.
THIS IS A LUCKY CHARM...
...TO ENSURE YOU HAVE A "SUNNY" FEELING FOREVER.
You'll have double luck since it's made out of priest's clothes.
THIS IS ALSO THE PROOF OF YOUR DESIRE...
...TO BE WITH YOUR SISTER.

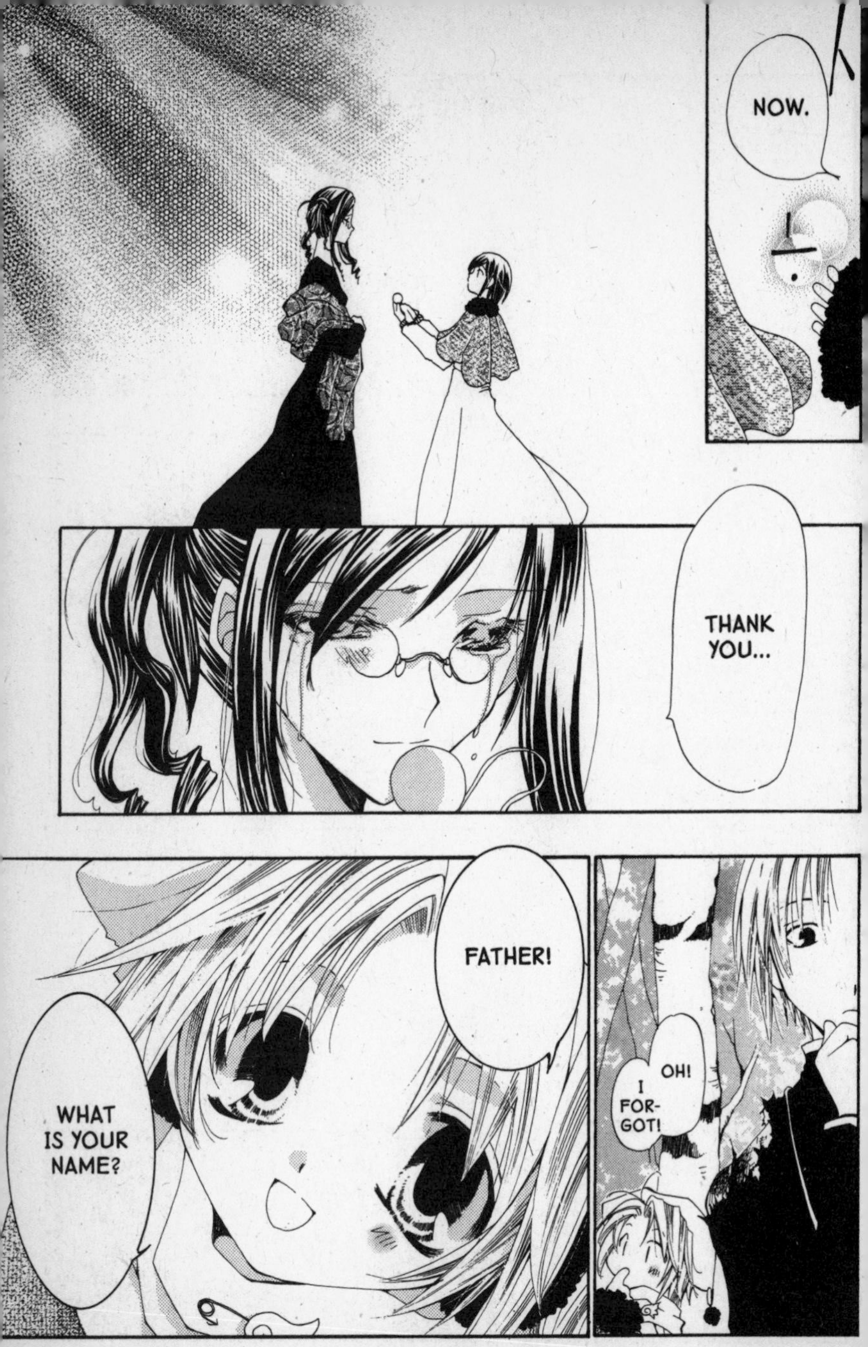
NOW.
THANK YOU...
OH! I FOR-GOT!
FATHER!
WHAT IS YOUR NAME?

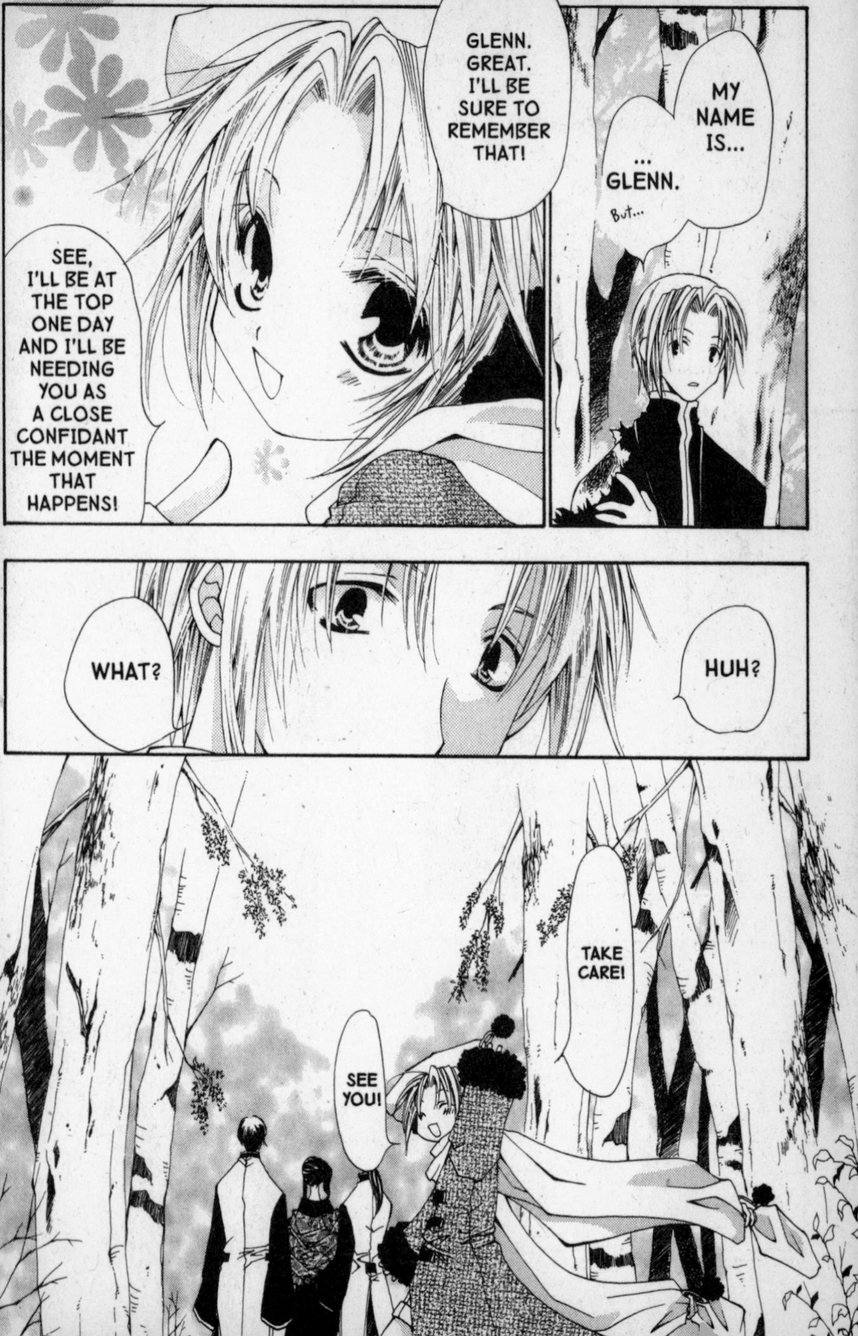
MY NAME IS...
... GLENN.
But...
GLENN. GREAT. I'LL BE SURE TO REMEMBER THAT!
SEE, I'LL BE AT THE TOP ONE DAY AND I'LL BE NEEDING YOU AS A CLOSE CONFIDANT THE MOMENT THAT HAPPENS!
HUH?
WHAT?
TAKE CARE!
SEE YOU!

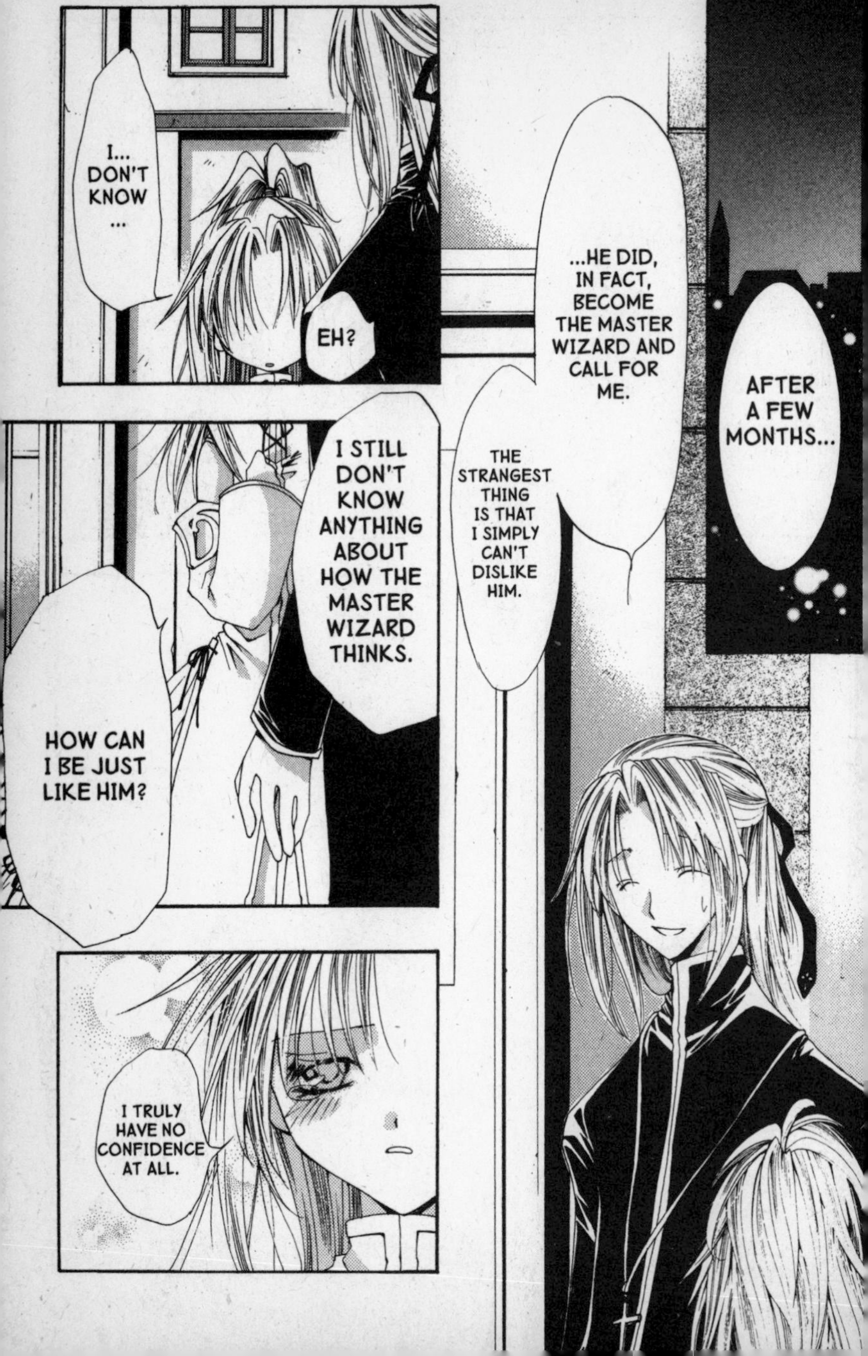
AFTER A FEW MONTHS...
...HE DID, IN FACT, BECOME THE MASTER WIZARD AND CALL FOR ME.
THE STRANGEST THING IS THAT I SIMPLY CAN'T DISLIKE HIM.
I... DON'T KNOW ...
EH?
I STILL DON'T KNOW ANYTHING ABOUT HOW THE MASTER WIZARD THINKS.
HOW CAN I BE JUST LIKE HIM?
I TRULY HAVE NO CONFIDENCE AT ALL.

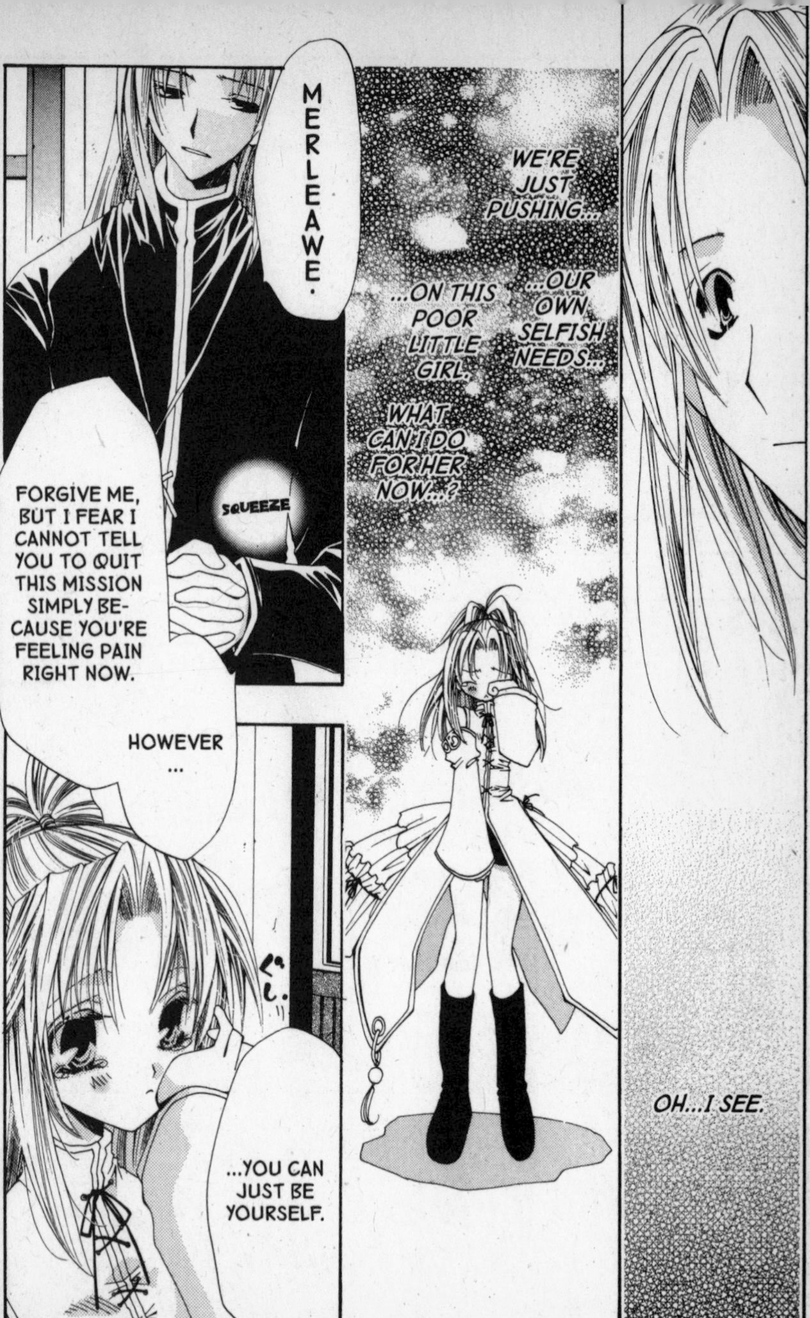

OH...I SEE.
WE'RE JUST PUSHING...
...OUR OWN SELFISH NEEDS...
...ON THIS POOR LITTLE GIRL.
WHAT CAN I DO FOR HER NOW...?
MERLEAWE.
FORGIVE ME, BUT I FEAR I CANNOT TELL YOU TO QUIT THIS MISSION SIMPLY BE-CAUSE YOU'RE FEELING PAIN RIGHT NOW.
SQUEEZE
HOWEVER ...
...YOU CAN JUST BE YOURSELF.

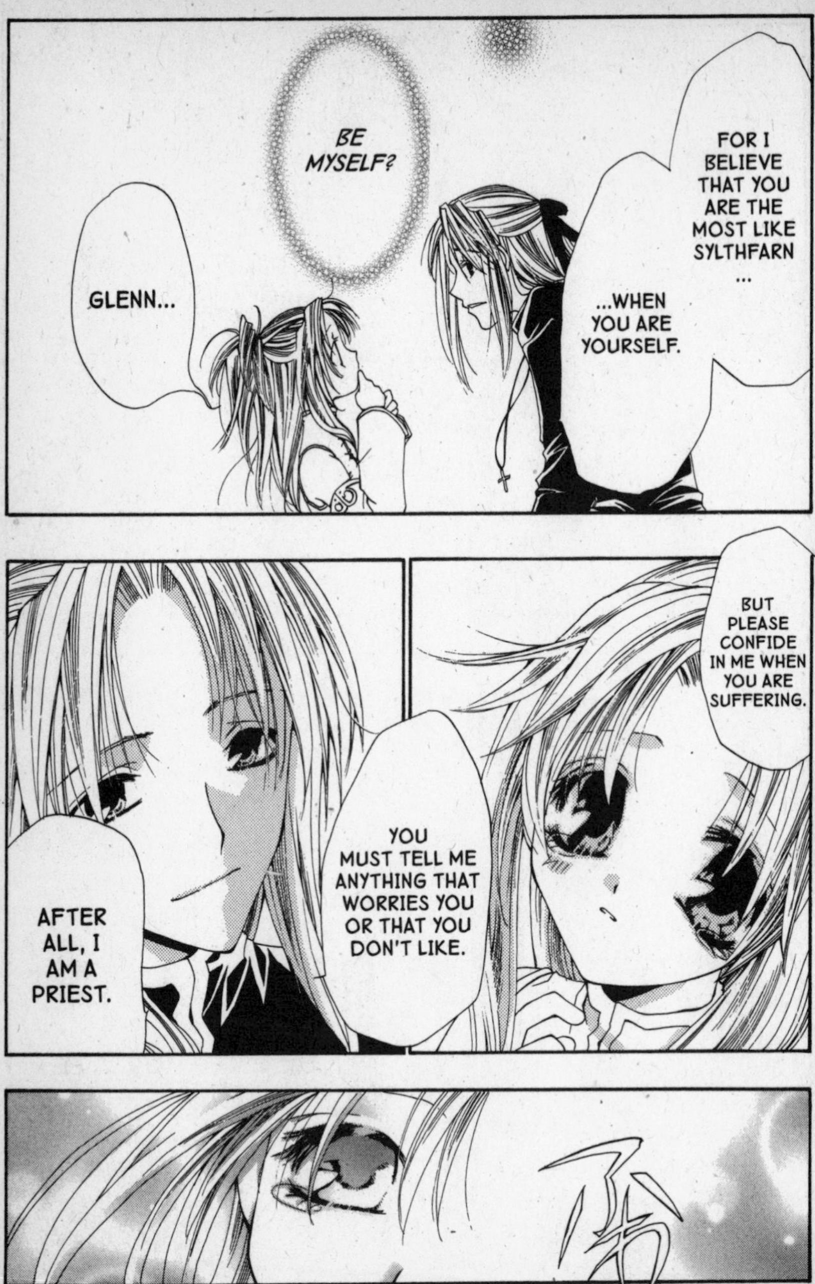
FOR I BELIEVE THAT YOU ARE THE MOST LIKE SYLTHFARN ...
...WHEN YOU ARE YOURSELF.
BE MYSELF?
GLENN...
BUT PLEASE CONFIDE IN ME WHEN YOU ARE SUFFERING.
YOU MUST TELL ME ANYTHING THAT WORRIES YOU OR THAT YOU DON'T LIKE.
AFTER ALL, I AM A PRIEST.

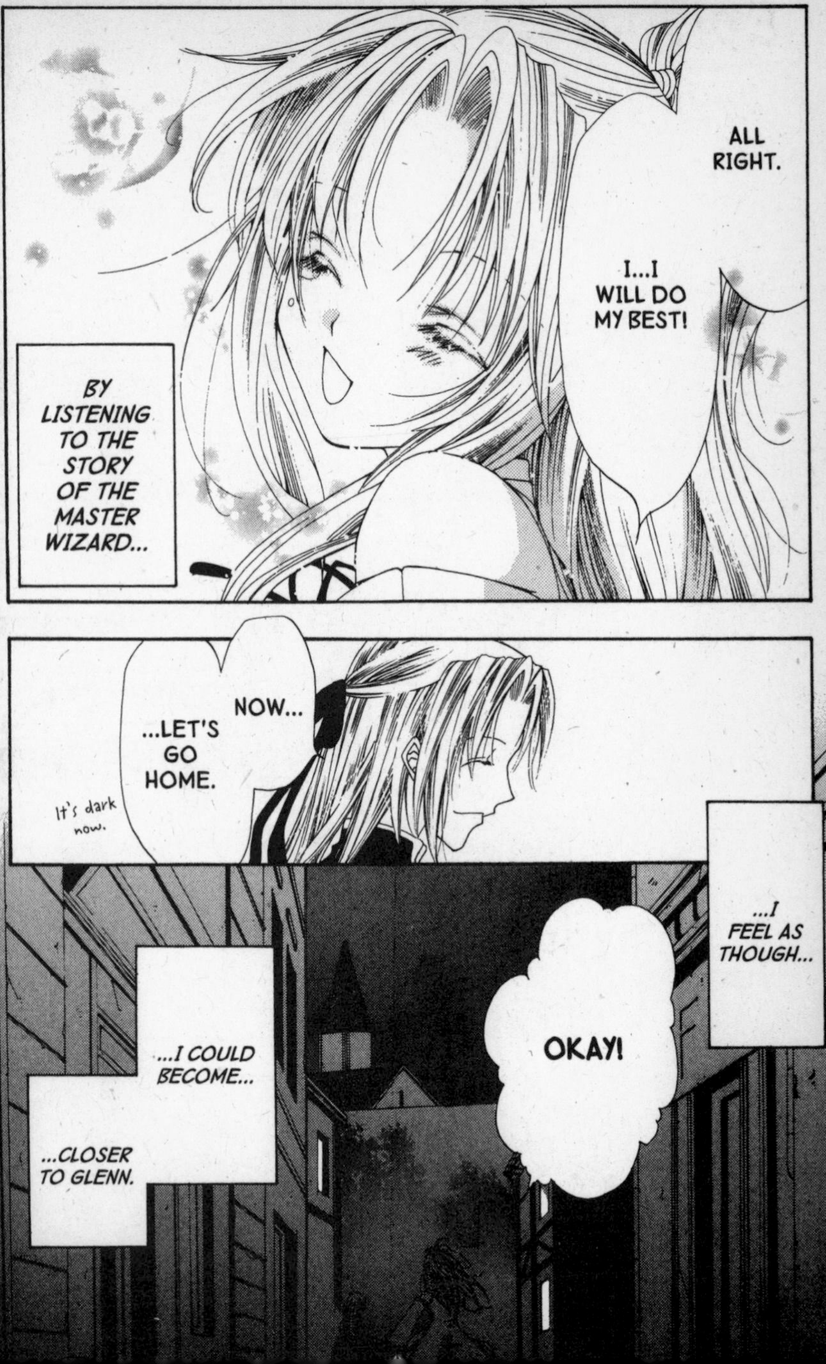
ALL RIGHT.
I...I WILL DO MY BEST!
BY LISTENING TO THE STORY OF THE MASTER WIZARD...
NOW...
...LET'S GO HOME.
It's dark now.
...I FEEL AS THOUGH...
OKAY!
...I COULD BECOME...
...CLOSER TO GLENN.

Episode.13

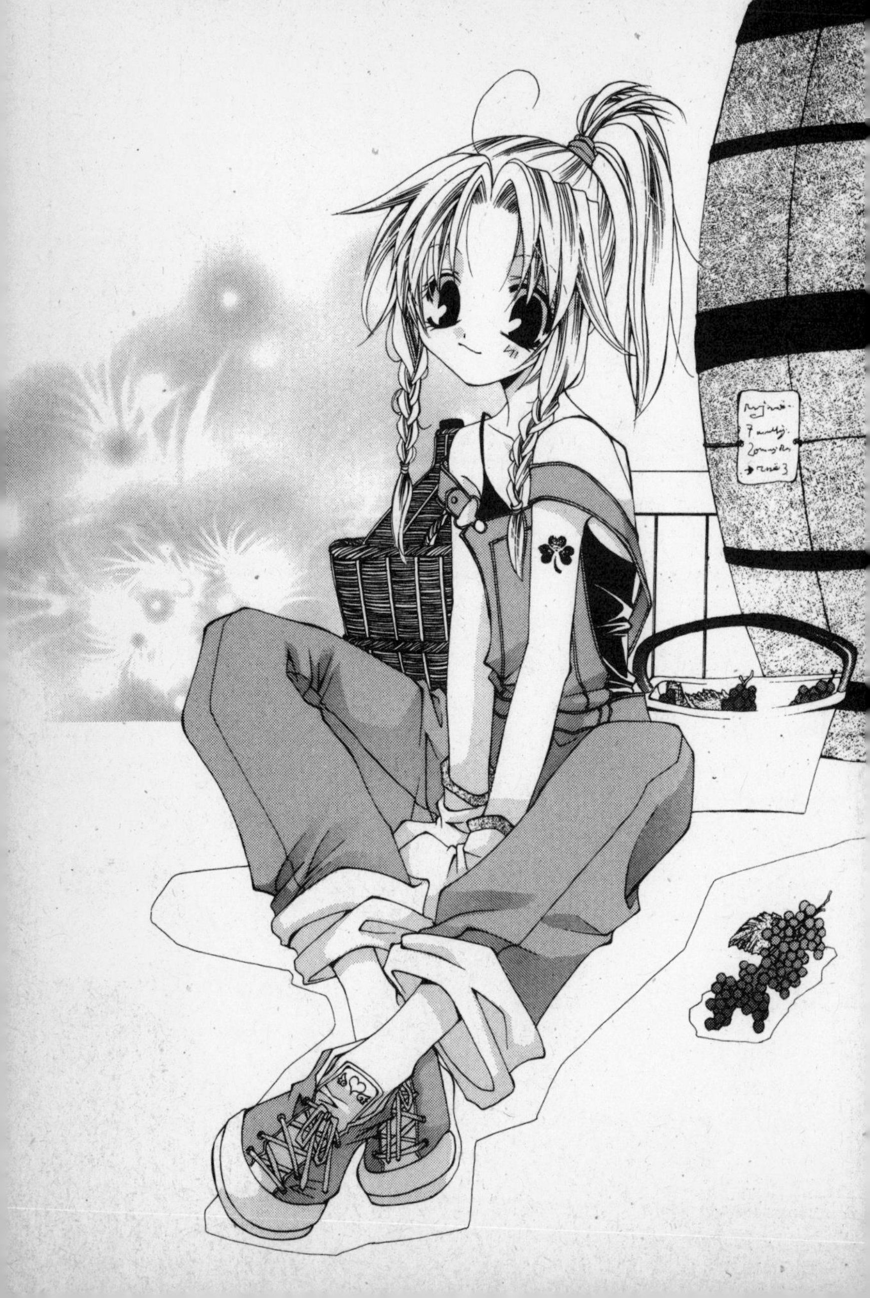

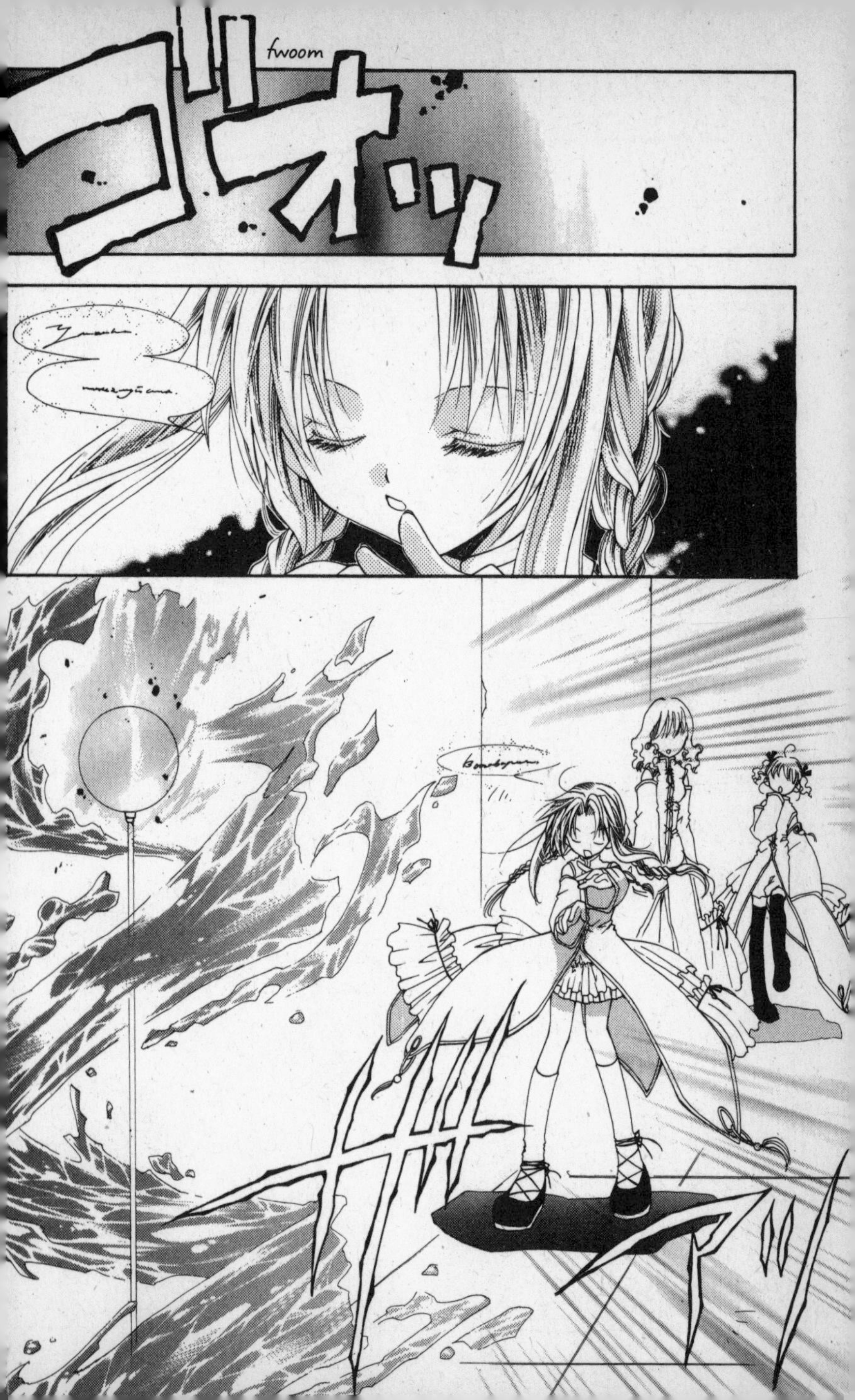
fwoom

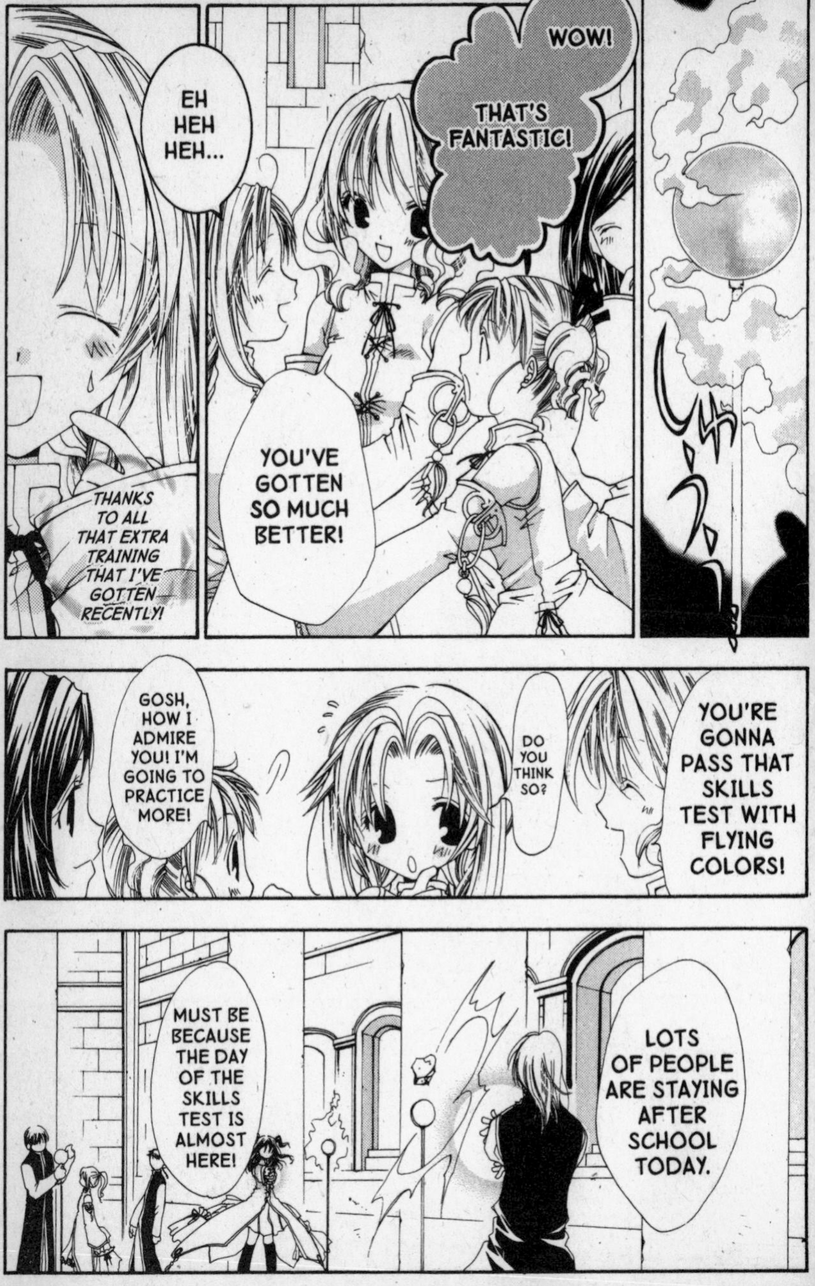
WOW! THAT'S FANTASTIC!
YOU'VE GOTTEN SO MUCH BETTER!
EH HEH HEH...
THANKS TO ALL THAT EXTRA TRAINING THAT I'VE GOTTEN RECENTLY!
YOU'RE GONNA PASS THAT SKILLS TEST WITH FLYING COLORS!
DO YOU THINK SO?
GOSH, HOW I ADMIRE YOU! I'M GOING TO PRACTICE MORE!
LOTS OF PEOPLE ARE STAYING AFTER SCHOOL TODAY.
MUST BE BECAUSE THE DAY OF THE SKILLS TEST IS ALMOST HERE!

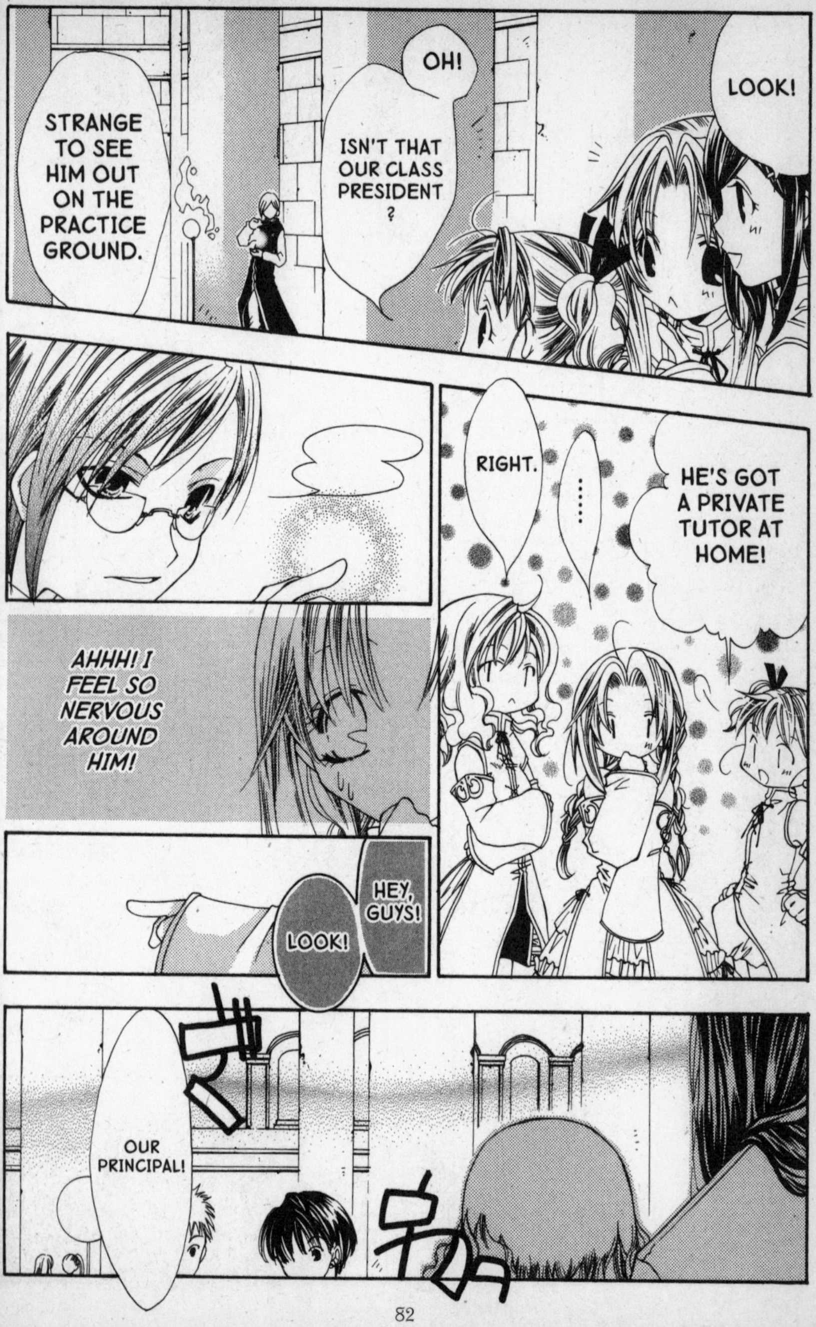
LOOK!
OH!
ISN'T THAT OUR CLASS PRESIDENT?
STRANGE TO SEE HIM OUT ON THE PRACTICE GROUND.
HE'S GOT A PRIVATE TUTOR AT HOME!
......
RIGHT.
AHHH! I FEEL SO NERVOUS AROUND HIM!
HEY, GUYS!
LOOK!
OUR PRINCIPAL!

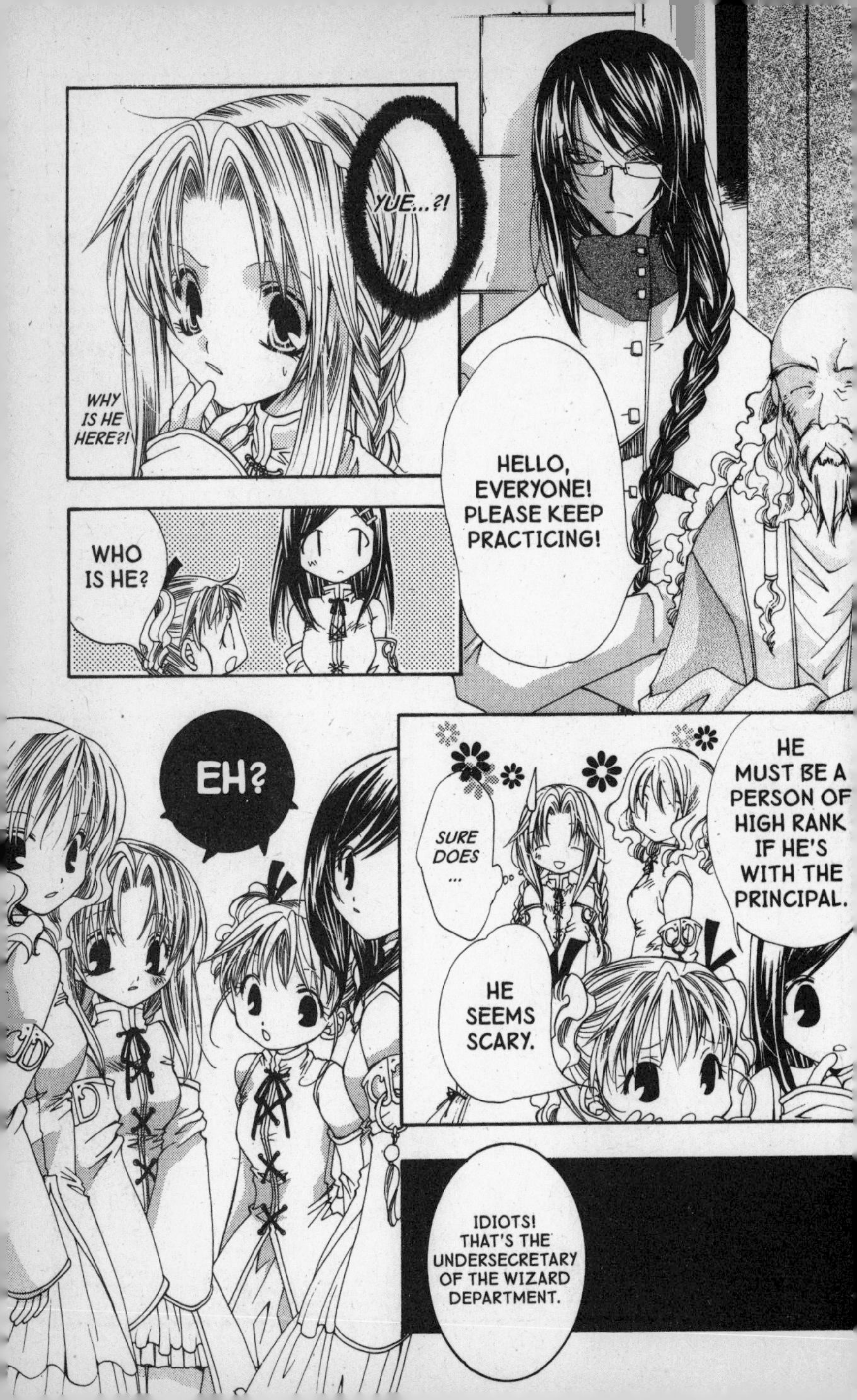
HELLO, EVERYONE! PLEASE KEEP PRACTICING!
YUE...?!
WHY IS HE HERE?!
WHO IS HE?
HE MUST BE A PERSON OF HIGH RANK IF HE'S WITH THE PRINCIPAL.
SURE DOES...
HE SEEMS SCARY.
IDIOTS! THAT'S THE UNDERSECRETARY OF THE WIZARD DEPARTMENT.
EH?

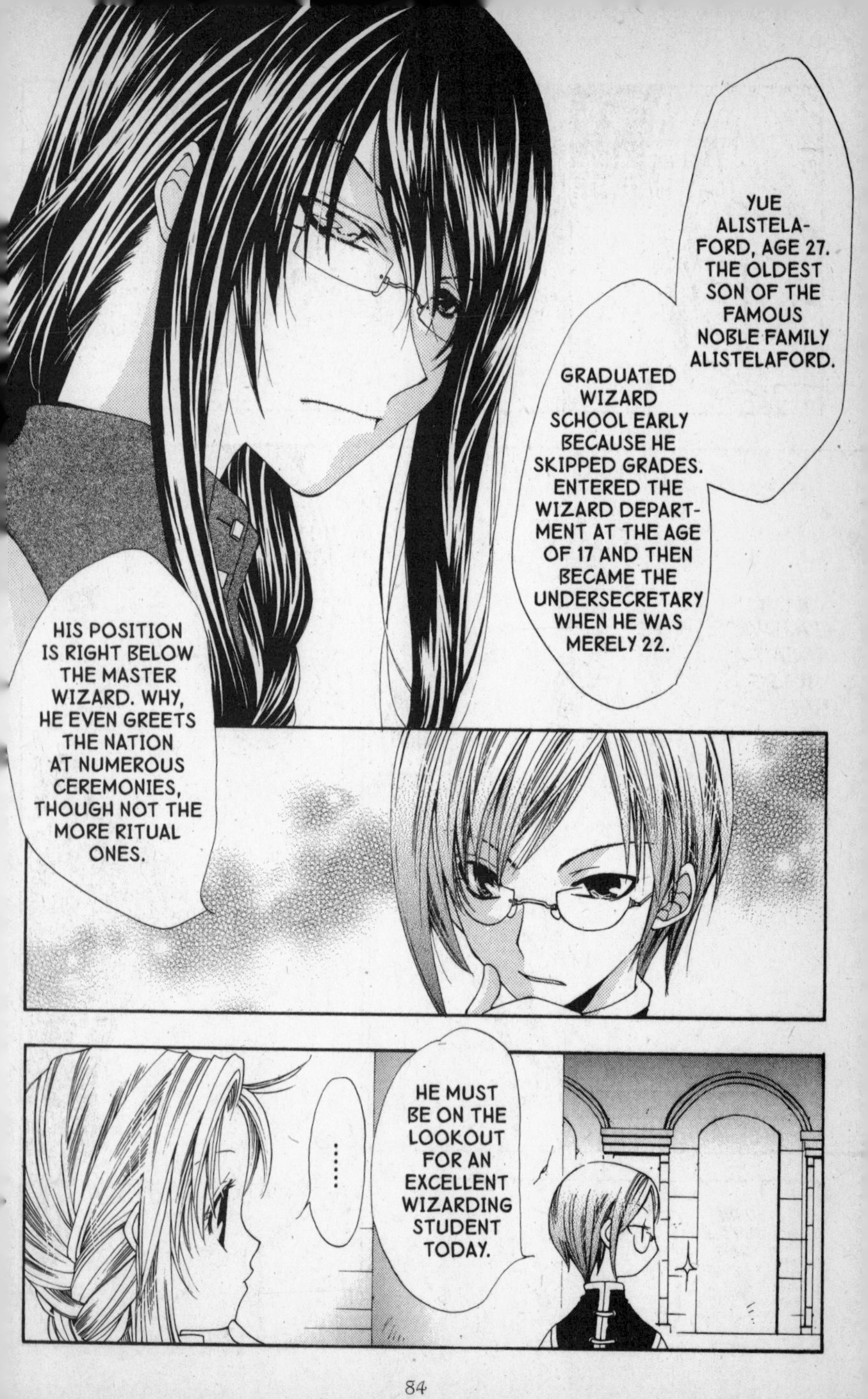
YUE ALISTELA-FORD, AGE 27. THE OLDEST SON OF THE FAMOUS NOBLE FAMILY ALISTELAFORD.
GRADUATED WIZARD SCHOOL EARLY BECAUSE HE SKIPPED GRADES. ENTERED THE WIZARD DEPART-MENT AT THE AGE OF 17 AND THEN BECAME THE UNDERSECRETARY WHEN HE WAS MERELY 22.
HIS POSITION IS RIGHT BELOW THE MASTER WIZARD. WHY, HE EVEN GREETS THE NATION AT NUMEROUS CEREMONIES, THOUGH NOT THE MORE RITUAL ONES.
HE MUST BE ON THE LOOKOUT FOR AN EXCELLENT WIZARDING STUDENT TODAY.
......

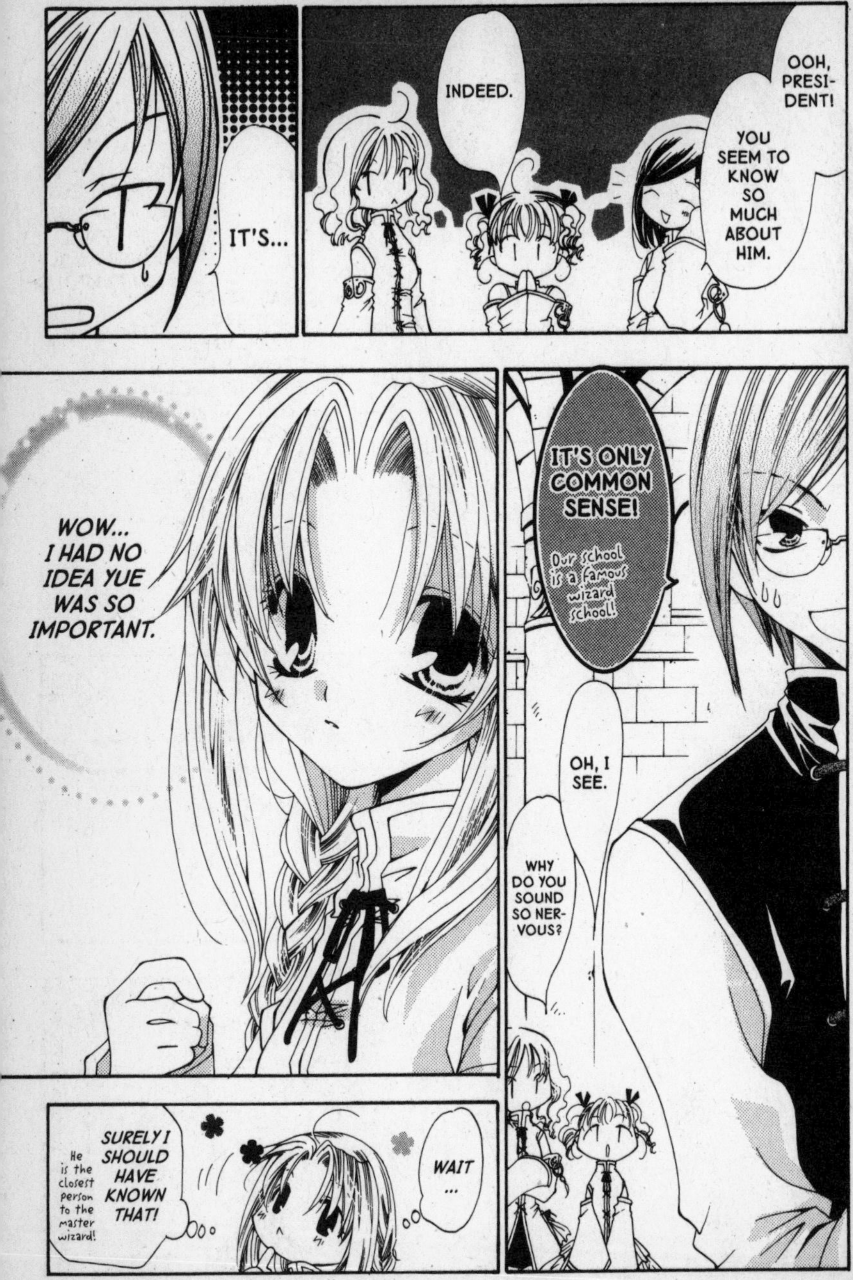
OOH, PRESIDENT!
YOU SEEM TO KNOW SO MUCH ABOUT HIM.
INDEED.
IT'S...
IT'S ONLY COMMON SENSE!
Our school is a famous wizard school!
OH, I SEE.
WHY DO YOU SOUND SO NERVOUS?
WOW... I HAD NO IDEA YUE WAS SO IMPORTANT.
WAIT...
SURELY I SHOULD HAVE KNOWN THAT!
He is the closest person to the master wizard!

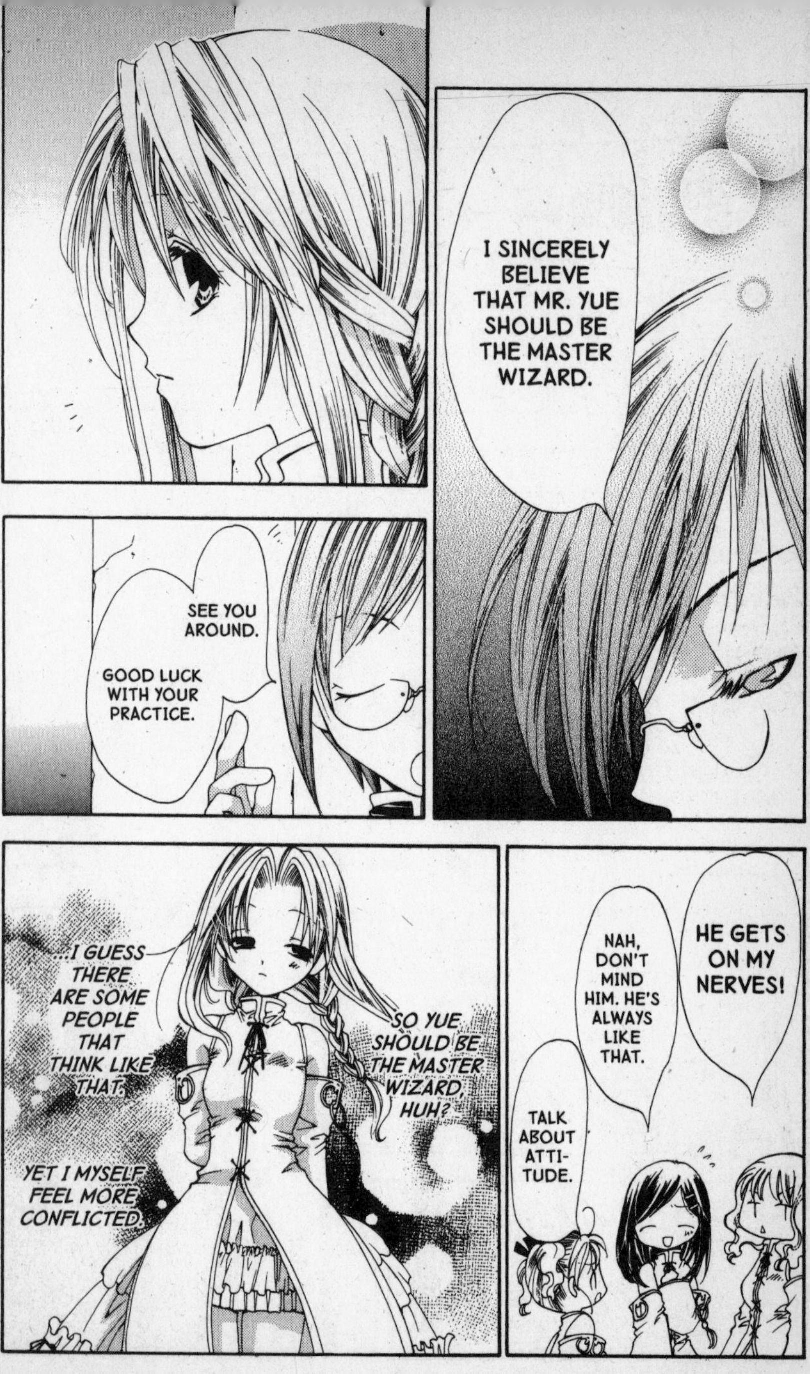
I SINCERELY BELIEVE THAT MR. YUE SHOULD BE THE MASTER WIZARD.
SEE YOU AROUND.
GOOD LUCK WITH YOUR PRACTICE.
HE GETS ON MY NERVES!
NAH, DON'T MIND HIM. HE'S ALWAYS LIKE THAT.
TALK ABOUT ATTI-TUDE.
SO YUE SHOULD BE THE MASTER WIZARD, HUH?
...I GUESS THERE ARE SOME PEOPLE THAT THINK LIKE THAT.
YET I MYSELF FEEL MORE CONFLICTED.

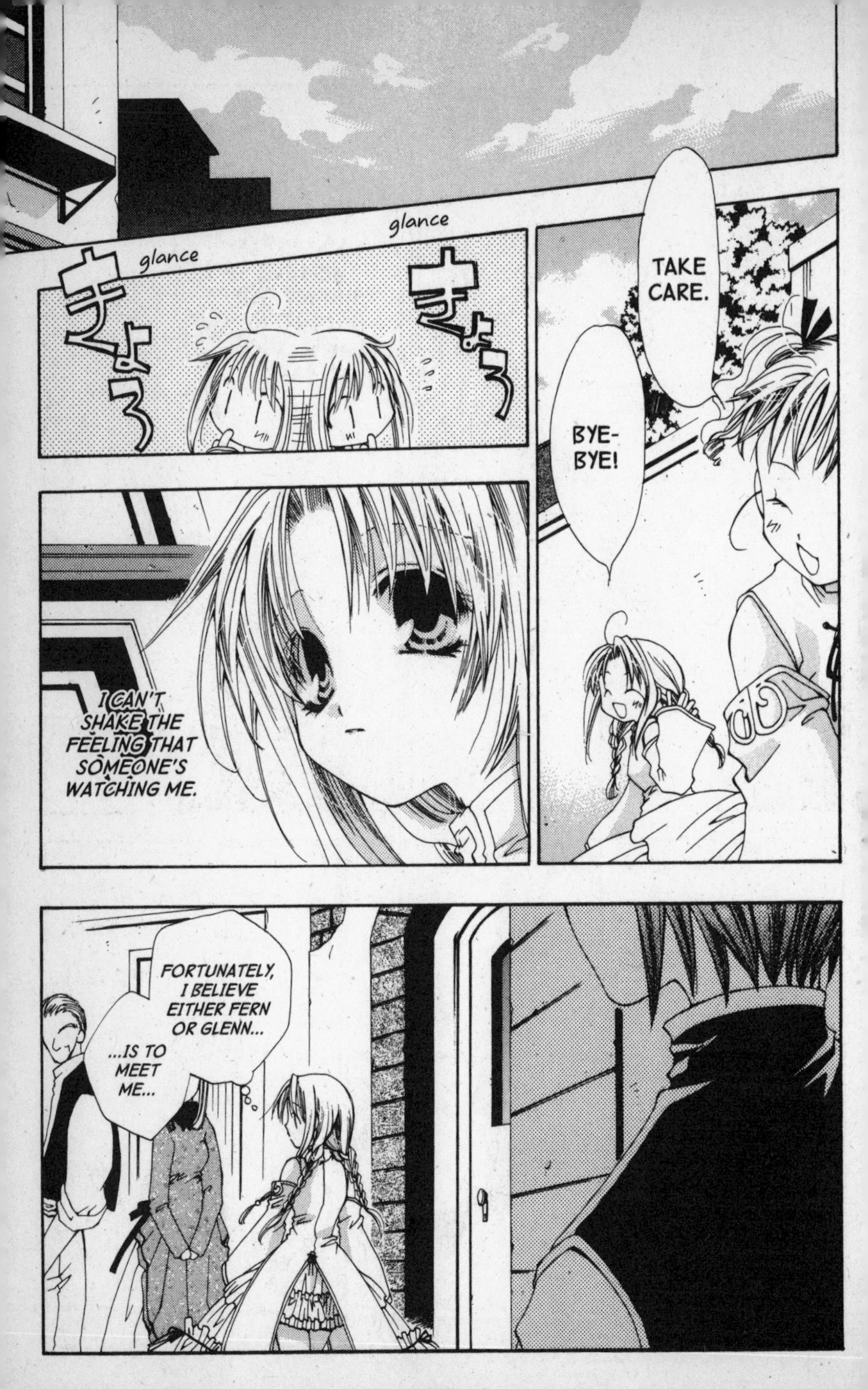

TAKE CARE.
BYE-BYE!
glance
きょろ
glance
きょろ
I CAN'T SHAKE THE FEELING THAT SOMEONE'S WATCHING ME.
FORTUNATELY, I BELIEVE EITHER FERN OR GLENN...
...IS TO MEET ME...

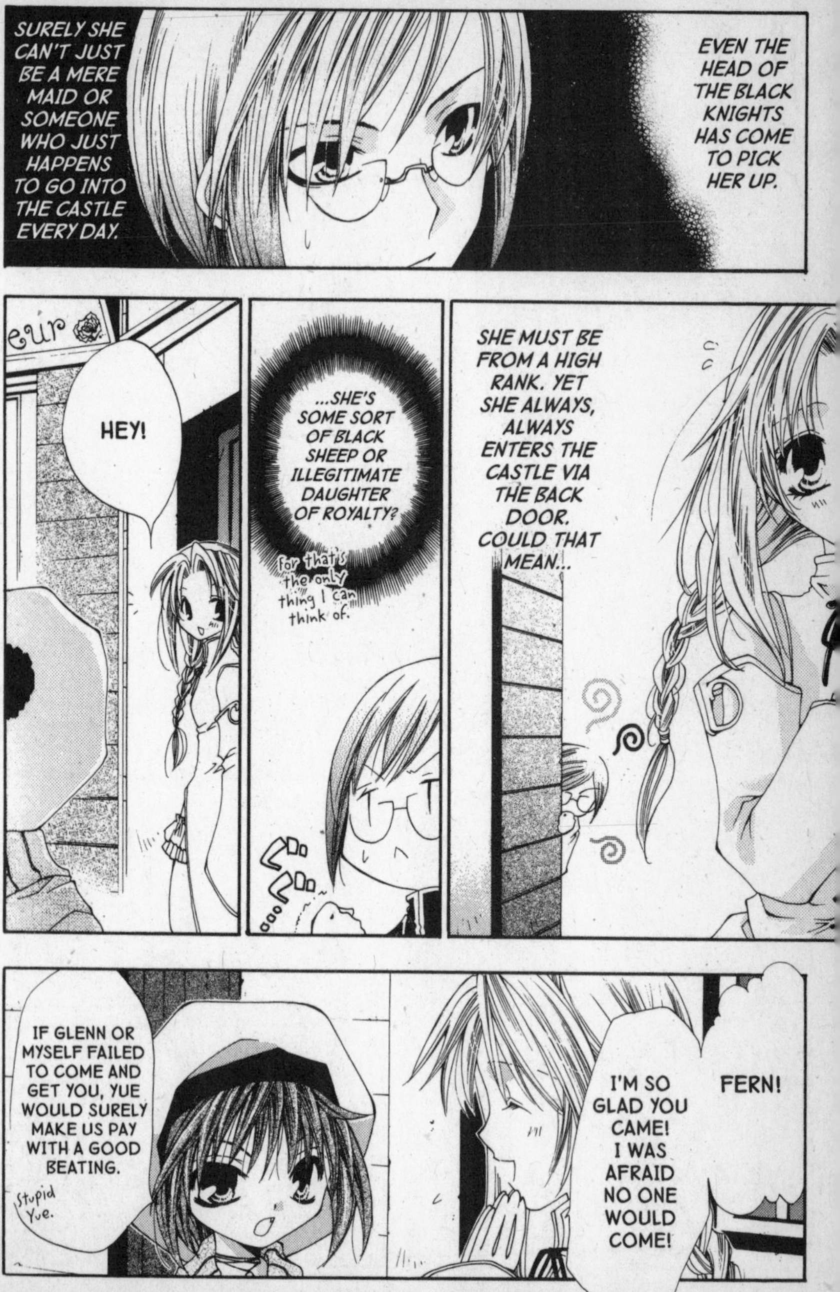
EVEN THE HEAD OF THE BLACK KNIGHTS HAS COME TO PICK HER UP.
SURELY SHE CAN'T JUST BE A MERE MAID OR SOMEONE WHO JUST HAPPENS TO GO INTO THE CASTLE EVERY DAY.
SHE MUST BE FROM A HIGH RANK. YET SHE ALWAYS, ALWAYS ENTERS THE CASTLE VIA THE BACK DOOR. COULD THAT MEAN...
...SHE'S SOME SORT OF BLACK SHEEP OR ILLEGITIMATE DAUGHTER OF ROYALTY?
for that's the only thing I can think of.
HEY!
FERN!
I'M SO GLAD YOU CAME! I WAS AFRAID NO ONE WOULD COME!
IF GLENN OR MYSELF FAILED TO COME AND GET YOU, YUE WOULD SURELY MAKE US PAY WITH A GOOD BEATING.
Stupid Yue.

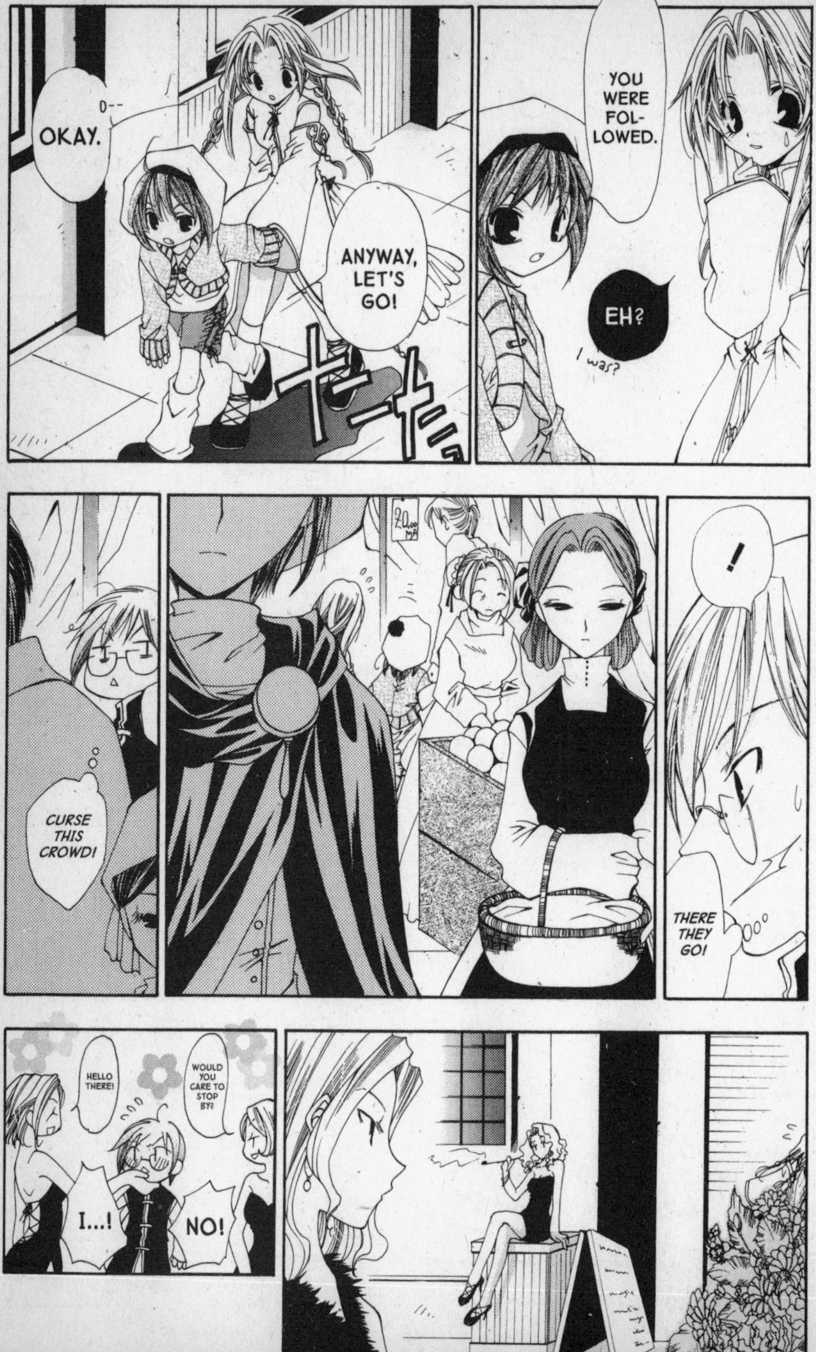
YOU WERE FOL-LOWED.
EH?
I was?
D--
OKAY.
ANYWAY, LET'S GO!
!
THERE THEY GO!
CURSE THIS CROWD!
WOULD YOU CARE TO STOP BY?
HELLO THERE!
NO!
I...!

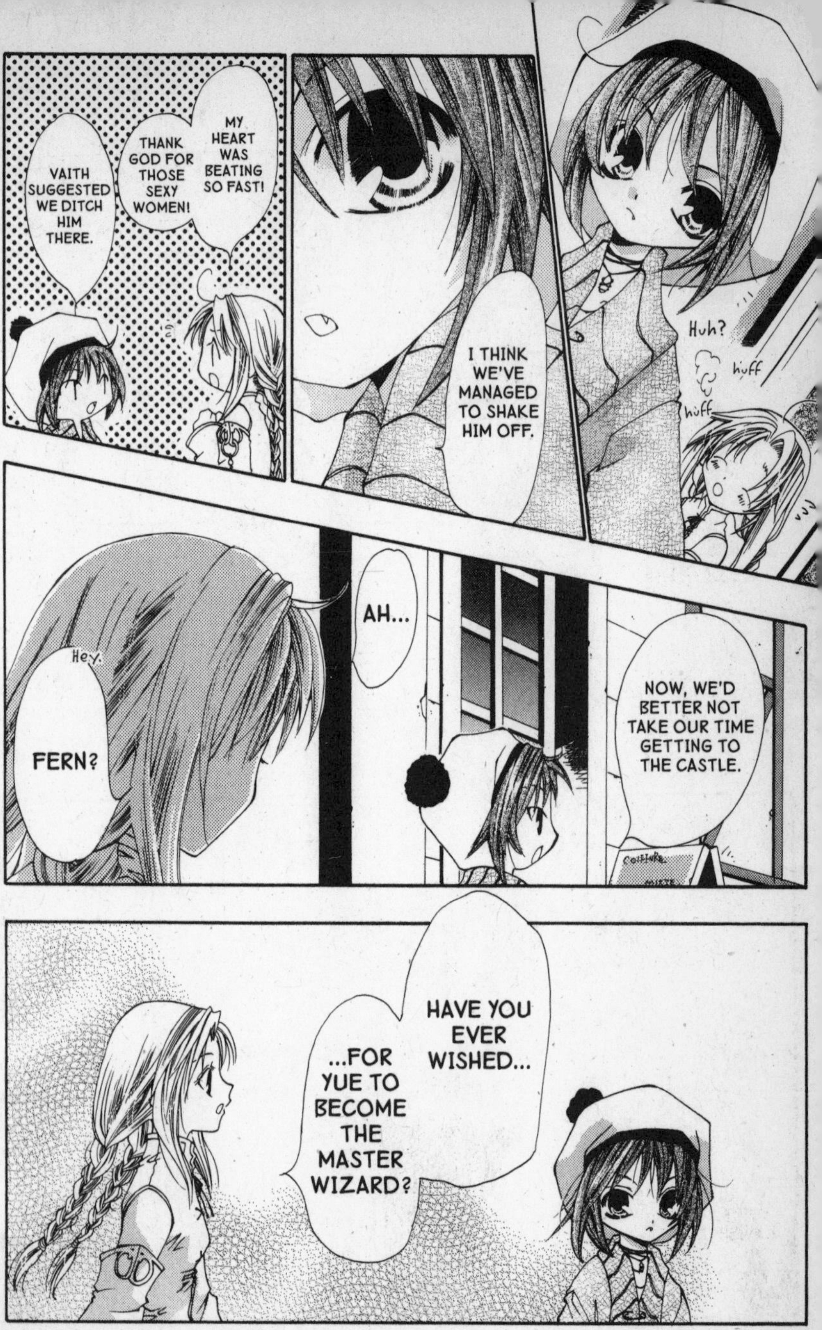
Huh?
huff
huff
I THINK WE'VE MANAGED TO SHAKE HIM OFF.
MY HEART WAS BEATING SO FAST!
THANK GOD FOR THOSE SEXY WOMEN!
VAITH SUGGESTED WE DITCH HIM THERE.
NOW, WE'D BETTER NOT TAKE OUR TIME GETTING TO THE CASTLE.
AH...
Hey.
FERN?
HAVE YOU EVER WISHED...
...FOR YUE TO BECOME THE MASTER WIZARD?

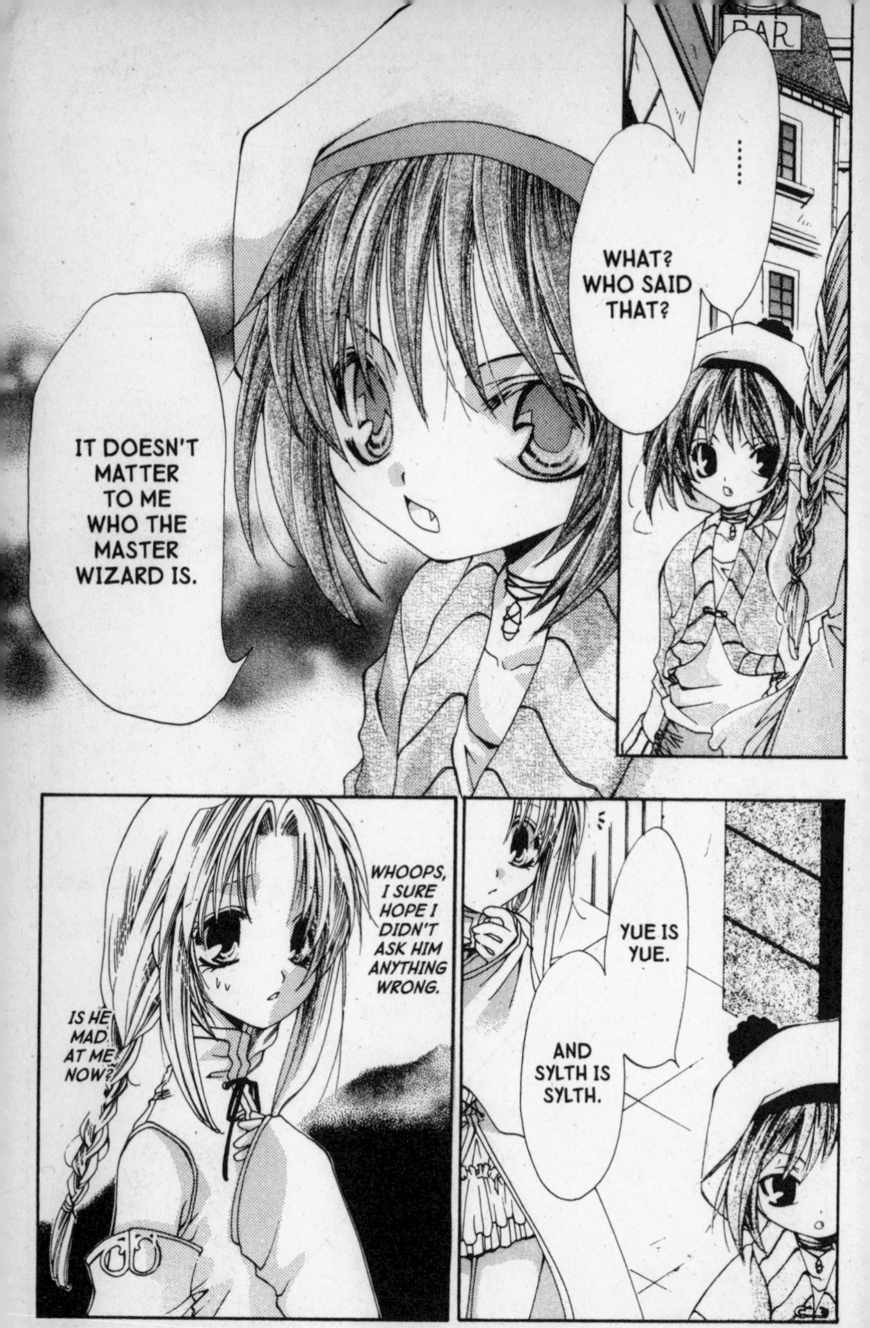
BAR
......
WHAT? WHO SAID THAT?
IT DOESN'T MATTER TO ME WHO THE MASTER WIZARD IS.
YUE IS YUE.
AND SYLTH IS SYLTH.
WHOOPS, I SURE HOPE I DIDN'T ASK HIM ANYTHING WRONG.
IS HE MAD AT ME NOW?

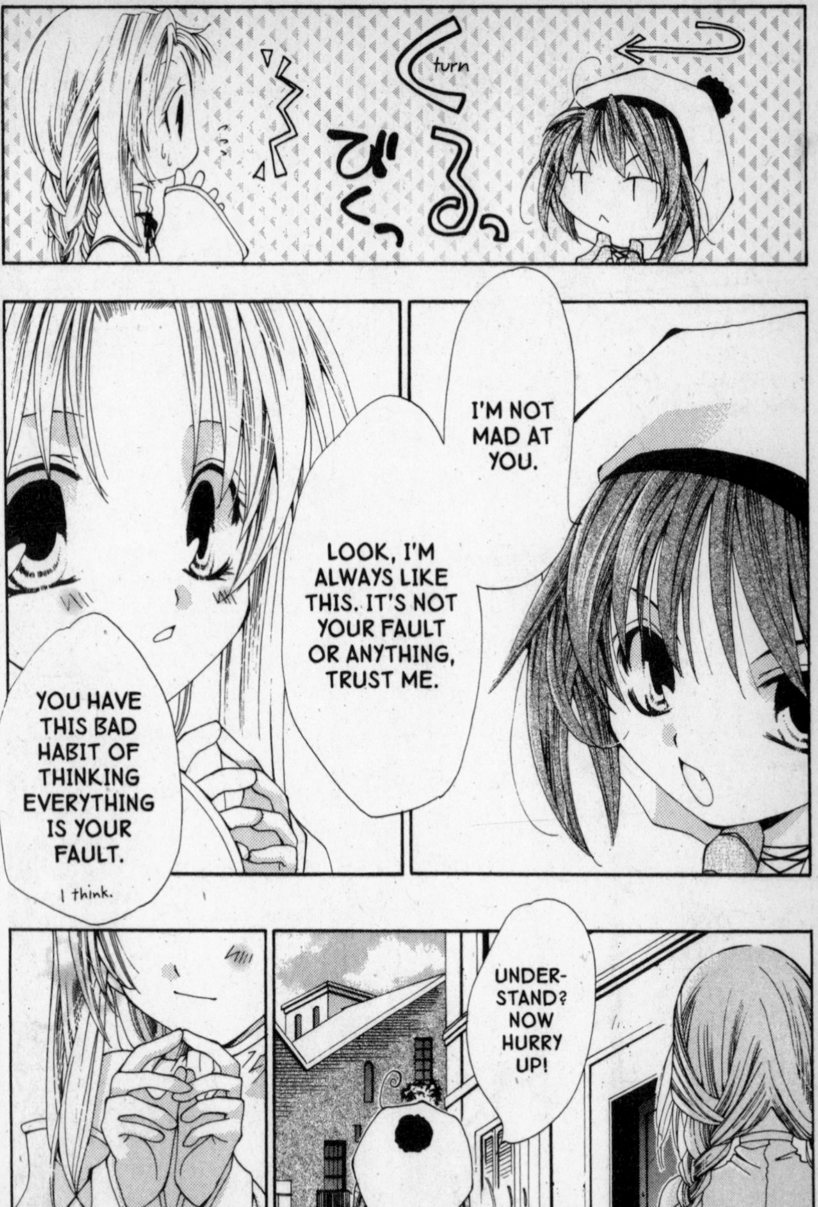
くるっ
turn
びくっ
I'M NOT MAD AT YOU.
LOOK, I'M ALWAYS LIKE THIS. IT'S NOT YOUR FAULT OR ANYTHING, TRUST ME.
YOU HAVE THIS BAD HABIT OF THINKING EVERYTHING IS YOUR FAULT.
I think.
UNDER-STAND? NOW HURRY UP!

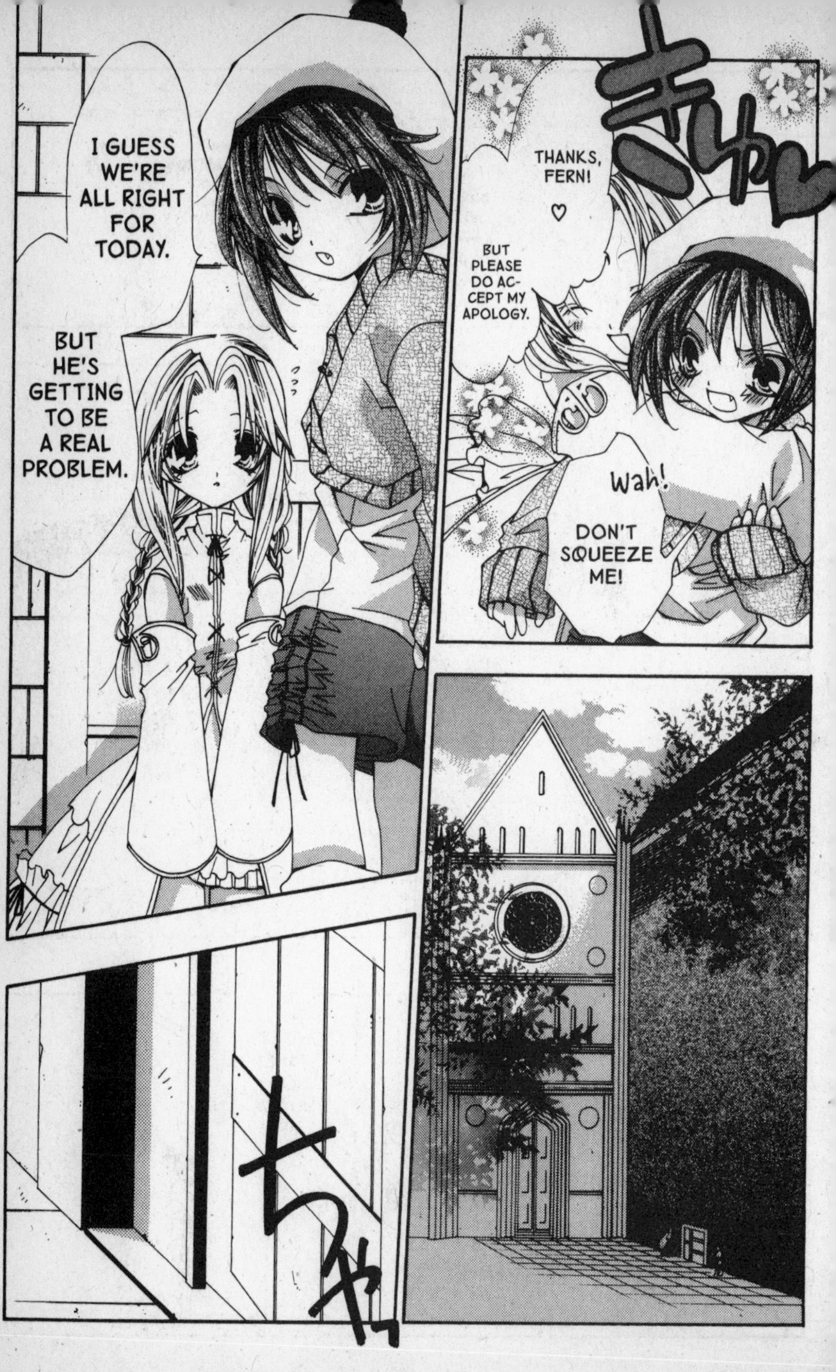
THANKS, FERN! ♡
BUT PLEASE DO AC-CEPT MY APOLOGY.
Wah!
DON'T SQUEEZE ME!
I GUESS WE'RE ALL RIGHT FOR TODAY.
BUT HE'S GETTING TO BE A REAL PROBLEM.

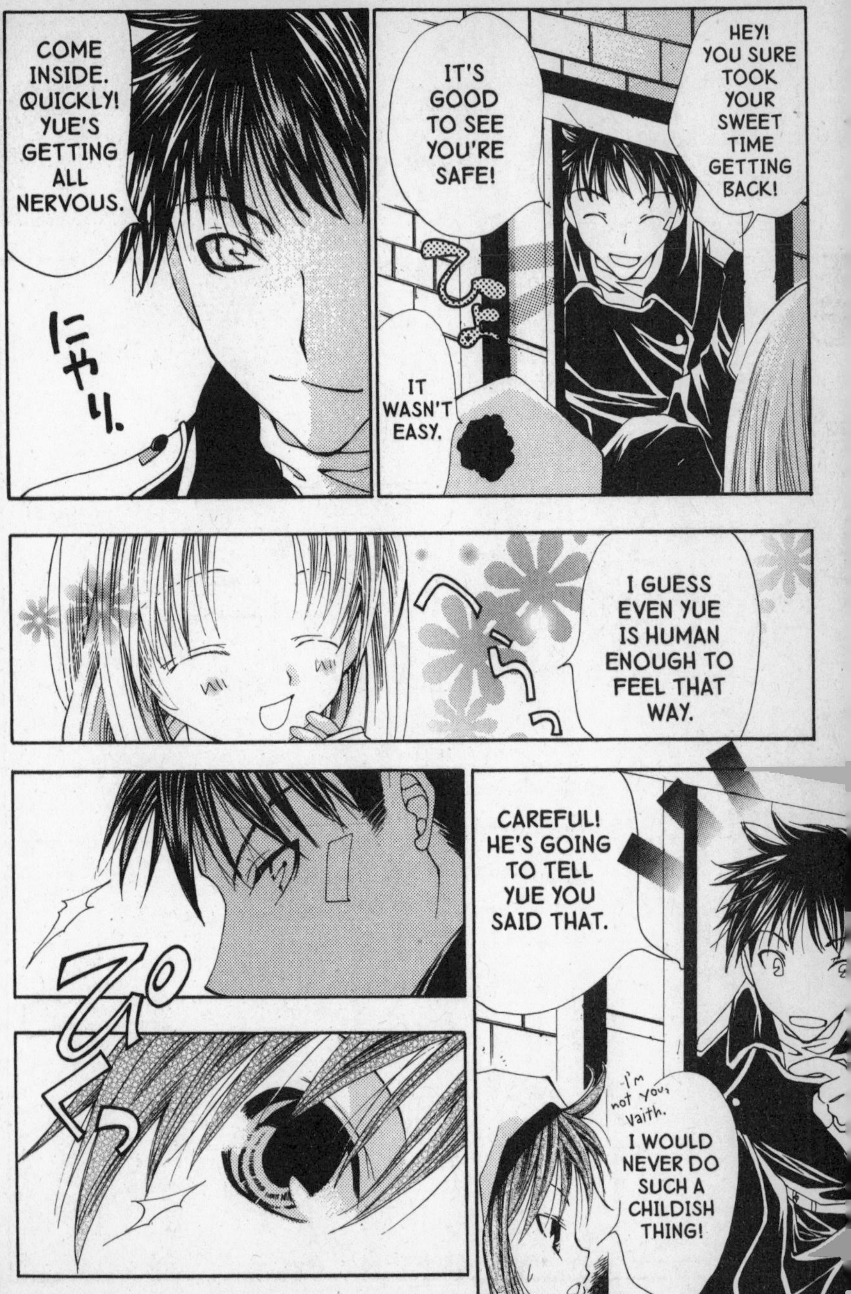
HEY! YOU SURE TOOK YOUR SWEET TIME GETTING BACK!
IT'S GOOD TO SEE YOU'RE SAFE!
IT WASN'T EASY.
COME INSIDE. QUICKLY! YUE'S GETTING ALL NERVOUS.
にやり。
I GUESS EVEN YUE IS HUMAN ENOUGH TO FEEL THAT WAY.
CAREFUL! HE'S GOING TO TELL YUE YOU SAID THAT.
I'm not your vaith.
I WOULD NEVER DO SUCH A CHILDISH THING!

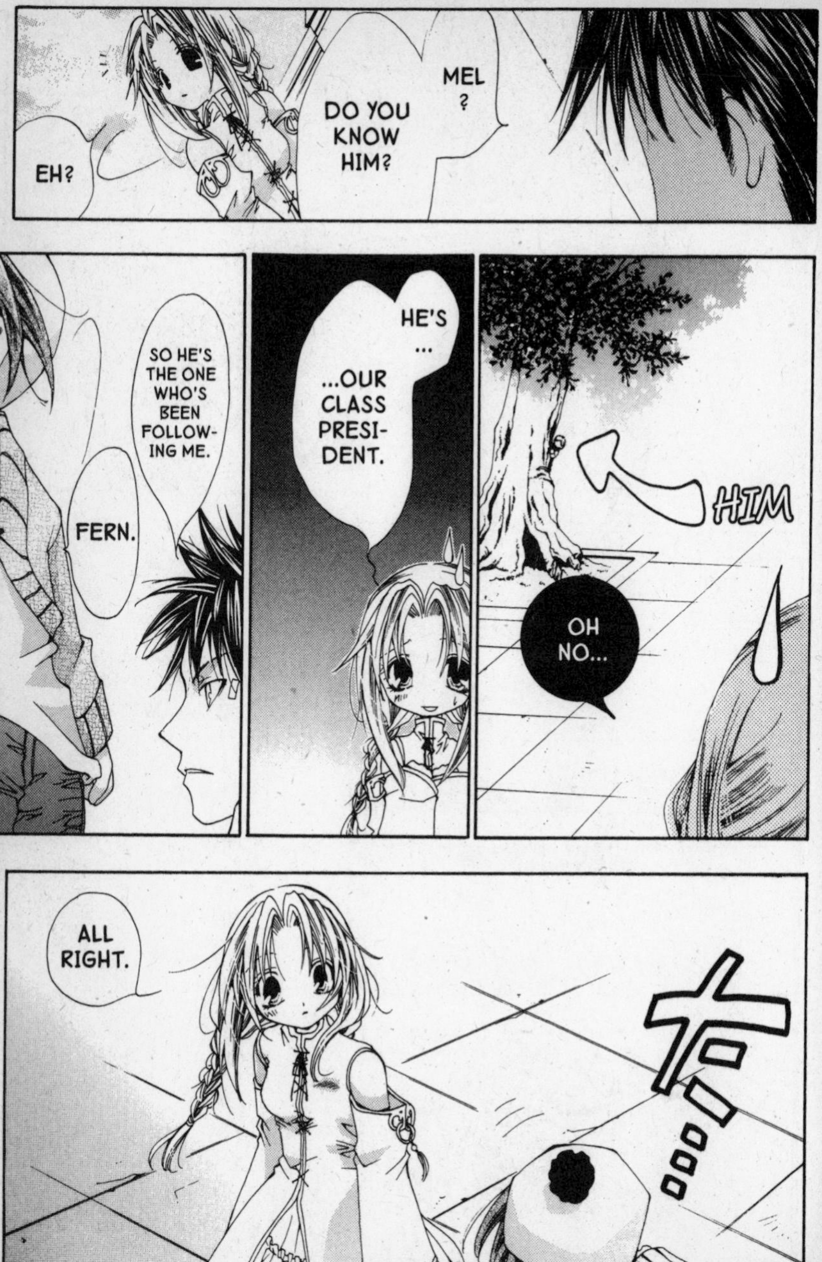
MEL ?
DO YOU KNOW HIM?
EH?
HIM
OH NO...
HE'S ...
...OUR CLASS PRESI-DENT.
SO HE'S THE ONE WHO'S BEEN FOLLOW-ING ME.
FERN.
ALL RIGHT.

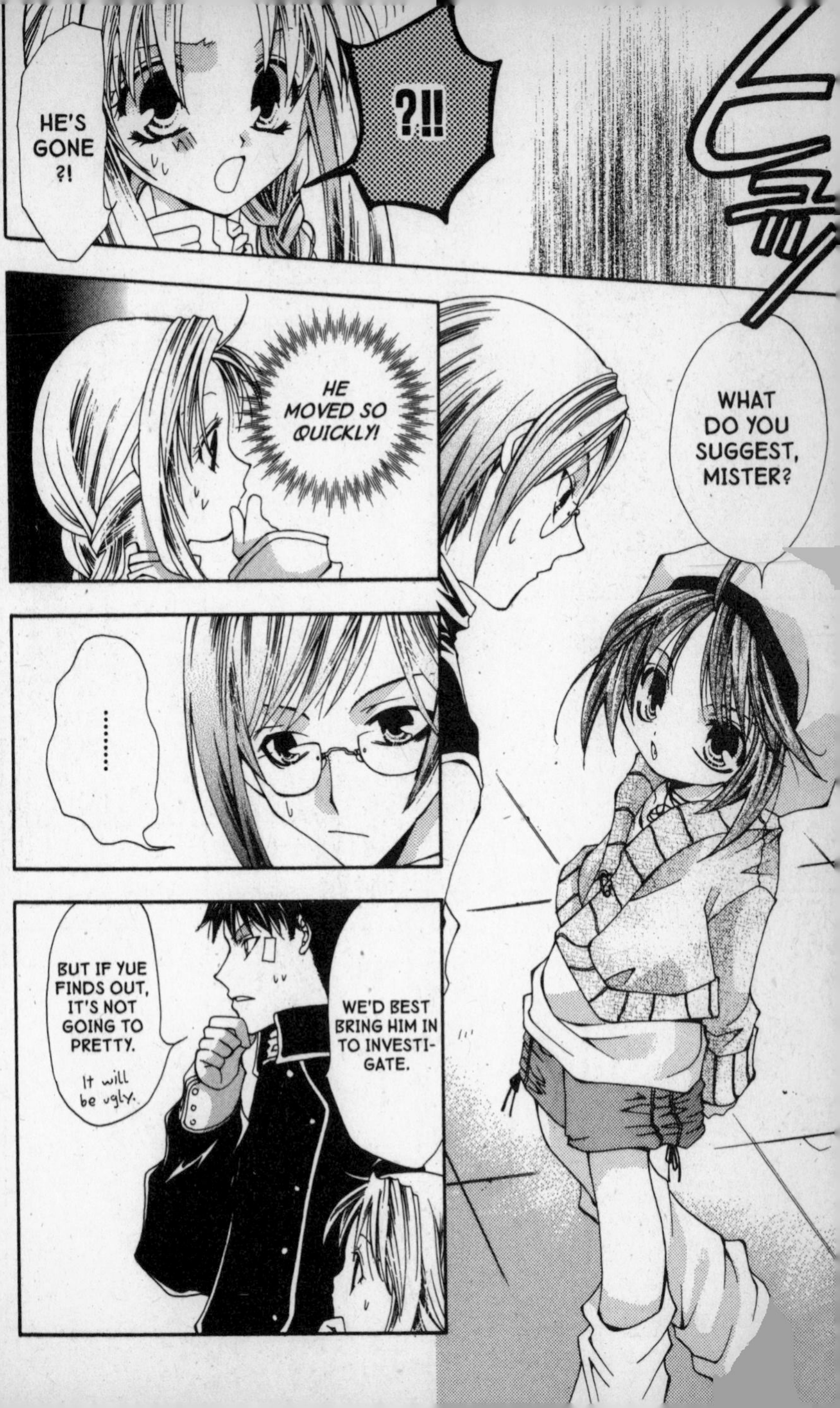
?!!
HE'S GONE ?!
WHAT DO YOU SUGGEST, MISTER?
HE MOVED SO QUICKLY!
....
WE'D BEST BRING HIM IN TO INVESTI-GATE.
BUT IF YUE FINDS OUT, IT'S NOT GOING TO PRETTY.
It will be ugly.

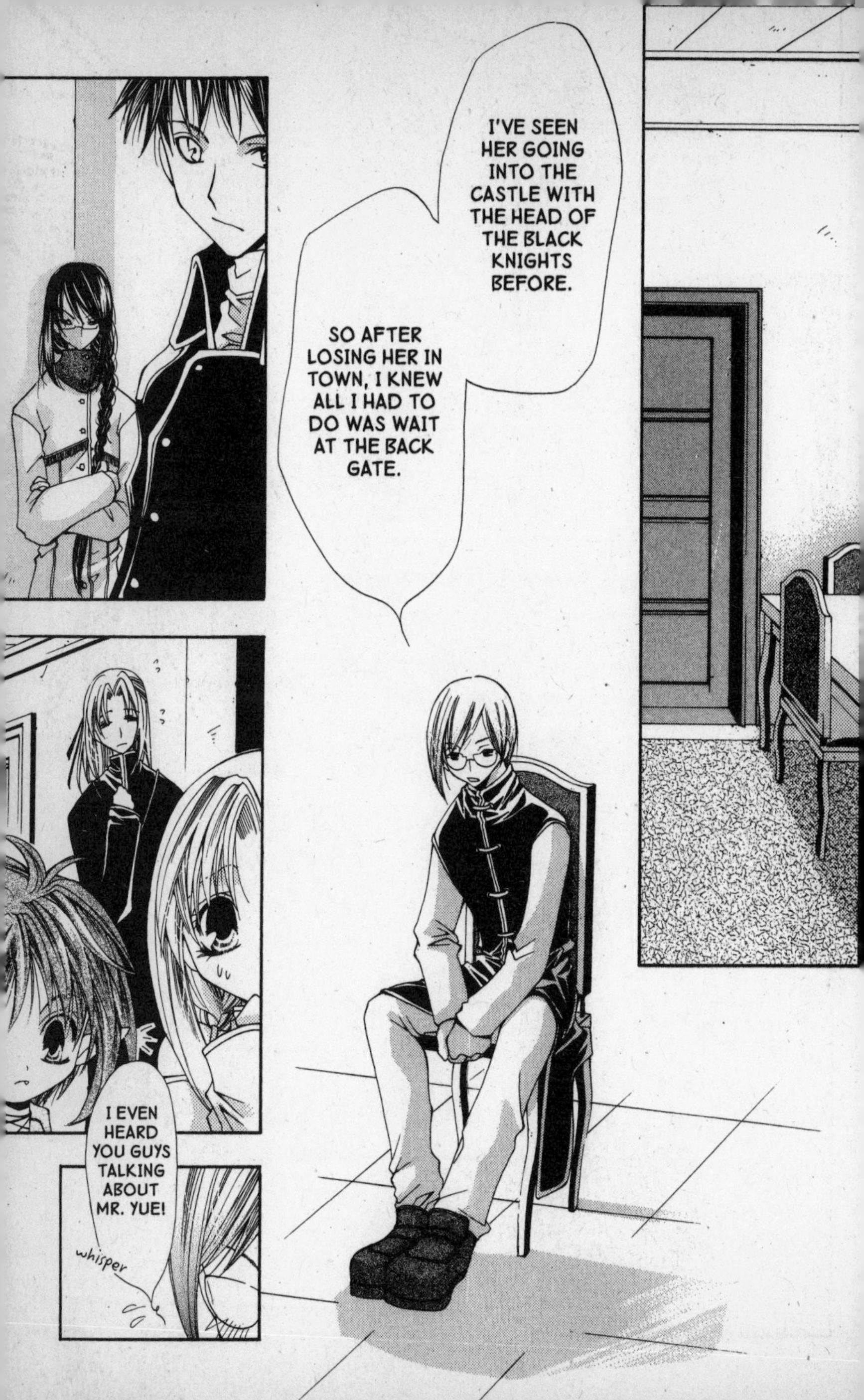
I'VE SEEN HER GOING INTO THE CASTLE WITH THE HEAD OF THE BLACK KNIGHTS BEFORE.
SO AFTER LOSING HER IN TOWN, I KNEW ALL I HAD TO DO WAS WAIT AT THE BACK GATE.
I EVEN HEARD YOU GUYS TALKING ABOUT MR. YUE!
whisper

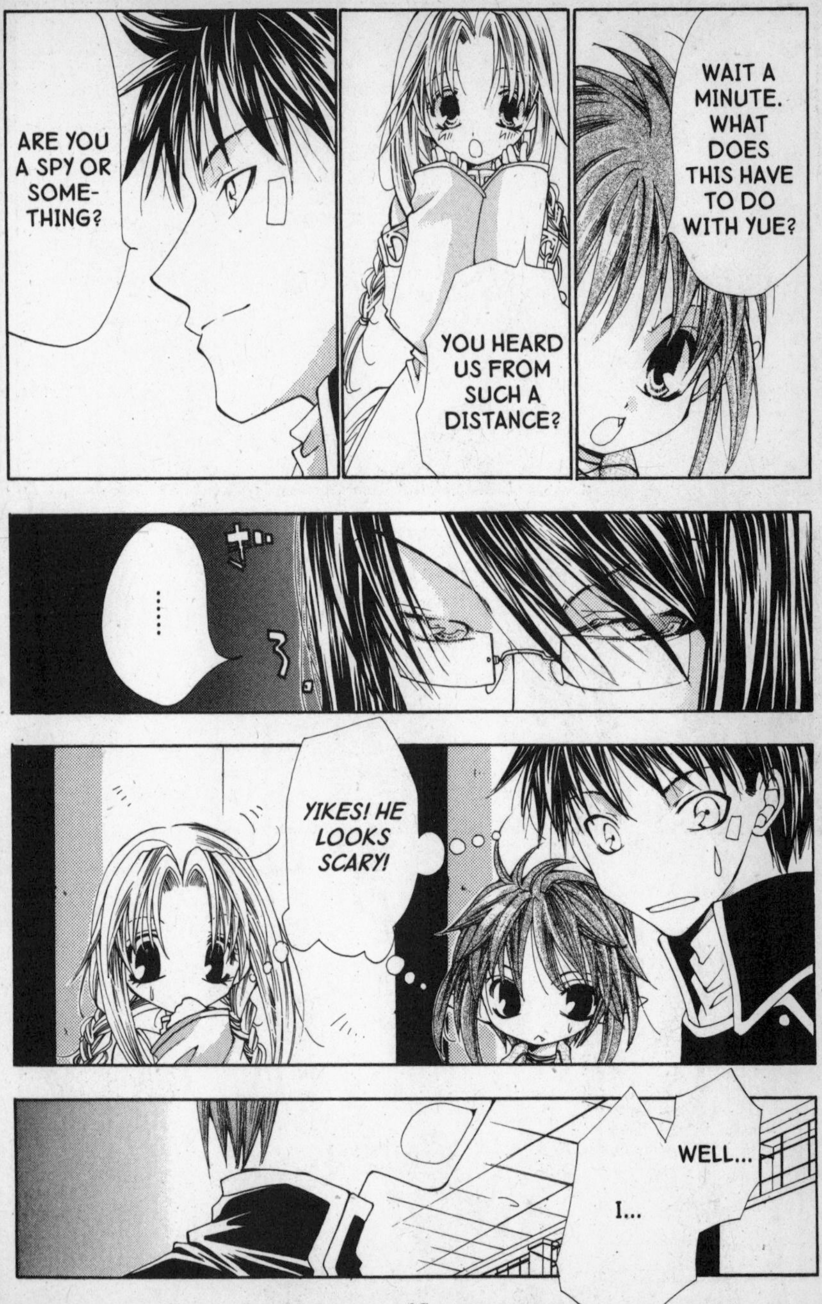
WAIT A MINUTE. WHAT DOES THIS HAVE TO DO WITH YUE?
YOU HEARD US FROM SUCH A DISTANCE?
ARE YOU A SPY OR SOME-THING?
……
YIKES! HE LOOKS SCARY!
WELL...
I...

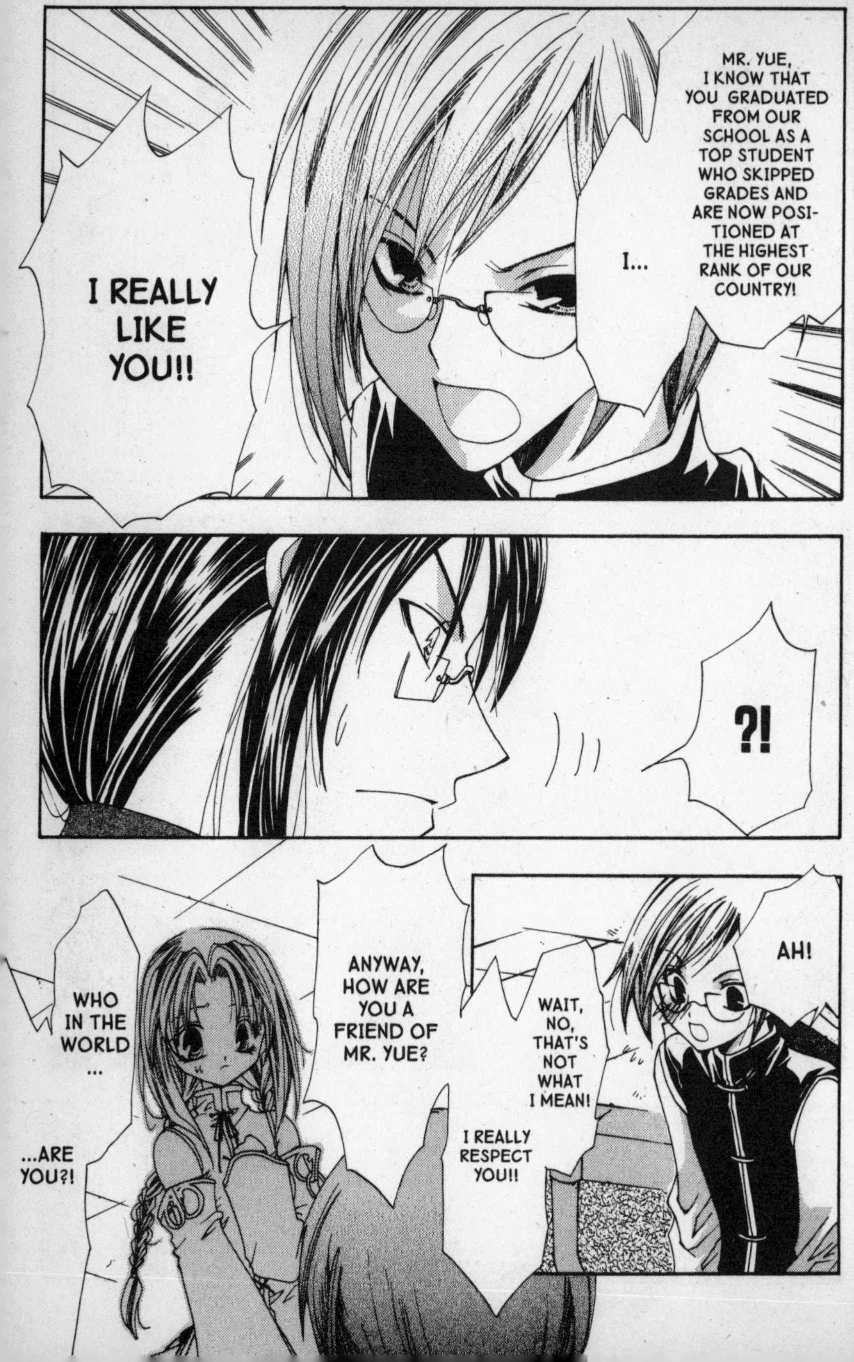
MR. YUE, I KNOW THAT YOU GRADUATED FROM OUR SCHOOL AS A TOP STUDENT WHO SKIPPED GRADES AND ARE NOW POSITIONED AT THE HIGHEST RANK OF OUR COUNTRY!
I...
I REALLY LIKE YOU!!
?!
AH!
WAIT, NO, THAT'S NOT WHAT I MEAN!
I REALLY RESPECT YOU!!
ANYWAY, HOW ARE YOU A FRIEND OF MR. YUE?
WHO IN THE WORLD ...
...ARE YOU?!

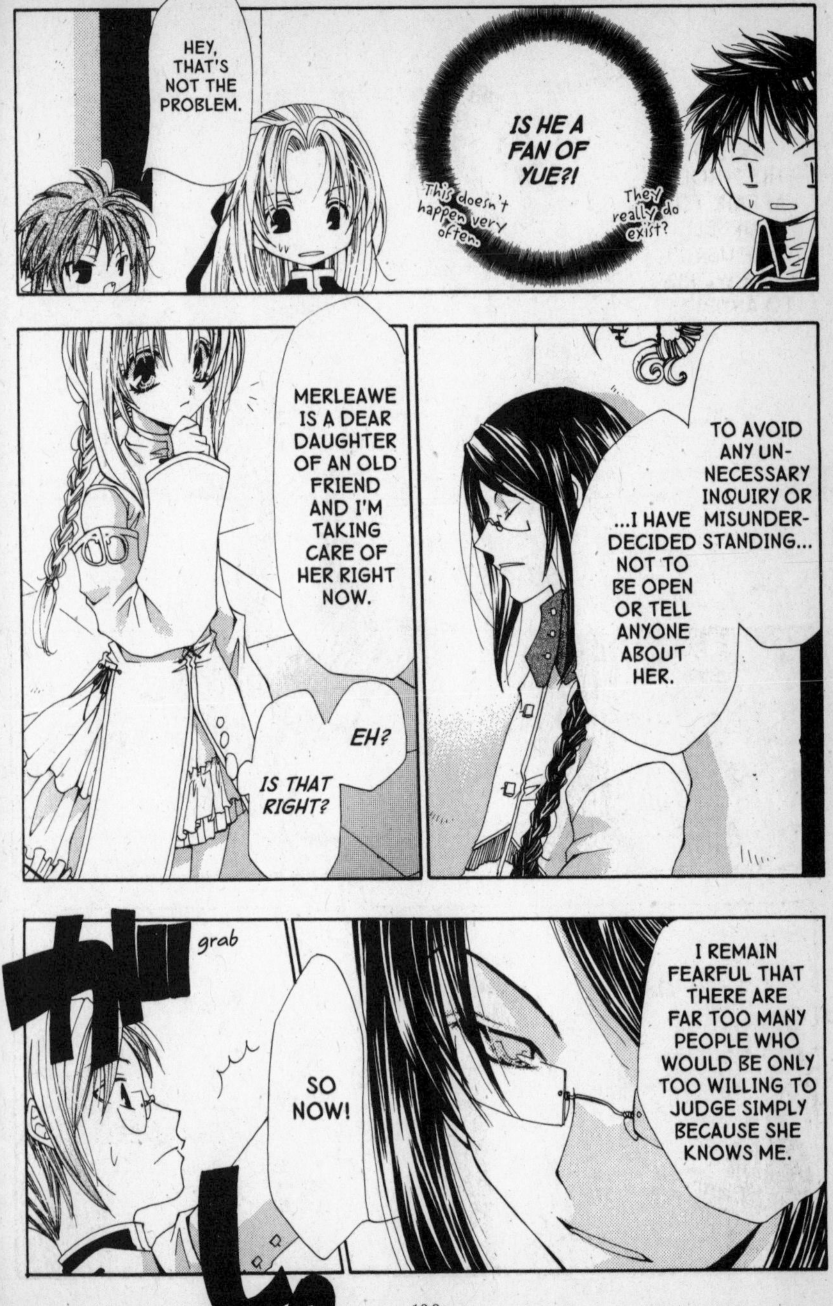
IS HE A FAN OF YUE?!
They really do exist?
This doesn't happen very often.
HEY, THAT'S NOT THE PROBLEM.
TO AVOID ANY UN-NECESSARY INQUIRY OR MISUNDER-STANDING...
...I HAVE DECIDED NOT TO BE OPEN OR TELL ANYONE ABOUT HER.
MERLEAWE IS A DEAR DAUGHTER OF AN OLD FRIEND AND I'M TAKING CARE OF HER RIGHT NOW.
EH?
IS THAT RIGHT?
I REMAIN FEARFUL THAT THERE ARE FAR TOO MANY PEOPLE WHO WOULD BE ONLY TOO WILLING TO JUDGE SIMPLY BECAUSE SHE KNOWS ME.
grab
SO NOW!

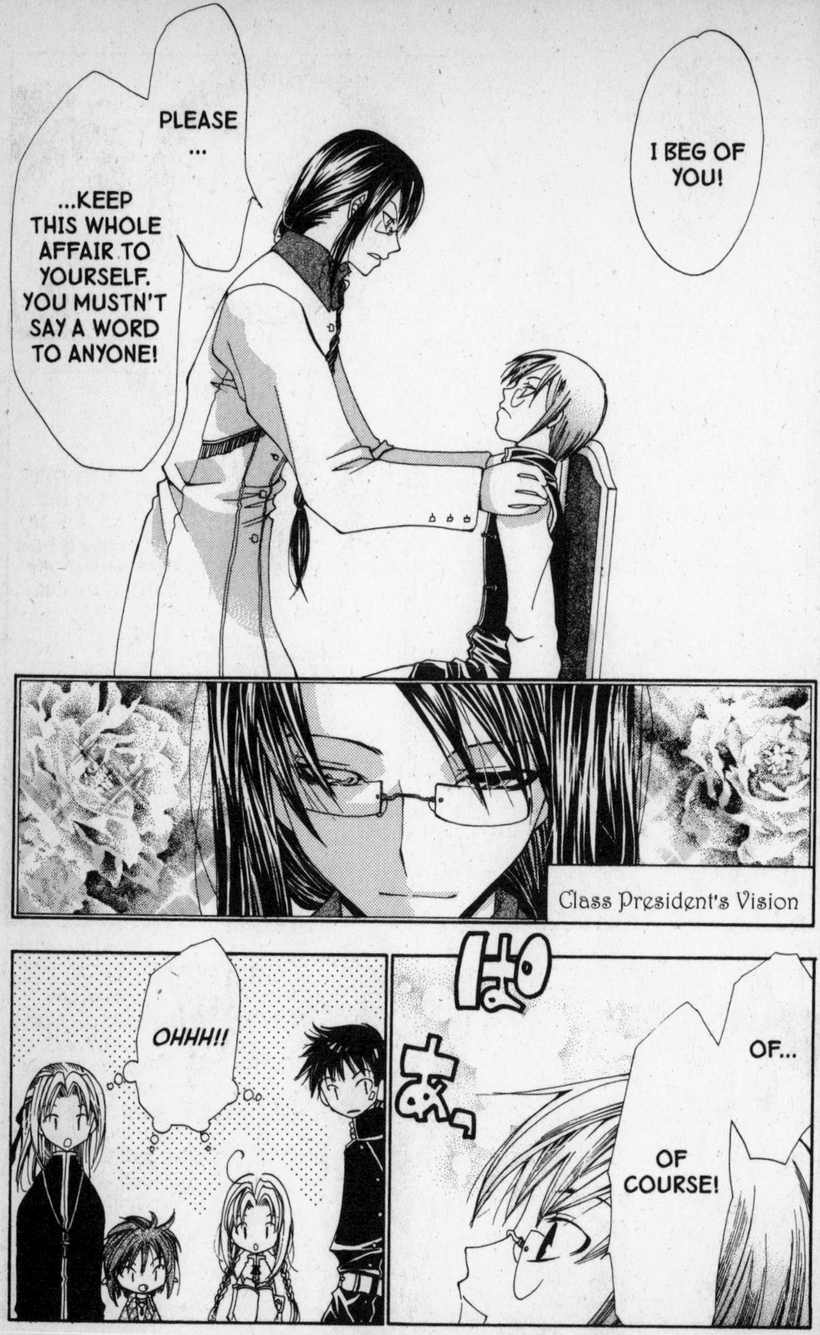
I BEG OF YOU!
PLEASE ...
...KEEP THIS WHOLE AFFAIR TO YOURSELF. YOU MUSTN'T SAY A WORD TO ANYONE!
Class President's Vision
はっ
あっ
OF...
OF COURSE!
OHHH!!

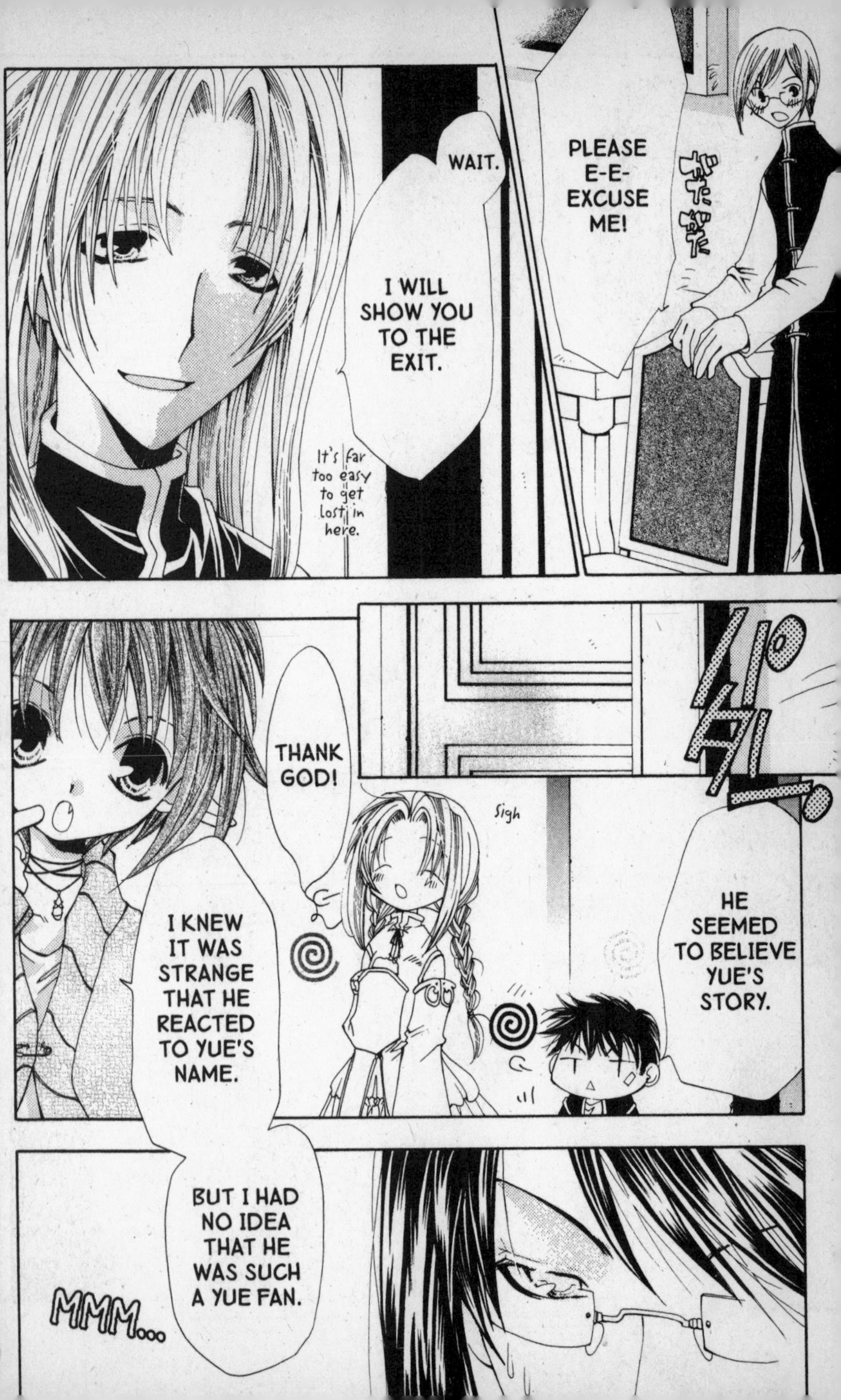
PLEASE E-E-EXCUSE ME!
WAIT.
I WILL SHOW YOU TO THE EXIT.
It's far too easy to get lost in here.
HE SEEMED TO BELIEVE YUE'S STORY.
THANK GOD!
Sigh
I KNEW IT WAS STRANGE THAT HE REACTED TO YUE'S NAME.
BUT I HAD NO IDEA THAT HE WAS SUCH A YUE FAN.
MMM...

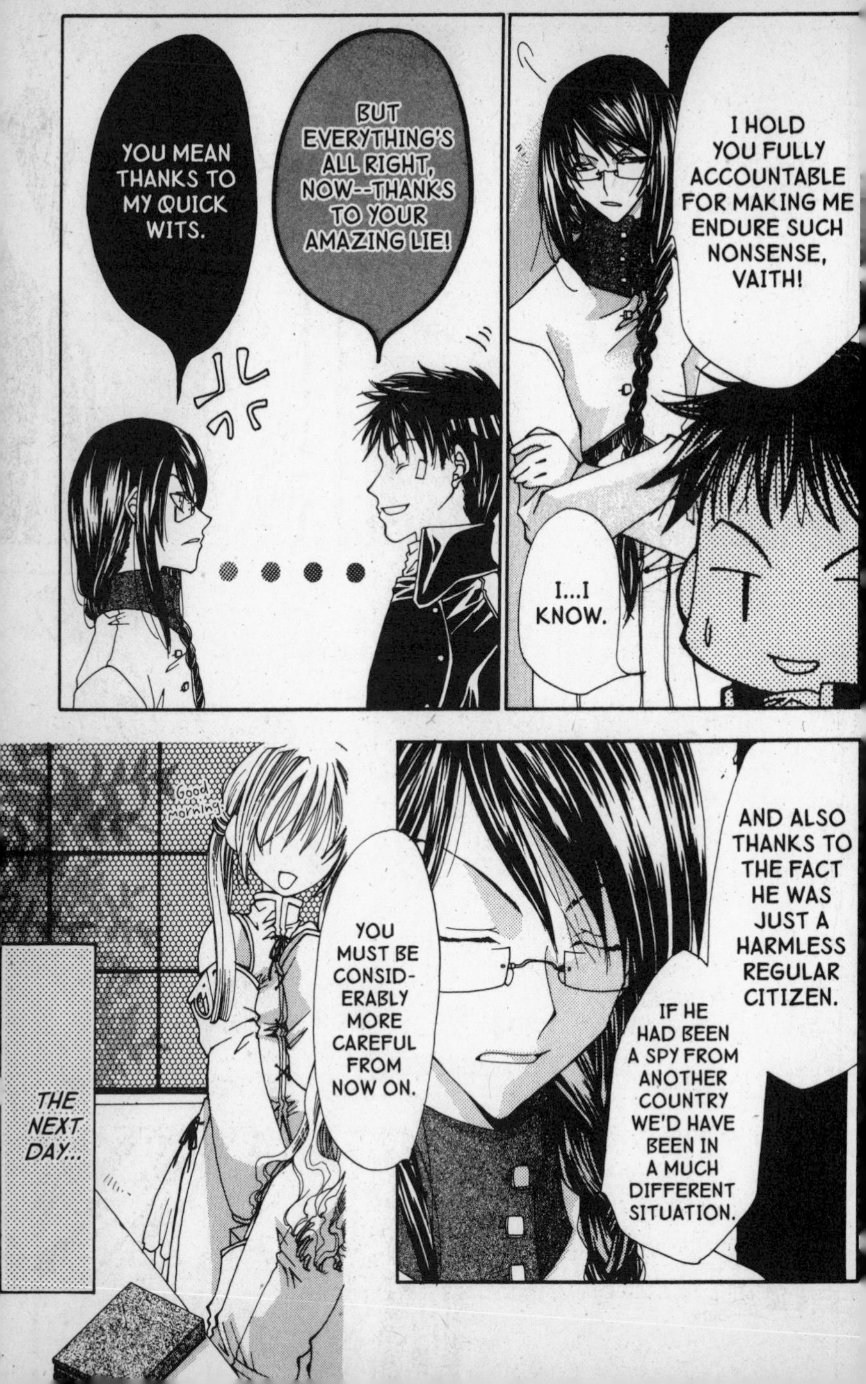
I HOLD YOU FULLY ACCOUNTABLE FOR MAKING ME ENDURE SUCH NONSENSE, VAITH!
I...I KNOW.
BUT EVERYTHING'S ALL RIGHT, NOW--THANKS TO YOUR AMAZING LIE!
YOU MEAN THANKS TO MY QUICK WITS.
....
AND ALSO THANKS TO THE FACT HE WAS JUST A HARMLESS REGULAR CITIZEN.
IF HE HAD BEEN A SPY FROM ANOTHER COUNTRY WE'D HAVE BEEN IN A MUCH DIFFERENT SITUATION.
YOU MUST BE CONSID-ERABLY MORE CAREFUL FROM NOW ON.
Good morning
THE NEXT DAY...

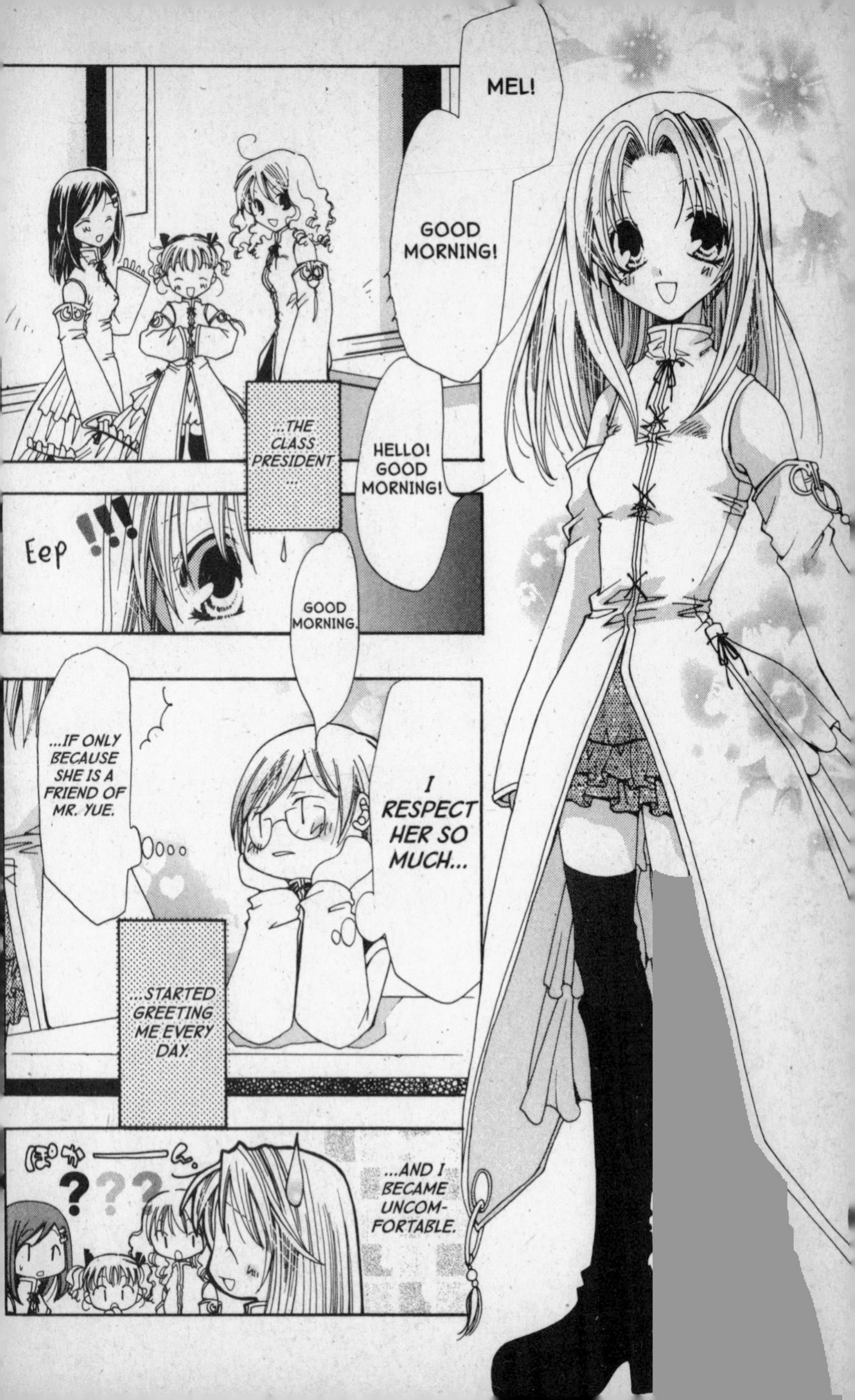
MEL!
GOOD MORNING!
HELLO! GOOD MORNING!
...THE CLASS PRESIDENT...
Eep !!!
GOOD MORNING.
I RESPECT HER SO MUCH...
...IF ONLY BECAUSE SHE IS A FRIEND OF MR. YUE.
...STARTED GREETING ME EVERY DAY.
...AND I BECAME UNCOMFORTABLE.
ぽか———ん。
???

Episode.14

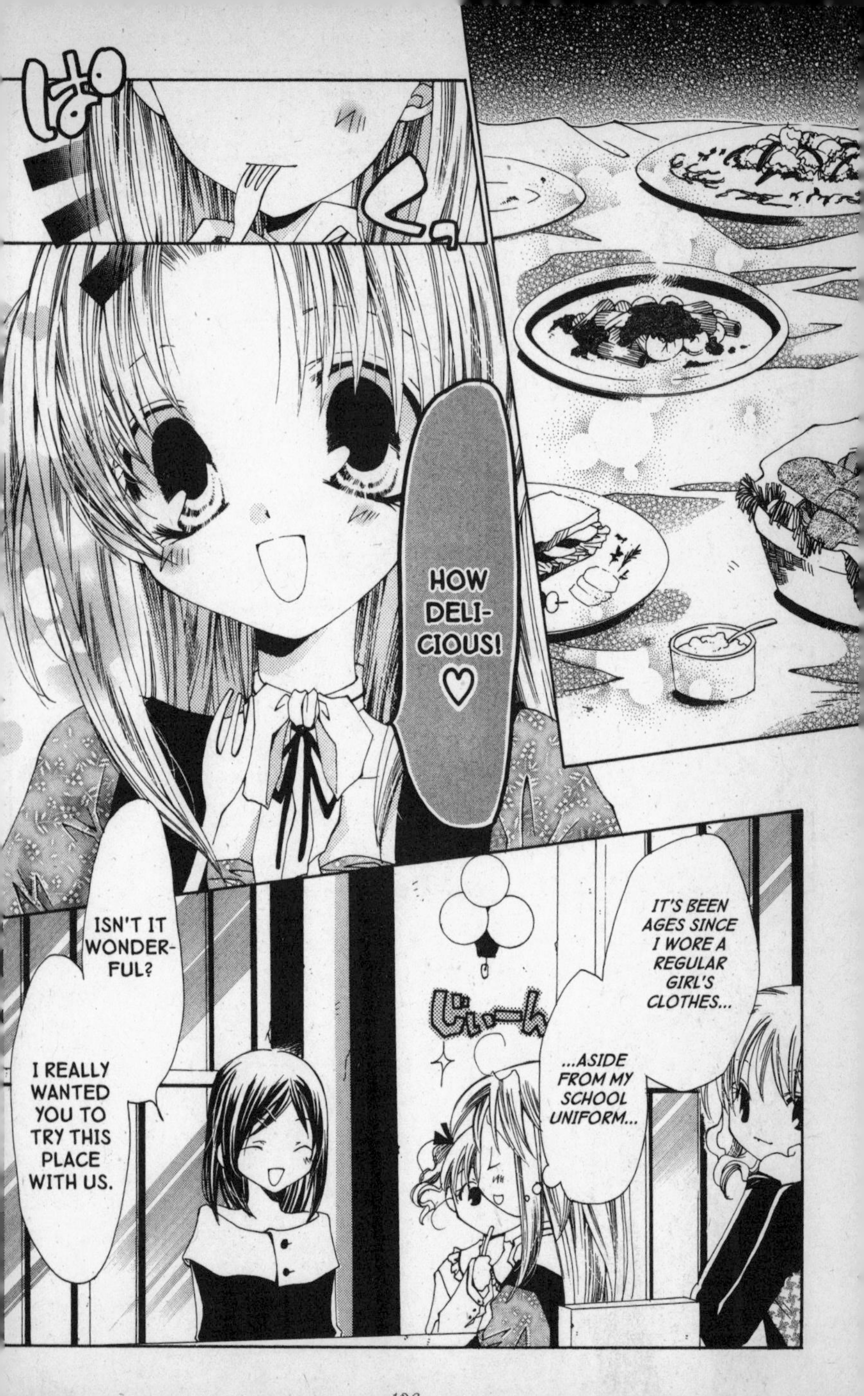
はっ
HOW DELICIOUS! ♡
IT'S BEEN AGES SINCE I WORE A REGULAR GIRL'S CLOTHES...
...ASIDE FROM MY SCHOOL UNIFORM...
じぃーん
ISN'T IT WONDERFUL?
I REALLY WANTED YOU TO TRY THIS PLACE WITH US.

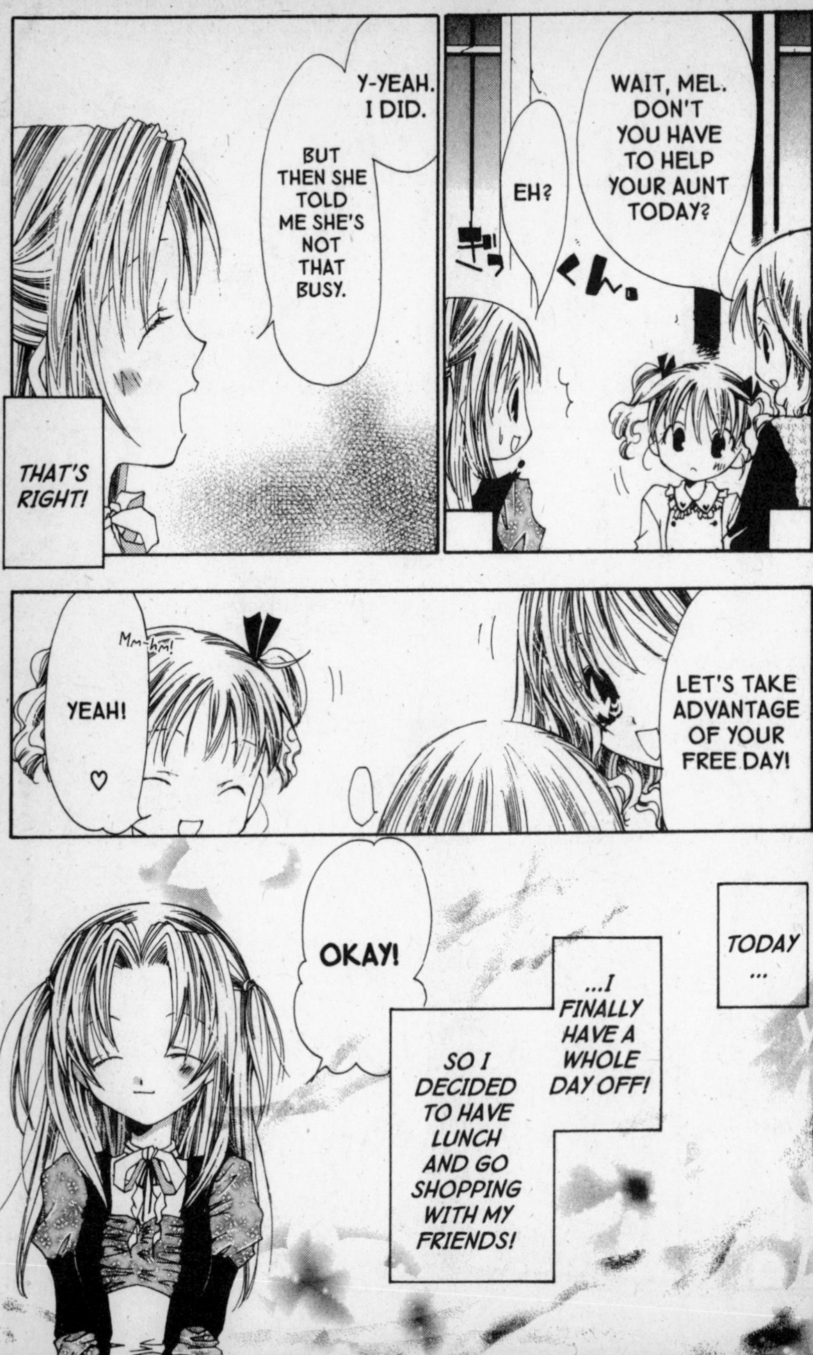
WAIT, MEL. DON'T YOU HAVE TO HELP YOUR AUNT TODAY?
EH?
Y-YEAH. I DID.
BUT THEN SHE TOLD ME SHE'S NOT THAT BUSY.
THAT'S RIGHT!
LET'S TAKE ADVANTAGE OF YOUR FREE DAY!
Mm-hm!
YEAH! ♡
TODAY ...
...I FINALLY HAVE A WHOLE DAY OFF!
SO I DECIDED TO HAVE LUNCH AND GO SHOPPING WITH MY FRIENDS!
OKAY!

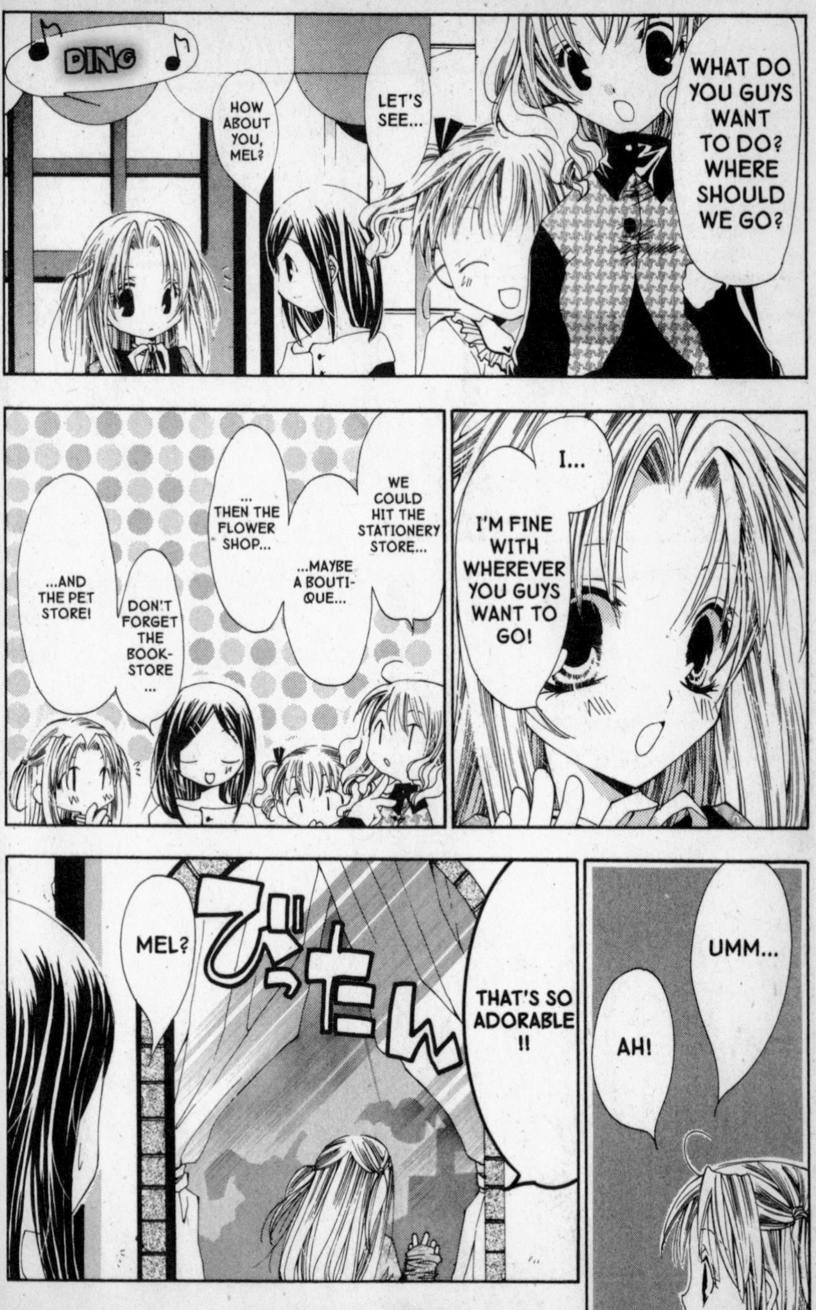
WHAT DO YOU GUYS WANT TO DO? WHERE SHOULD WE GO?
LET'S SEE...
HOW ABOUT YOU, MEL?
DING
I...
I'M FINE WITH WHEREVER YOU GUYS WANT TO GO!
WE COULD HIT THE STATIONERY STORE...
...MAYBE A BOUTIQUE...
...THEN THE FLOWER SHOP...
DON'T FORGET THE BOOKSTORE...
...AND THE PET STORE!
UMM...
AH!
THAT'S SO ADORABLE!!
びったん
MEL?

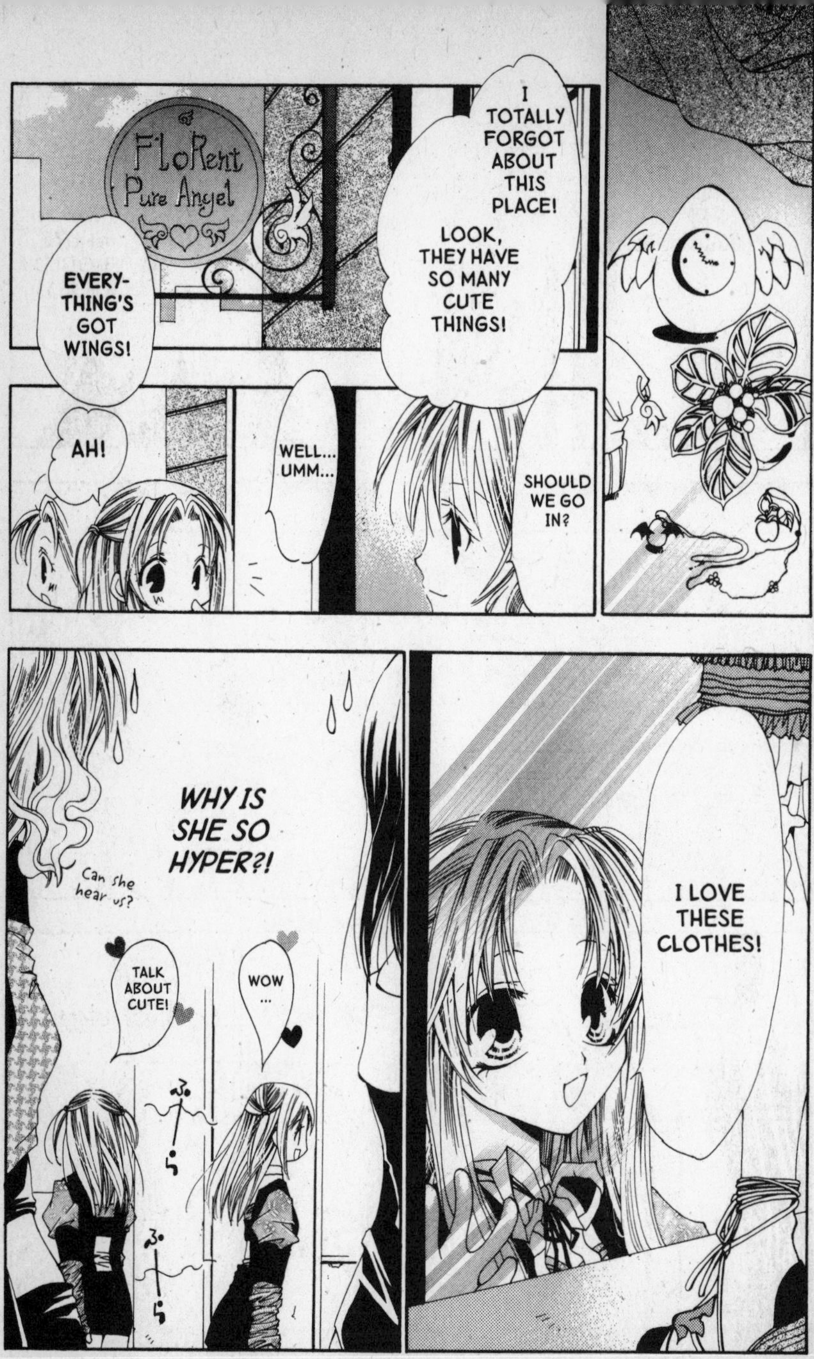
I TOTALLY FORGOT ABOUT THIS PLACE!
LOOK, THEY HAVE SO MANY CUTE THINGS!
FloRent Pure Angel
EVERY-THING'S GOT WINGS!
SHOULD WE GO IN?
WELL... UMM...
AH!
I LOVE THESE CLOTHES!
WHY IS SHE SO HYPER?!
Can she hear us?
WOW ...
TALK ABOUT CUTE!

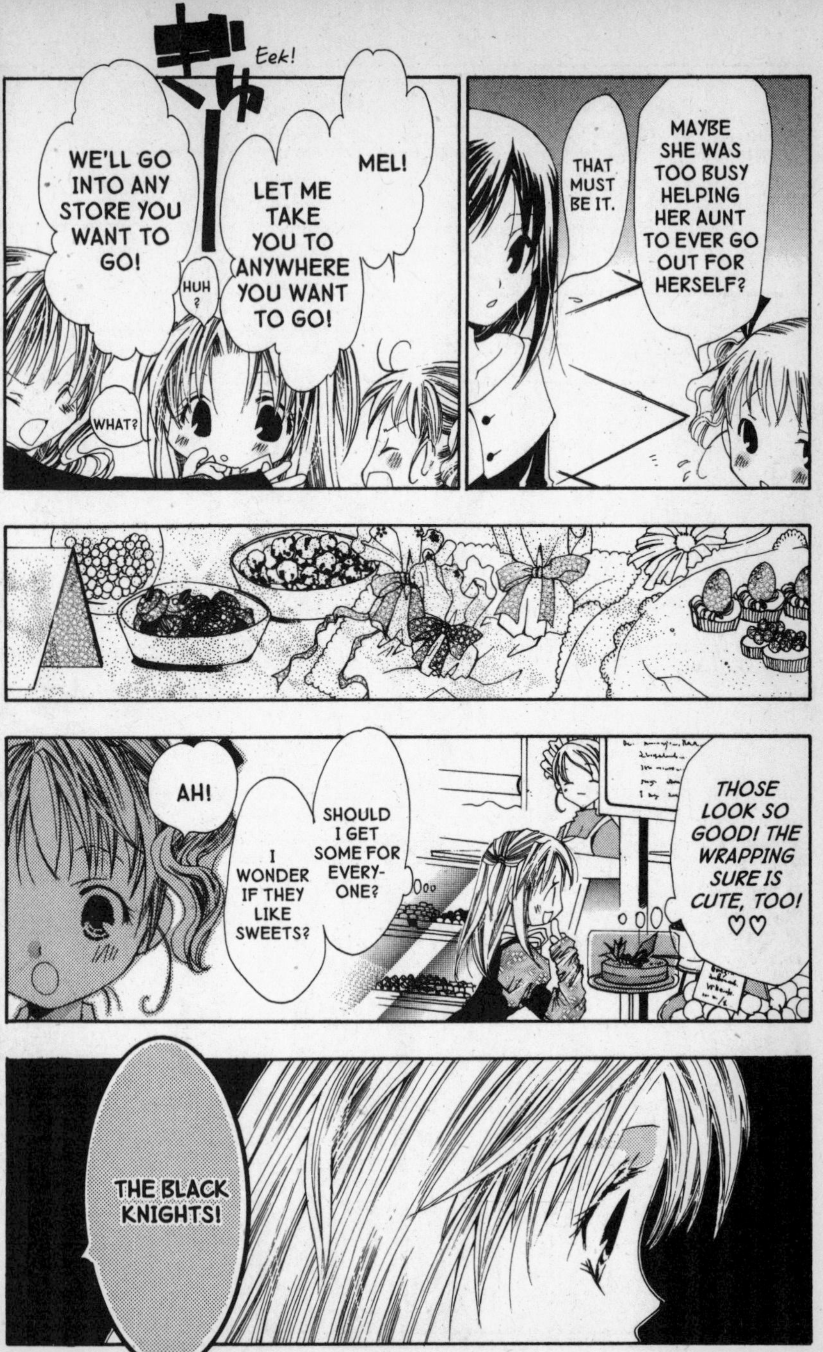
MAYBE SHE WAS TOO BUSY HELPING HER AUNT TO EVER GO OUT FOR HERSELF?
THAT MUST BE IT.
Eek!
MEL!
LET ME TAKE YOU TO ANYWHERE YOU WANT TO GO!
WE'LL GO INTO ANY STORE YOU WANT TO GO!
HUH?
WHAT?
THOSE LOOK SO GOOD! THE WRAPPING SURE IS CUTE, TOO! ♡♡
SHOULD I GET SOME FOR EVERY-ONE?
I WONDER IF THEY LIKE SWEETS?
AH!
THE BLACK KNIGHTS!

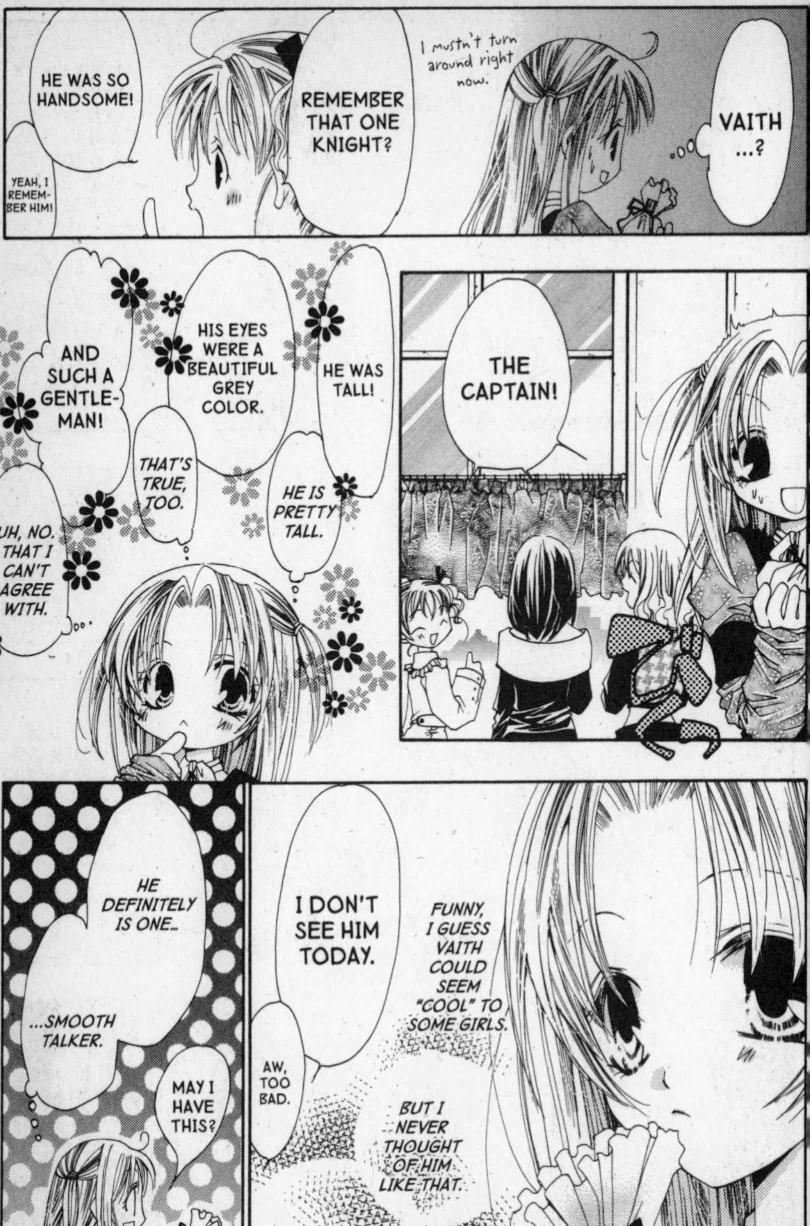
VAITH ...?
I mustn't turn around right now.
REMEMBER THAT ONE KNIGHT?
HE WAS SO HANDSOME!
YEAH, I REMEMBER HIM!
THE CAPTAIN!
HE WAS TALL!
HE IS PRETTY TALL.
HIS EYES WERE A BEAUTIFUL GREY COLOR.
THAT'S TRUE, TOO.
AND SUCH A GENTLE-MAN!
UH, NO. THAT I CAN'T AGREE WITH.
I DON'T SEE HIM TODAY.
AW, TOO BAD.
FUNNY, I GUESS VAITH COULD SEEM "COOL" TO SOME GIRLS.
BUT I NEVER THOUGHT OF HIM LIKE THAT.
HE DEFINITELY IS ONE..
...SMOOTH TALKER.
MAY I HAVE THIS?

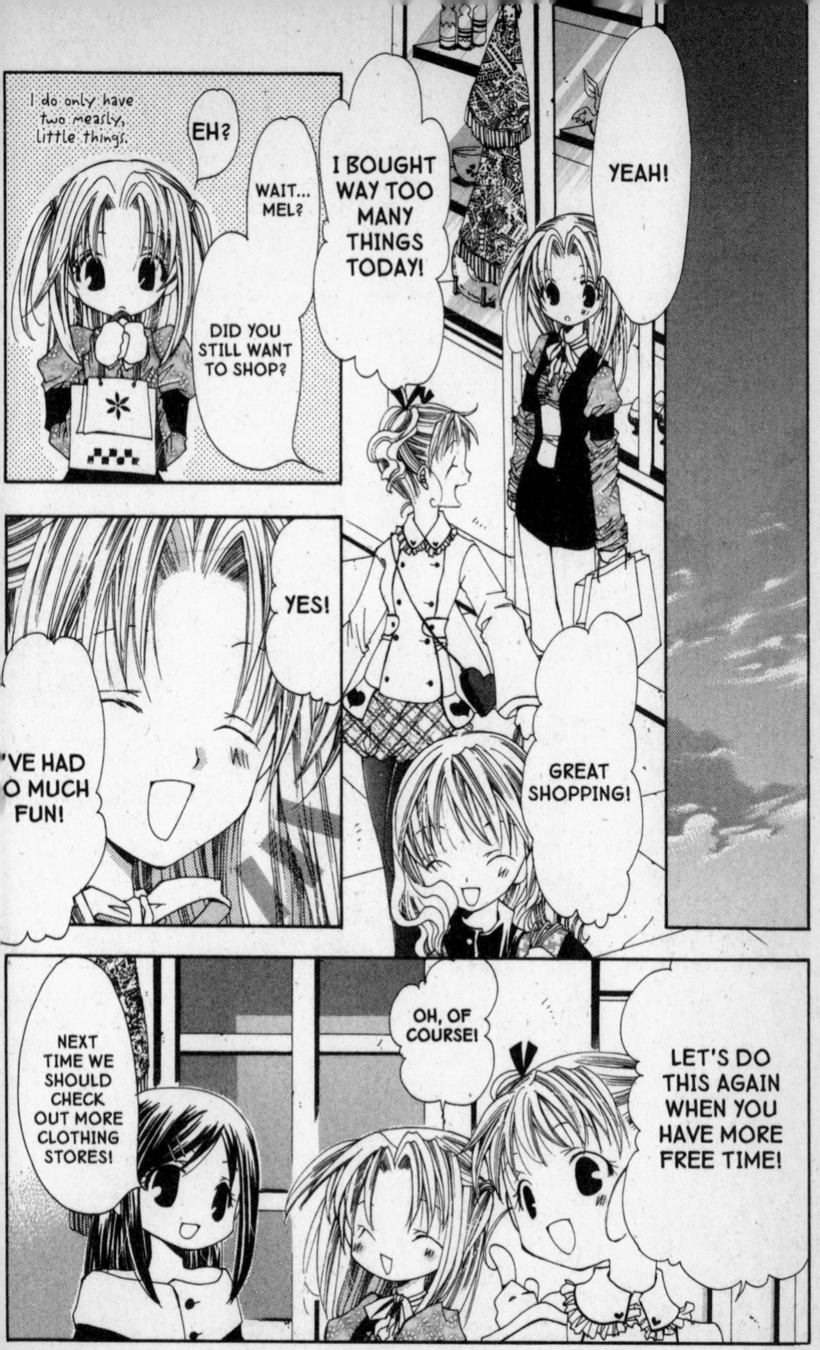
YEAH!
I BOUGHT WAY TOO MANY THINGS TODAY!
GREAT SHOPPING!
EH?
WAIT... MEL?
DID YOU STILL WANT TO SHOP?
I do only have two measly, little things.
YES!
'VE HAD O MUCH FUN!
LET'S DO THIS AGAIN WHEN YOU HAVE MORE FREE TIME!
OH, OF COURSE!
NEXT TIME WE SHOULD CHECK OUT MORE CLOTHING STORES!

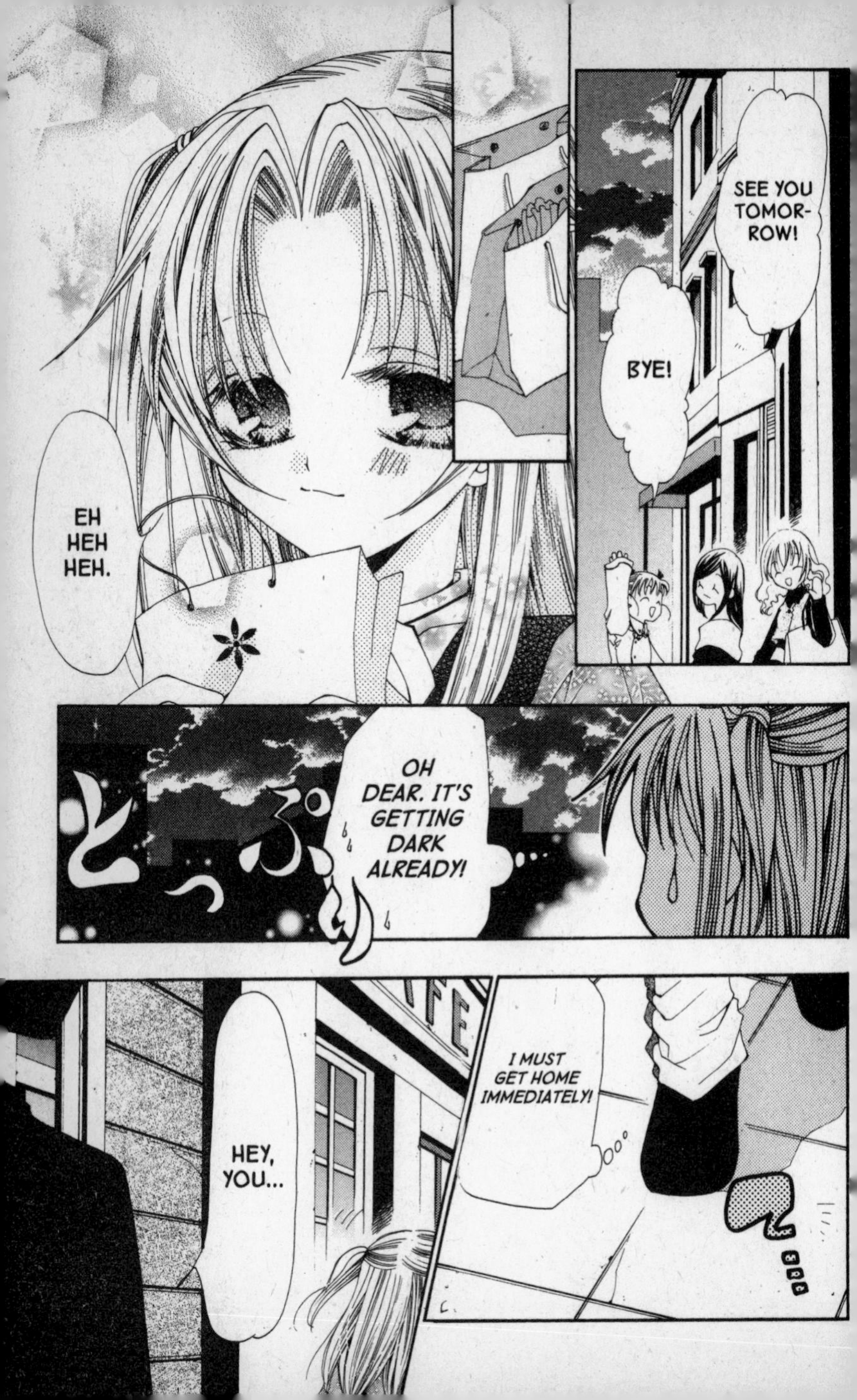
SEE YOU TOMORROW!
BYE!
EH HEH HEH.
OH DEAR. IT'S GETTING DARK ALREADY!
I MUST GET HOME IMMEDIATELY!
HEY, YOU...

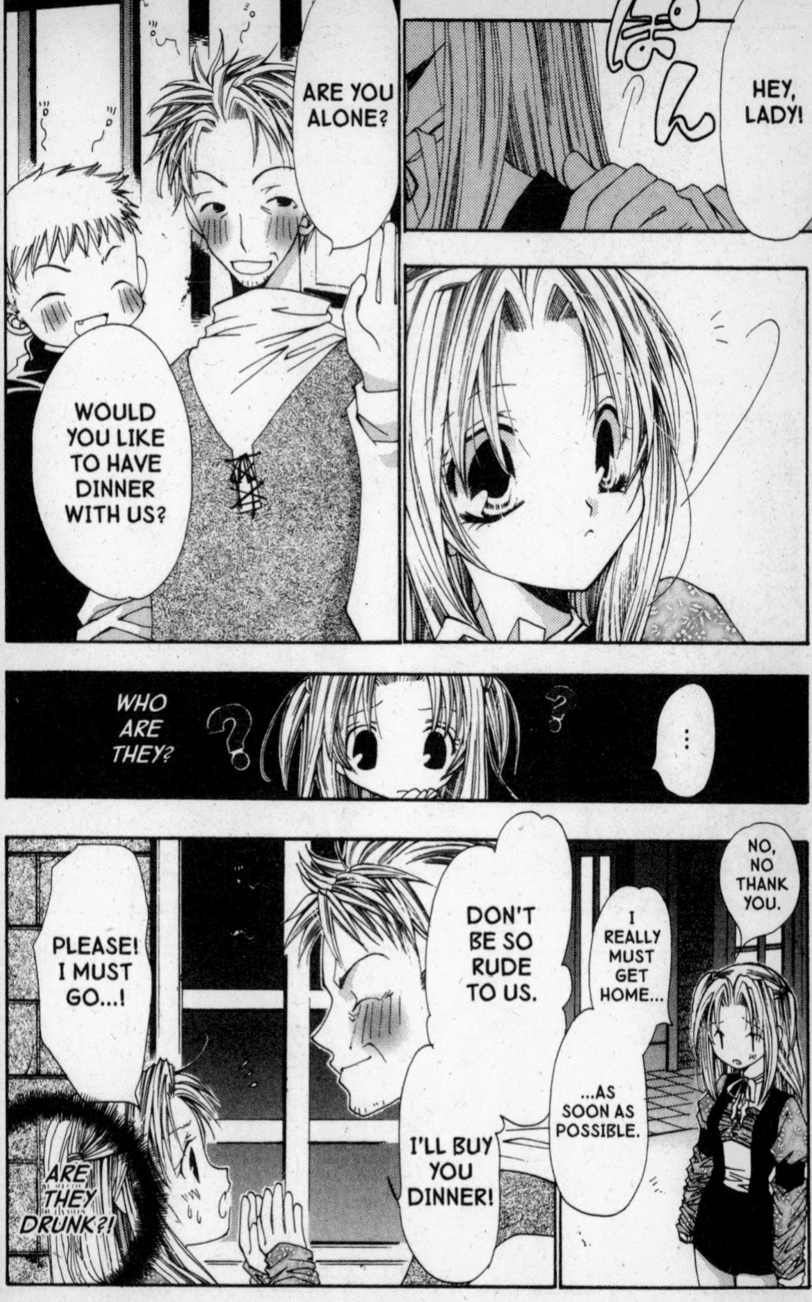
ぽん
HEY, LADY!
ARE YOU ALONE?
WOULD YOU LIKE TO HAVE DINNER WITH US?
...
WHO ARE THEY?
NO, NO THANK YOU.
I REALLY MUST GET HOME...
...AS SOON AS POSSIBLE.
DON'T BE SO RUDE TO US.
I'LL BUY YOU DINNER!
PLEASE! I MUST GO...!
ARE THEY DRUNK?!

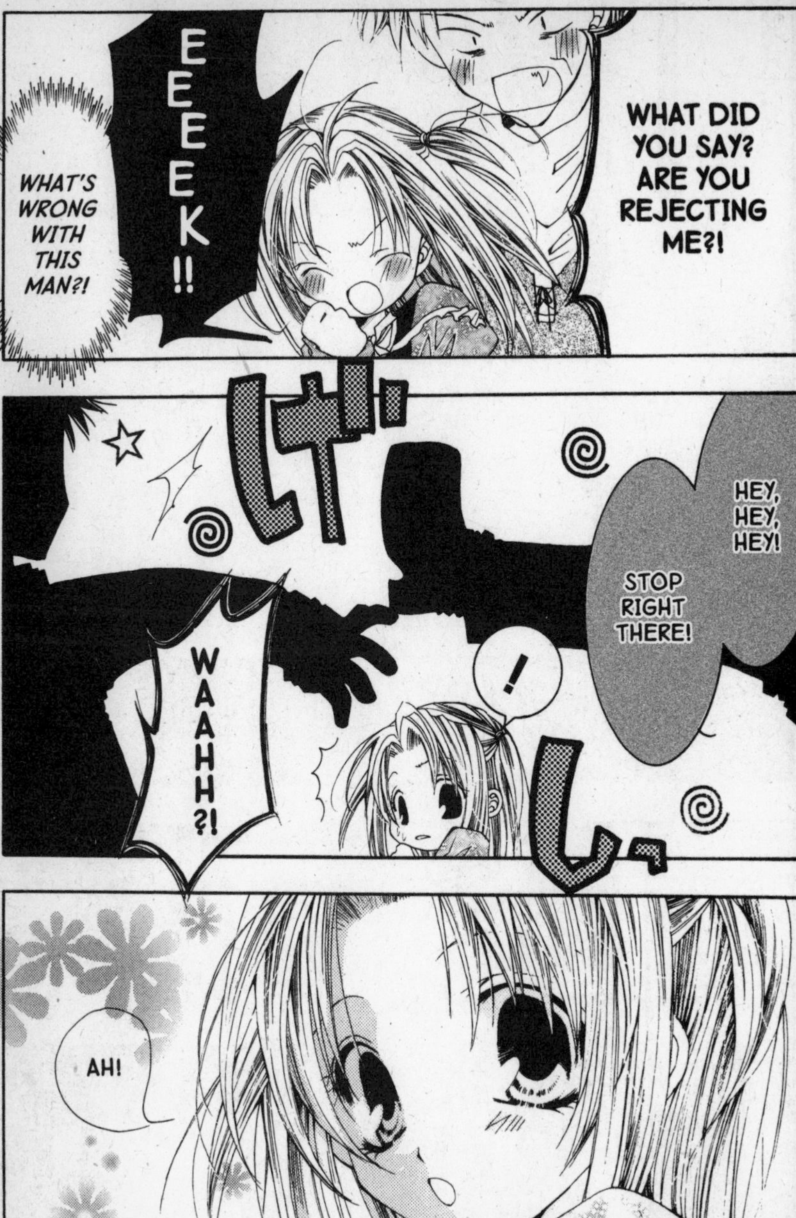
WHAT DID YOU SAY? ARE YOU REJECTING ME?!
EEEEK!!
WHAT'S WRONG WITH THIS MAN?!
HEY, HEY, HEY!
STOP RIGHT THERE!
!
WAAAHH?!
AH!

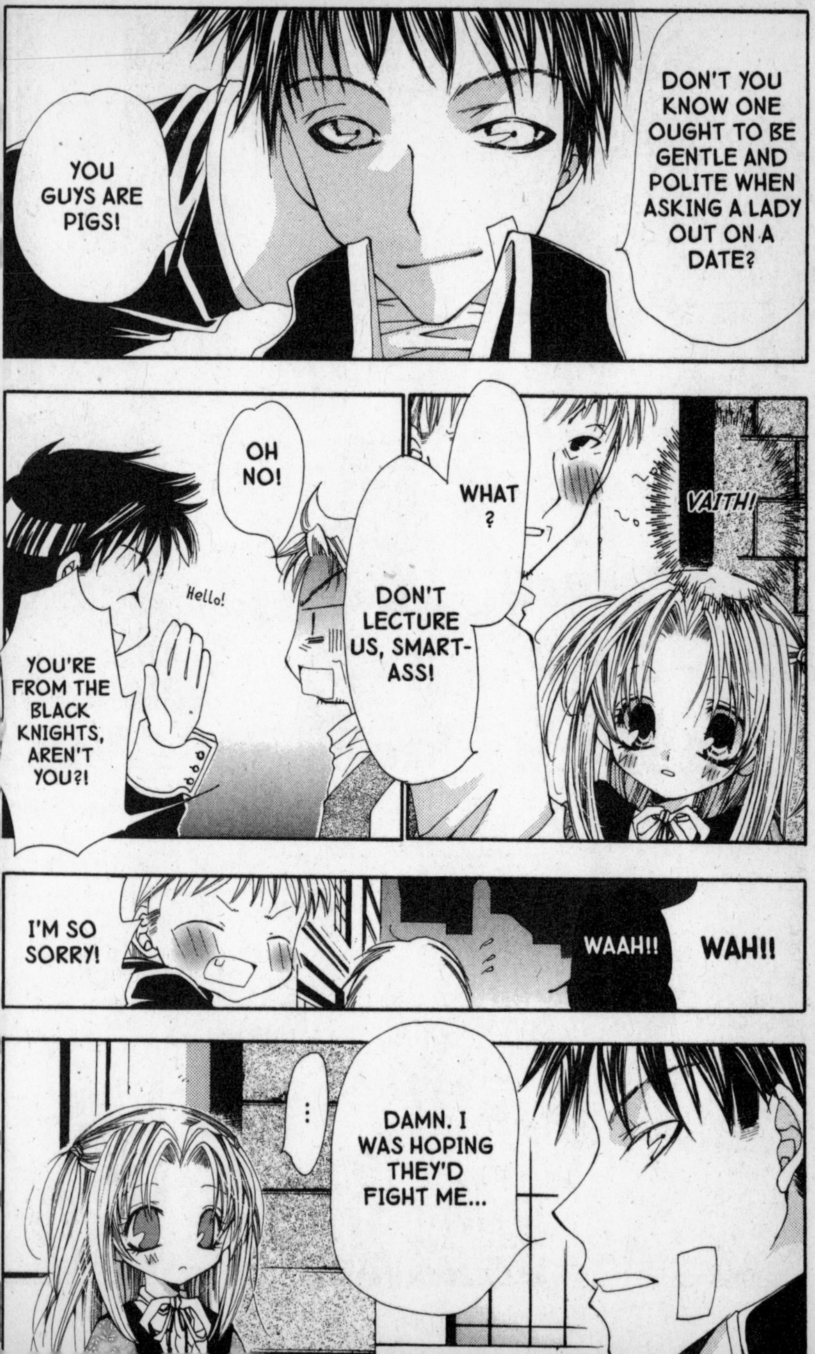
DON'T YOU KNOW ONE OUGHT TO BE GENTLE AND POLITE WHEN ASKING A LADY OUT ON A DATE?
YOU GUYS ARE PIGS!
WHAT?
VAITH!
DON'T LECTURE US, SMART-ASS!
OH NO!
Hello!
YOU'RE FROM THE BLACK KNIGHTS, AREN'T YOU?!
WAH!!
WAAH!!
I'M SO SORRY!
DAMN. I WAS HOPING THEY'D FIGHT ME...
...

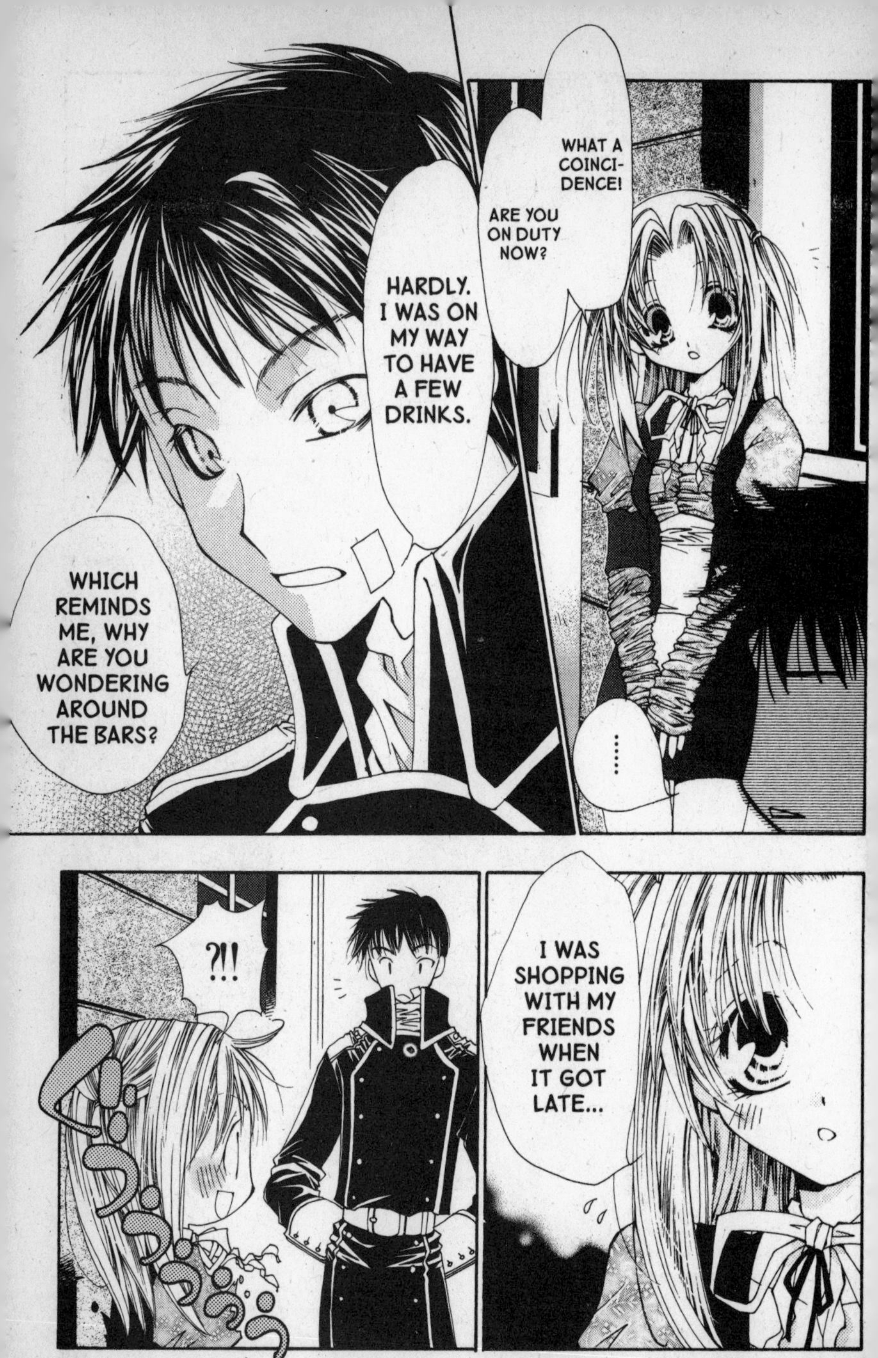
WHAT A COINCIDENCE!
ARE YOU ON DUTY NOW?
HARDLY. I WAS ON MY WAY TO HAVE A FEW DRINKS.
WHICH REMINDS ME, WHY ARE YOU WONDERING AROUND THE BARS?
......
I WAS SHOPPING WITH MY FRIENDS WHEN IT GOT LATE...
?!!
grooowl

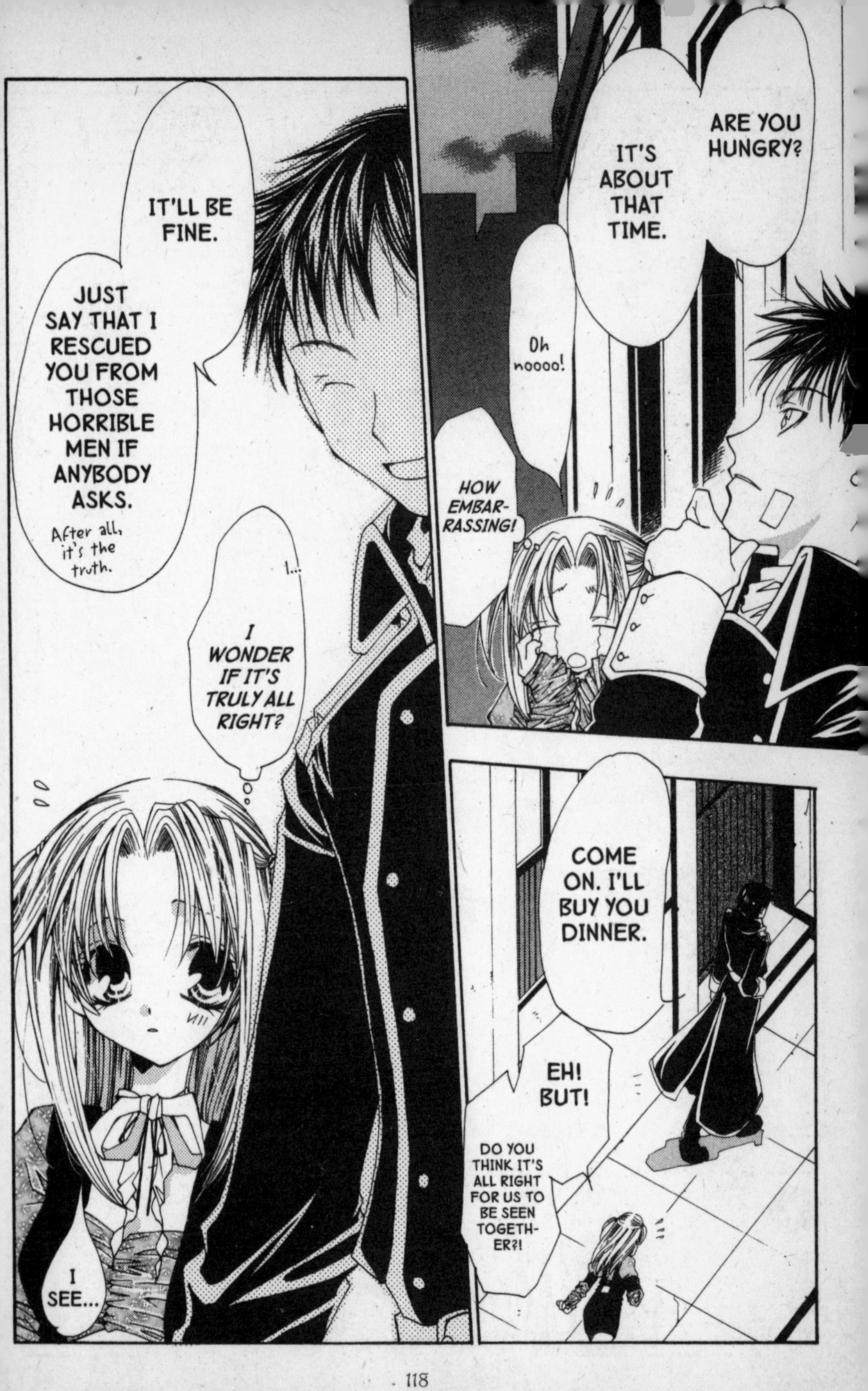
ARE YOU HUNGRY?
IT'S ABOUT THAT TIME.
Oh noooo!
HOW EMBAR-RASSING!
COME ON. I'LL BUY YOU DINNER.
EH! BUT!
DO YOU THINK IT'S ALL RIGHT FOR US TO BE SEEN TOGETH-ER?!
IT'LL BE FINE.
JUST SAY THAT I RESCUED YOU FROM THOSE HORRIBLE MEN IF ANYBODY ASKS.
After all, it's the truth.
I...
I WONDER IF IT'S TRULY ALL RIGHT?
I SEE...

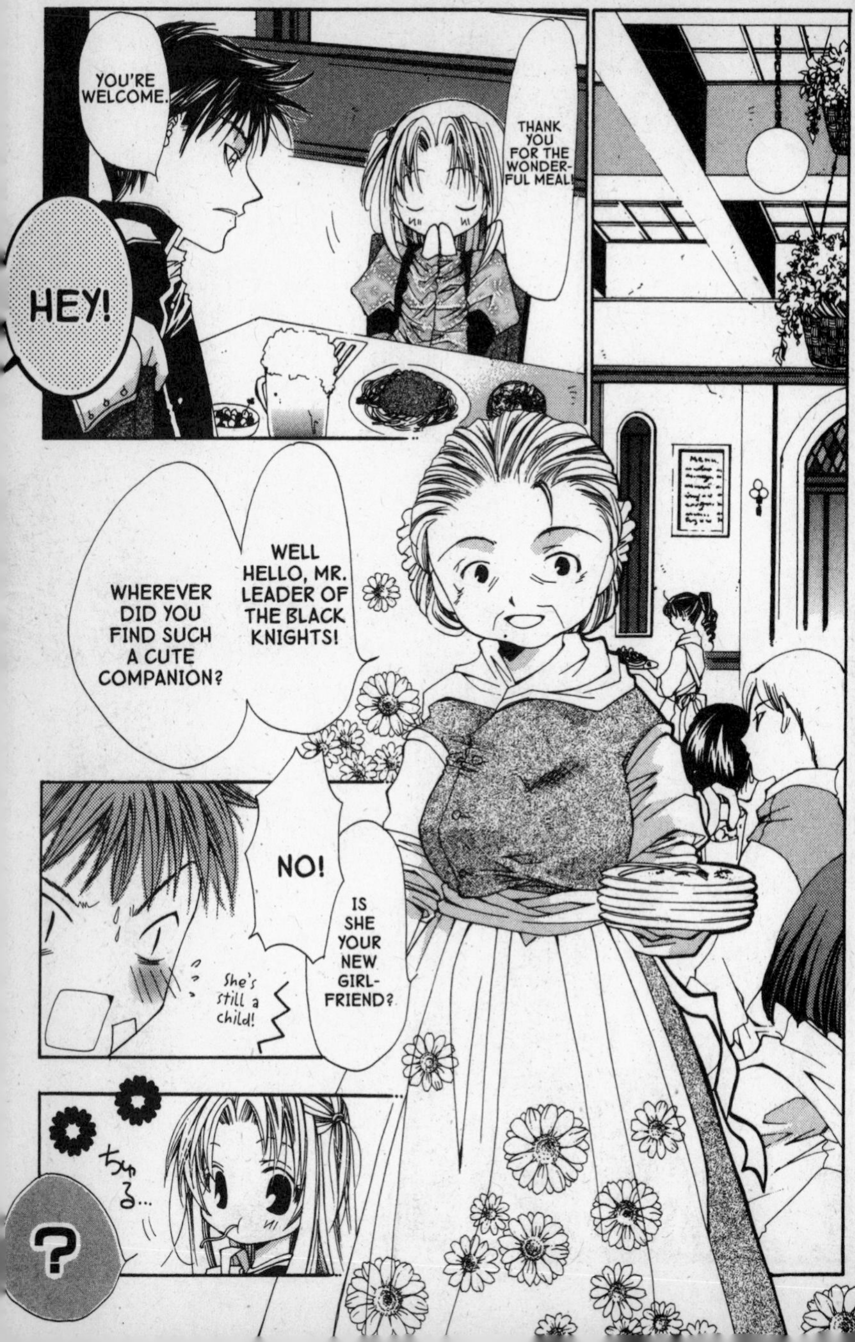
THANK YOU FOR THE WONDERFUL MEAL!
YOU'RE WELCOME.
HEY!
WELL HELLO, MR. LEADER OF THE BLACK KNIGHTS!
WHEREVER DID YOU FIND SUCH A CUTE COMPANION?
IS SHE YOUR NEW GIRLFRIEND?
NO!
She's still a child!
ちゅる...
?

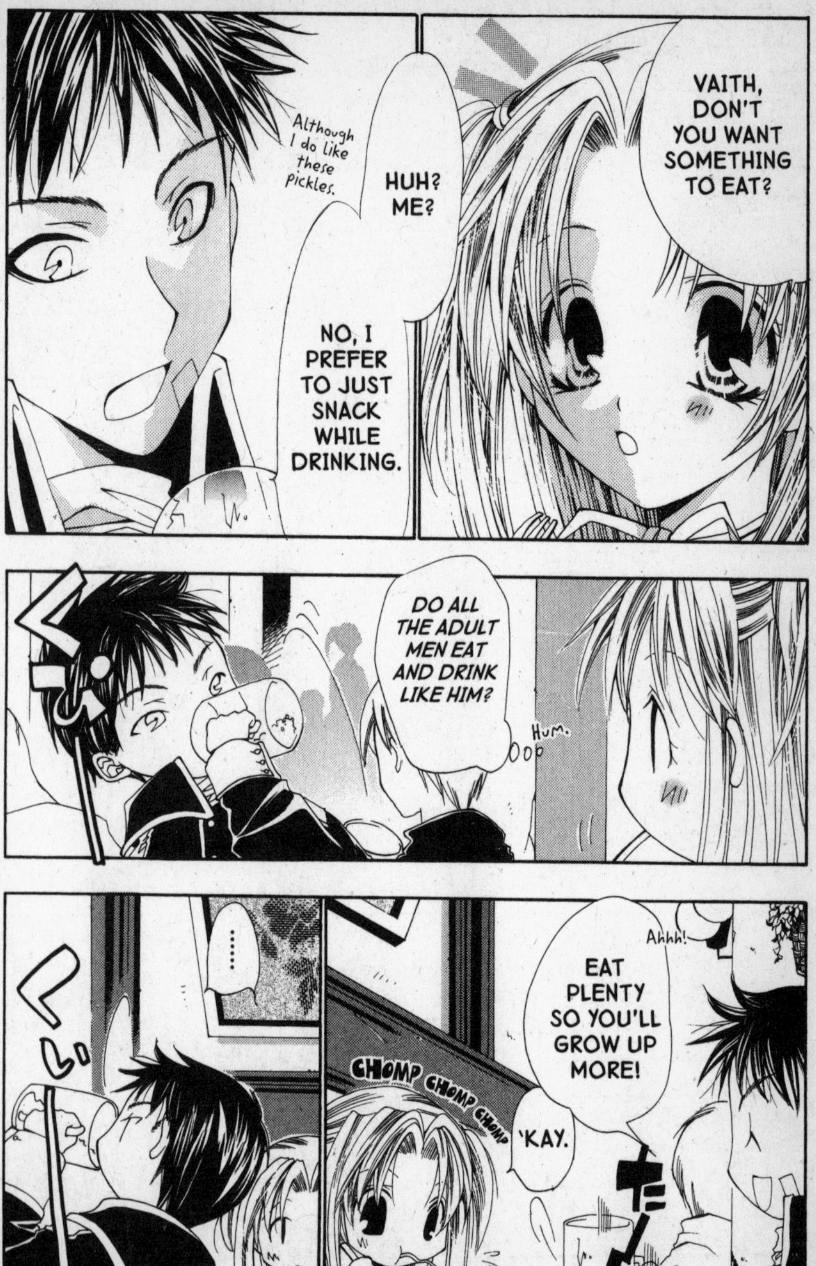
VAITH, DON'T YOU WANT SOMETHING TO EAT?
HUH? ME?
NO, I PREFER TO JUST SNACK WHILE DRINKING.
Although I do like these pickles.
Hum.
DO ALL THE ADULT MEN EAT AND DRINK LIKE HIM?
Ahhh!
EAT PLENTY SO YOU'LL GROW UP MORE!
'KAY.
CHOMP CHOMP CHOMP
......

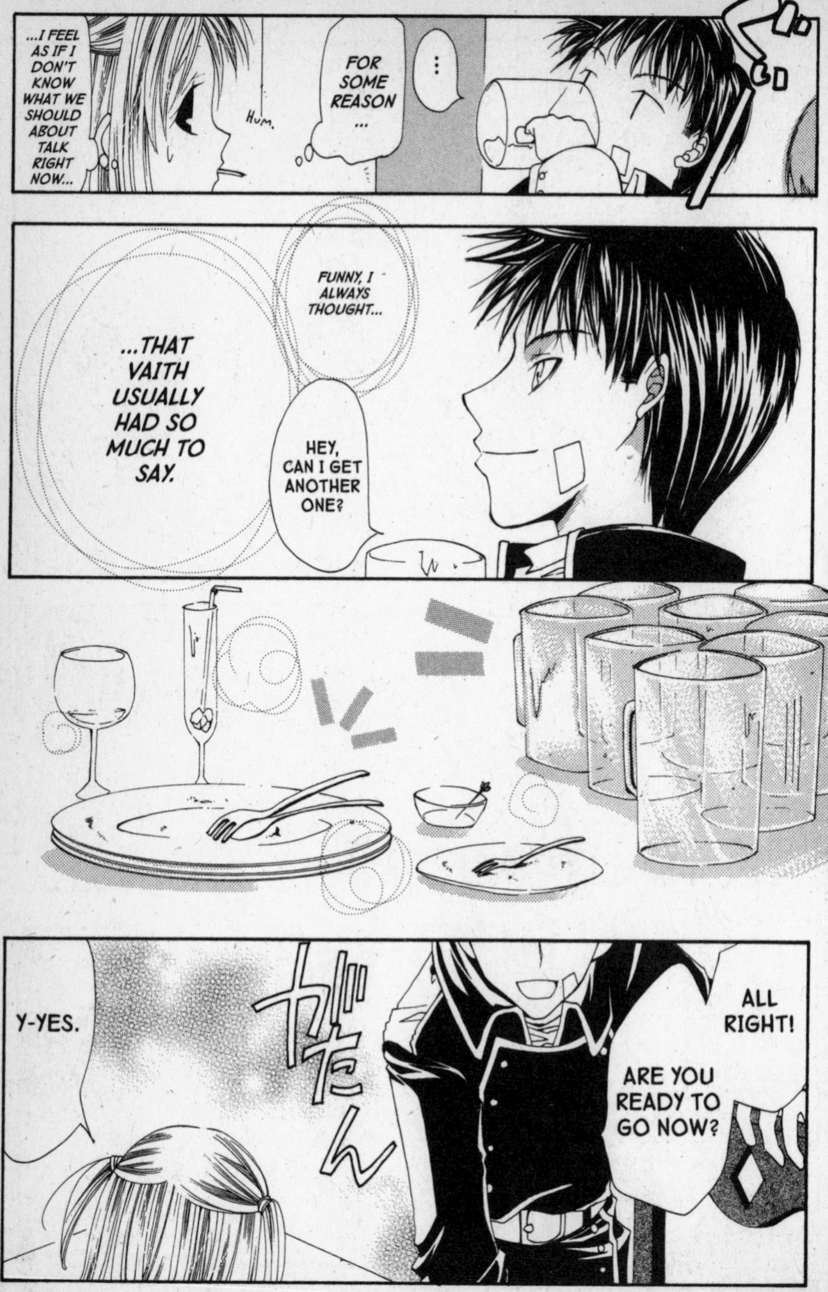
...
FOR SOME REASON ...
HUM.
...I FEEL AS IF I DON'T KNOW WHAT WE SHOULD ABOUT TALK RIGHT NOW...
FUNNY, I ALWAYS THOUGHT...
...THAT VAITH USUALLY HAD SO MUCH TO SAY.
HEY, CAN I GET ANOTHER ONE?
ALL RIGHT!
ARE YOU READY TO GO NOW?
がたん
Y-YES.

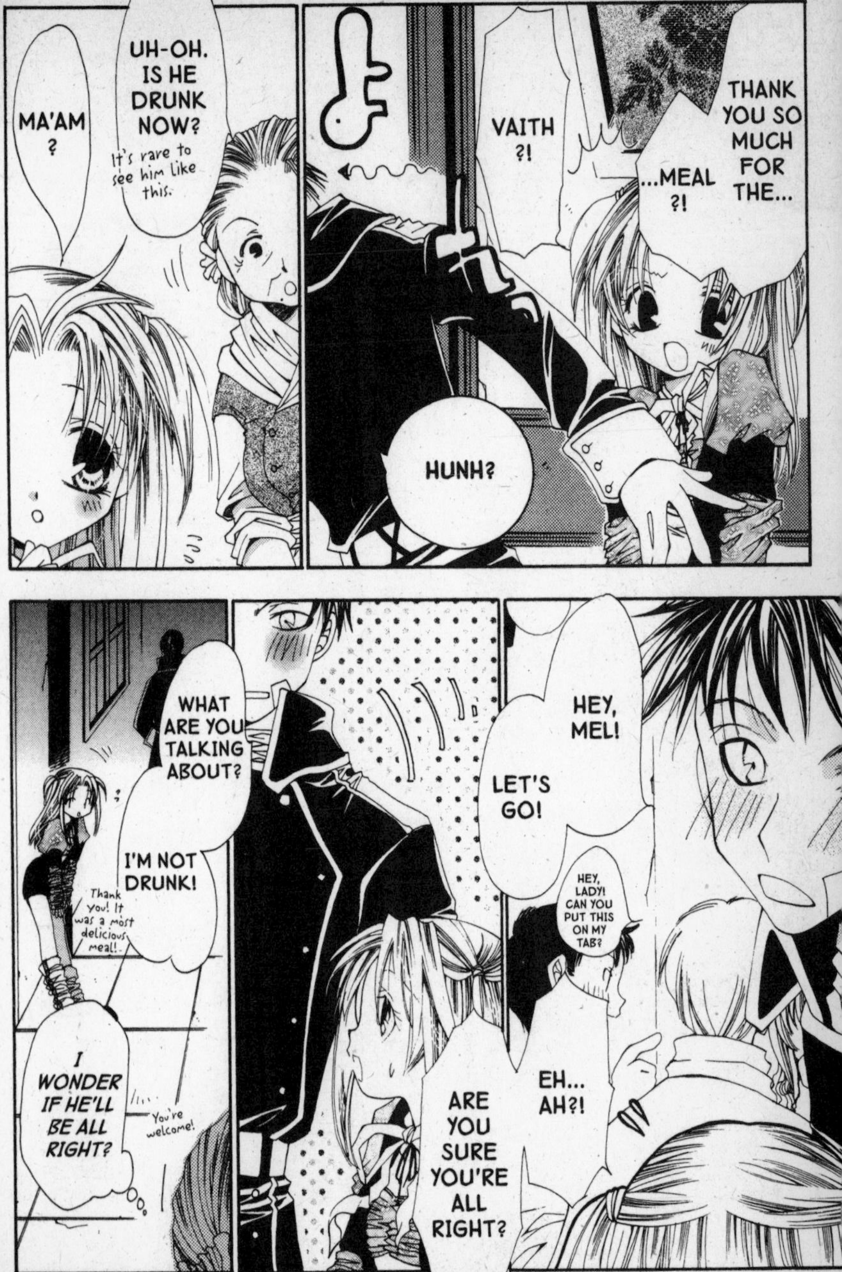
THANK YOU SO MUCH FOR THE...
...MEAL ?!
VAITH ?!
HUNH?
UH-OH. IS HE DRUNK NOW?
It's rare to see him like this.
MA'AM ?
HEY, MEL!
LET'S GO!
HEY, LADY! CAN YOU PUT THIS ON MY TAB?
EH... AH?!
ARE YOU SURE YOU'RE ALL RIGHT?
WHAT ARE YOU TALKING ABOUT?
I'M NOT DRUNK!
Thank you! It was a most delicious meal!
I WONDER IF HE'LL BE ALL RIGHT?
You're welcome!

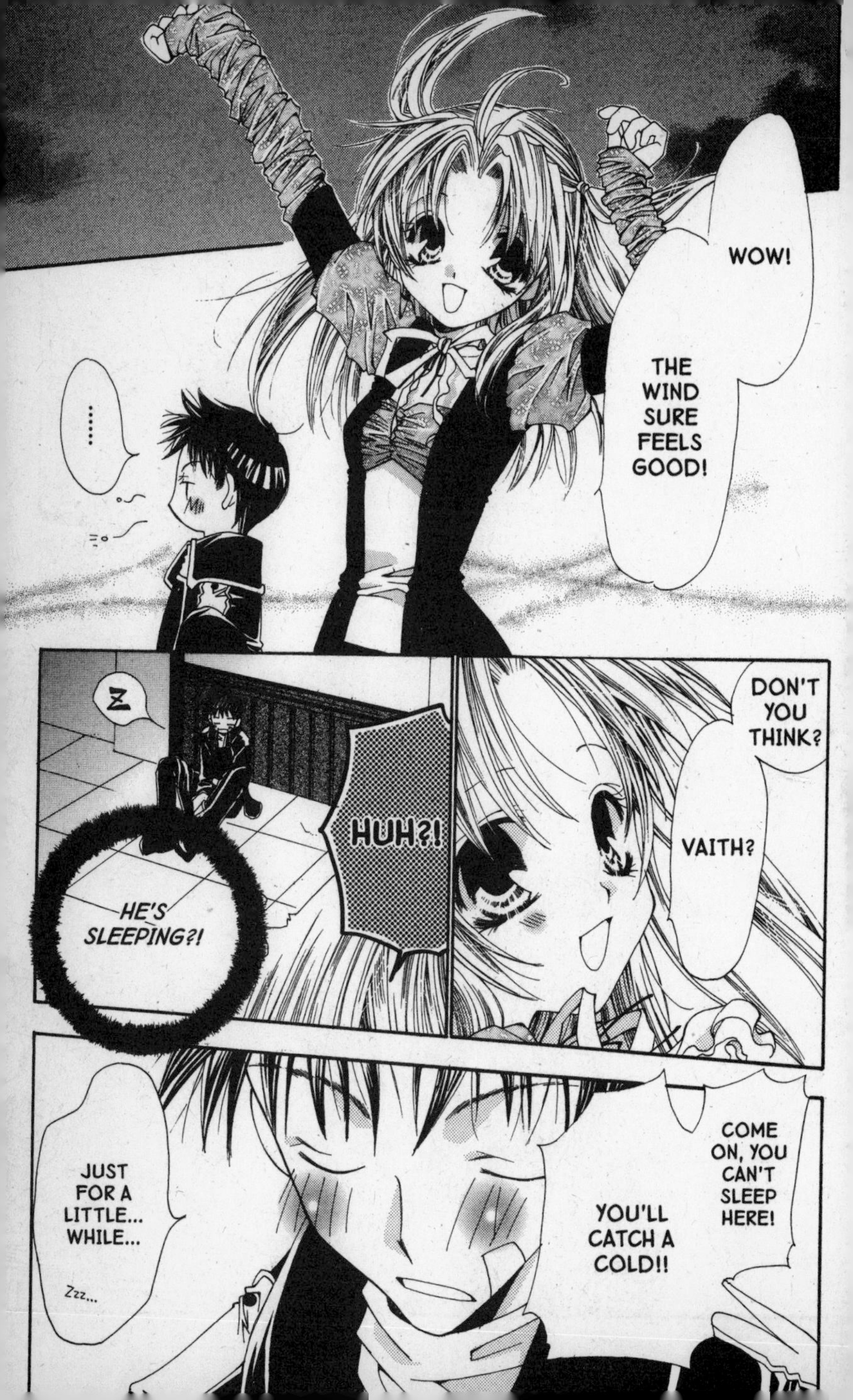
WOW!
THE WIND SURE FEELS GOOD!
......
DON'T YOU THINK?
VAITH?
HUH?!
Z
HE'S SLEEPING?!
COME ON, YOU CAN'T SLEEP HERE!
YOU'LL CATCH A COLD!!
JUST FOR A LITTLE... WHILE...
Zzz...

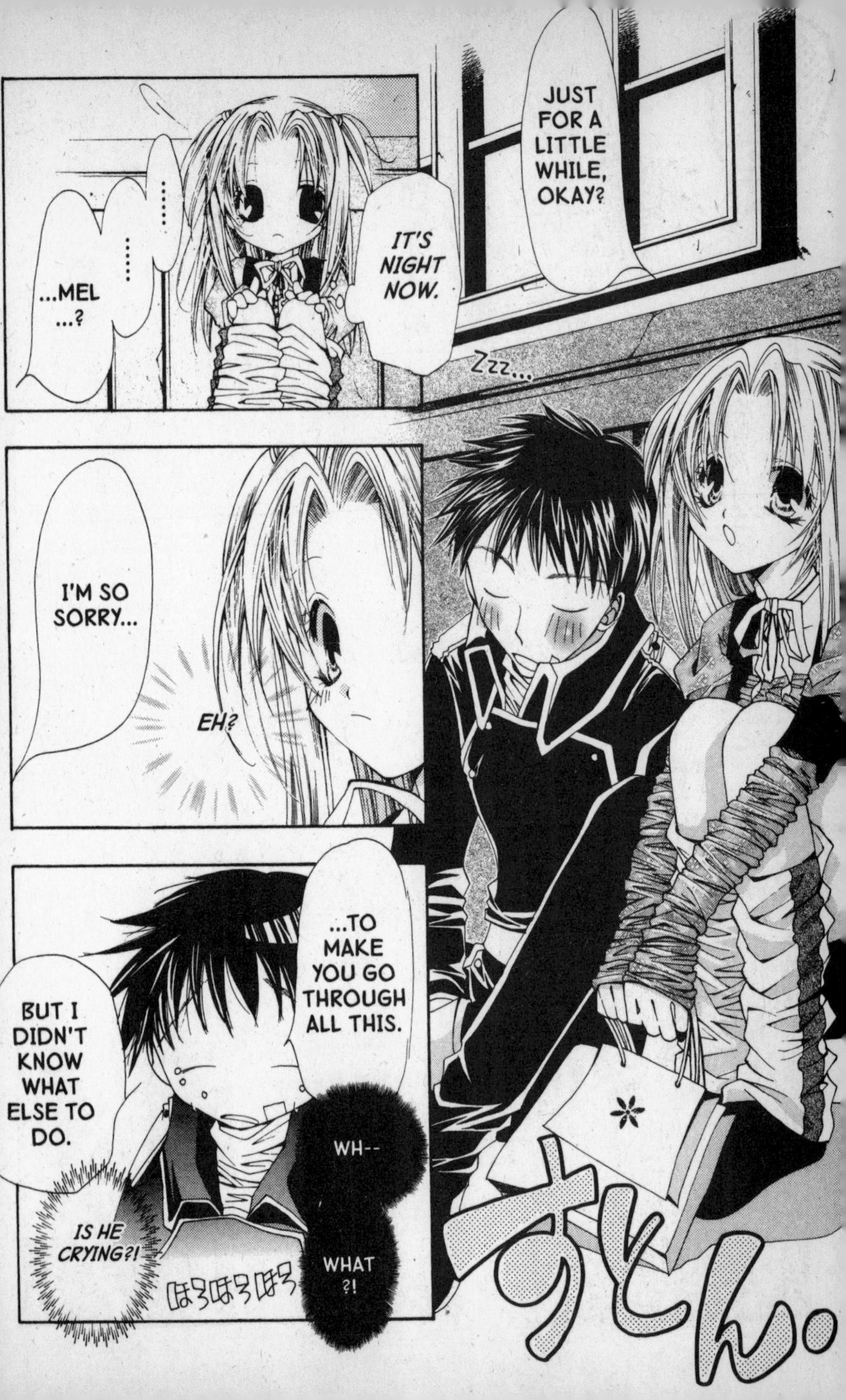
JUST FOR A LITTLE WHILE, OKAY?
Zzz...
すとん
IT'S NIGHT NOW.
......
...MEL ...?
I'M SO SORRY...
EH?
...TO MAKE YOU GO THROUGH ALL THIS.
WH--
WHAT ?!
BUT I DIDN'T KNOW WHAT ELSE TO DO.
IS HE CRYING?!
ほろほろほろ

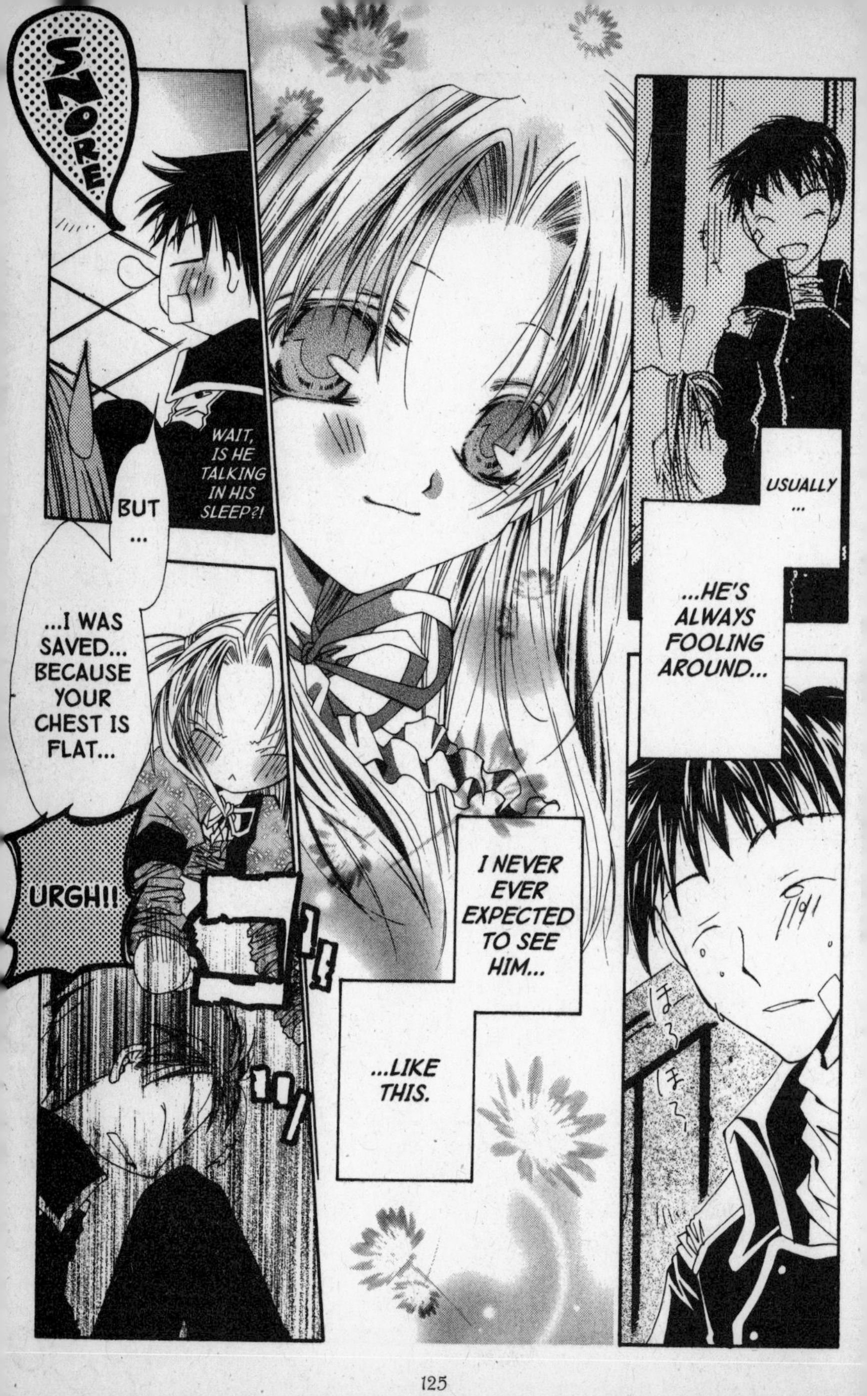

USUALLY ...
...HE'S ALWAYS FOOLING AROUND...
I NEVER EVER EXPECTED TO SEE HIM...
...LIKE THIS.
SNORE
WAIT, IS HE TALKING IN HIS SLEEP?!
BUT ...
...I WAS SAVED... BECAUSE YOUR CHEST IS FLAT...
URGH!!

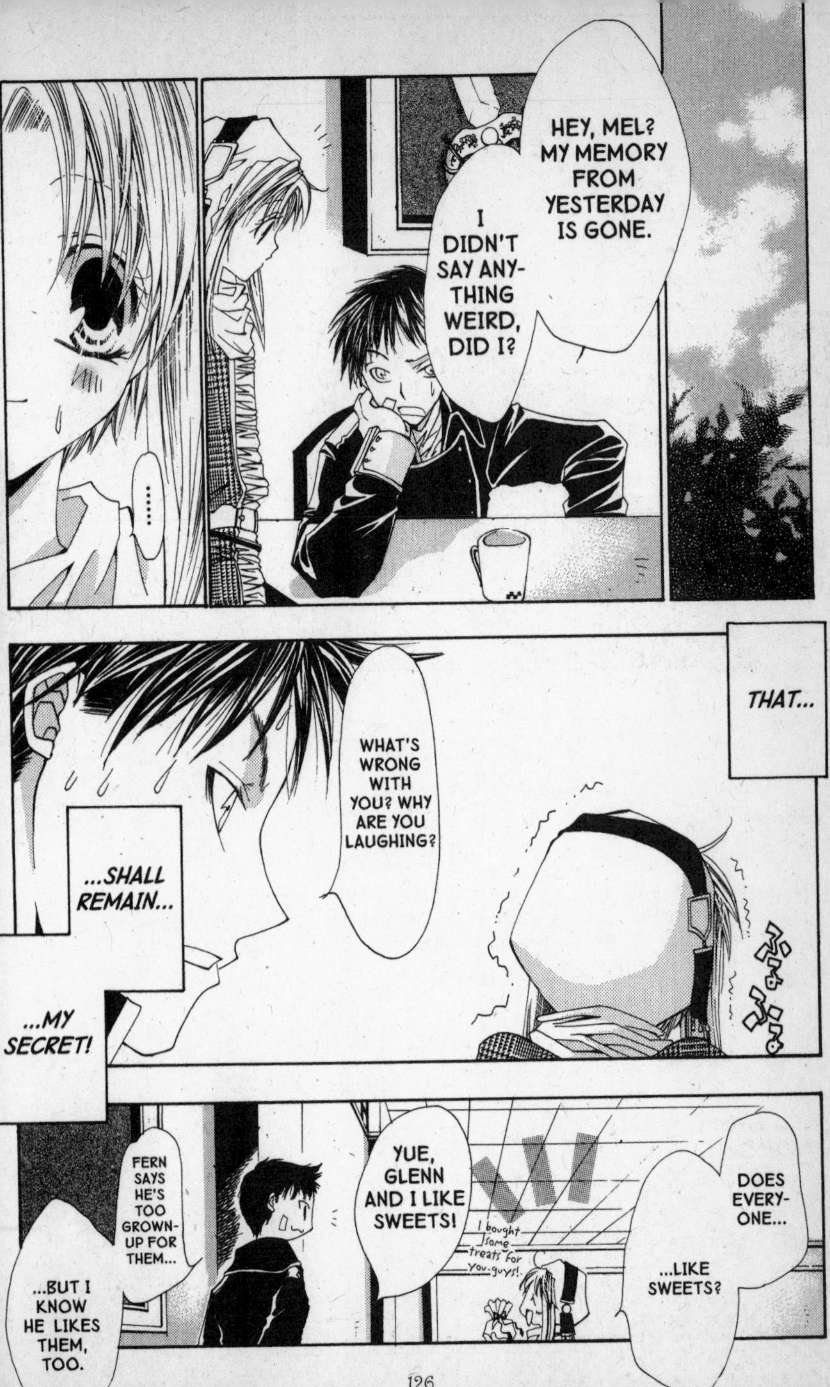
HEY, MEL? MY MEMORY FROM YESTERDAY IS GONE.
I DIDN'T SAY ANY-THING WEIRD, DID I?
......
THAT...
WHAT'S WRONG WITH YOU? WHY ARE YOU LAUGHING?
...SHALL REMAIN...
...MY SECRET!
DOES EVERY-ONE...
...LIKE SWEETS?
YUE, GLENN AND I LIKE SWEETS!
I bought some treats for you guys!
FERN SAYS HE'S TOO GROWN-UP FOR THEM...
...BUT I KNOW HE LIKES THEM, TOO.

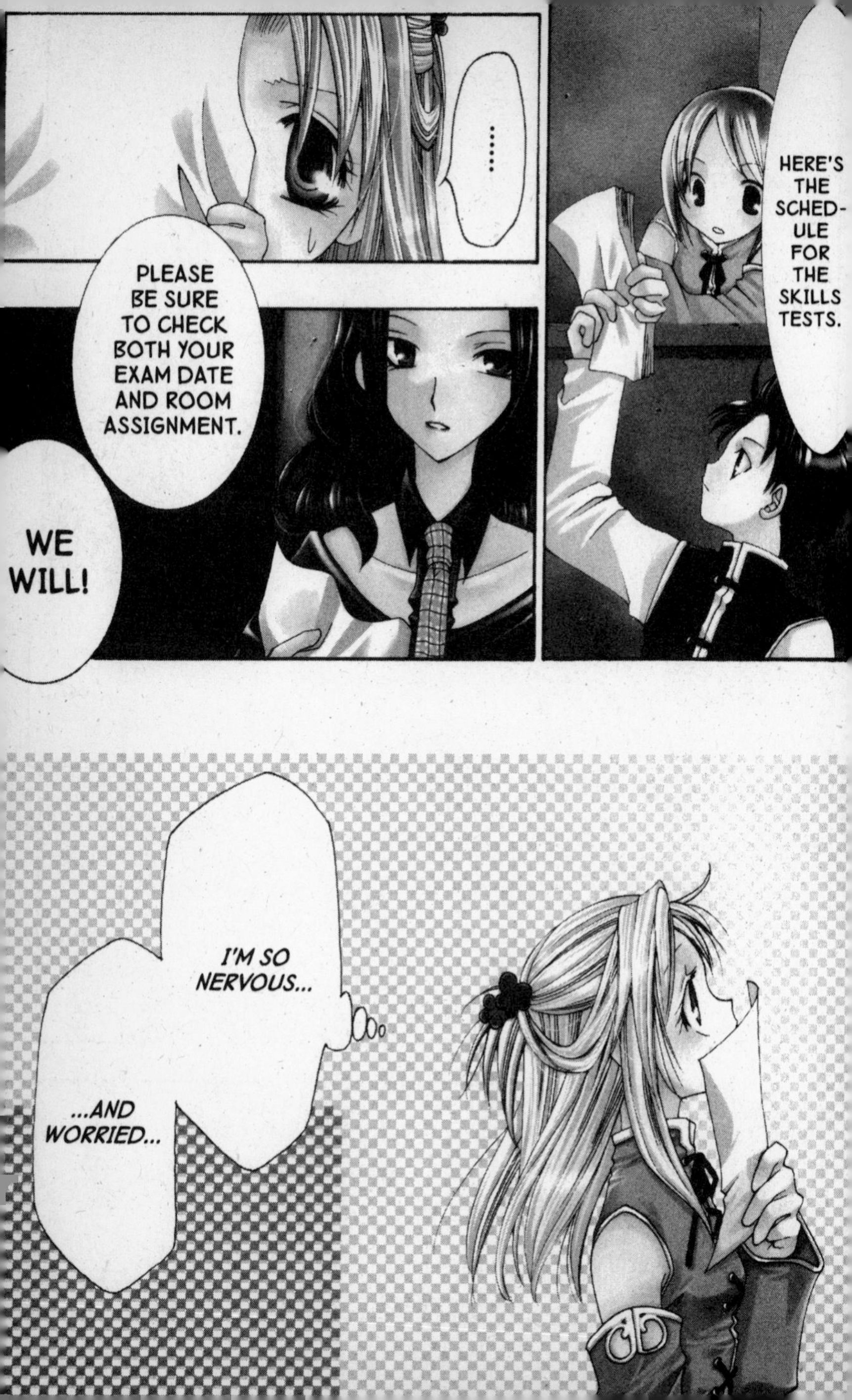
HERE'S THE SCHEDULE FOR THE SKILLS TESTS.
......
PLEASE BE SURE TO CHECK BOTH YOUR EXAM DATE AND ROOM ASSIGNMENT.
WE WILL!
I'M SO NERVOUS...
...AND WORRIED...

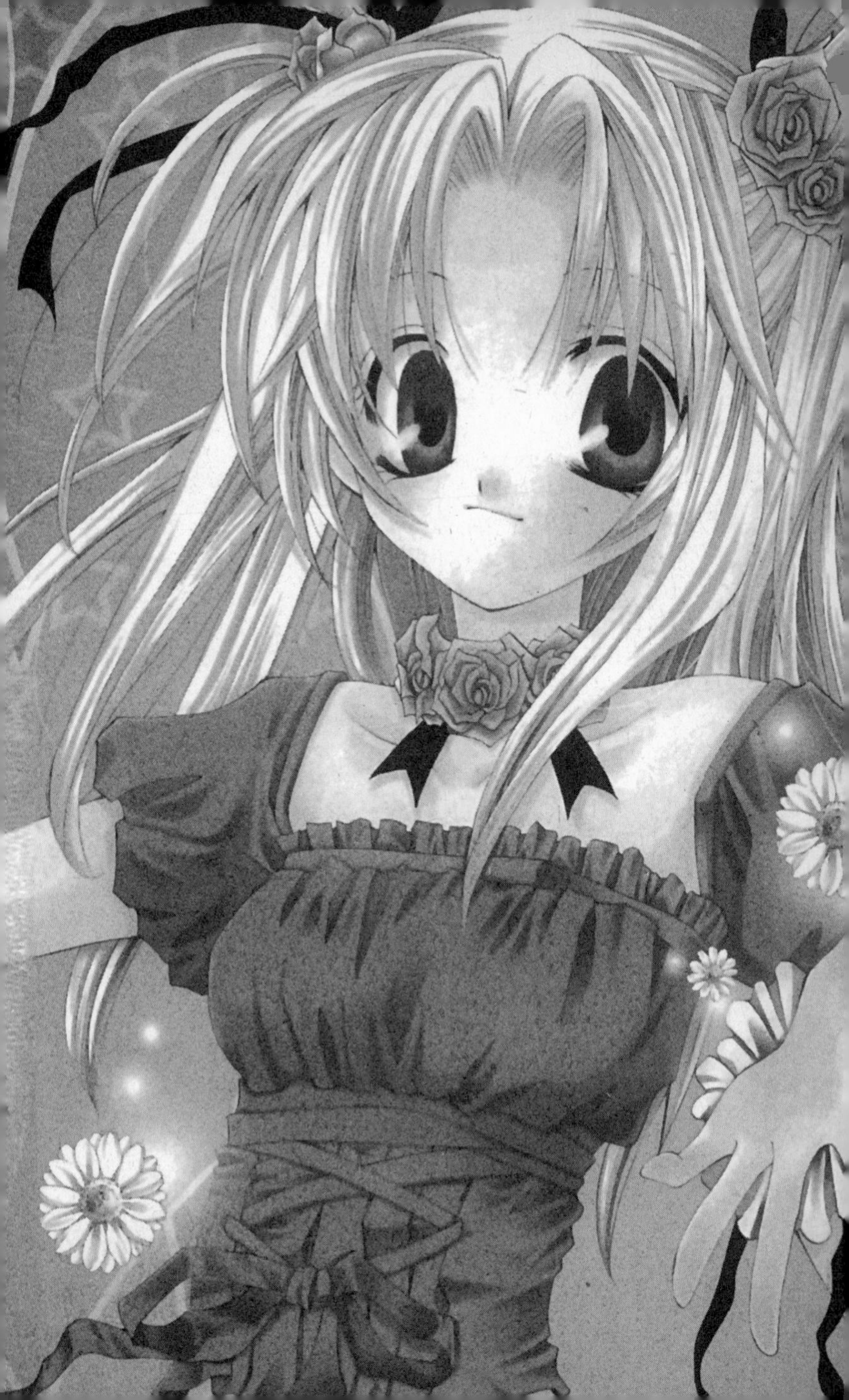

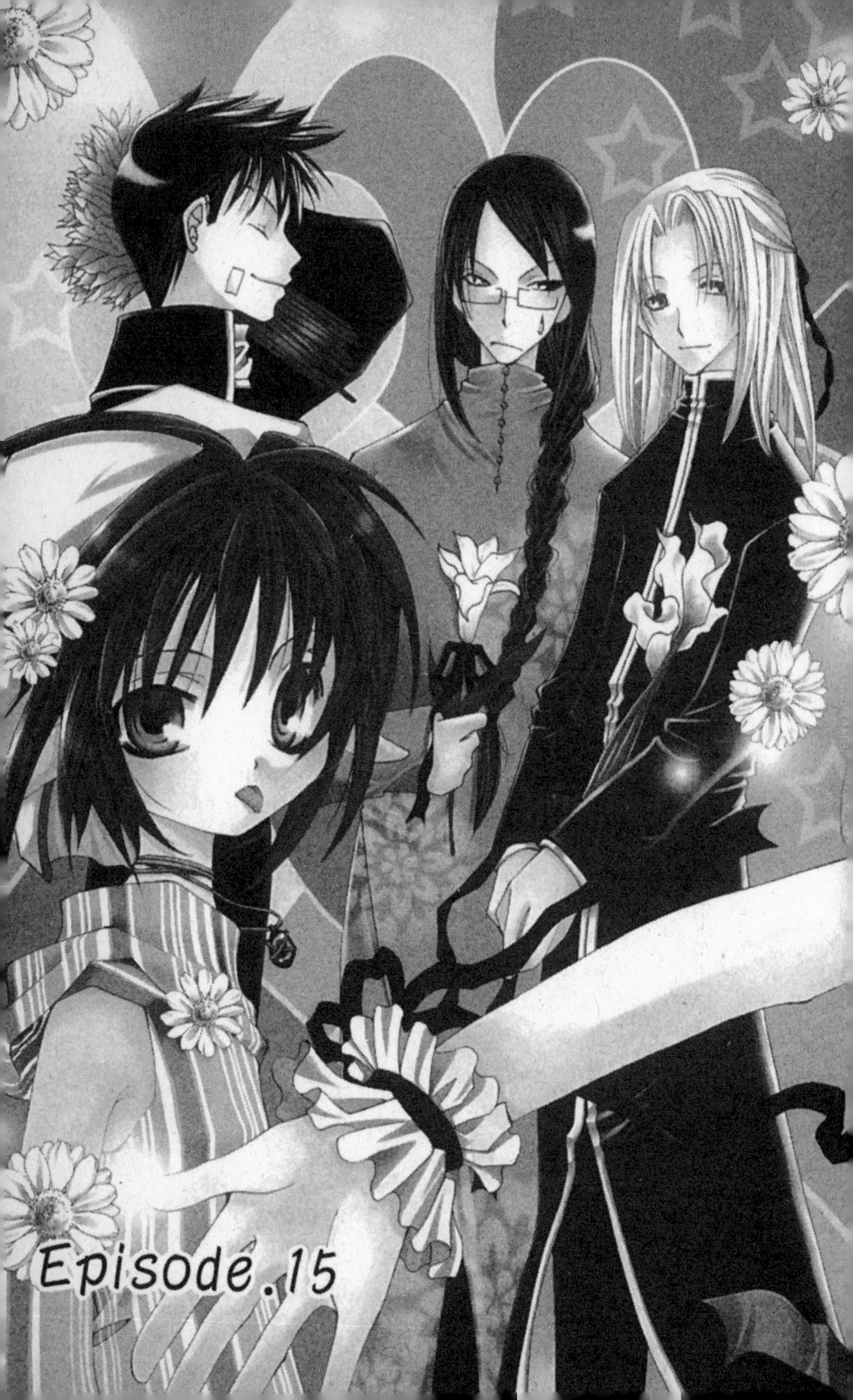
Episode.15

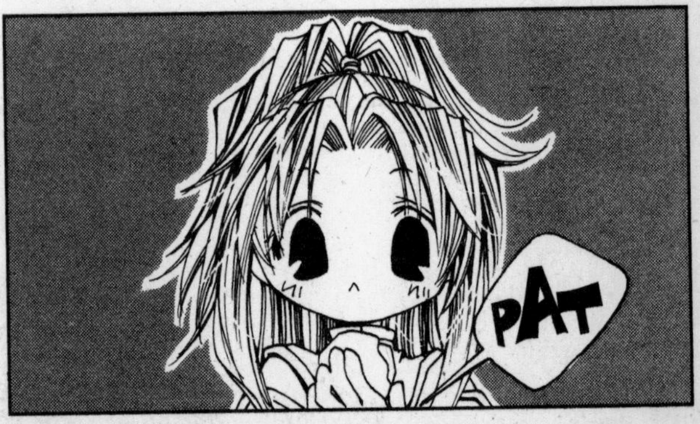
PAT

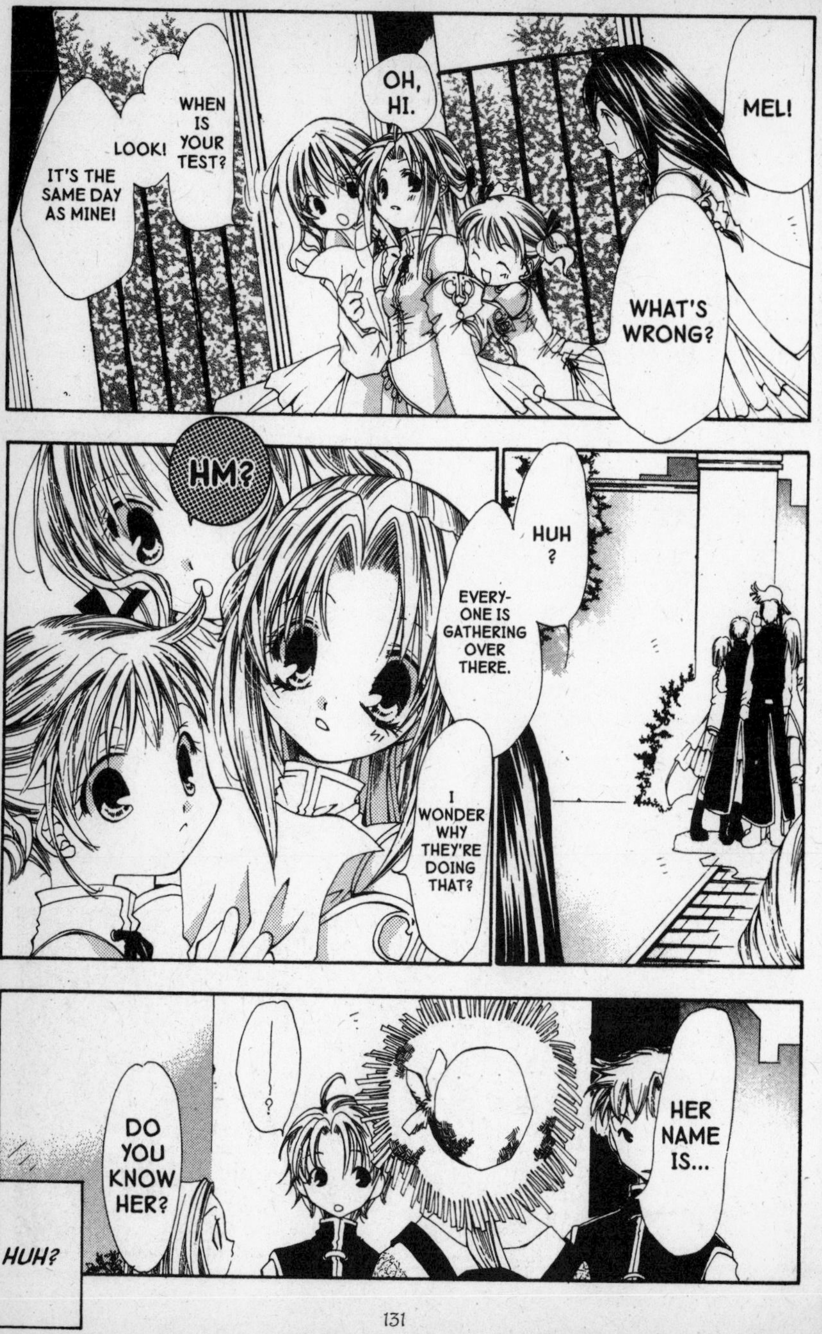
MEL!
WHAT'S WRONG?
OH, HI.
WHEN IS YOUR TEST?
LOOK! IT'S THE SAME DAY AS MINE!
HUH?
EVERY-ONE IS GATHERING OVER THERE.
I WONDER WHY THEY'RE DOING THAT?
HM?
HER NAME IS...
!?
DO YOU KNOW HER?
HUH?

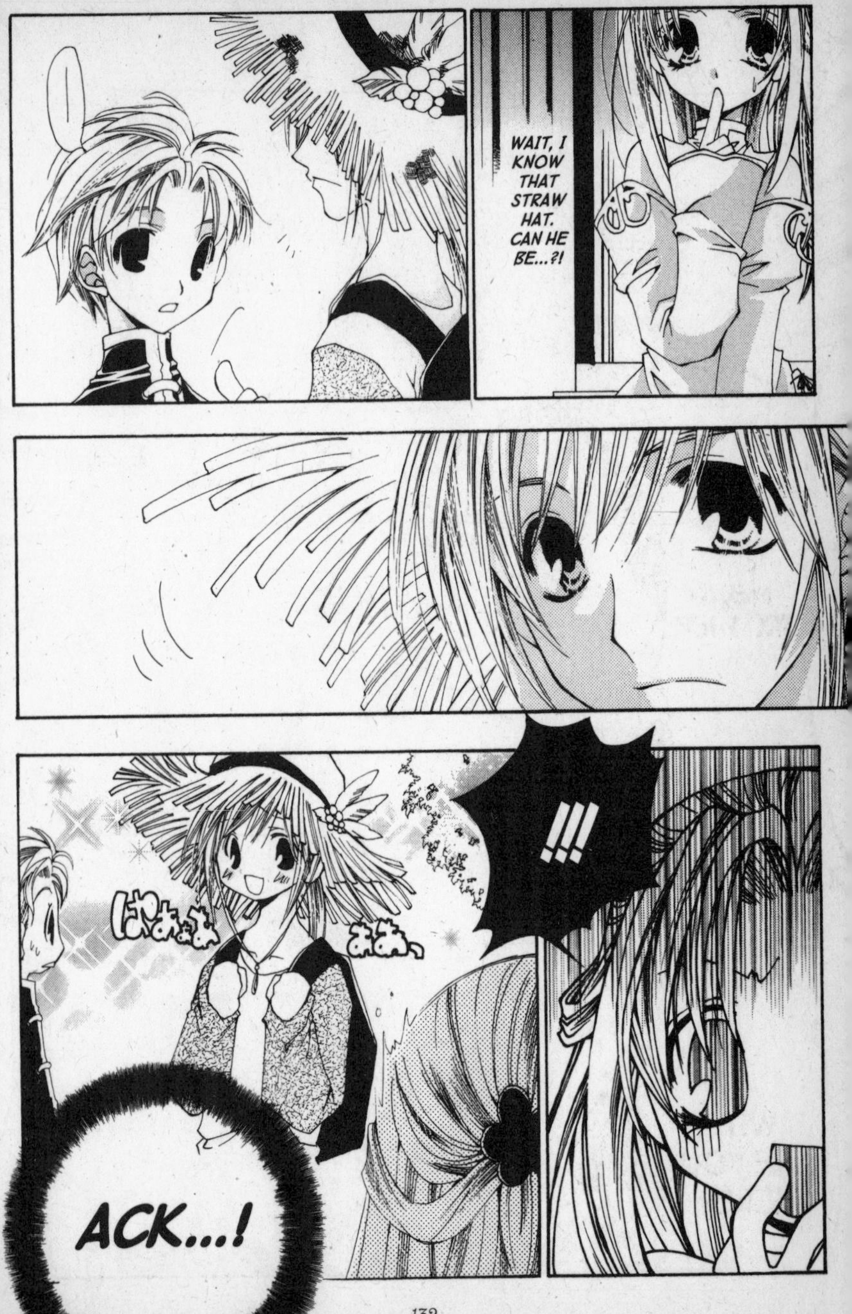
WAIT, I KNOW THAT STRAW HAT. CAN HE BE...?!
!!!
ACK...!

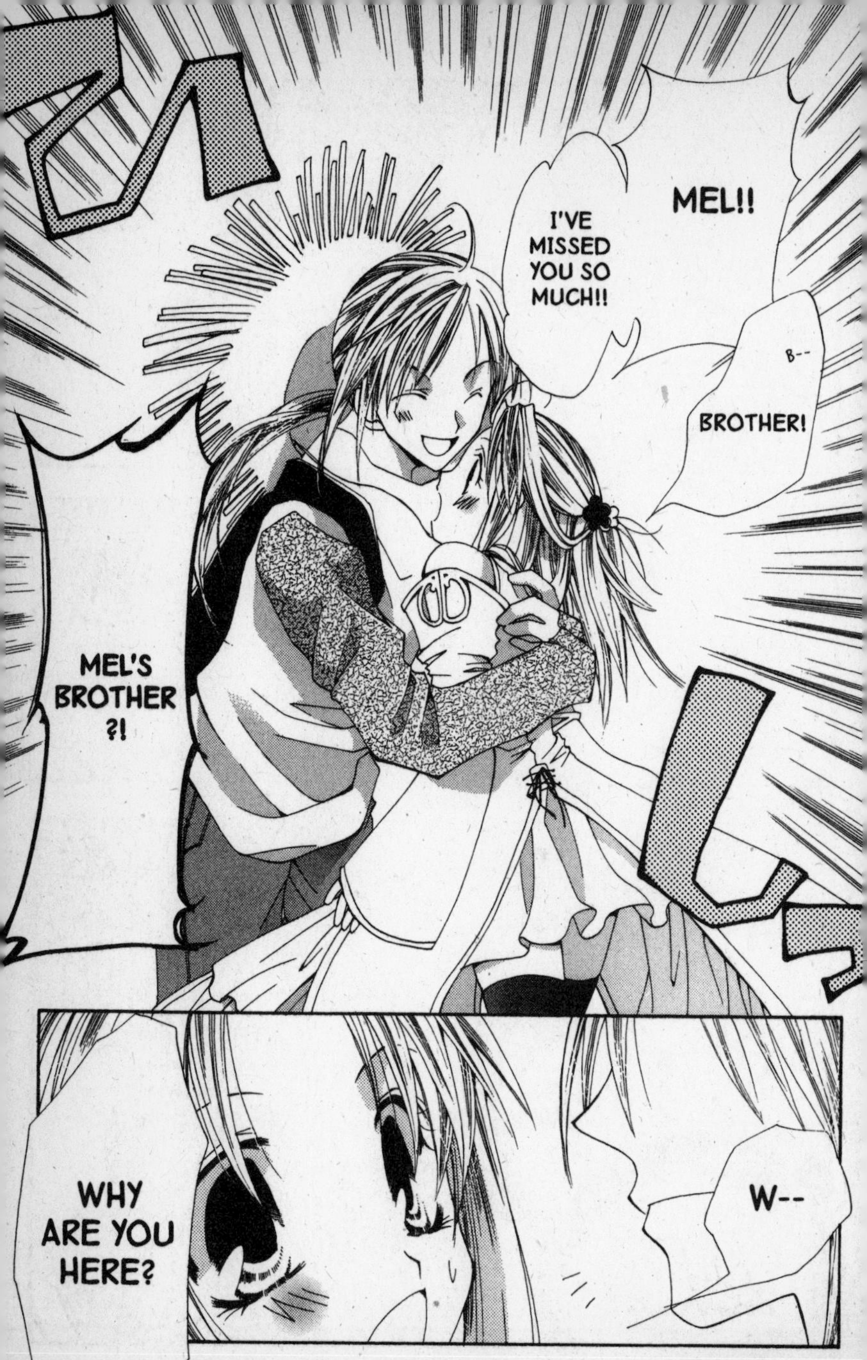
MEL!!
I'VE MISSED YOU SO MUCH!!
B-- BROTHER!
MEL'S BROTHER ?!
W--
WHY ARE YOU HERE?

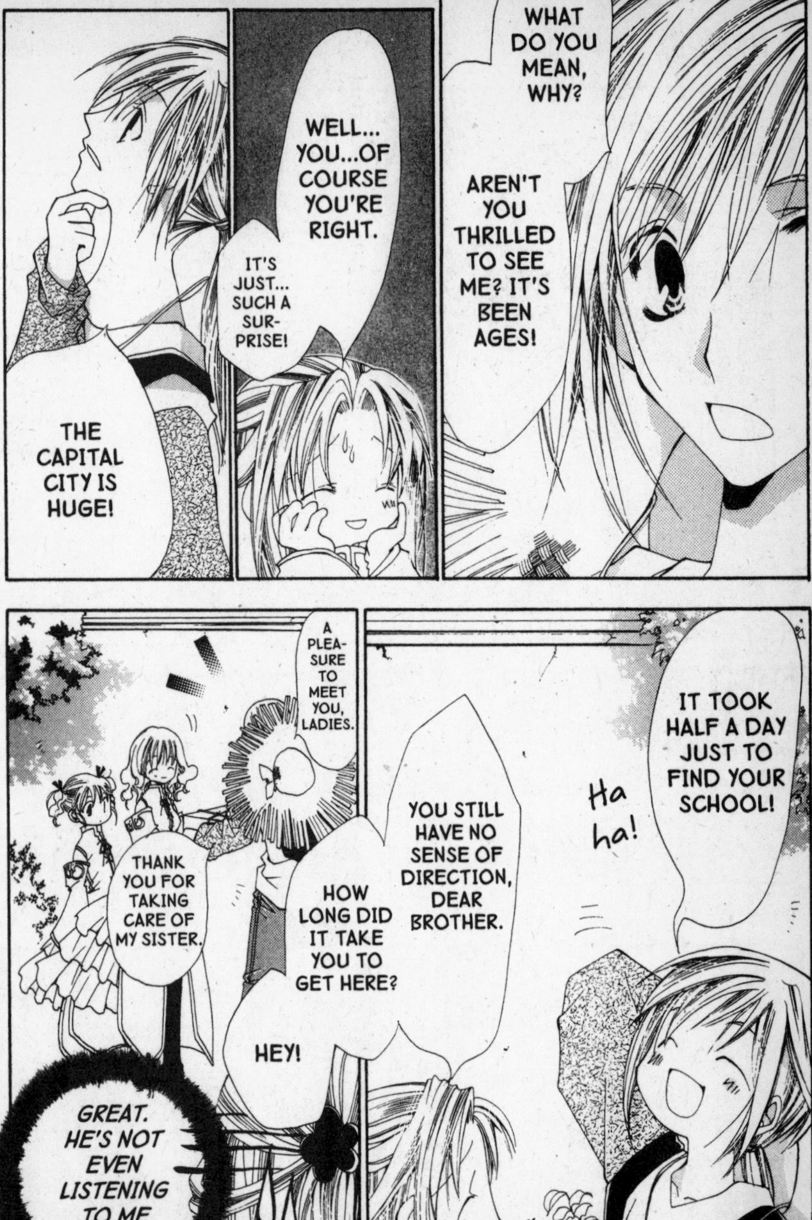

WHAT DO YOU MEAN, WHY?
AREN'T YOU THRILLED TO SEE ME? IT'S BEEN AGES!
WELL... YOU...OF COURSE YOU'RE RIGHT.
IT'S JUST... SUCH A SUR-PRISE!
THE CAPITAL CITY IS HUGE!
IT TOOK HALF A DAY JUST TO FIND YOUR SCHOOL!
Ha ha!
YOU STILL HAVE NO SENSE OF DIRECTION, DEAR BROTHER.
HOW LONG DID IT TAKE YOU TO GET HERE?
HEY!
A PLEA-SURE TO MEET YOU, LADIES.
THANK YOU FOR TAKING CARE OF MY SISTER.
GREAT. HE'S NOT EVEN LISTENING TO ME ANYMORE.

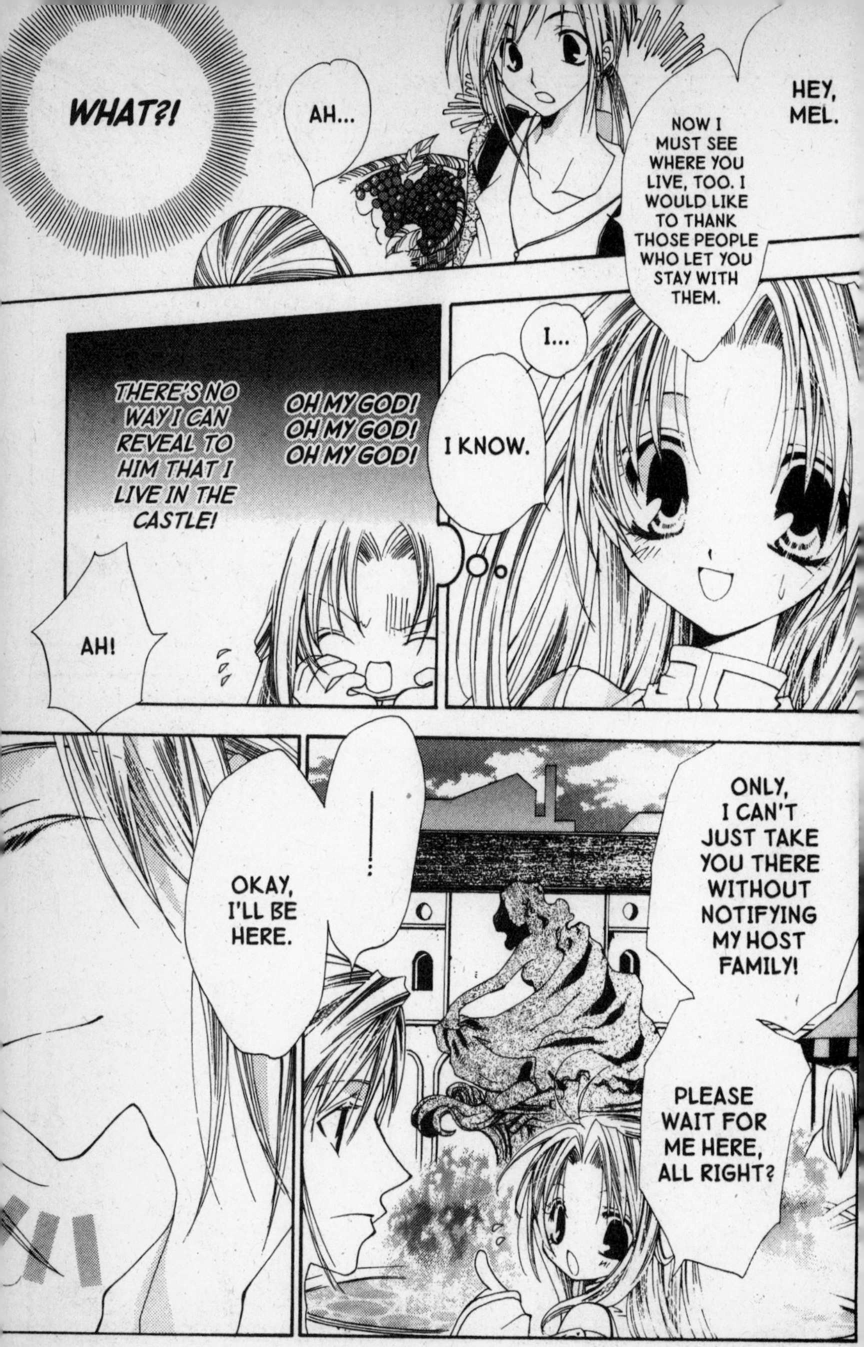
HEY, MEL.
NOW I MUST SEE WHERE YOU LIVE, TOO. I WOULD LIKE TO THANK THOSE PEOPLE WHO LET YOU STAY WITH THEM.
AH...
WHAT?!
I...
I KNOW.
OH MY GOD! OH MY GOD! OH MY GOD!
THERE'S NO WAY I CAN REVEAL TO HIM THAT I LIVE IN THE CASTLE!
AH!
ONLY, I CAN'T JUST TAKE YOU THERE WITHOUT NOTIFYING MY HOST FAMILY!
PLEASE WAIT FOR ME HERE, ALL RIGHT?
...!
OKAY, I'LL BE HERE.

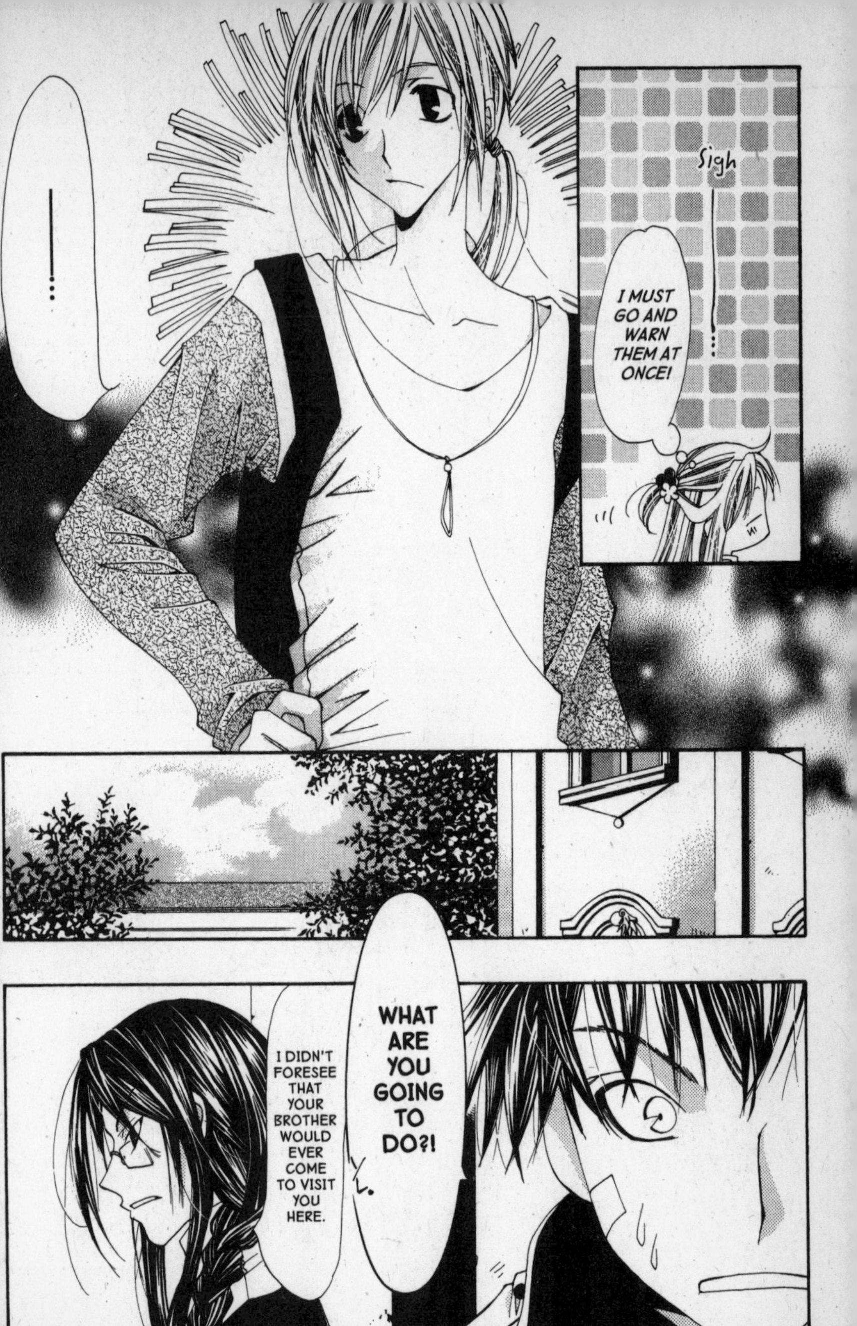
Sigh
......
I MUST GO AND WARN THEM AT ONCE!
......
WHAT ARE YOU GOING TO DO?!
I DIDN'T FORESEE THAT YOUR BROTHER WOULD EVER COME TO VISIT YOU HERE.

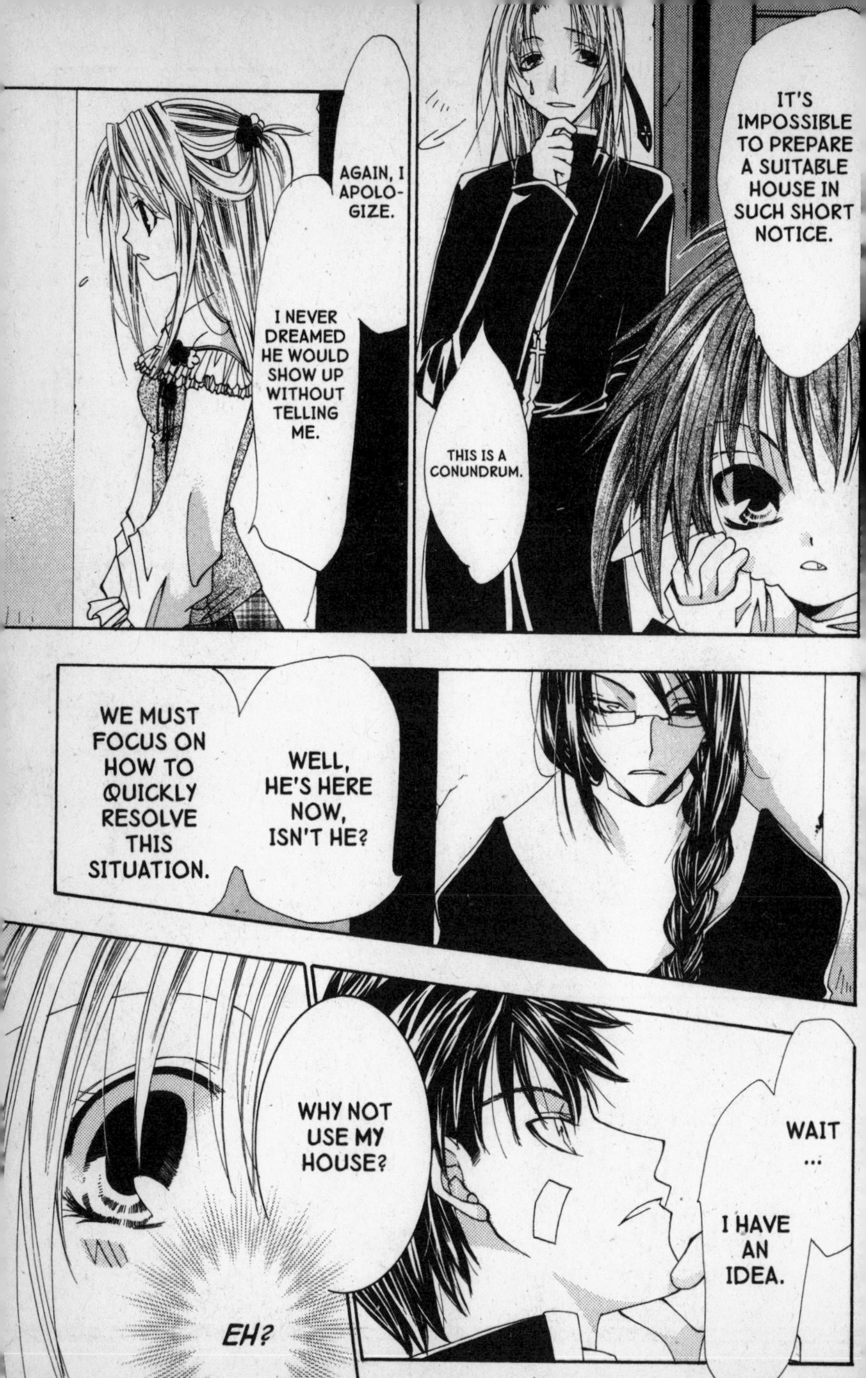
IT'S IMPOSSIBLE TO PREPARE A SUITABLE HOUSE IN SUCH SHORT NOTICE.
THIS IS A CONUNDRUM.
AGAIN, I APOLOGIZE.
I NEVER DREAMED HE WOULD SHOW UP WITHOUT TELLING ME.
WELL, HE'S HERE NOW, ISN'T HE?
WE MUST FOCUS ON HOW TO QUICKLY RESOLVE THIS SITUATION.
WAIT ...
I HAVE AN IDEA.
WHY NOT USE MY HOUSE?
EH?

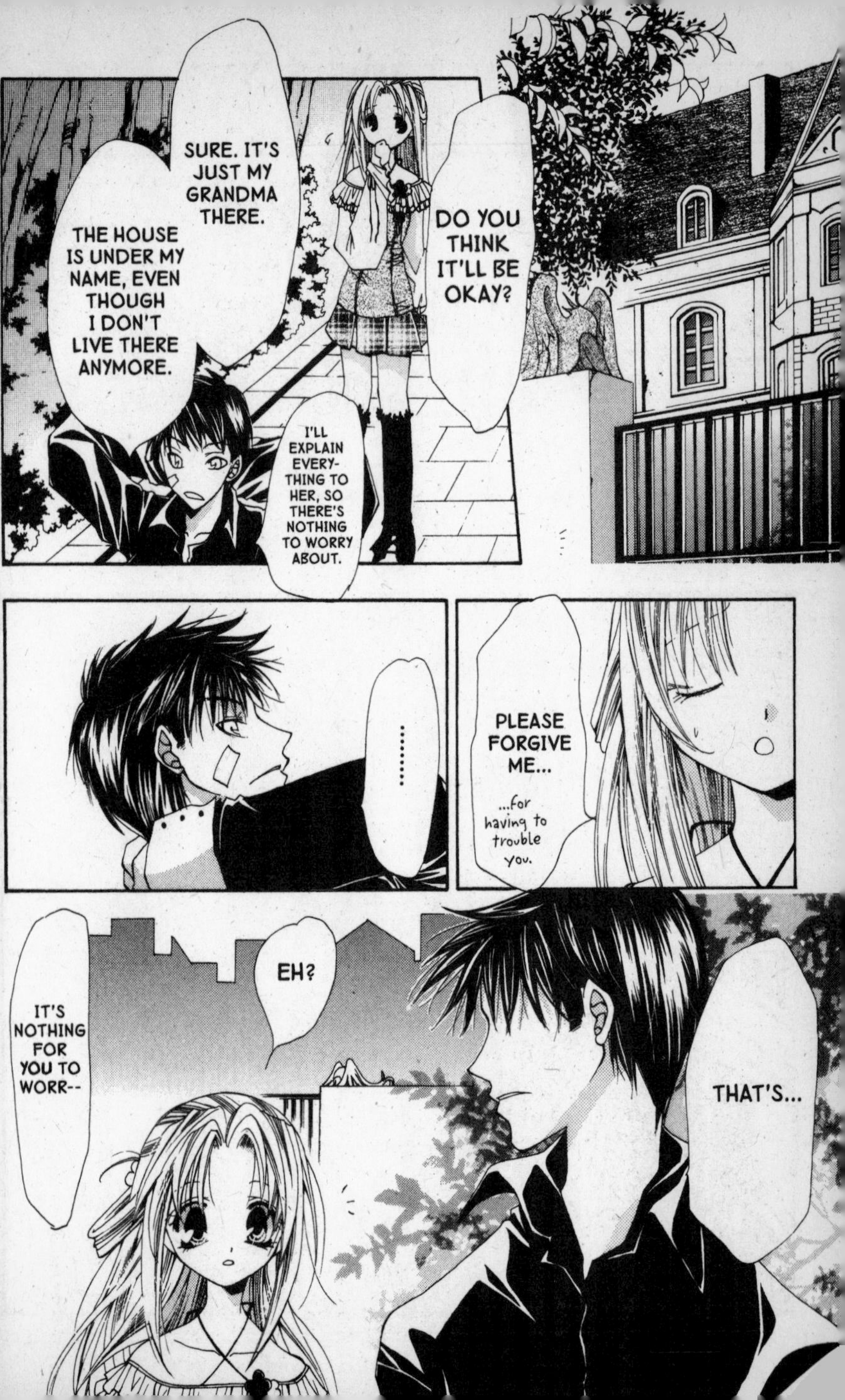
DO YOU THINK IT'LL BE OKAY?
SURE. IT'S JUST MY GRANDMA THERE.
THE HOUSE IS UNDER MY NAME, EVEN THOUGH I DON'T LIVE THERE ANYMORE.
I'LL EXPLAIN EVERYTHING TO HER, SO THERE'S NOTHING TO WORRY ABOUT.
PLEASE FORGIVE ME...
...for having to trouble you.
....
THAT'S...
EH?
IT'S NOTHING FOR YOU TO WORR--

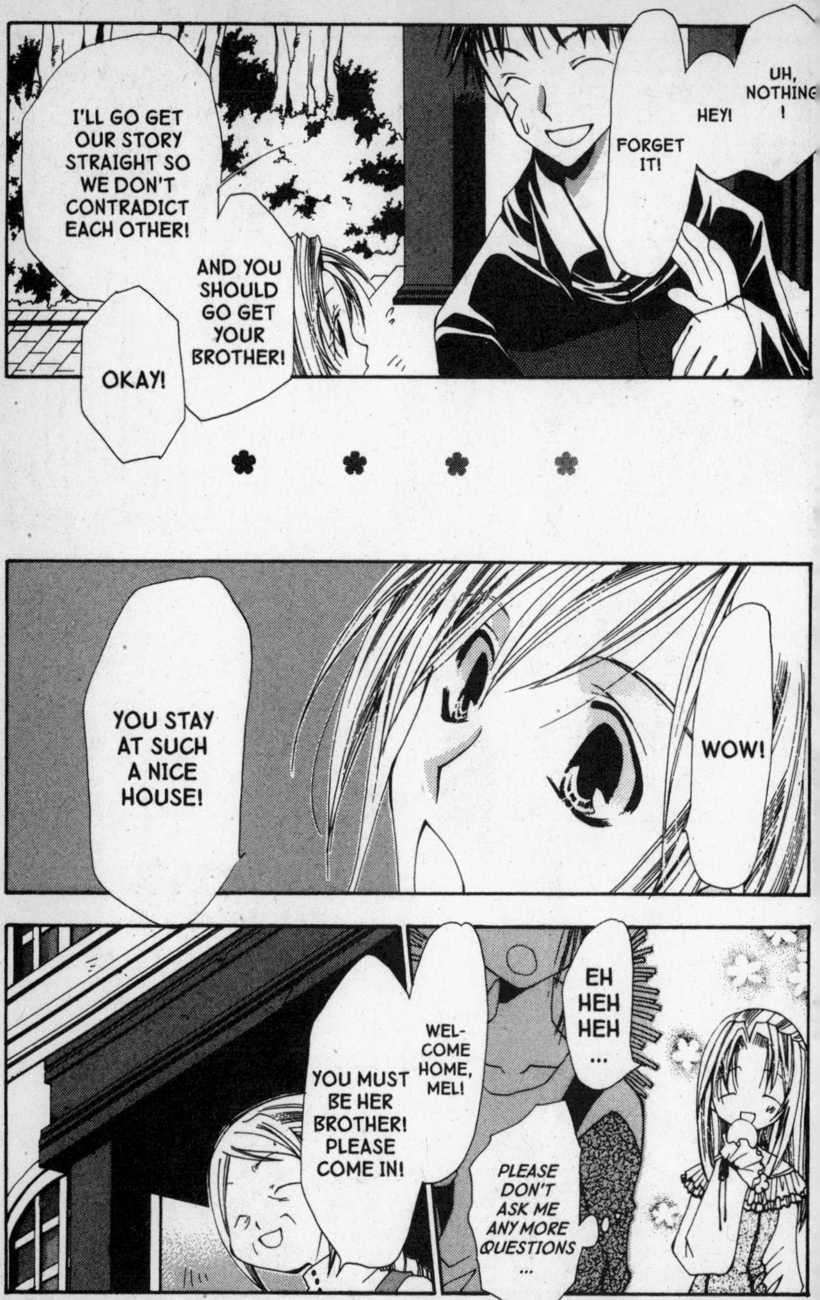
UH, NOTHING!
HEY!
FORGET IT!
I'LL GO GET OUR STORY STRAIGHT SO WE DON'T CONTRADICT EACH OTHER!
AND YOU SHOULD GO GET YOUR BROTHER!
OKAY!
WOW!
YOU STAY AT SUCH A NICE HOUSE!
EH HEH HEH...
WEL-COME HOME, MEL!
YOU MUST BE HER BROTHER! PLEASE COME IN!
PLEASE DON'T ASK ME ANY MORE QUESTIONS...

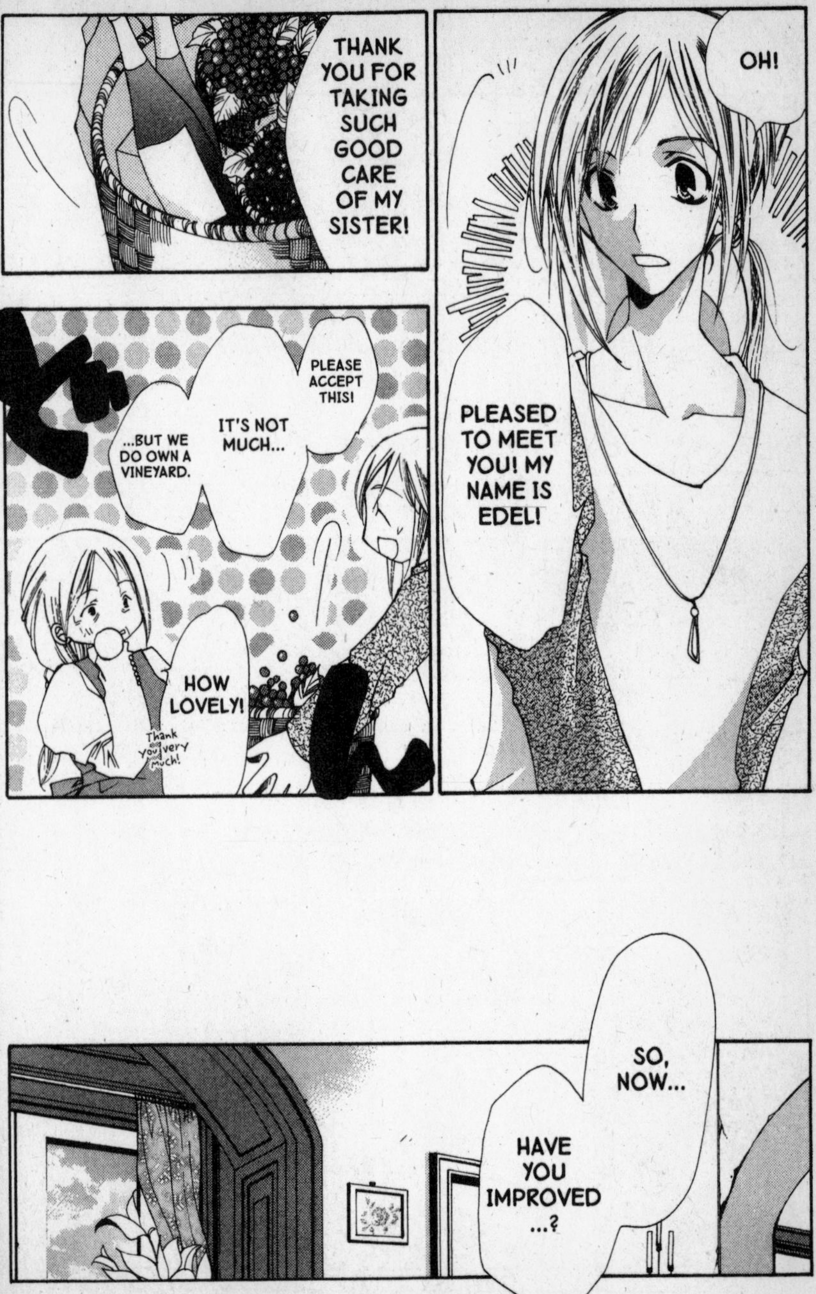
OH!
PLEASED TO MEET YOU! MY NAME IS EDEL!
THANK YOU FOR TAKING SUCH GOOD CARE OF MY SISTER!
PLEASE ACCEPT THIS!
IT'S NOT MUCH...
...BUT WE DO OWN A VINEYARD.
HOW LOVELY!
Thank you very much!
SO, NOW...
HAVE YOU IMPROVED ...?

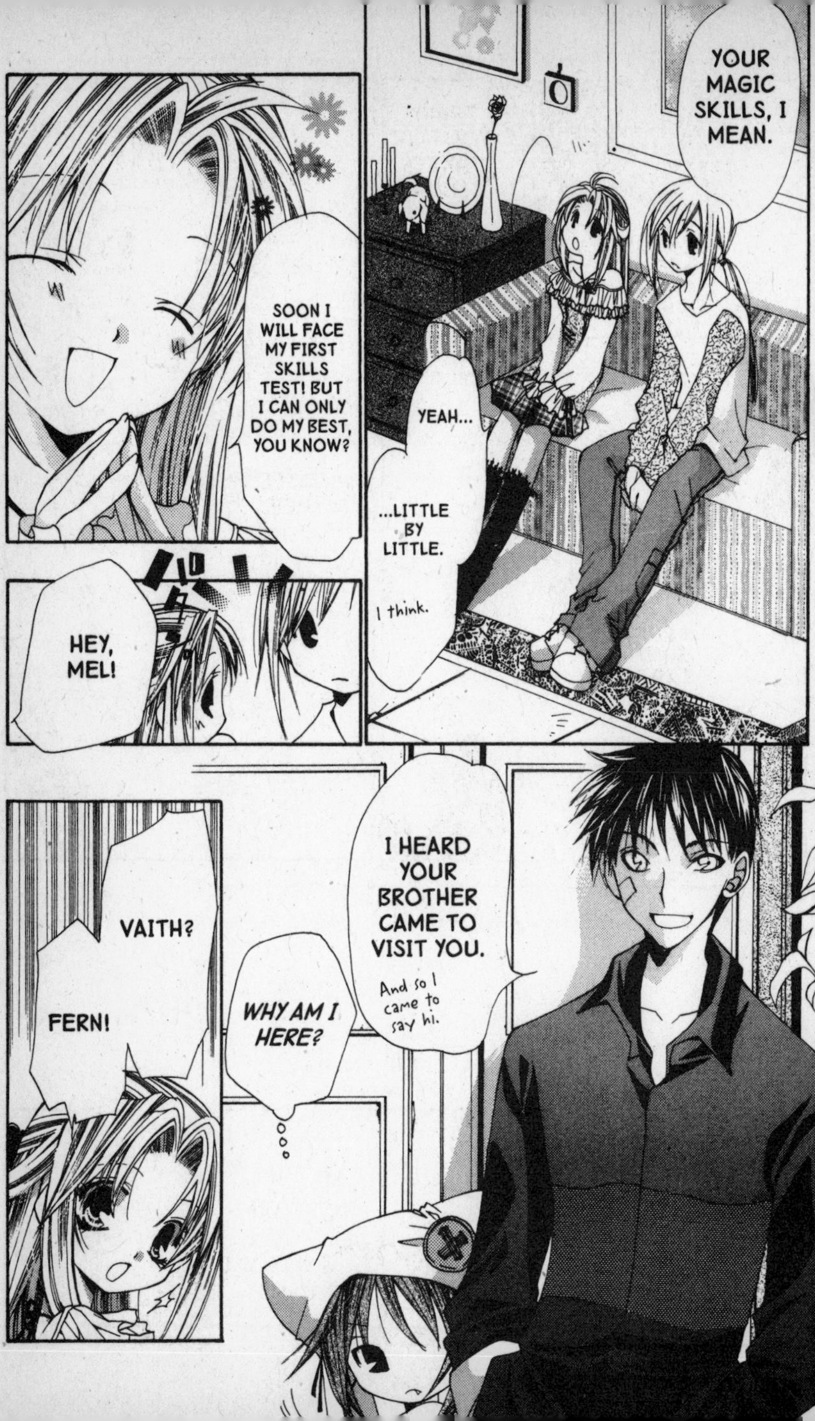
YOUR MAGIC SKILLS, I MEAN.
YEAH...
...LITTLE BY LITTLE.
I think.
SOON I WILL FACE MY FIRST SKILLS TEST! BUT I CAN ONLY DO MY BEST, YOU KNOW?
HEY, MEL!
I HEARD YOUR BROTHER CAME TO VISIT YOU.
And so I came to say hi.
WHY AM I HERE?
VAITH?
FERN!

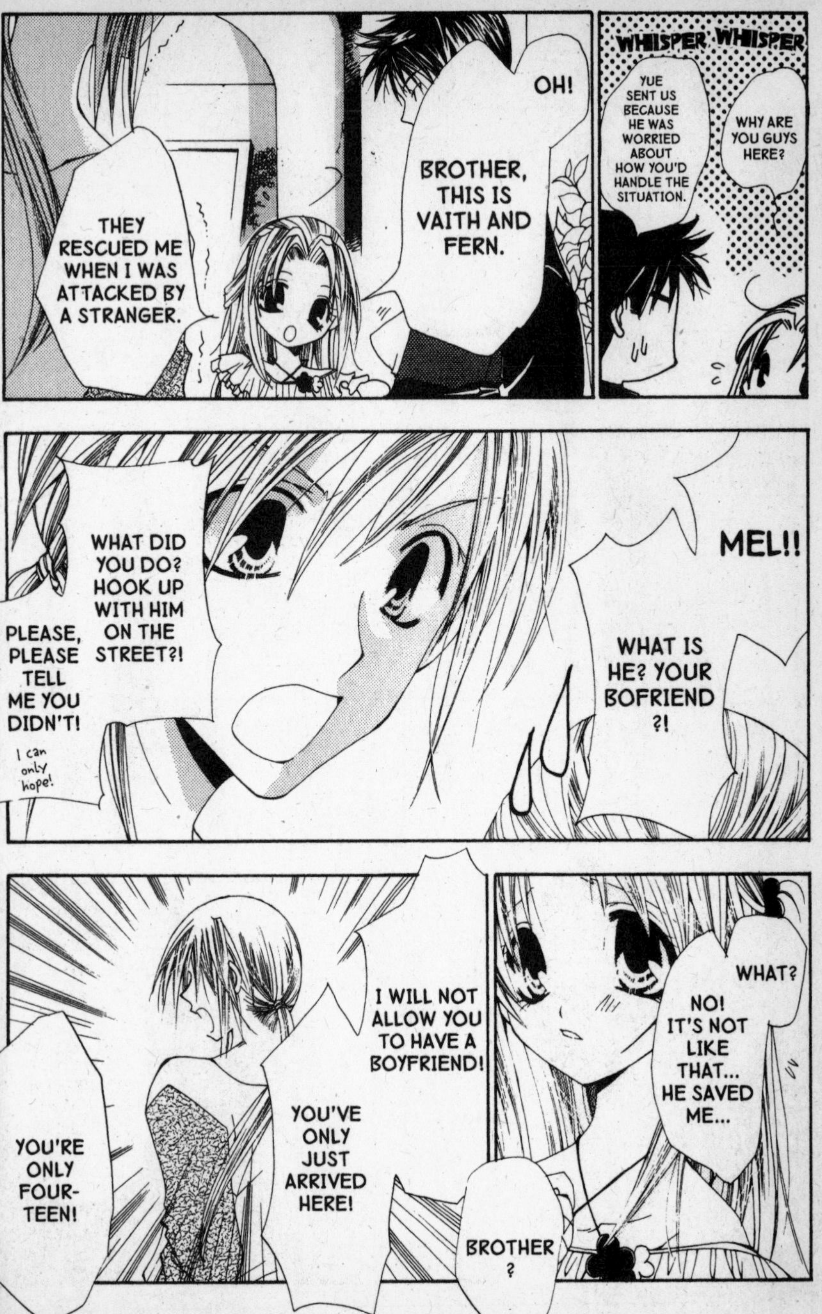
WHISPER WHISPER
WHY ARE YOU GUYS HERE?
YUE SENT US BECAUSE HE WAS WORRIED ABOUT HOW YOU'D HANDLE THE SITUATION.
OH!
BROTHER, THIS IS VAITH AND FERN.
THEY RESCUED ME WHEN I WAS ATTACKED BY A STRANGER.
MEL!!
WHAT IS HE? YOUR BOFRIEND ?!
WHAT DID YOU DO? HOOK UP WITH HIM ON THE STREET?!
PLEASE, PLEASE TELL ME YOU DIDN'T!
I can only hope!
WHAT?
NO! IT'S NOT LIKE THAT... HE SAVED ME...
BROTHER ?
I WILL NOT ALLOW YOU TO HAVE A BOYFRIEND!
YOU'VE ONLY JUST ARRIVED HERE!
YOU'RE ONLY FOUR-TEEN!

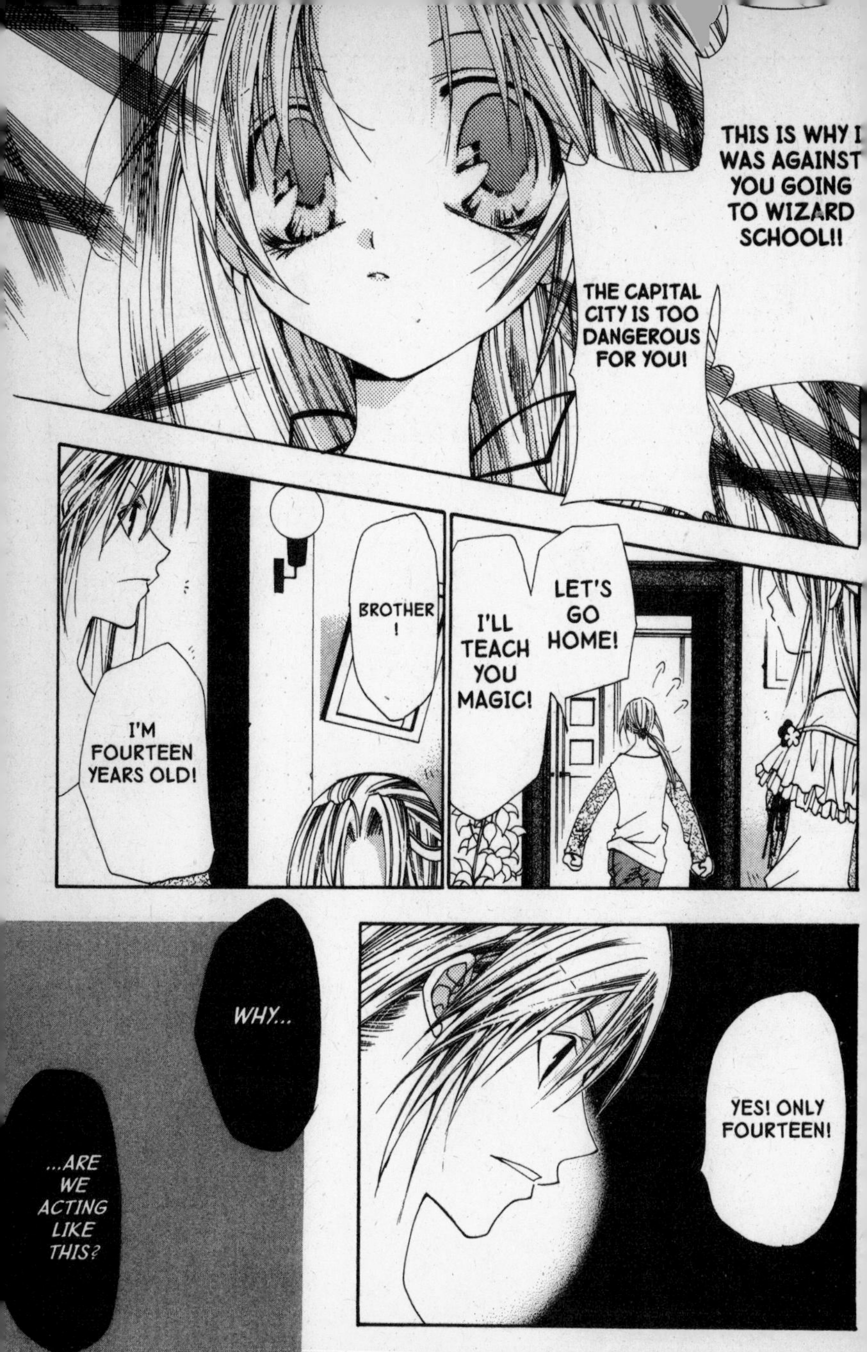
THIS IS WHY I WAS AGAINST YOU GOING TO WIZARD SCHOOL!!
THE CAPITAL CITY IS TOO DANGEROUS FOR YOU!
LET'S GO HOME!
I'LL TEACH YOU MAGIC!
BROTHER!
I'M FOURTEEN YEARS OLD!
YES! ONLY FOURTEEN!
WHY...
...ARE WE ACTING LIKE THIS?

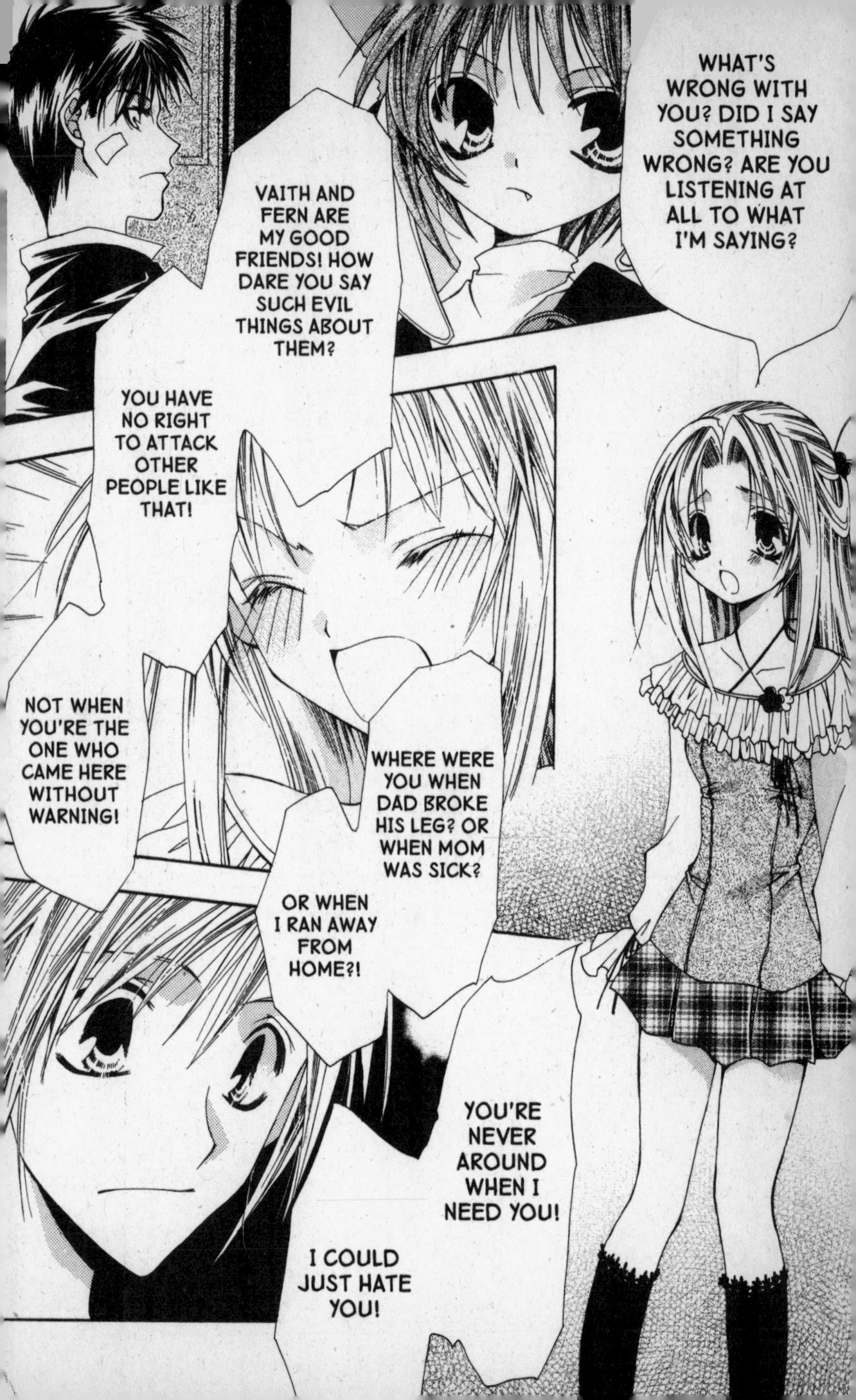
WHAT'S WRONG WITH YOU? DID I SAY SOMETHING WRONG? ARE YOU LISTENING AT ALL TO WHAT I'M SAYING?
VAITH AND FERN ARE MY GOOD FRIENDS! HOW DARE YOU SAY SUCH EVIL THINGS ABOUT THEM?
YOU HAVE NO RIGHT TO ATTACK OTHER PEOPLE LIKE THAT!
NOT WHEN YOU'RE THE ONE WHO CAME HERE WITHOUT WARNING!
WHERE WERE YOU WHEN DAD BROKE HIS LEG? OR WHEN MOM WAS SICK?
OR WHEN I RAN AWAY FROM HOME?!
YOU'RE NEVER AROUND WHEN I NEED YOU!
I COULD JUST HATE YOU!

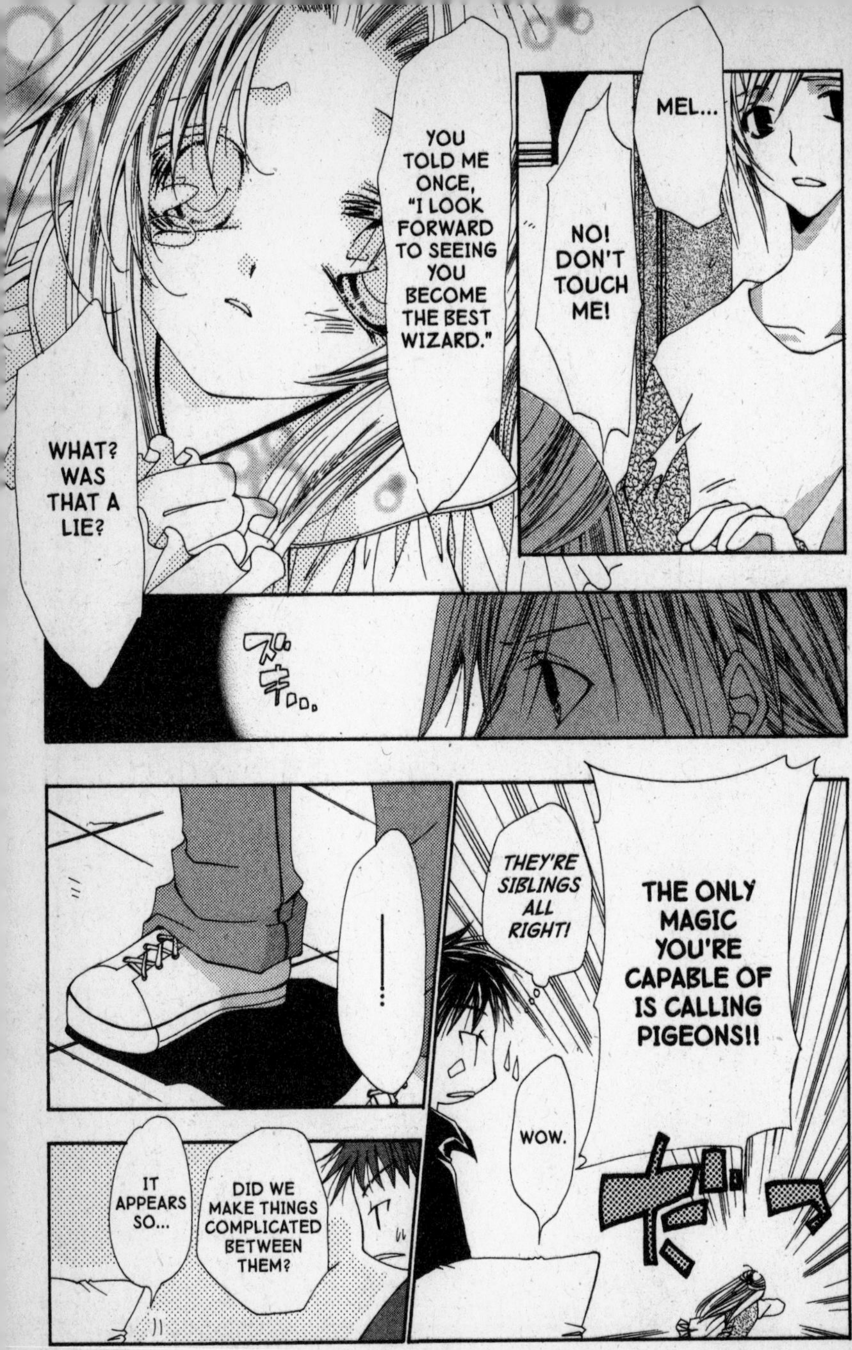
MEL...
NO! DON'T TOUCH ME!
YOU TOLD ME ONCE, "I LOOK FORWARD TO SEEING YOU BECOME THE BEST WIZARD."
WHAT? WAS THAT A LIE?
ズキ...
THE ONLY MAGIC YOU'RE CAPABLE OF IS CALLING PIGEONS!!
THEY'RE SIBLINGS ALL RIGHT!
WOW.
......
DID WE MAKE THINGS COMPLICATED BETWEEN THEM?
IT APPEARS SO...

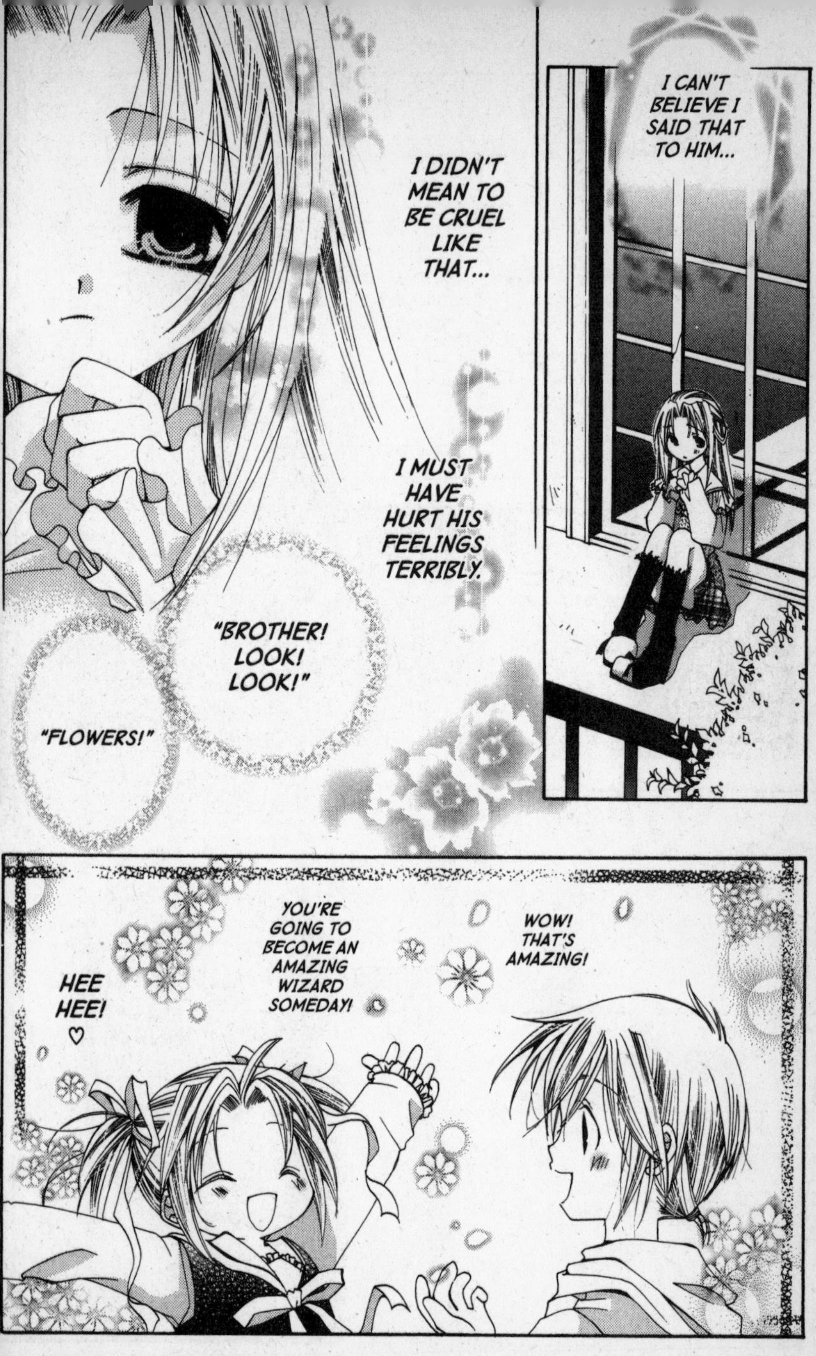
I CAN'T BELIEVE I SAID THAT TO HIM...
I DIDN'T MEAN TO BE CRUEL LIKE THAT...
I MUST HAVE HURT HIS FEELINGS TERRIBLY.
"BROTHER! LOOK! LOOK!"
"FLOWERS!"
WOW! THAT'S AMAZING!
YOU'RE GOING TO BECOME AN AMAZING WIZARD SOMEDAY!
HEE HEE! ♡

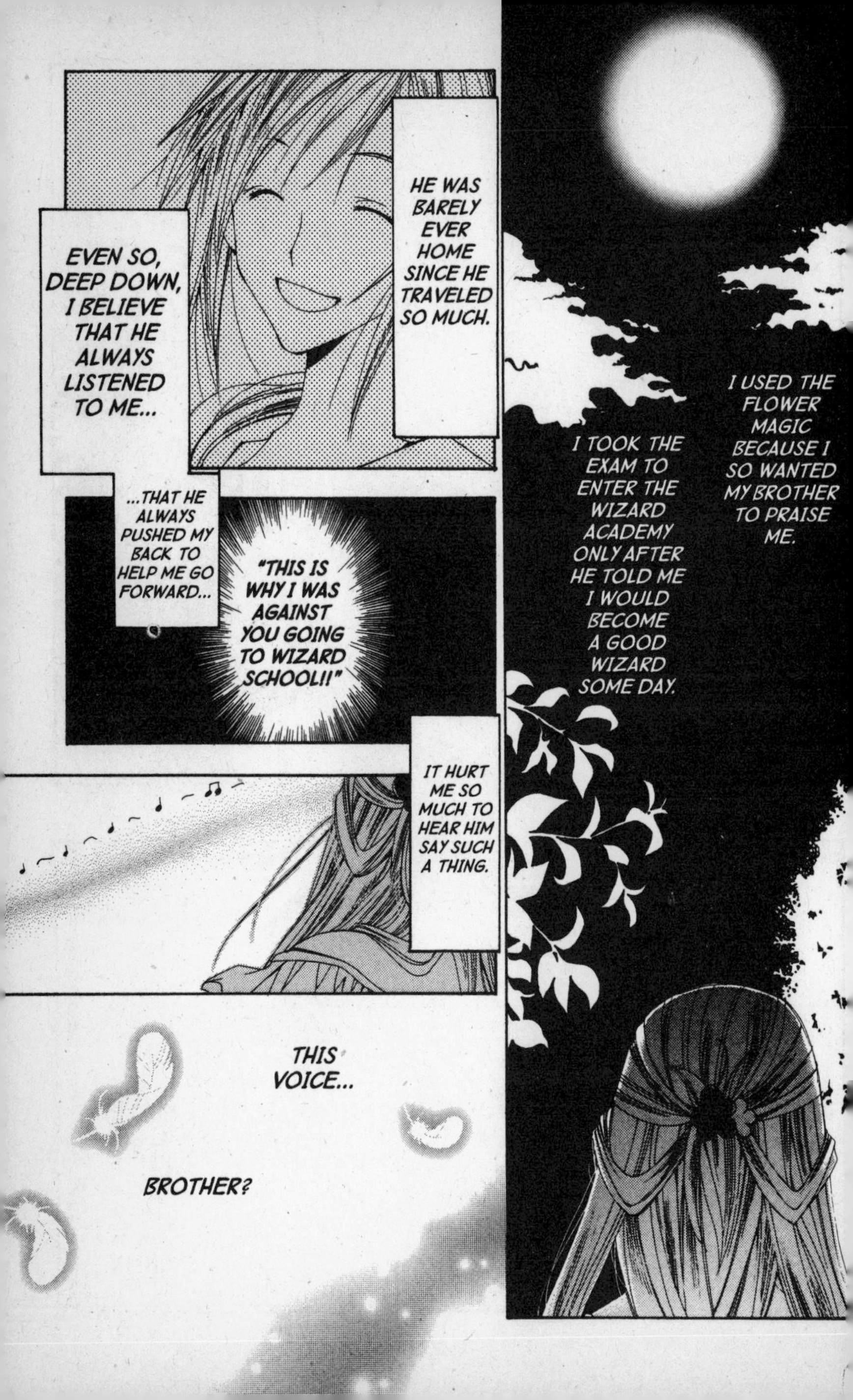
I USED THE FLOWER MAGIC BECAUSE I SO WANTED MY BROTHER TO PRAISE ME.
I TOOK THE EXAM TO ENTER THE WIZARD ACADEMY ONLY AFTER HE TOLD ME I WOULD BECOME A GOOD WIZARD SOME DAY.
HE WAS BARELY EVER HOME SINCE HE TRAVELED SO MUCH.
EVEN SO, DEEP DOWN, I BELIEVE THAT HE ALWAYS LISTENED TO ME...
...THAT HE ALWAYS PUSHED MY BACK TO HELP ME GO FORWARD...
"THIS IS WHY I WAS AGAINST YOU GOING TO WIZARD SCHOOL!!"
IT HURT ME SO MUCH TO HEAR HIM SAY SUCH A THING.
THIS VOICE...
BROTHER?

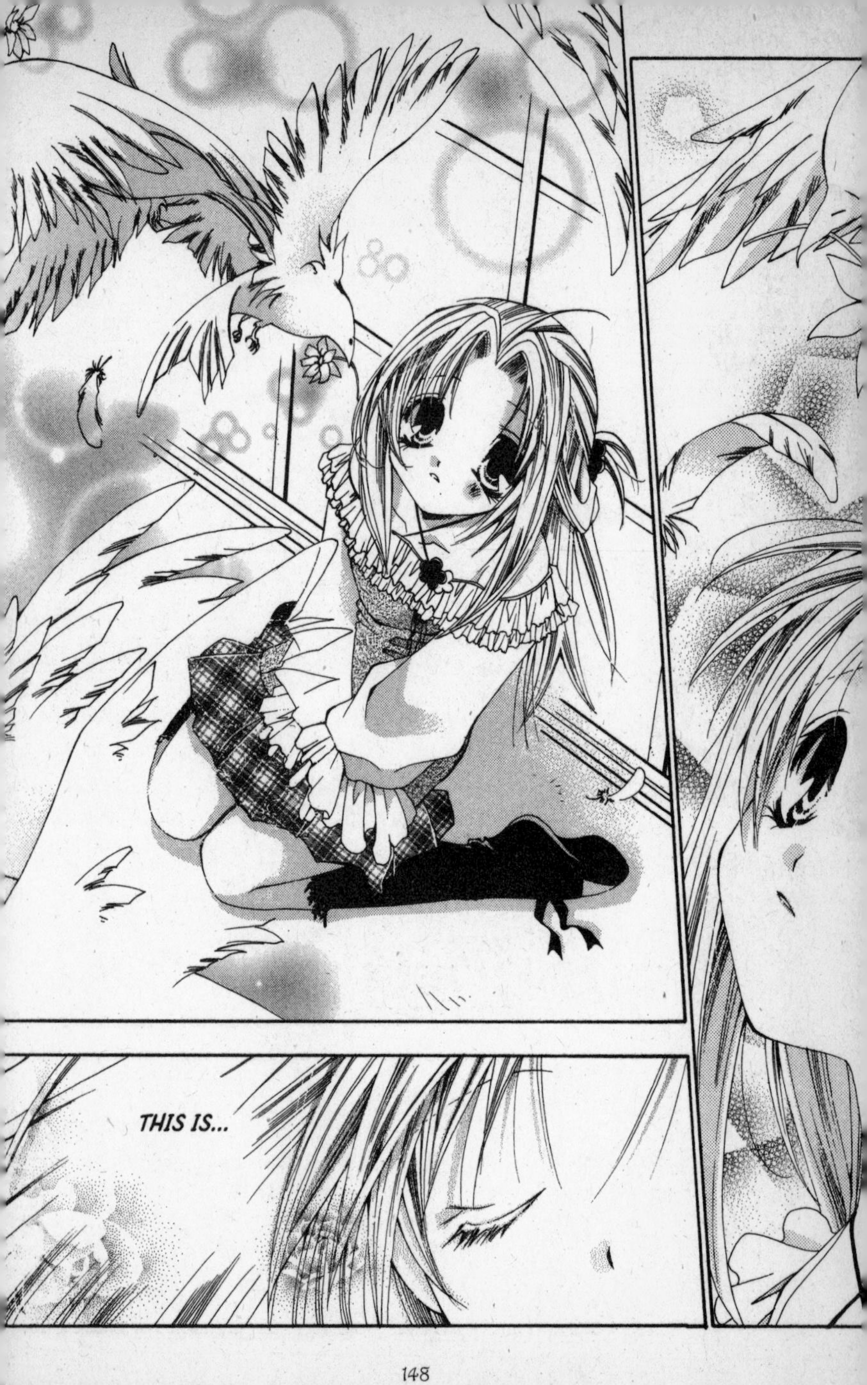
THIS IS...

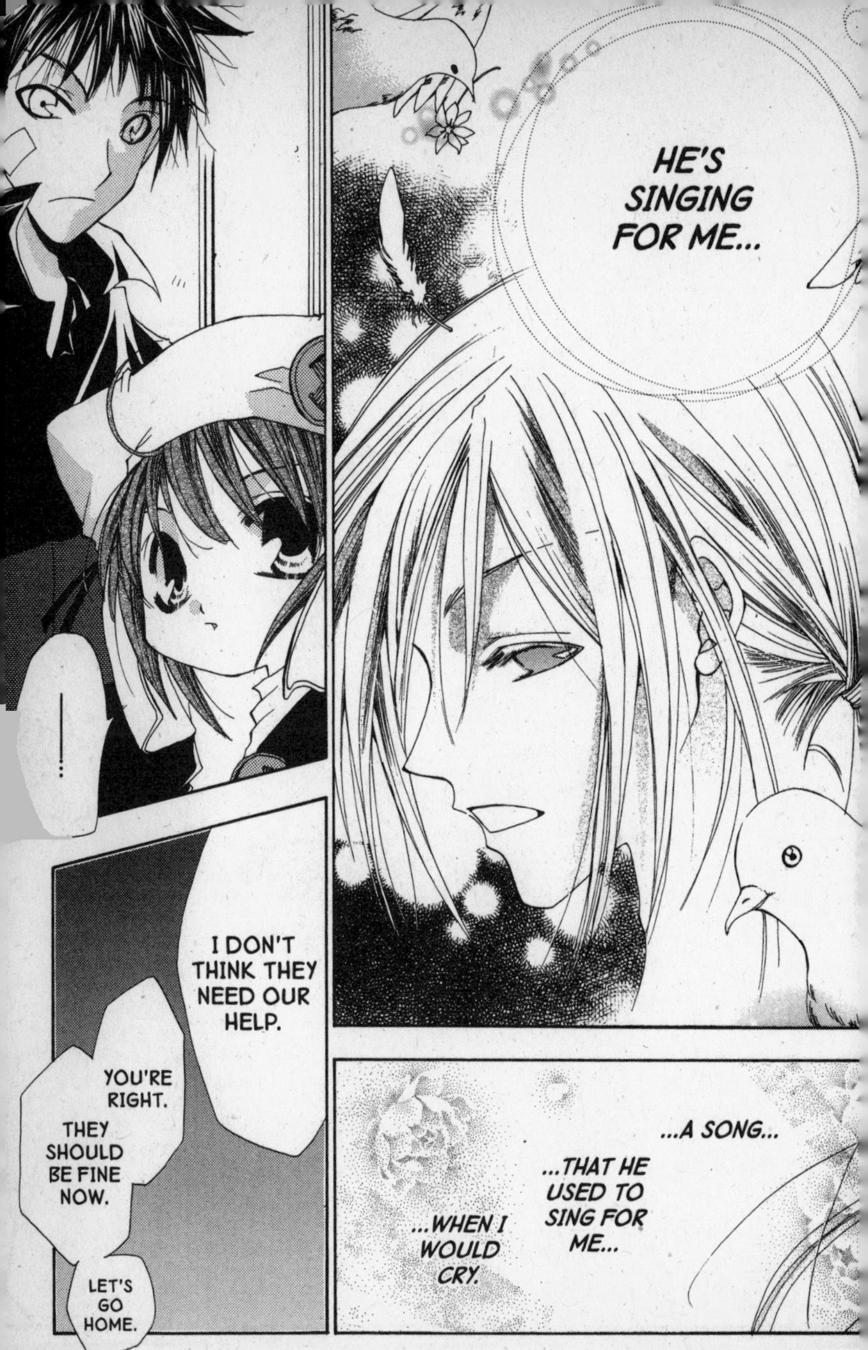
HE'S SINGING FOR ME...
I DON'T THINK THEY NEED OUR HELP.
YOU'RE RIGHT.
THEY SHOULD BE FINE NOW.
LET'S GO HOME.
...A SONG...
...THAT HE USED TO SING FOR ME...
...WHEN I WOULD CRY.

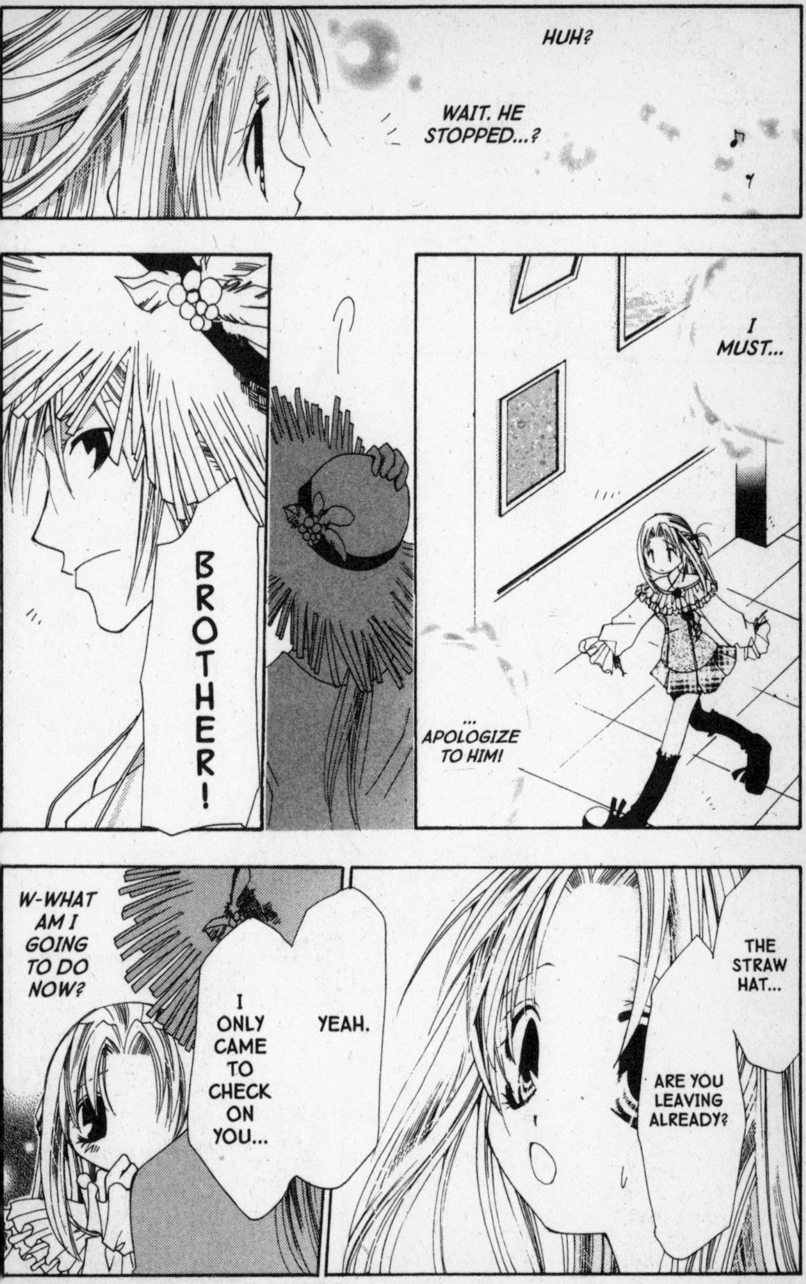
HUH?
WAIT. HE STOPPED...?
I MUST...
... APOLOGIZE TO HIM!
BROTHER!
THE STRAW HAT...
ARE YOU LEAVING ALREADY?
YEAH.
I ONLY CAME TO CHECK ON YOU...
W-WHAT AM I GOING TO DO NOW?

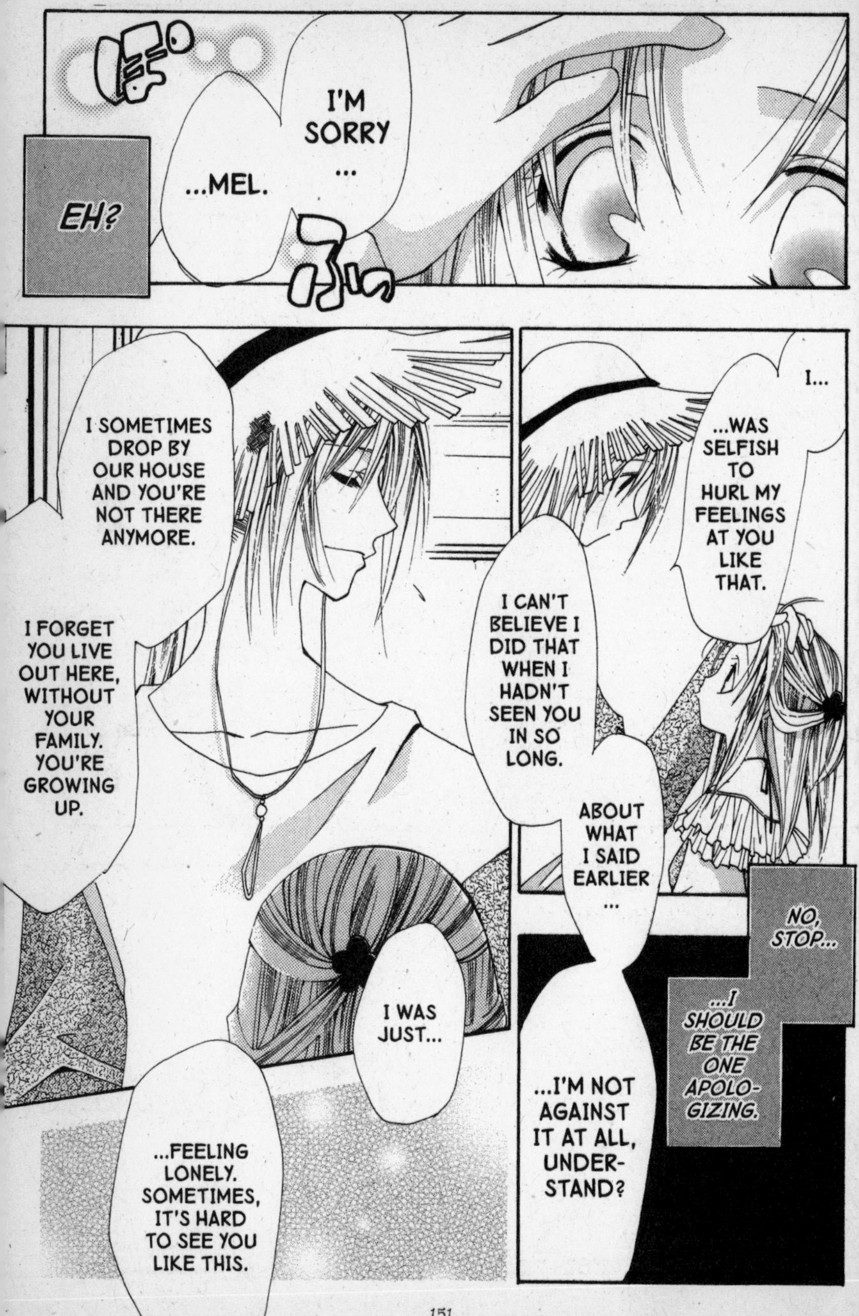
I'M SORRY ...
...MEL.
EH?
I...
...WAS SELFISH TO HURL MY FEELINGS AT YOU LIKE THAT.
I CAN'T BELIEVE I DID THAT WHEN I HADN'T SEEN YOU IN SO LONG.
ABOUT WHAT I SAID EARLIER ...
NO, STOP...
...I SHOULD BE THE ONE APOLO-GIZING.
...I'M NOT AGAINST IT AT ALL, UNDER-STAND?
I SOMETIMES DROP BY OUR HOUSE AND YOU'RE NOT THERE ANYMORE.
I FORGET YOU LIVE OUT HERE, WITHOUT YOUR FAMILY. YOU'RE GROWING UP.
I WAS JUST...
...FEELING LONELY. SOMETIMES, IT'S HARD TO SEE YOU LIKE THIS.

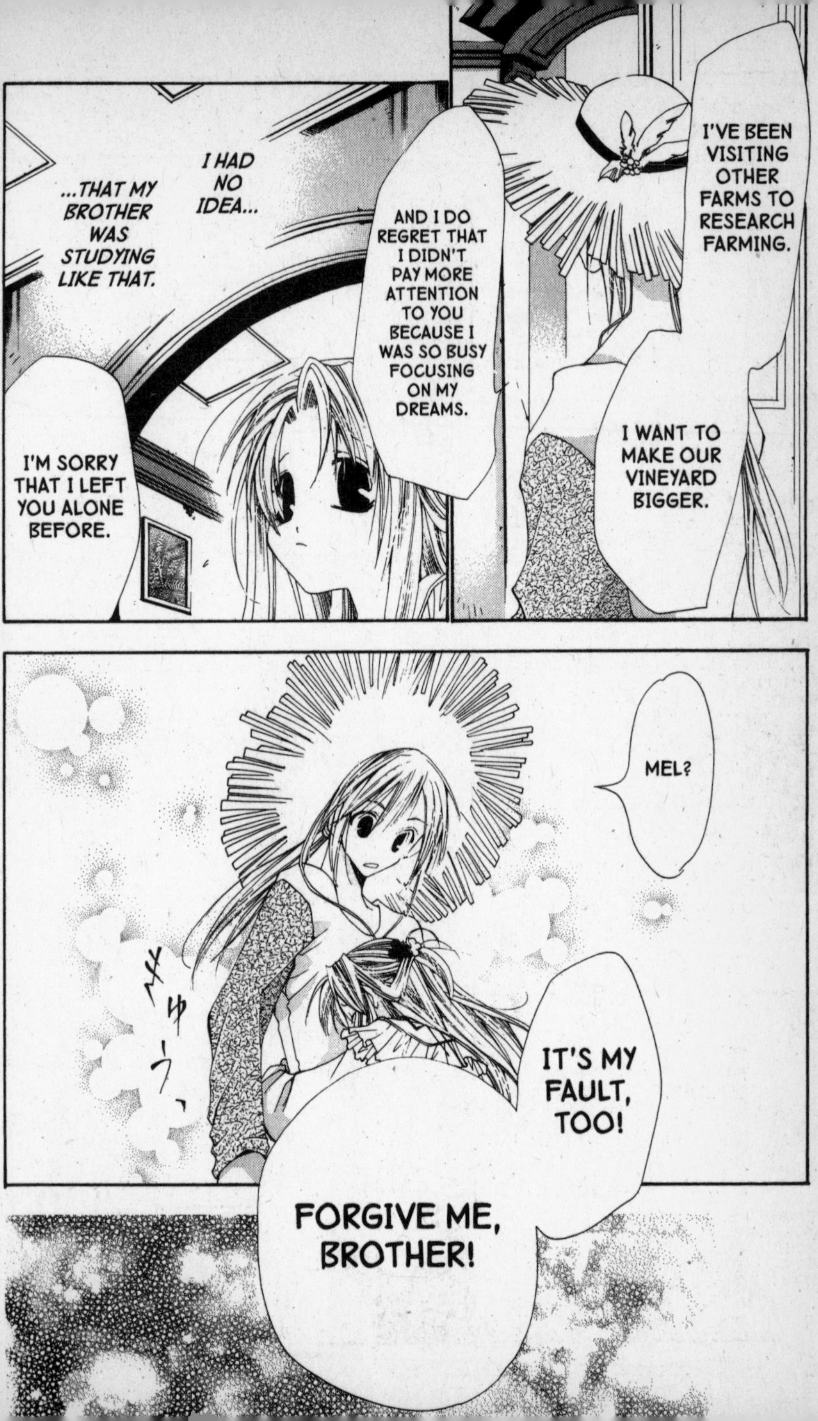
I'VE BEEN VISITING OTHER FARMS TO RESEARCH FARMING.
I WANT TO MAKE OUR VINEYARD BIGGER.
AND I DO REGRET THAT I DIDN'T PAY MORE ATTENTION TO YOU BECAUSE I WAS SO BUSY FOCUSING ON MY DREAMS.
I HAD NO IDEA...
...THAT MY BROTHER WAS STUDYING LIKE THAT.
I'M SORRY THAT I LEFT YOU ALONE BEFORE.
MEL?
ぎゅう
IT'S MY FAULT, TOO!
FORGIVE ME, BROTHER!

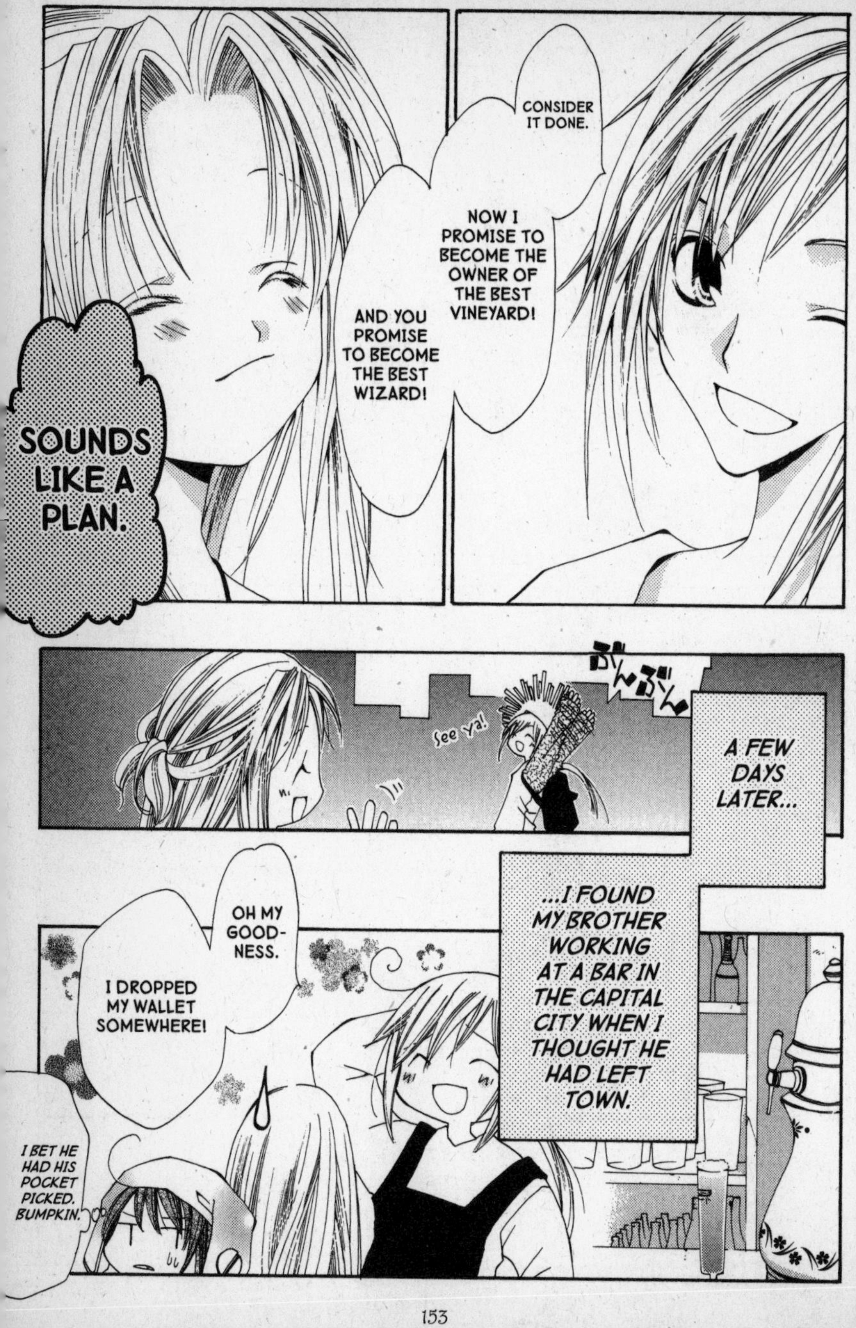
CONSIDER IT DONE.
NOW I PROMISE TO BECOME THE OWNER OF THE BEST VINEYARD!
AND YOU PROMISE TO BECOME THE BEST WIZARD!
SOUNDS LIKE A PLAN.
ぶんぶん
See ya!
A FEW DAYS LATER...
...I FOUND MY BROTHER WORKING AT A BAR IN THE CAPITAL CITY WHEN I THOUGHT HE HAD LEFT TOWN.
OH MY GOODNESS.
I DROPPED MY WALLET SOMEWHERE!
I BET HE HAD HIS POCKET PICKED. BUMPKIN.

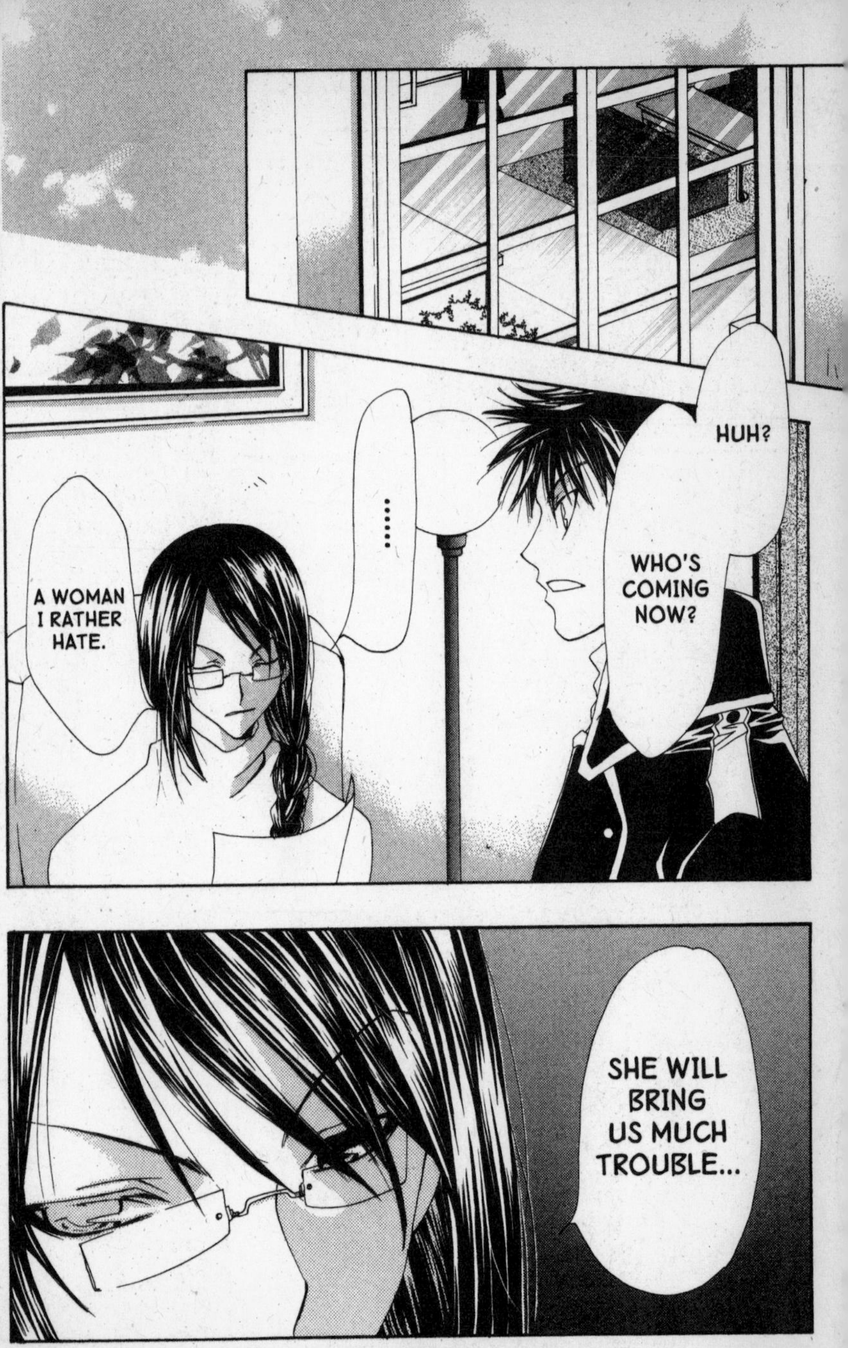
HUH?
WHO'S COMING NOW?
......
A WOMAN I RATHER HATE.
SHE WILL BRING US MUCH TROUBLE...

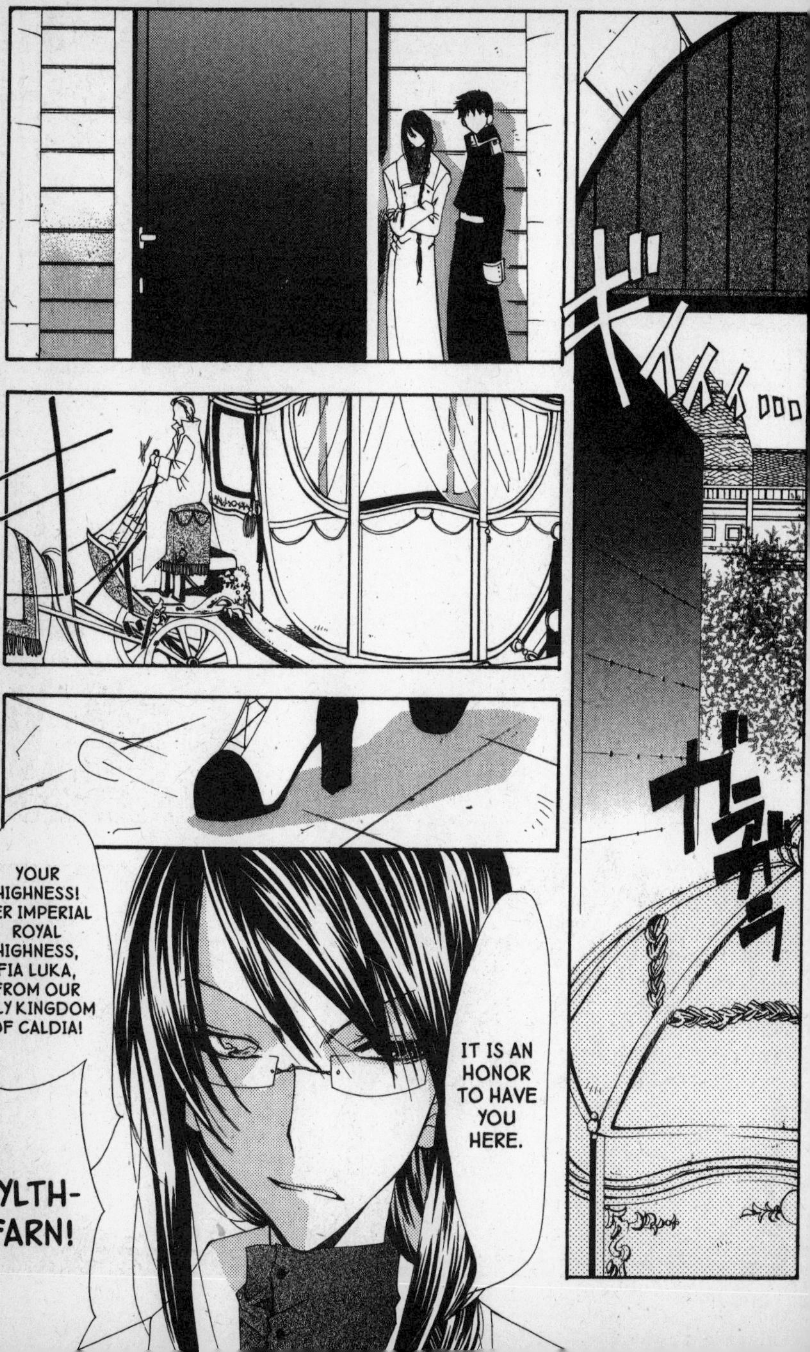
ギィィィ…
ガラガラ
YOUR HIGHNESS! HER IMPERIAL ROYAL HIGHNESS, FIA LUKA, FROM OUR ALLY KINGDOM OF CALDIA!
IT IS AN HONOR TO HAVE YOU HERE.
SYLTH-FARN!

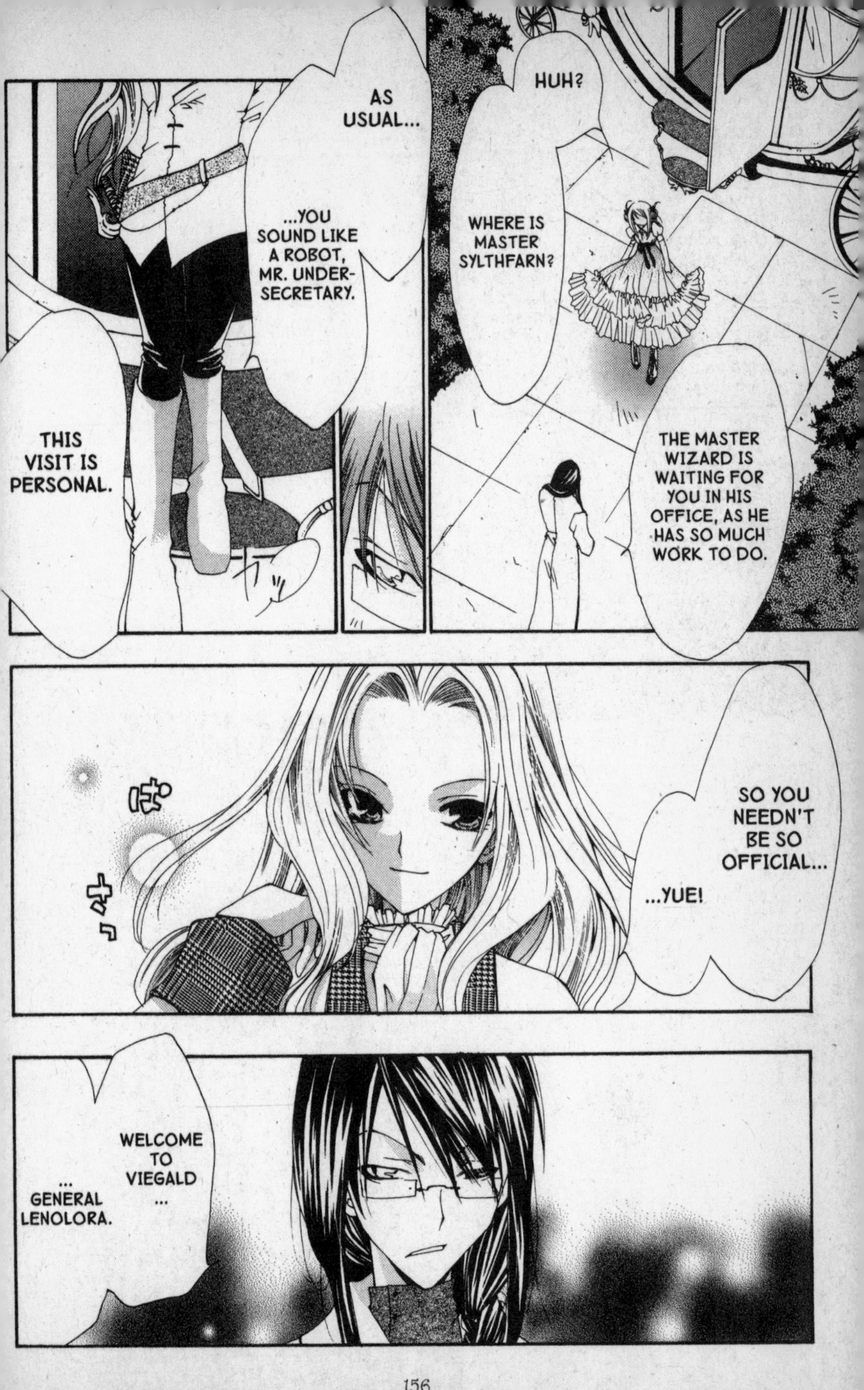
HUH?
WHERE IS MASTER SYLTHFARN?
THE MASTER WIZARD IS WAITING FOR YOU IN HIS OFFICE, AS HE HAS SO MUCH WORK TO DO.
AS USUAL...
...YOU SOUND LIKE A ROBOT, MR. UNDER-SECRETARY.
THIS VISIT IS PERSONAL.
SO YOU NEEDN'T BE SO OFFICIAL...
...YUE!
WELCOME TO VIEGALD ...
... GENERAL LENOLORA.

Episode.16

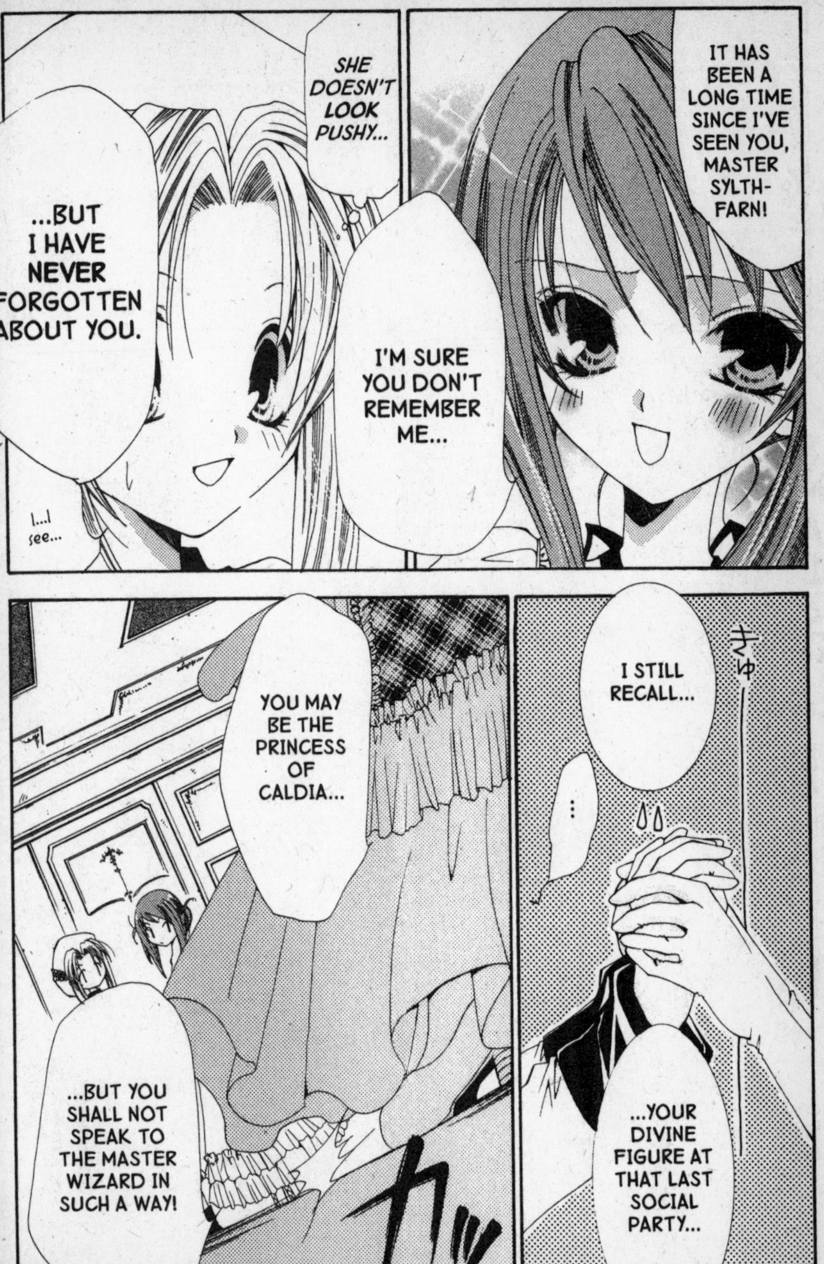
IT HAS BEEN A LONG TIME SINCE I'VE SEEN YOU, MASTER SYLTH-FARN!
I'M SURE YOU DON'T REMEMBER ME...
...BUT I HAVE NEVER FORGOTTEN ABOUT YOU.
SHE DOESN'T LOOK PUSHY...
I...I see...
きゅー
I STILL RECALL...
...
...YOUR DIVINE FIGURE AT THAT LAST SOCIAL PARTY...
YOU MAY BE THE PRINCESS OF CALDIA...
...BUT YOU SHALL NOT SPEAK TO THE MASTER WIZARD IN SUCH A WAY!
カッ

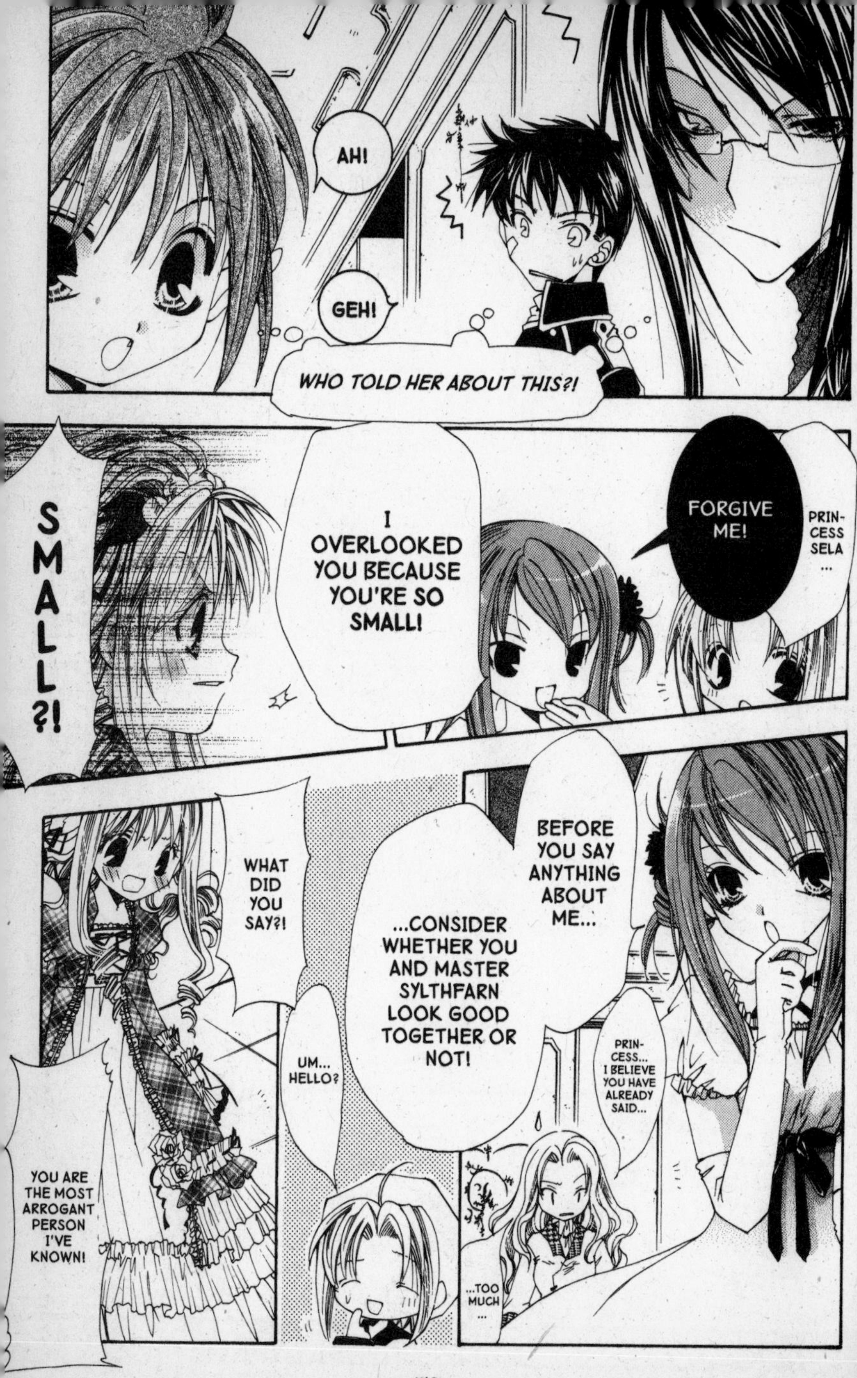
AH!
GEH!
WHO TOLD HER ABOUT THIS?!
PRIN-CESS SELA...
FORGIVE ME!
I OVERLOOKED YOU BECAUSE YOU'RE SO SMALL!
SMALL?!
BEFORE YOU SAY ANYTHING ABOUT ME...
...CONSIDER WHETHER YOU AND MASTER SYLTHFARN LOOK GOOD TOGETHER OR NOT!
PRIN-CESS... I BELIEVE YOU HAVE ALREADY SAID...
...TOO MUCH...
UM... HELLO?
WHAT DID YOU SAY?!
YOU ARE THE MOST ARROGANT PERSON I'VE KNOWN!

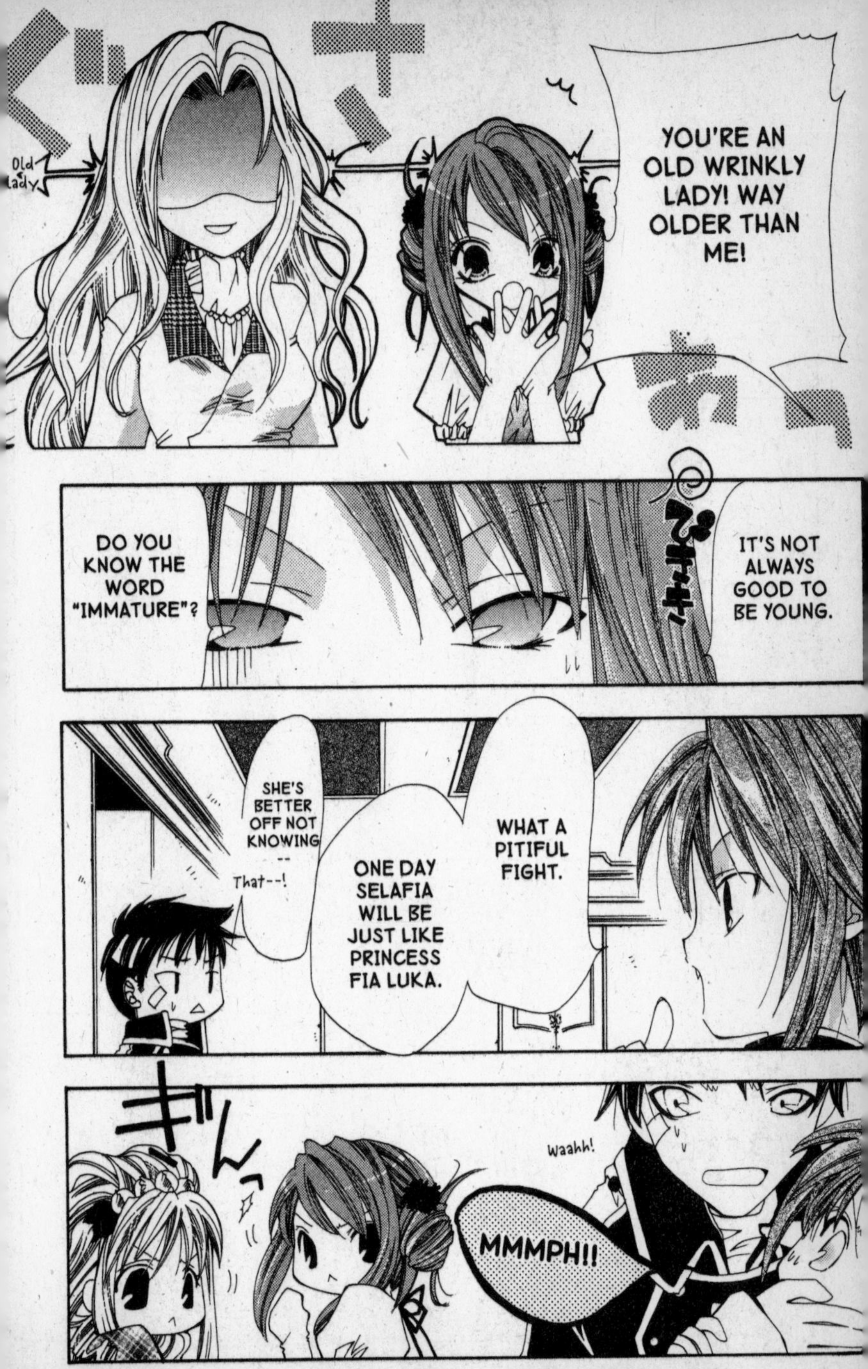
YOU'RE AN OLD WRINKLY LADY! WAY OLDER THAN ME!
Old lady
IT'S NOT ALWAYS GOOD TO BE YOUNG.
DO YOU KNOW THE WORD "IMMATURE"?
WHAT A PITIFUL FIGHT.
ONE DAY SELAFIA WILL BE JUST LIKE PRINCESS FIA LUKA.
SHE'S BETTER OFF NOT KNOWING --
That--!
Waahh!
MMMPH!!

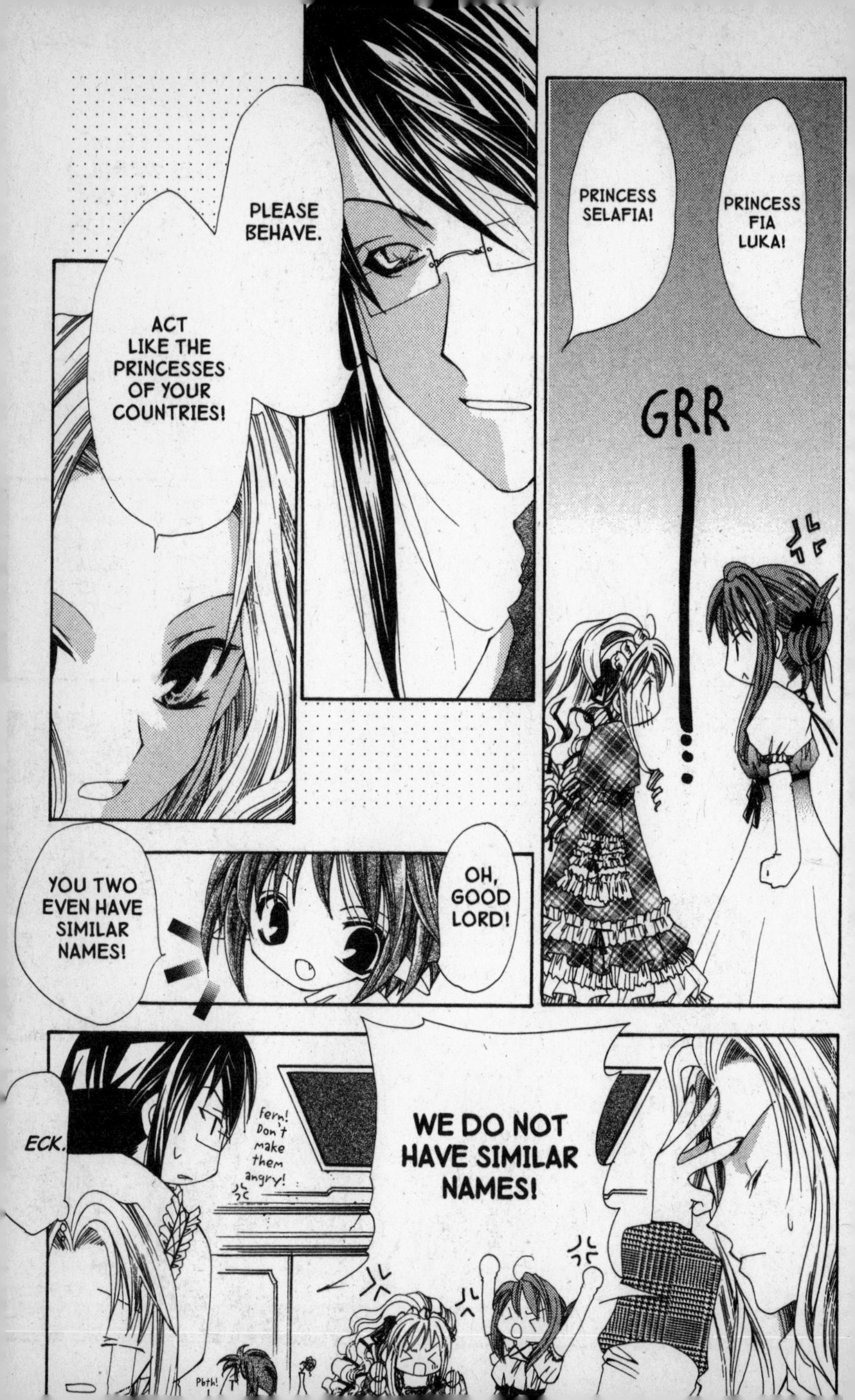
PRINCESS FIA LUKA!
PRINCESS SELAFIA!
GRR
PLEASE BEHAVE.
ACT LIKE THE PRINCESSES OF YOUR COUNTRIES!
OH, GOOD LORD!
YOU TWO EVEN HAVE SIMILAR NAMES!
WE DO NOT HAVE SIMILAR NAMES!
Fern! Don't make them angry!
ECK.
Pbth!

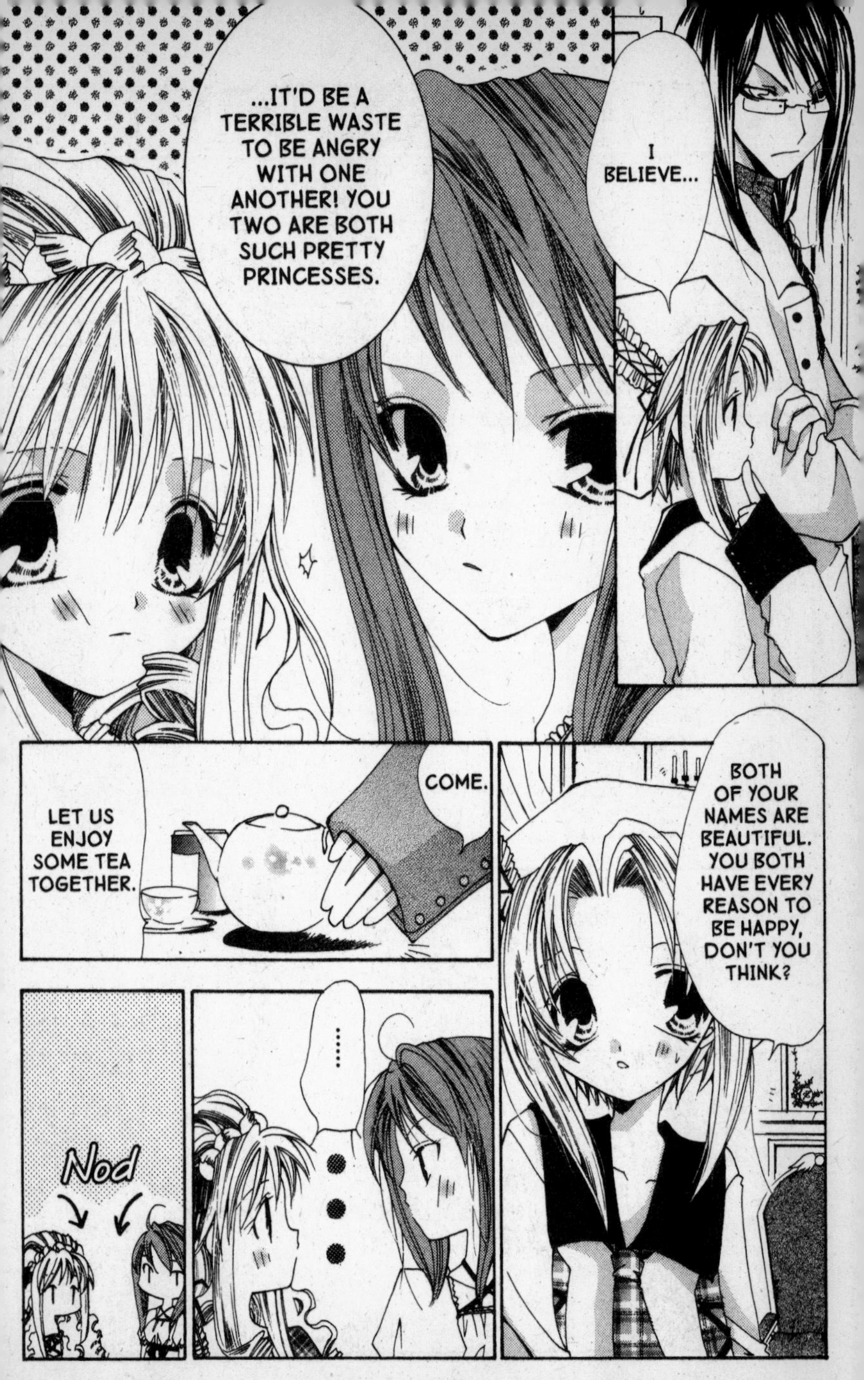
I BELIEVE...
...IT'D BE A TERRIBLE WASTE TO BE ANGRY WITH ONE ANOTHER! YOU TWO ARE BOTH SUCH PRETTY PRINCESSES.
BOTH OF YOUR NAMES ARE BEAUTIFUL. YOU BOTH HAVE EVERY REASON TO BE HAPPY, DON'T YOU THINK?
COME.
LET US ENJOY SOME TEA TOGETHER.
......
Nod

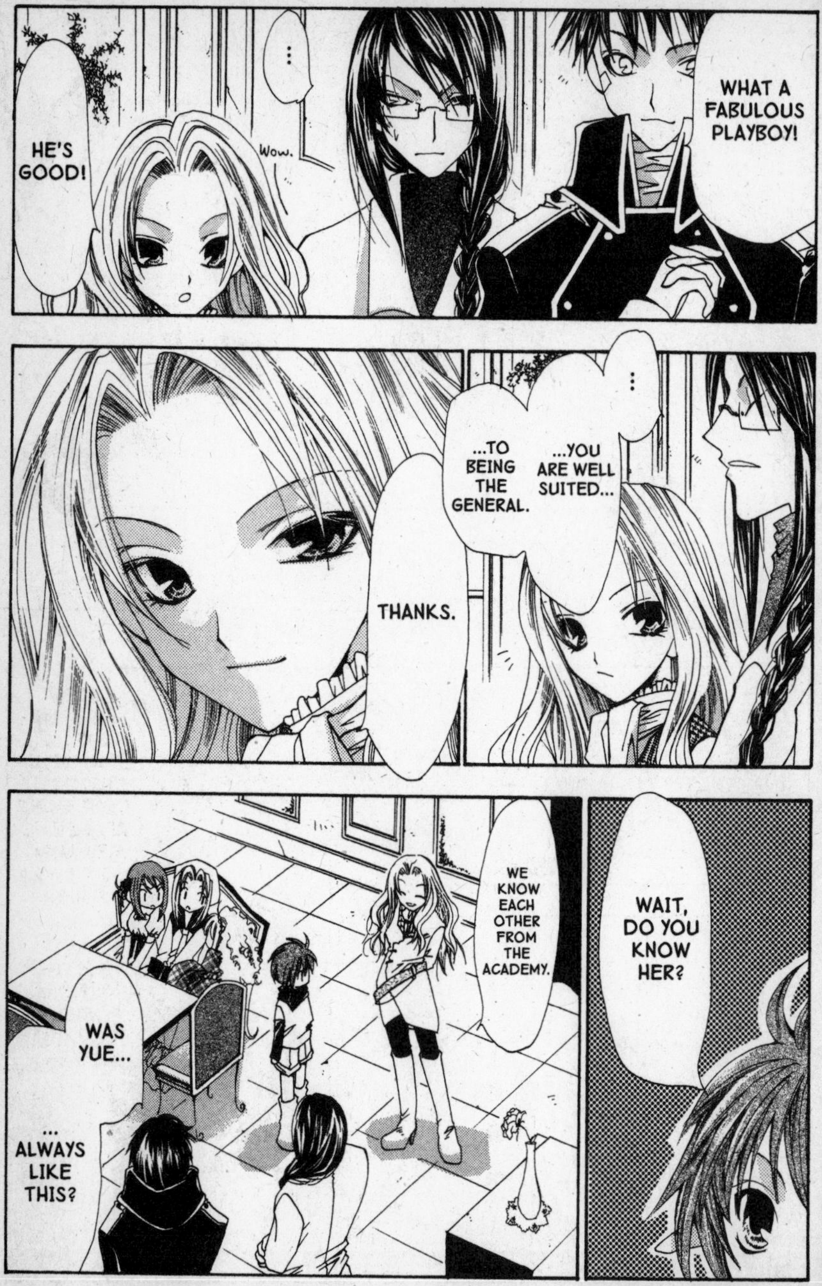
WHAT A FABULOUS PLAYBOY!
...
Wow.
HE'S GOOD!
...
...YOU ARE WELL SUITED...
...TO BEING THE GENERAL.
THANKS.
WAIT, DO YOU KNOW HER?
WE KNOW EACH OTHER FROM THE ACADEMY.
WAS YUE...
...ALWAYS LIKE THIS?

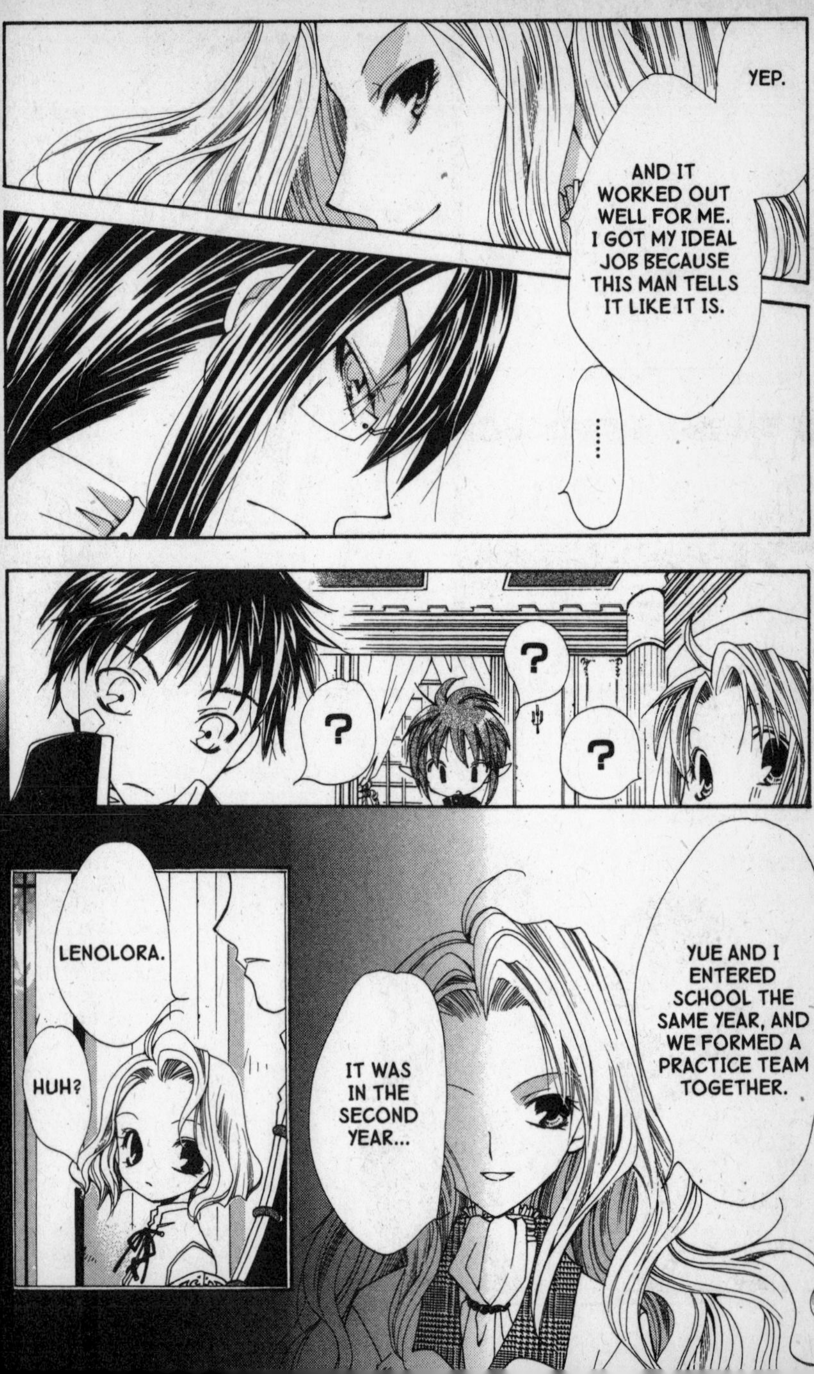
YEP.
AND IT WORKED OUT WELL FOR ME. I GOT MY IDEAL JOB BECAUSE THIS MAN TELLS IT LIKE IT IS.
......
?
?
?
YUE AND I ENTERED SCHOOL THE SAME YEAR, AND WE FORMED A PRACTICE TEAM TOGETHER.
IT WAS IN THE SECOND YEAR...
LENOLORA.
HUH?

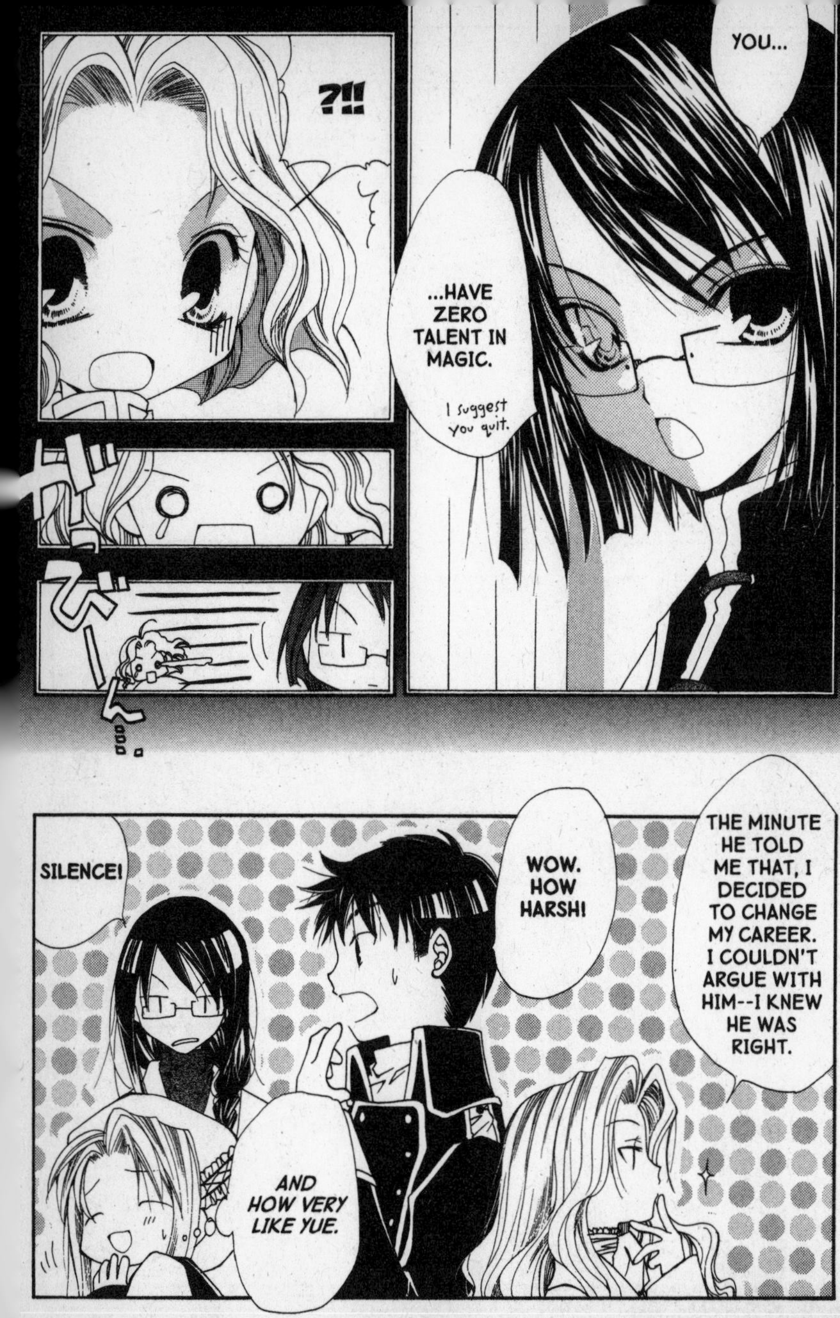
YOU...
...HAVE ZERO TALENT IN MAGIC.
I suggest you quit.
?!!
THE MINUTE HE TOLD ME THAT, I DECIDED TO CHANGE MY CAREER. I COULDN'T ARGUE WITH HIM--I KNEW HE WAS RIGHT.
WOW. HOW HARSH!
AND HOW VERY LIKE YUE.
SILENCE!

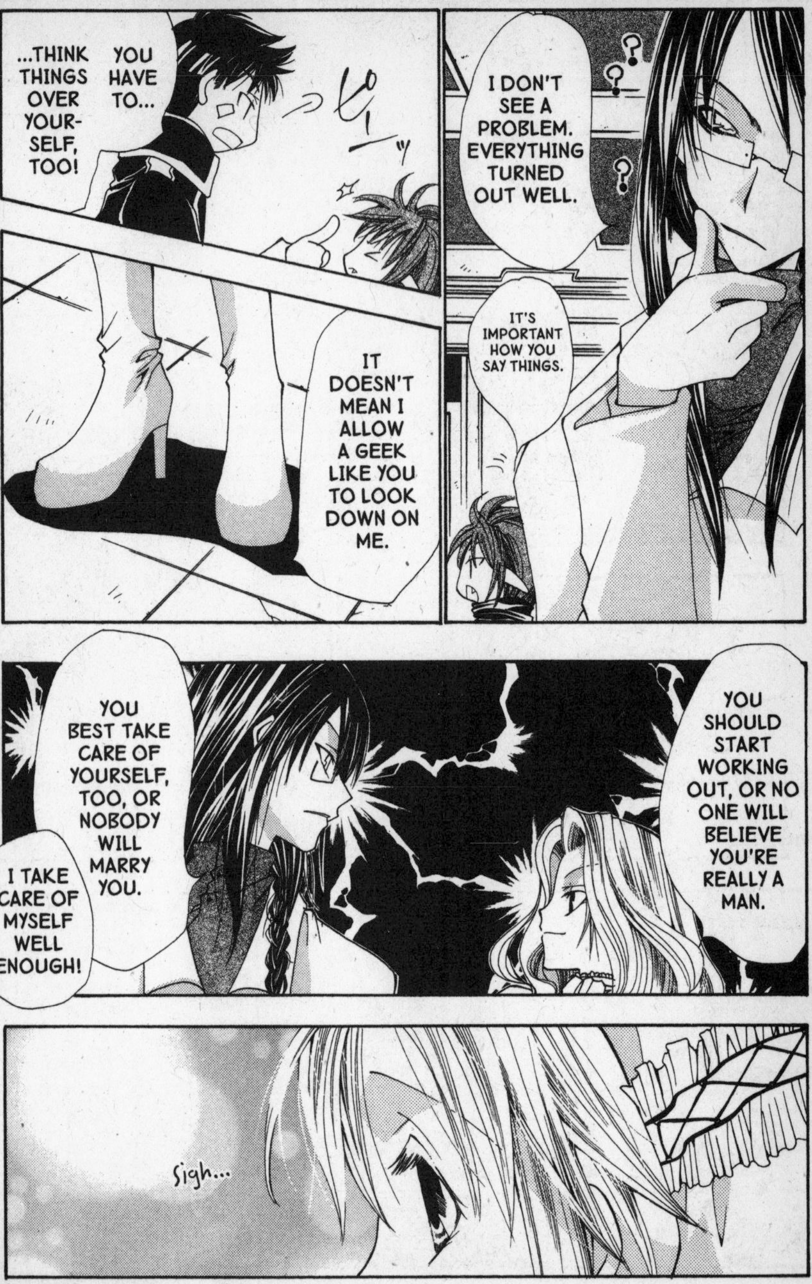
I DON'T SEE A PROBLEM. EVERYTHING TURNED OUT WELL.
IT'S IMPORTANT HOW YOU SAY THINGS.
YOU HAVE TO...
...THINK THINGS OVER YOURSELF, TOO!
IT DOESN'T MEAN I ALLOW A GEEK LIKE YOU TO LOOK DOWN ON ME.
YOU SHOULD START WORKING OUT, OR NO ONE WILL BELIEVE YOU'RE REALLY A MAN.
YOU BEST TAKE CARE OF YOURSELF, TOO, OR NOBODY WILL MARRY YOU.
I TAKE CARE OF MYSELF WELL ENOUGH!
Sigh...

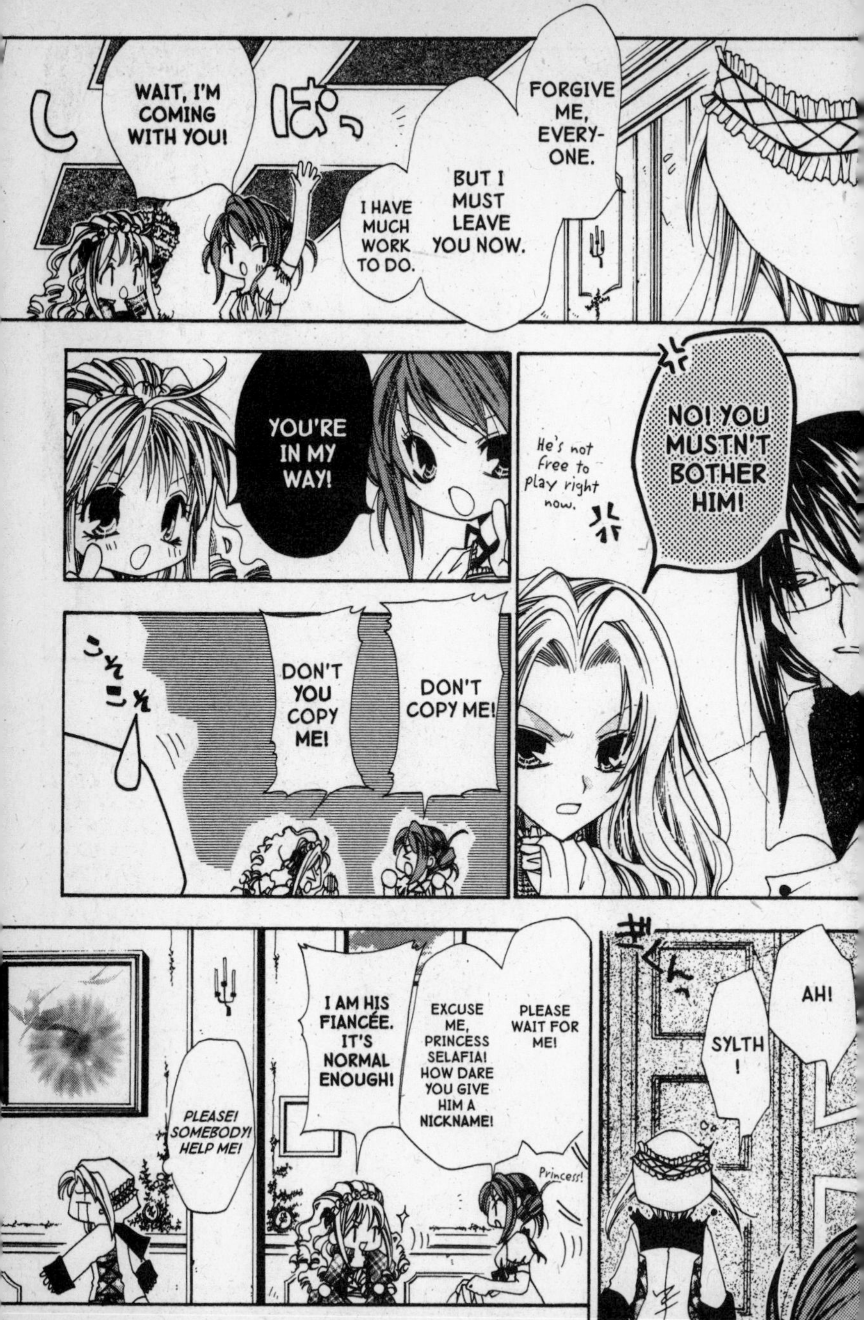
FORGIVE ME, EVERY-ONE.
BUT I MUST LEAVE YOU NOW.
I HAVE MUCH WORK TO DO.
ぱっ
WAIT, I'M COMING WITH YOU!
し
NO! YOU MUSTN'T BOTHER HIM!
He's not free to play right now.
YOU'RE IN MY WAY!
DON'T COPY ME!
DON'T YOU COPY ME!
こそこそ
ぎくっ
AH!
SYLTH!
PLEASE WAIT FOR ME!
EXCUSE ME, PRINCESS SELAFIA! HOW DARE YOU GIVE HIM A NICKNAME!
Princess!
I AM HIS FIANCÉE. IT'S NORMAL ENOUGH!
PLEASE! SOMEBODY! HELP ME!

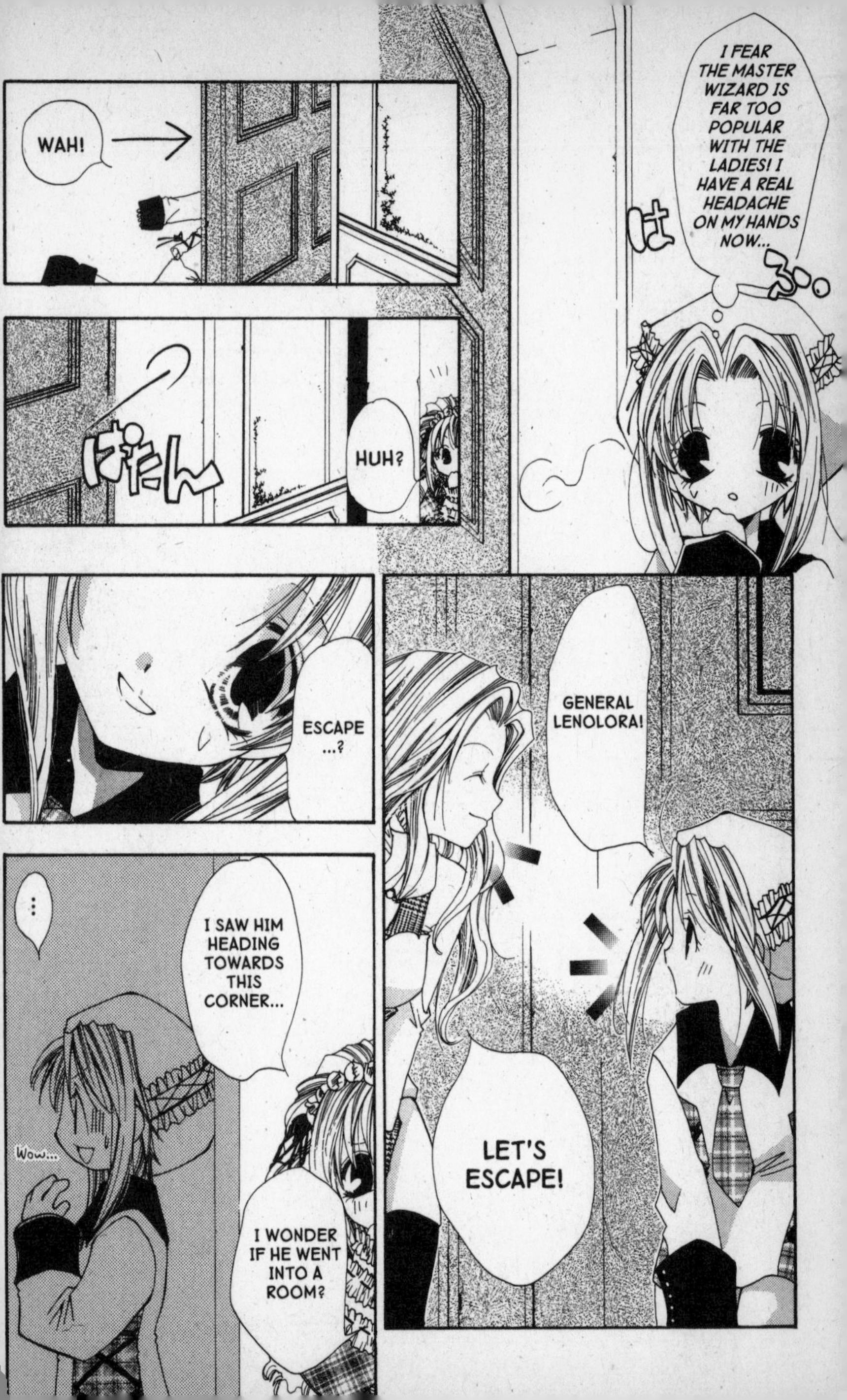
I FEAR THE MASTER WIZARD IS FAR TOO POPULAR WITH THE LADIES! I HAVE A REAL HEADACHE ON MY HANDS NOW...
はふ。
WAH!
ぱたん
HUH?
GENERAL LENOLORA!
LET'S ESCAPE!
ESCAPE ...?
I SAW HIM HEADING TOWARDS THIS CORNER...
...
I WONDER IF HE WENT INTO A ROOM?
Wow...

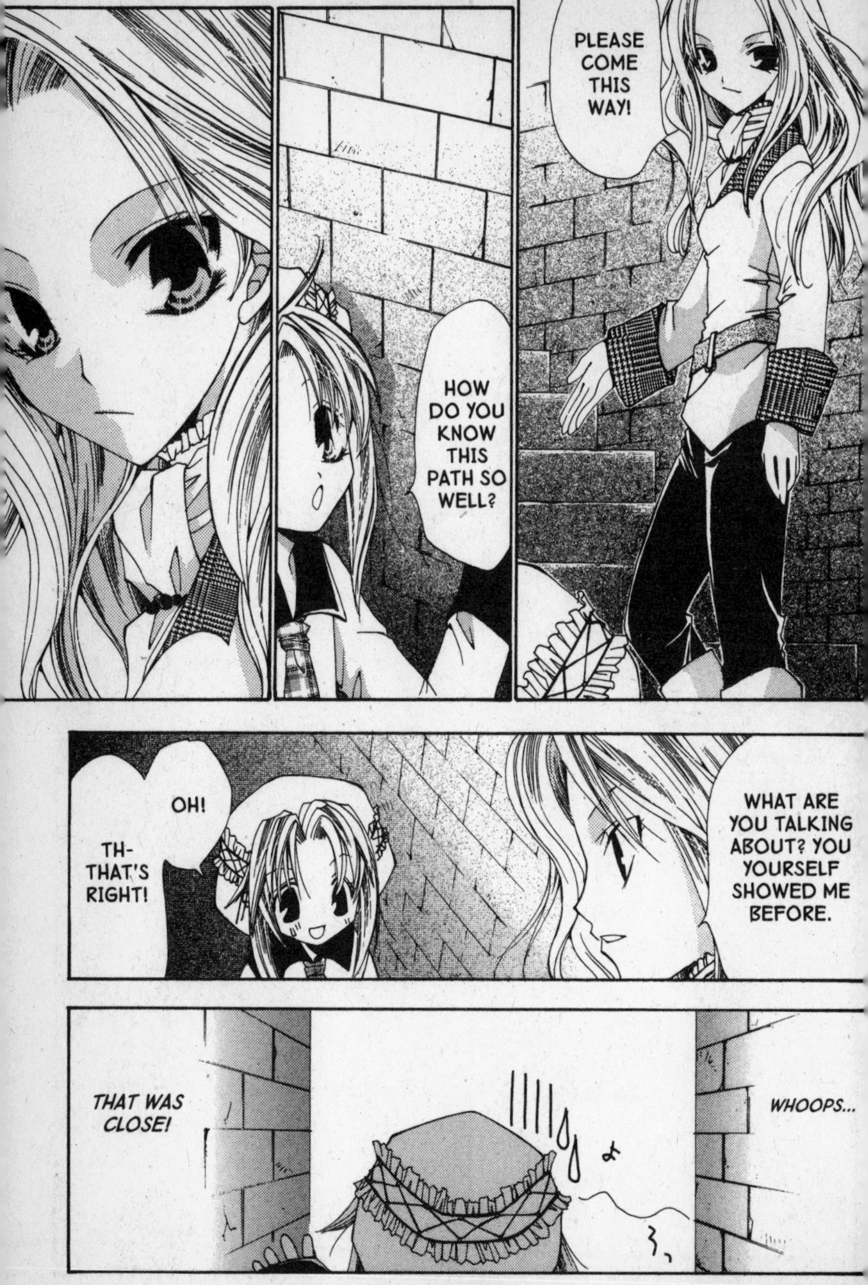
PLEASE COME THIS WAY!
HOW DO YOU KNOW THIS PATH SO WELL?
WHAT ARE YOU TALKING ABOUT? YOU YOURSELF SHOWED ME BEFORE.
OH!
TH- THAT'S RIGHT!
WHOOPS...
THAT WAS CLOSE!

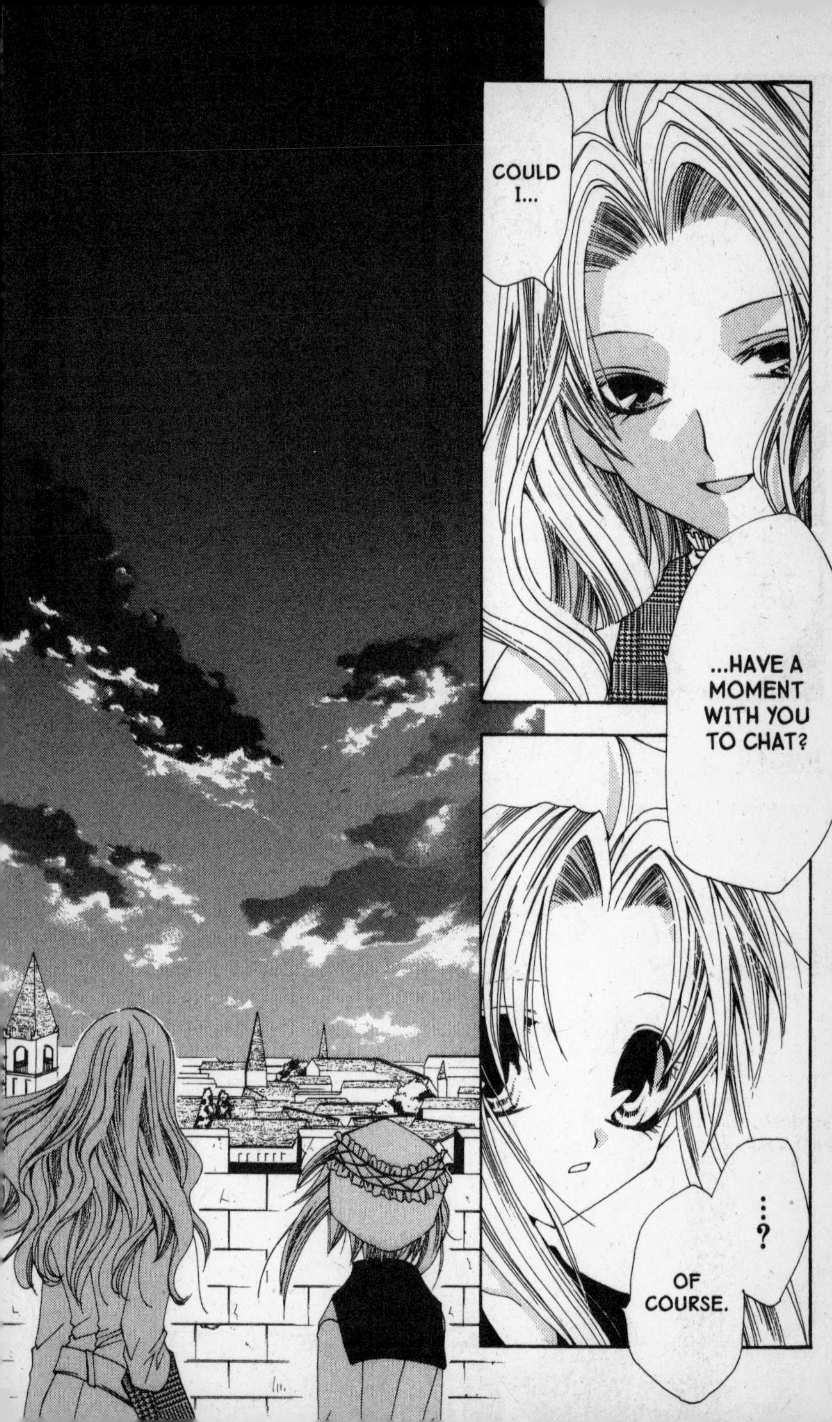
COULD I...
...HAVE A MOMENT WITH YOU TO CHAT?
...?
OF COURSE.

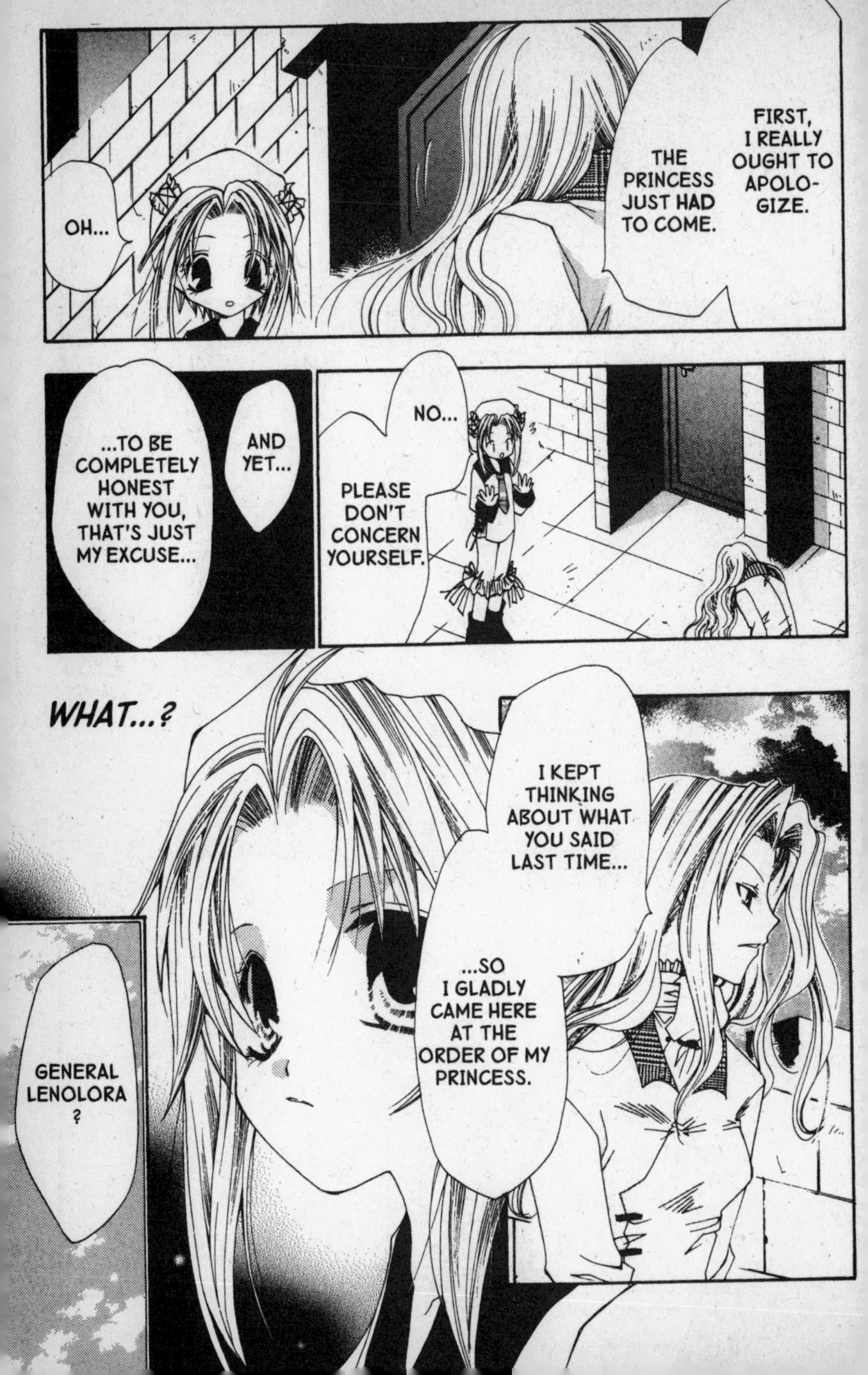
FIRST, I REALLY OUGHT TO APOLOGIZE.
THE PRINCESS JUST HAD TO COME.
OH...
NO...
PLEASE DON'T CONCERN YOURSELF.
AND YET...
...TO BE COMPLETELY HONEST WITH YOU, THAT'S JUST MY EXCUSE...
I KEPT THINKING ABOUT WHAT YOU SAID LAST TIME...
...SO I GLADLY CAME HERE AT THE ORDER OF MY PRINCESS.
WHAT...?
GENERAL LENOLORA?

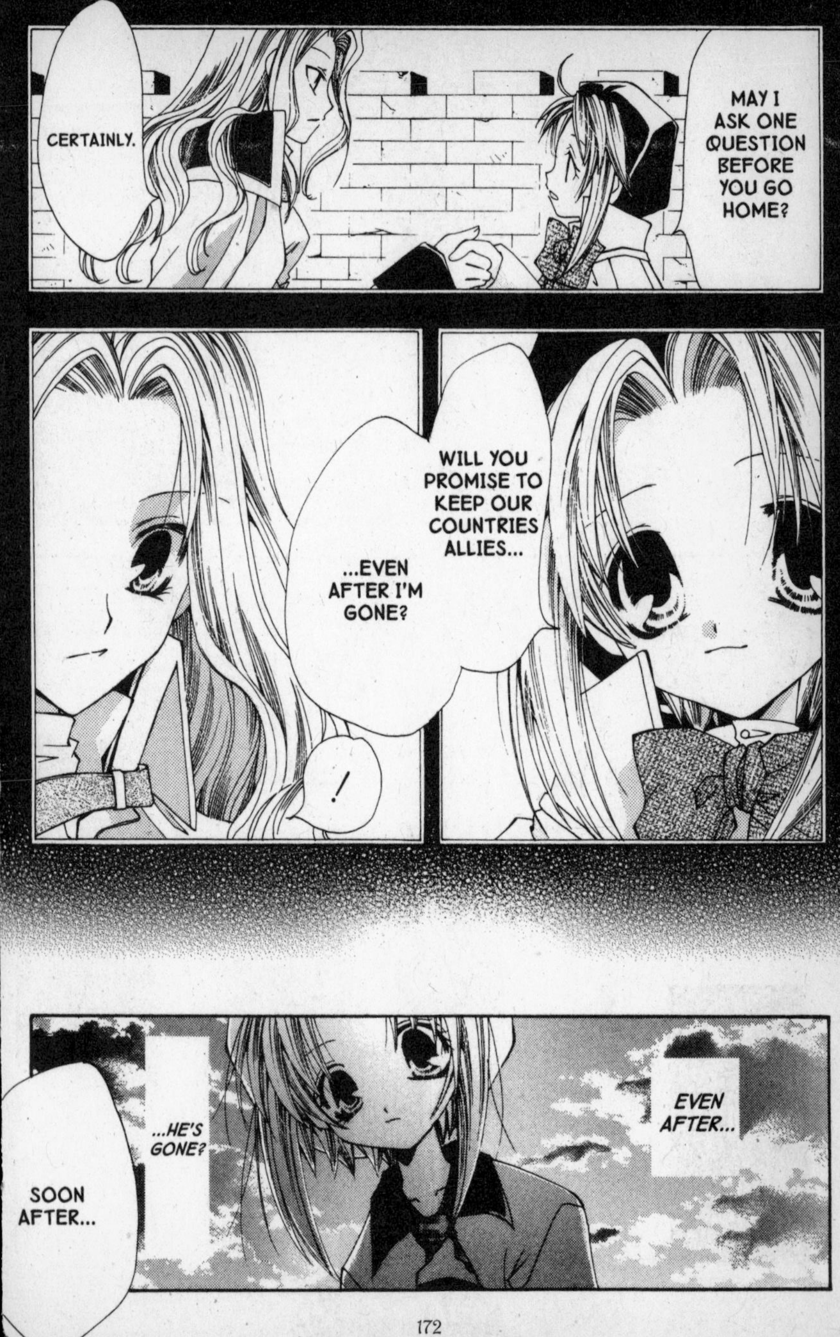
MAY I ASK ONE QUESTION BEFORE YOU GO HOME?
CERTAINLY.
WILL YOU PROMISE TO KEEP OUR COUNTRIES ALLIES...
...EVEN AFTER I'M GONE?
!
EVEN AFTER...
...HE'S GONE?
SOON AFTER...

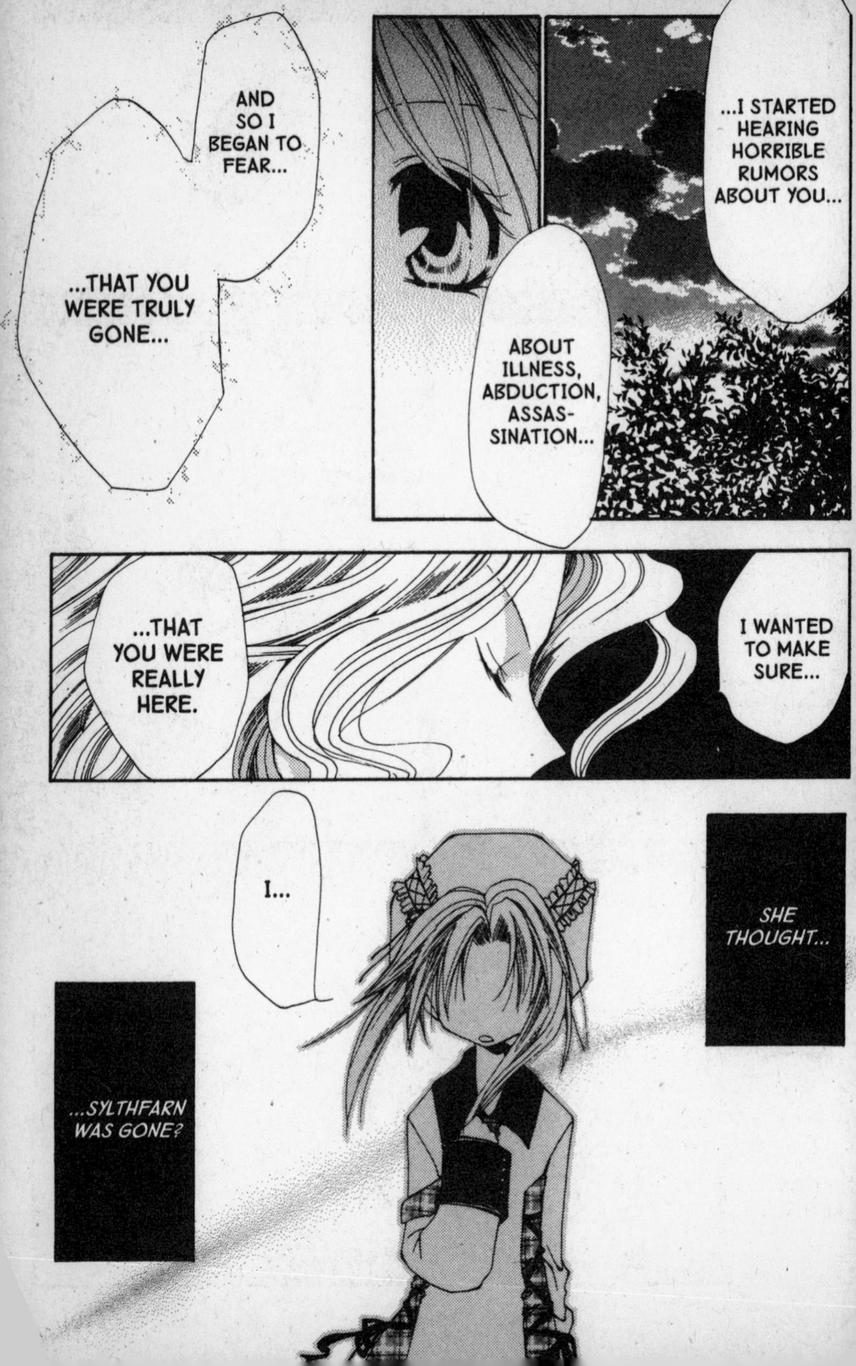
...I STARTED HEARING HORRIBLE RUMORS ABOUT YOU...
ABOUT ILLNESS, ABDUCTION, ASSAS-SINATION...
AND SO I BEGAN TO FEAR...
...THAT YOU WERE TRULY GONE...
I WANTED TO MAKE SURE...
...THAT YOU WERE REALLY HERE.
SHE THOUGHT...
I...
...SYLTHFARN WAS GONE?

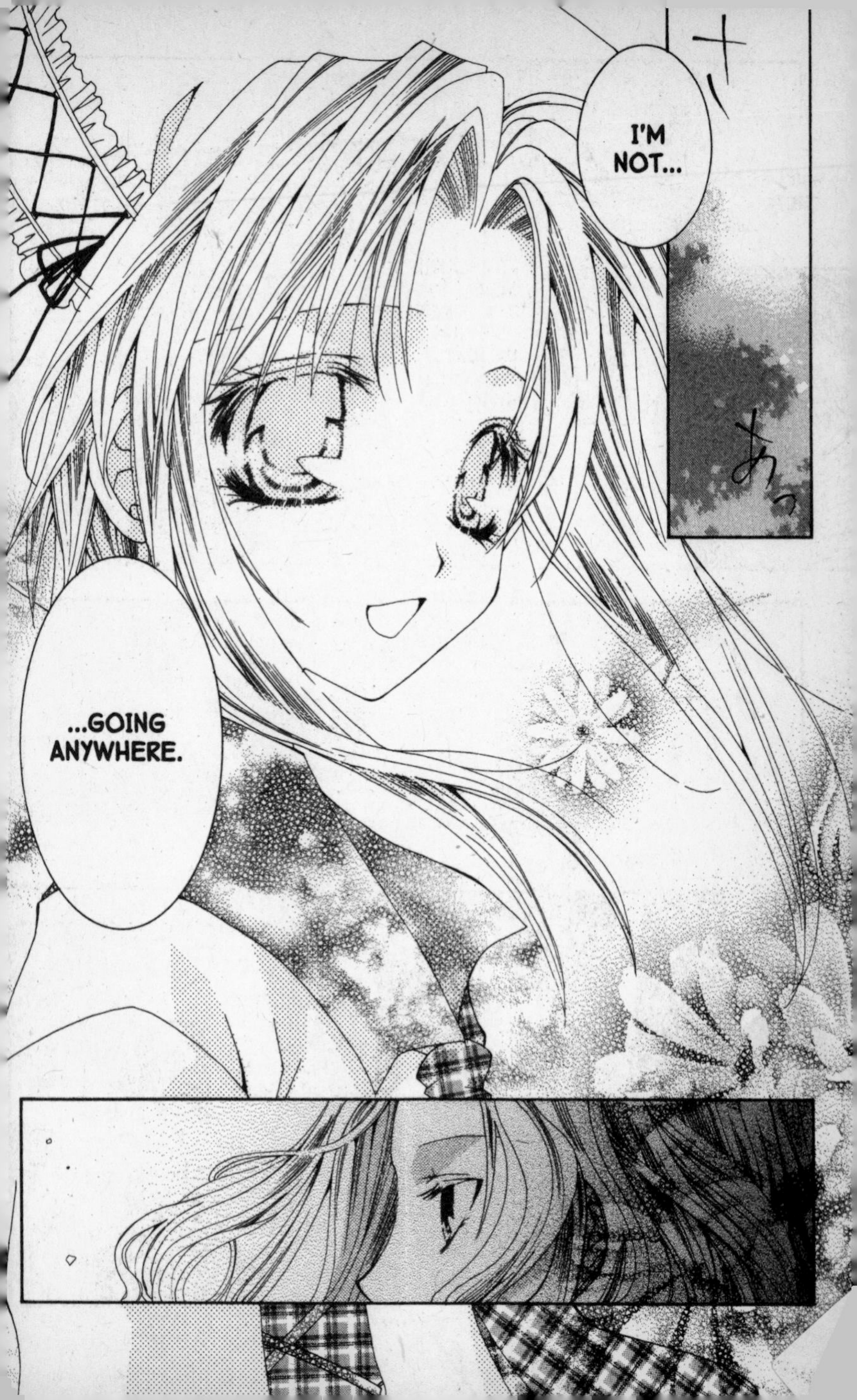
I'M NOT...
あっ
...GOING ANYWHERE.

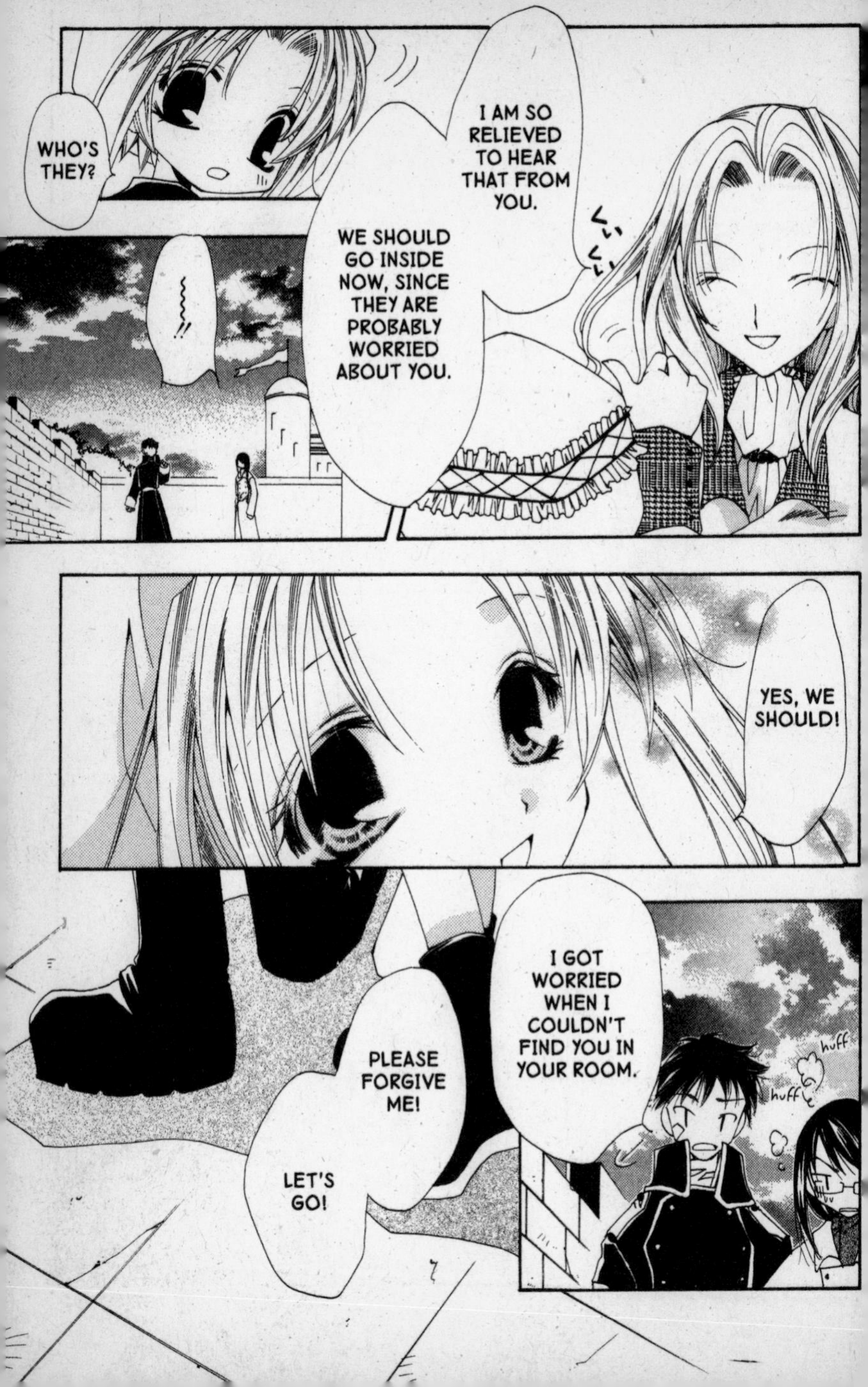

I AM SO RELIEVED TO HEAR THAT FROM YOU.
WE SHOULD GO INSIDE NOW, SINCE THEY ARE PROBABLY WORRIED ABOUT YOU.
WHO'S THEY?
...!!
YES, WE SHOULD!
I GOT WORRIED WHEN I COULDN'T FIND YOU IN YOUR ROOM.
huff
huff
PLEASE FORGIVE ME!
LET'S GO!

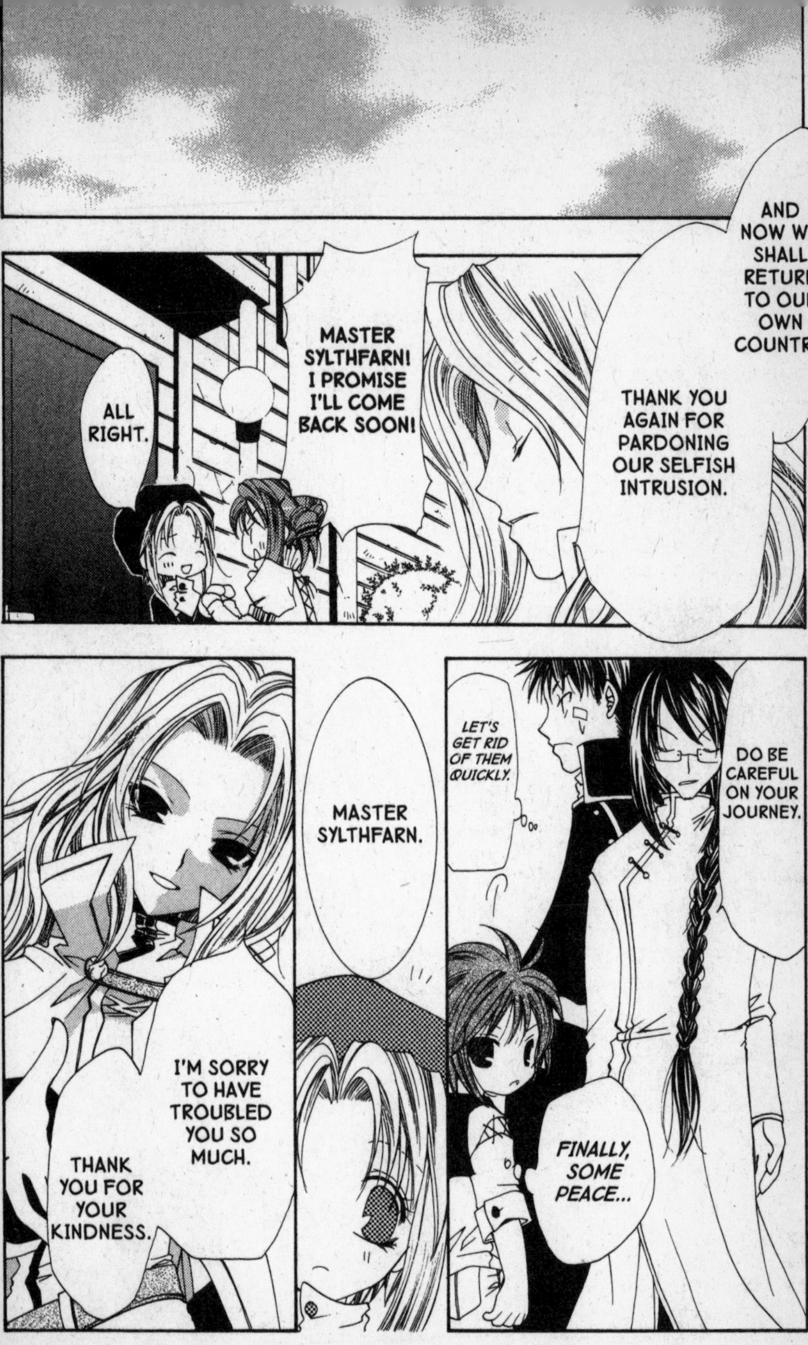
AND NOW WE SHALL RETURN TO OUR OWN COUNTRY.
THANK YOU AGAIN FOR PARDONING OUR SELFISH INTRUSION.
MASTER SYLTHFARN! I PROMISE I'LL COME BACK SOON!
ALL RIGHT.
DO BE CAREFUL ON YOUR JOURNEY.
LET'S GET RID OF THEM QUICKLY.
FINALLY, SOME PEACE...
MASTER SYLTHFARN.
I'M SORRY TO HAVE TROUBLED YOU SO MUCH.
THANK YOU FOR YOUR KINDNESS.

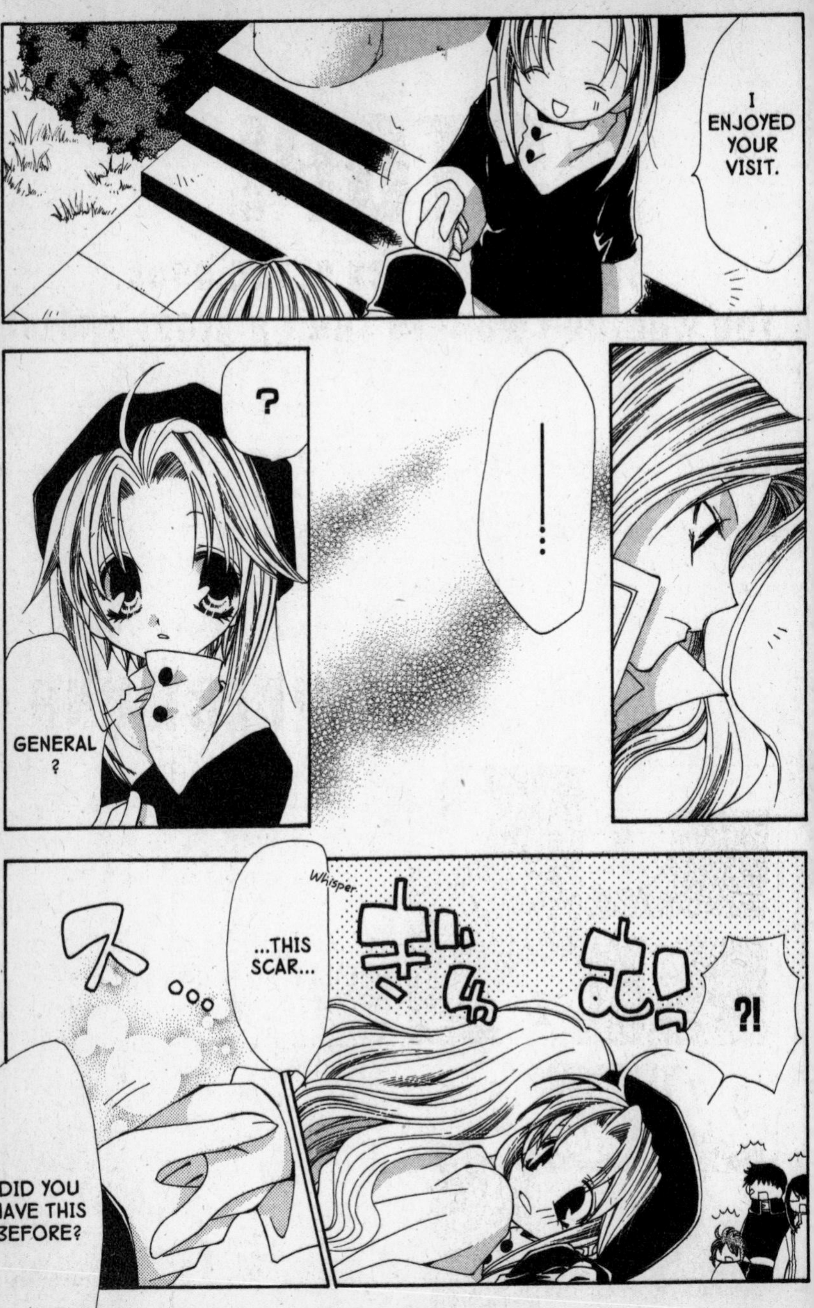
I ENJOYED YOUR VISIT.
...!
?
GENERAL?
?!
Whisper
...THIS SCAR...
DID YOU HAVE THIS BEFORE?

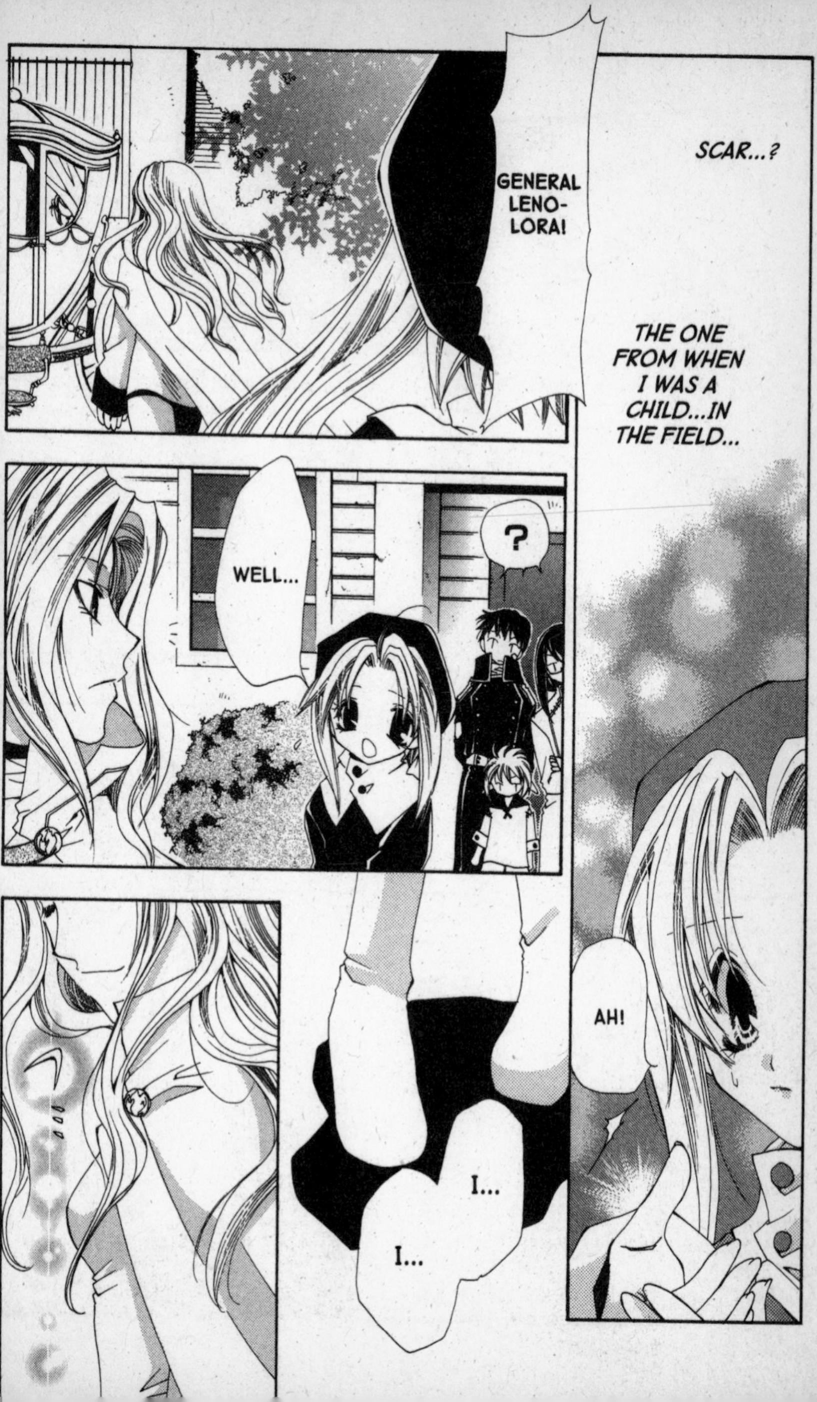
SCAR...?
THE ONE FROM WHEN I WAS A CHILD...IN THE FIELD...
AH!
GENERAL LENO-LORA!
?
WELL...
I...
I...

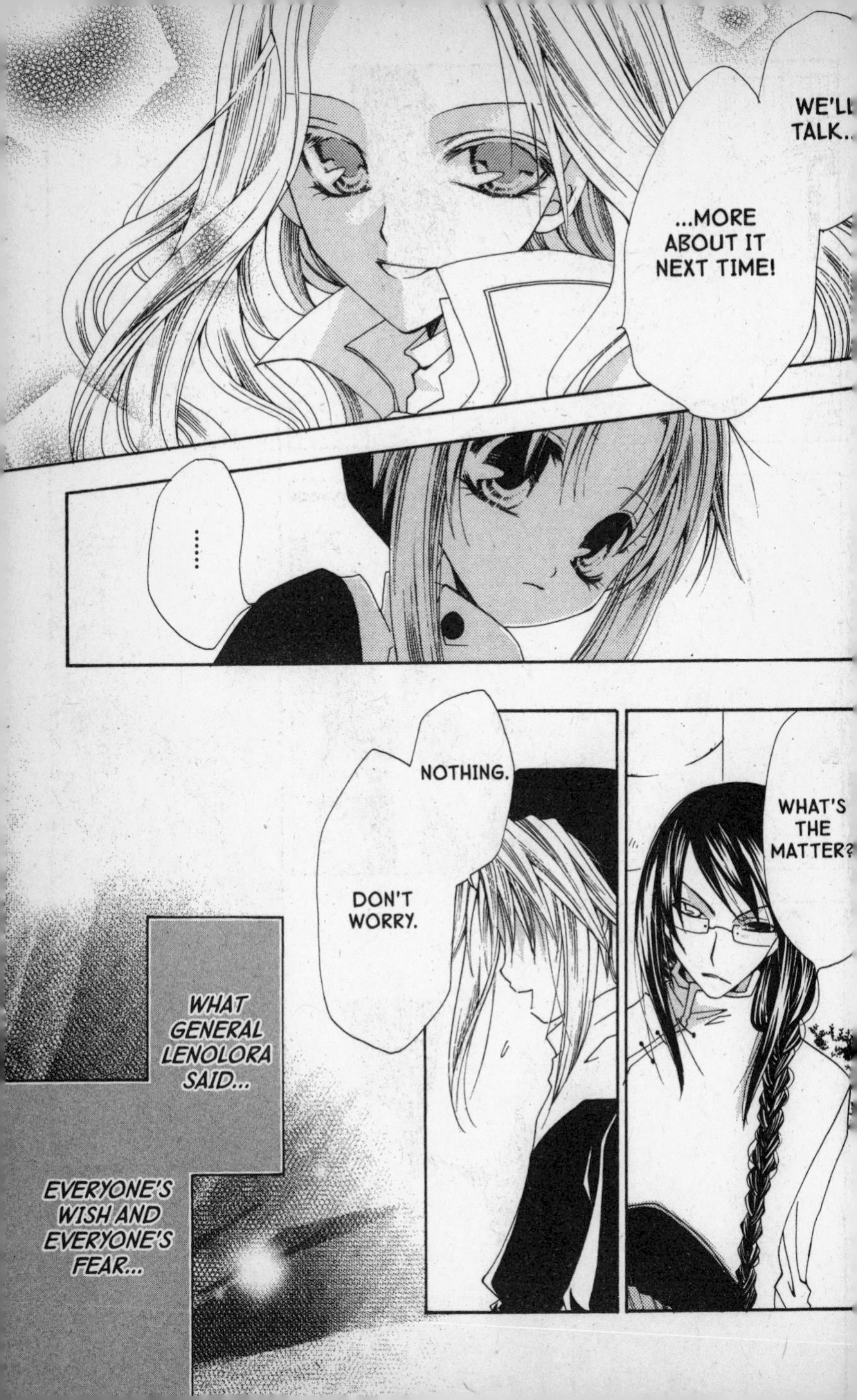
WE'LL TALK...
...MORE ABOUT IT NEXT TIME!
......
WHAT'S THE MATTER?
NOTHING.
DON'T WORRY.
WHAT GENERAL LENOLORA SAID...
EVERYONE'S WISH AND EVERYONE'S FEAR...

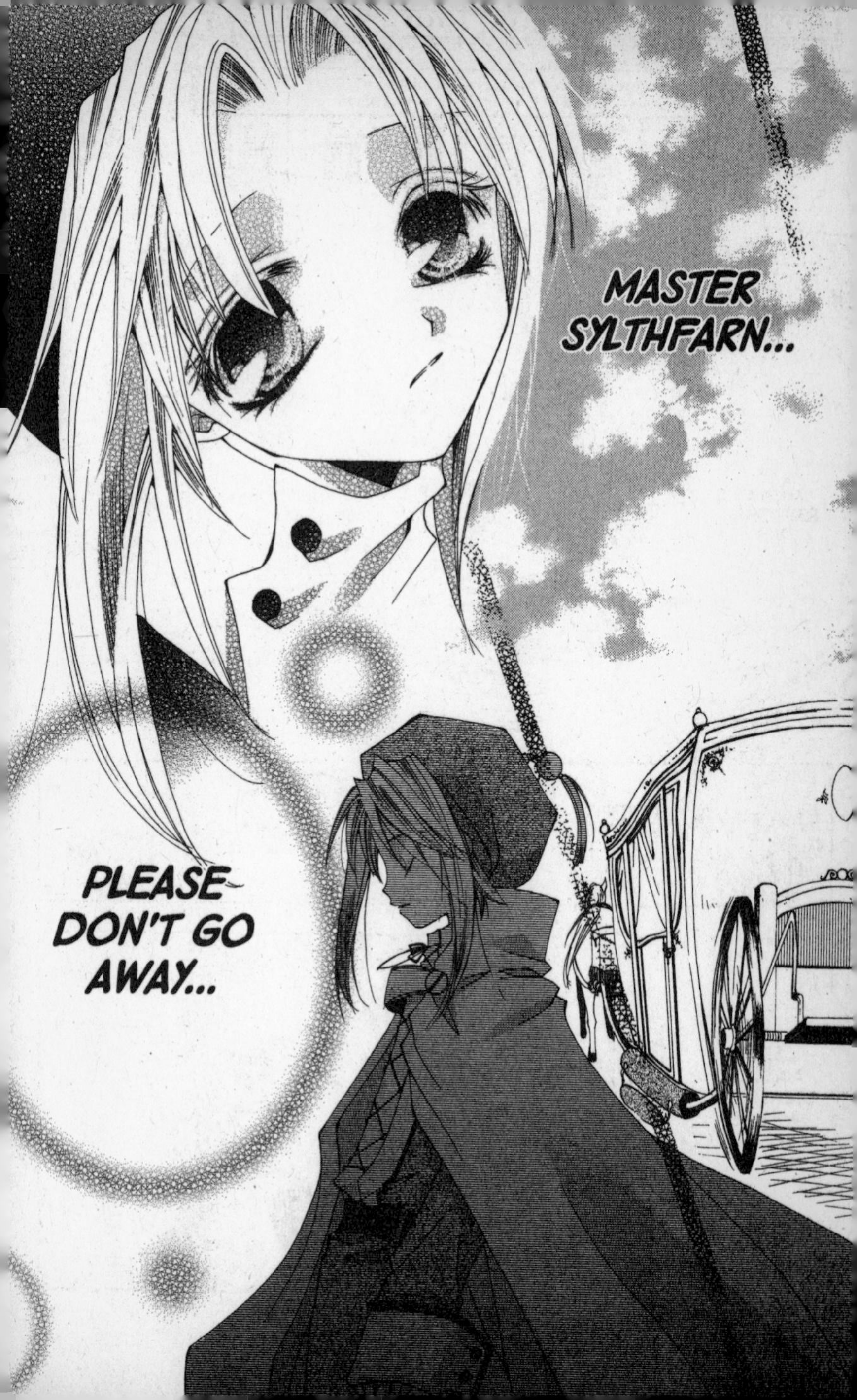
MASTER SYLTHFARN...
PLEASE DON'T GO AWAY...

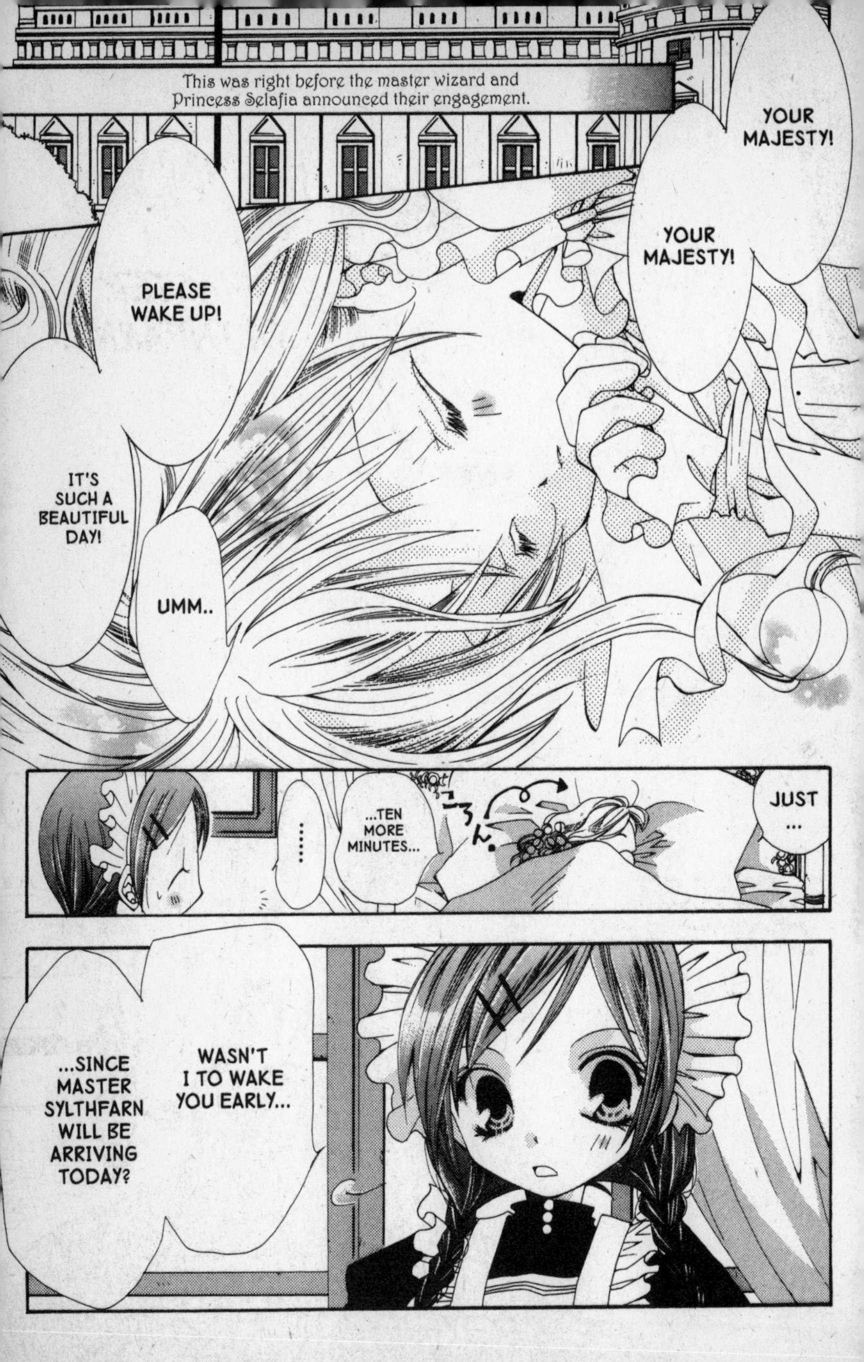
This was right before the master wizard and Princess Selafia announced their engagement.
YOUR MAJESTY!
YOUR MAJESTY!
PLEASE WAKE UP!
IT'S SUCH A BEAUTIFUL DAY!
UMM..
JUST ...
...TEN MORE MINUTES...
......
WASN'T I TO WAKE YOU EARLY...
...SINCE MASTER SYLTHFARN WILL BE ARRIVING TODAY?

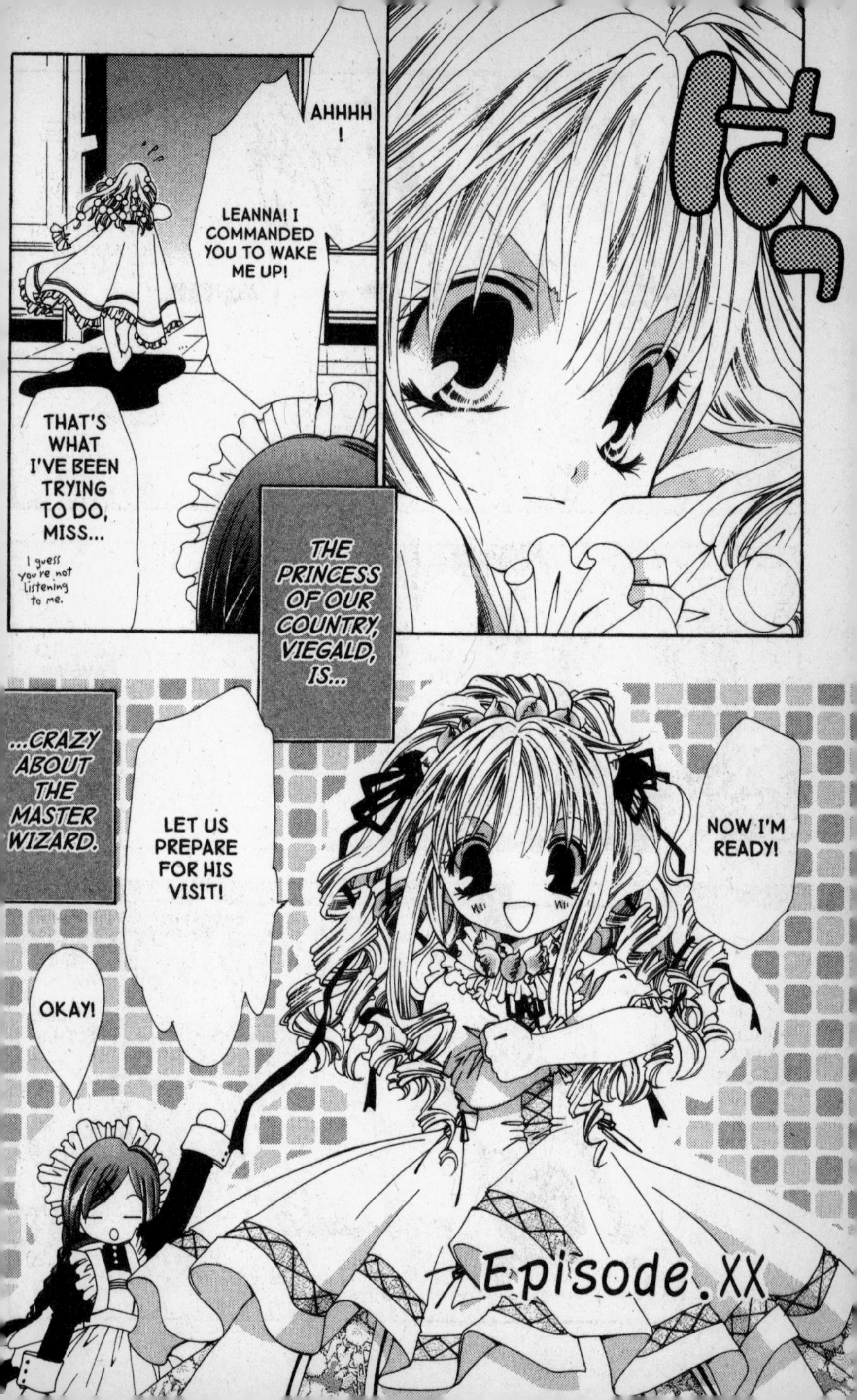
はっ
AHHHH!
LEANNA! I COMMANDED YOU TO WAKE ME UP!
THAT'S WHAT I'VE BEEN TRYING TO DO, MISS...
I guess you're not listening to me.
THE PRINCESS OF OUR COUNTRY, VIEGALD, IS...
...CRAZY ABOUT THE MASTER WIZARD.
NOW I'M READY!
LET US PREPARE FOR HIS VISIT!
OKAY!
Episode. XX

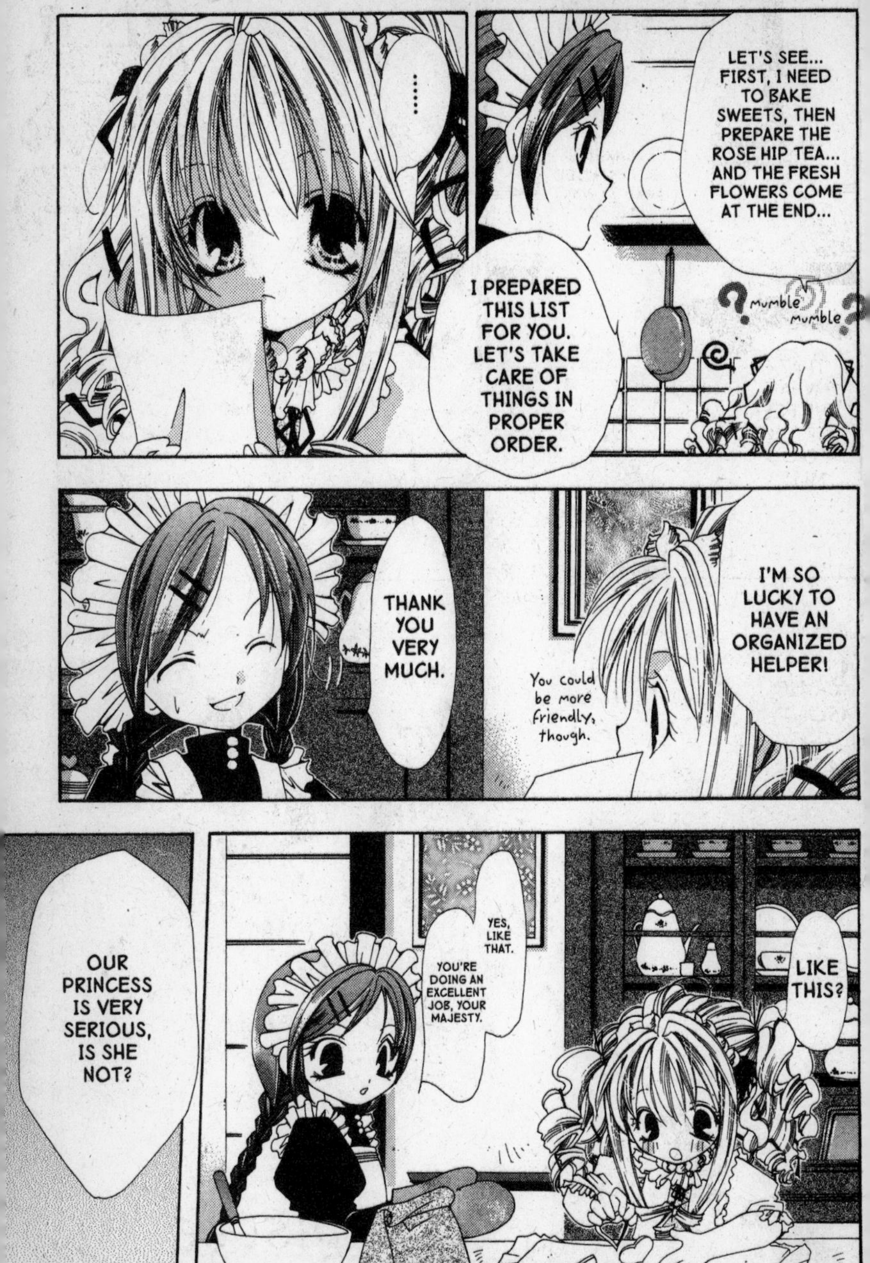
LET'S SEE... FIRST, I NEED TO BAKE SWEETS, THEN PREPARE THE ROSE HIP TEA... AND THE FRESH FLOWERS COME AT THE END...
mumble mumble
I PREPARED THIS LIST FOR YOU. LET'S TAKE CARE OF THINGS IN PROPER ORDER.
......
I'M SO LUCKY TO HAVE AN ORGANIZED HELPER!
You could be more friendly, though.
THANK YOU VERY MUCH.
LIKE THIS?
YES, LIKE THAT.
YOU'RE DOING AN EXCELLENT JOB, YOUR MAJESTY.
OUR PRINCESS IS VERY SERIOUS, IS SHE NOT?

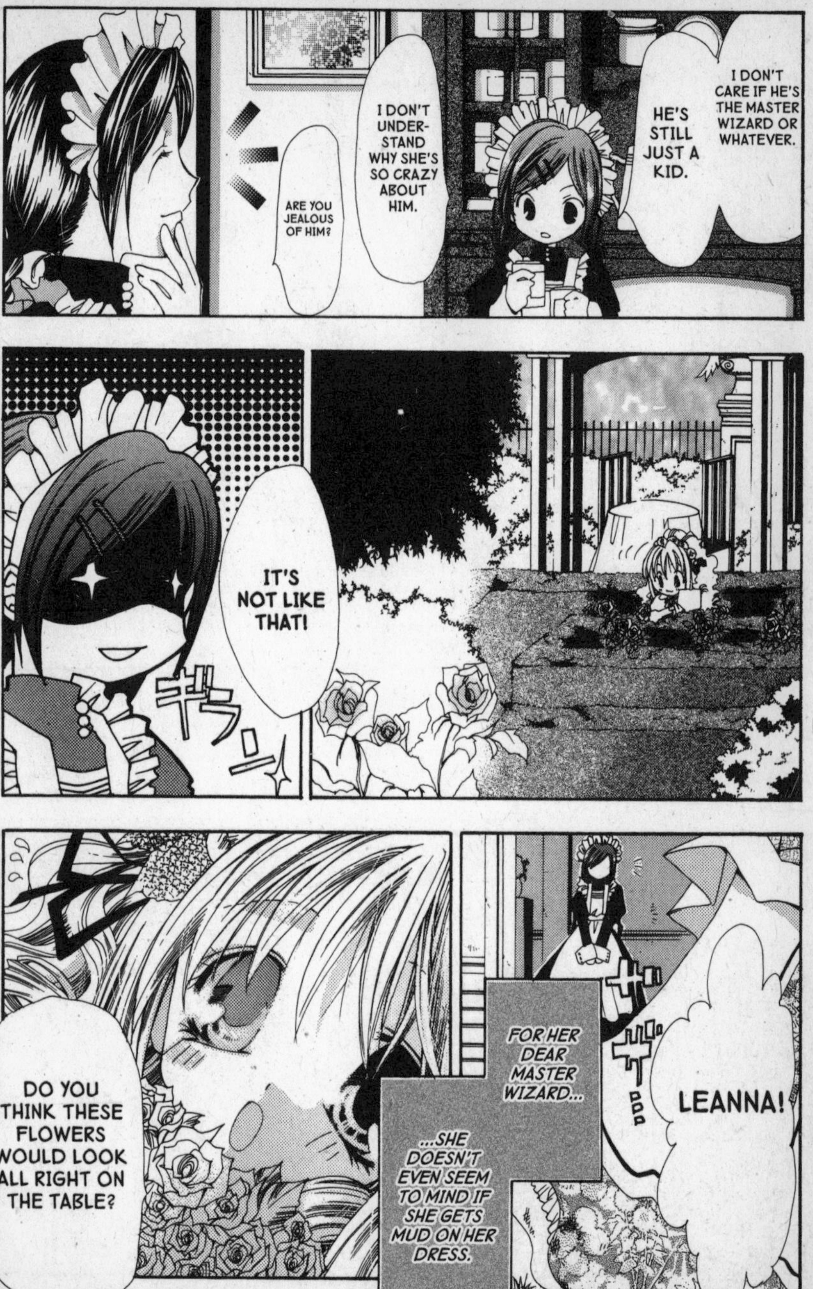
I DON'T CARE IF HE'S THE MASTER WIZARD OR WHATEVER.
HE'S STILL JUST A KID.
I DON'T UNDERSTAND WHY SHE'S SO CRAZY ABOUT HIM.
ARE YOU JEALOUS OF HIM?
IT'S NOT LIKE THAT!
LEANNA!
FOR HER DEAR MASTER WIZARD...
...SHE DOESN'T EVEN SEEM TO MIND IF SHE GETS MUD ON HER DRESS.
DO YOU THINK THESE FLOWERS WOULD LOOK ALL RIGHT ON THE TABLE?

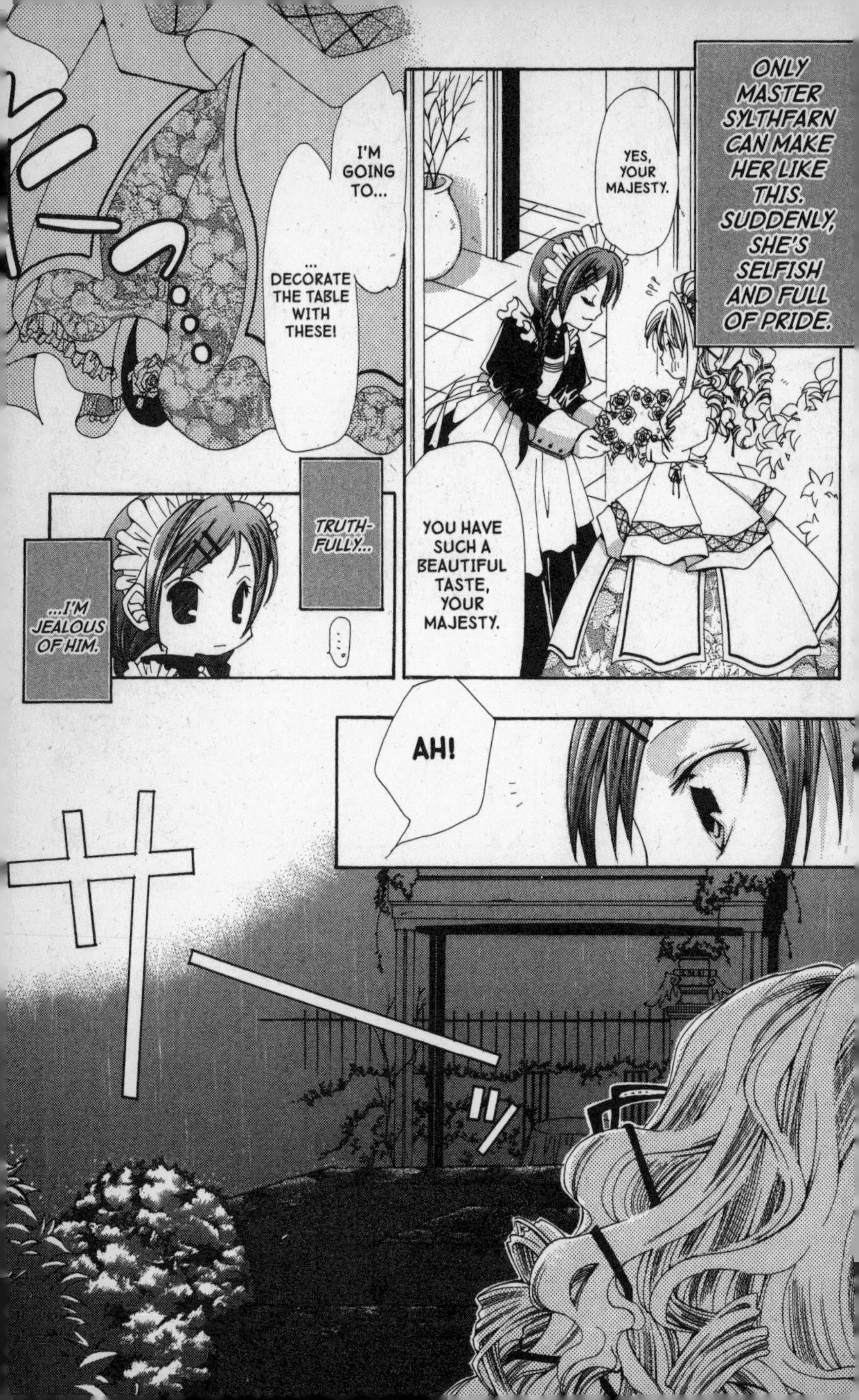
ONLY MASTER SYLTHFARN CAN MAKE HER LIKE THIS. SUDDENLY, SHE'S SELFISH AND FULL OF PRIDE.
YES, YOUR MAJESTY.
YOU HAVE SUCH A BEAUTIFUL TASTE, YOUR MAJESTY.
I'M GOING TO...
... DECORATE THE TABLE WITH THESE!
TRUTHFULLY...
...
...I'M JEALOUS OF HIM.
AH!

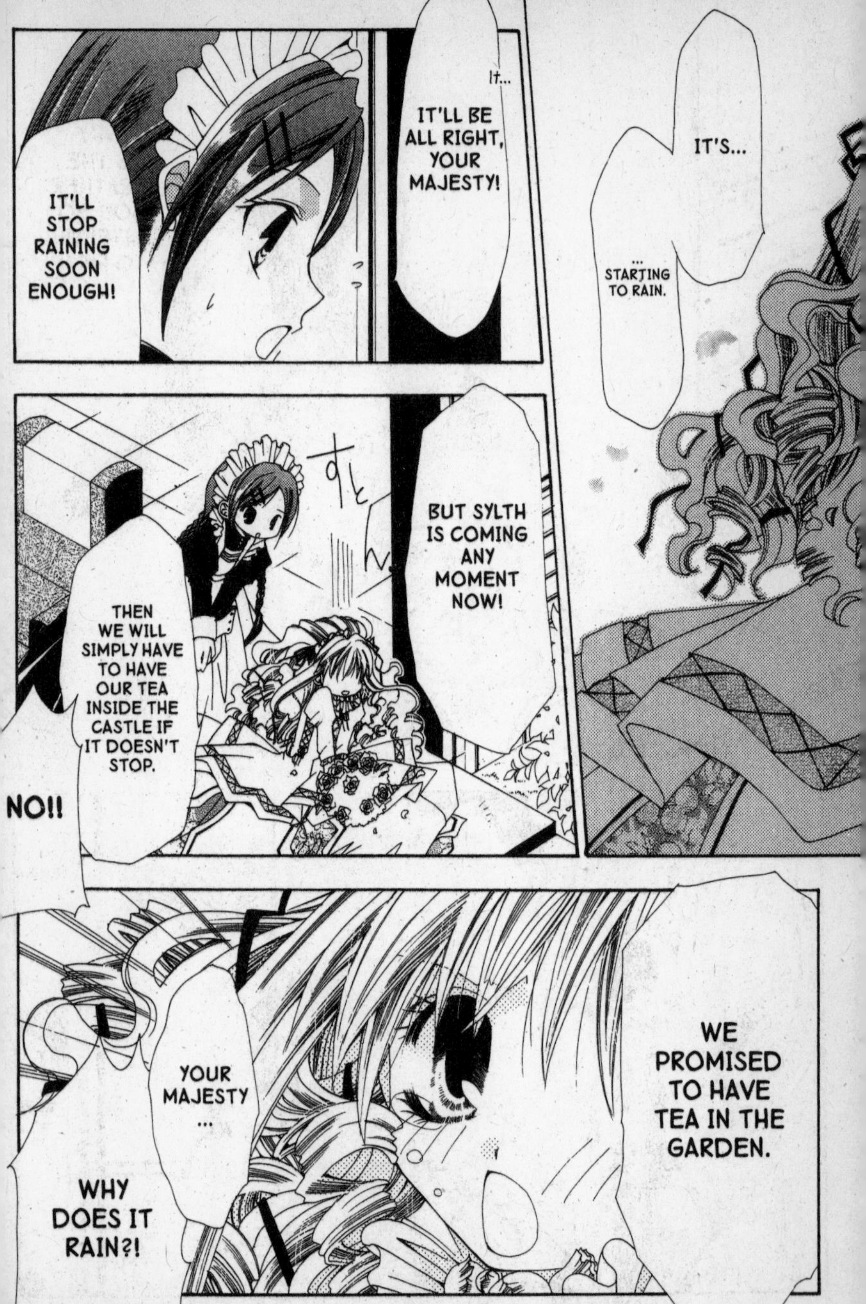

IT'S...
...STARTING TO RAIN.
It...
IT'LL BE ALL RIGHT, YOUR MAJESTY!
IT'LL STOP RAINING SOON ENOUGH!
BUT SYLTH IS COMING ANY MOMENT NOW!
THEN WE WILL SIMPLY HAVE TO HAVE OUR TEA INSIDE THE CASTLE IF IT DOESN'T STOP.
NO!!
WE PROMISED TO HAVE TEA IN THE GARDEN.
YOUR MAJESTY...
WHY DOES IT RAIN?!

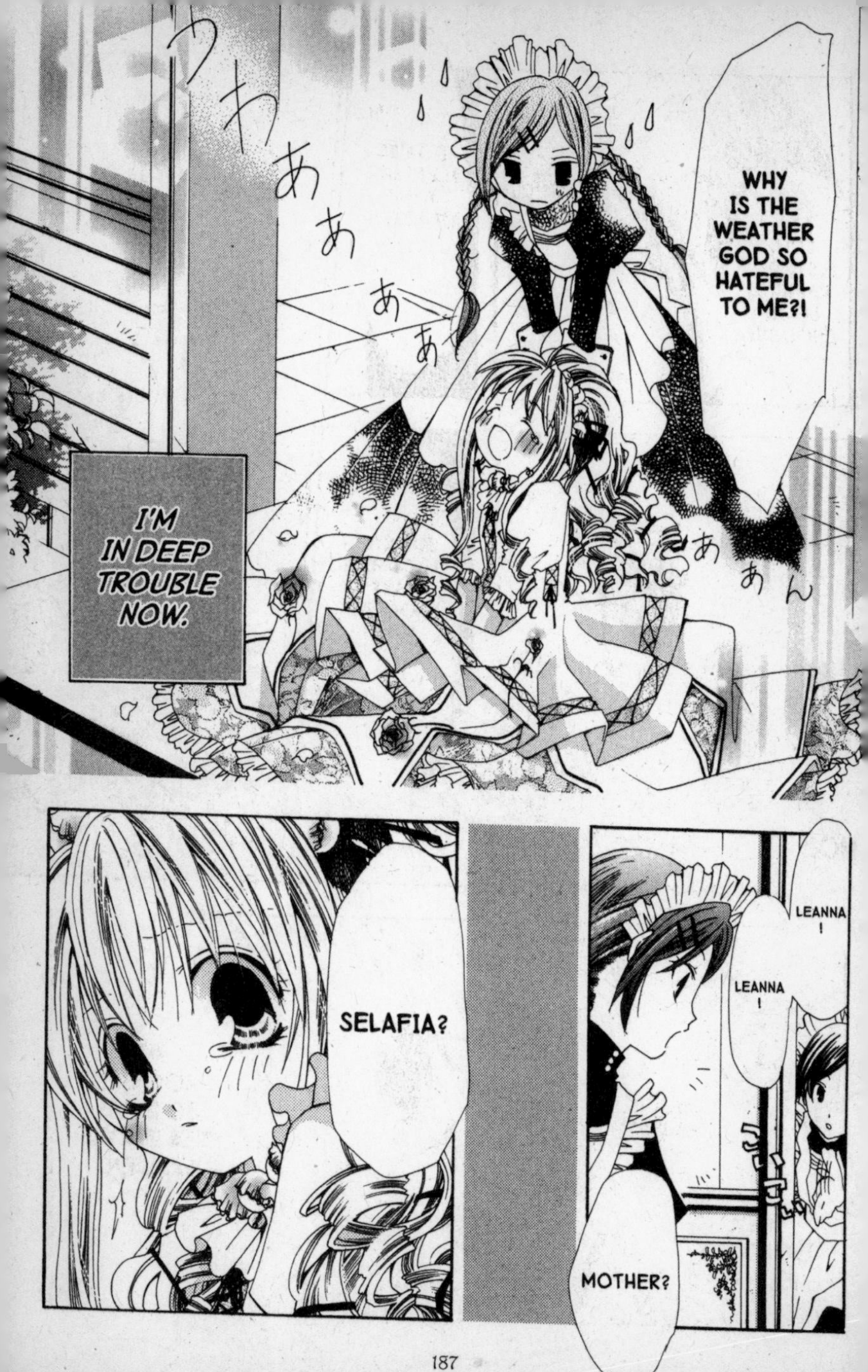
WHY IS THE WEATHER GOD SO HATEFUL TO ME?!
うわああああ
ああん
I'M IN DEEP TROUBLE NOW.
LEANNA!
LEANNA!
MOTHER?
SELAFIA?

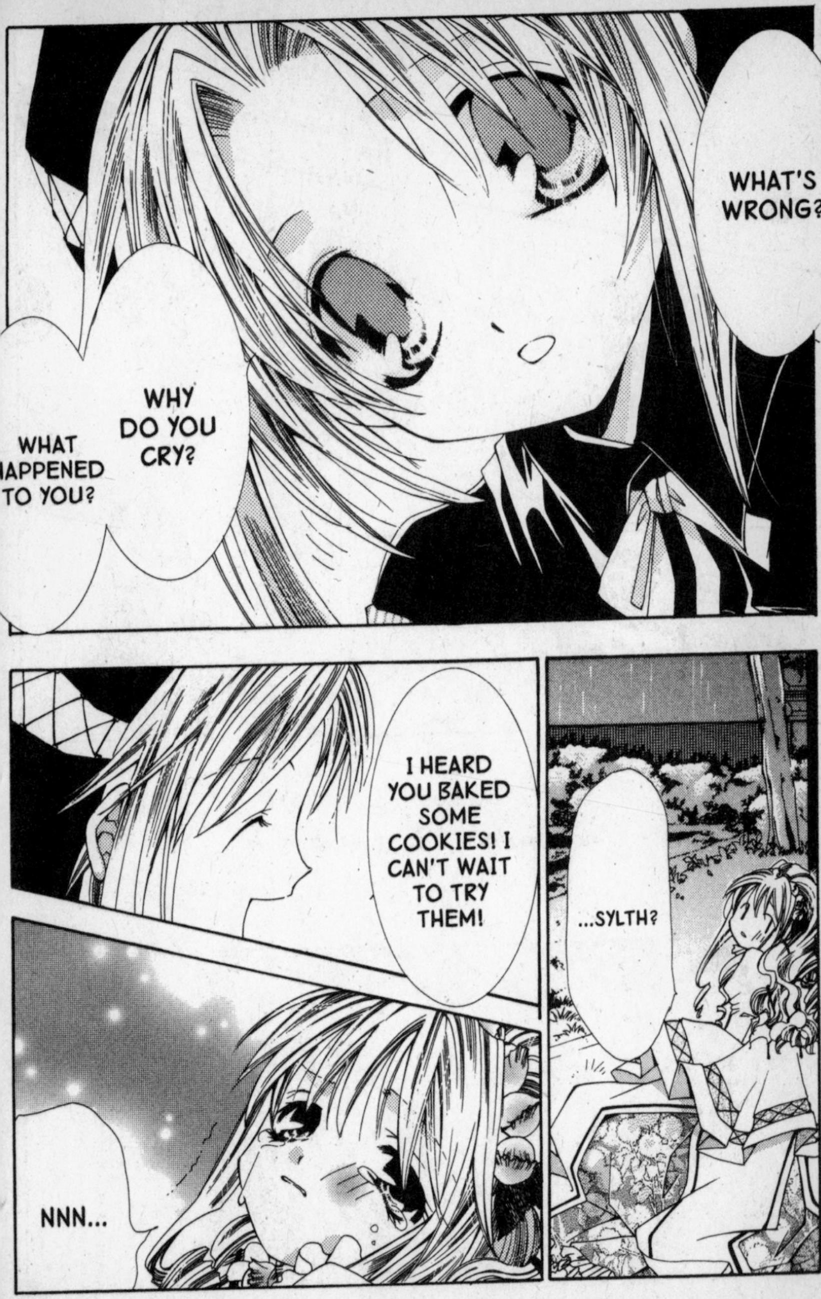
WHAT'S WRONG?
WHY DO YOU CRY?
WHAT APPENED TO YOU?
...SYLTH?
I HEARD YOU BAKED SOME COOKIES! I CAN'T WAIT TO TRY THEM!
NNN...

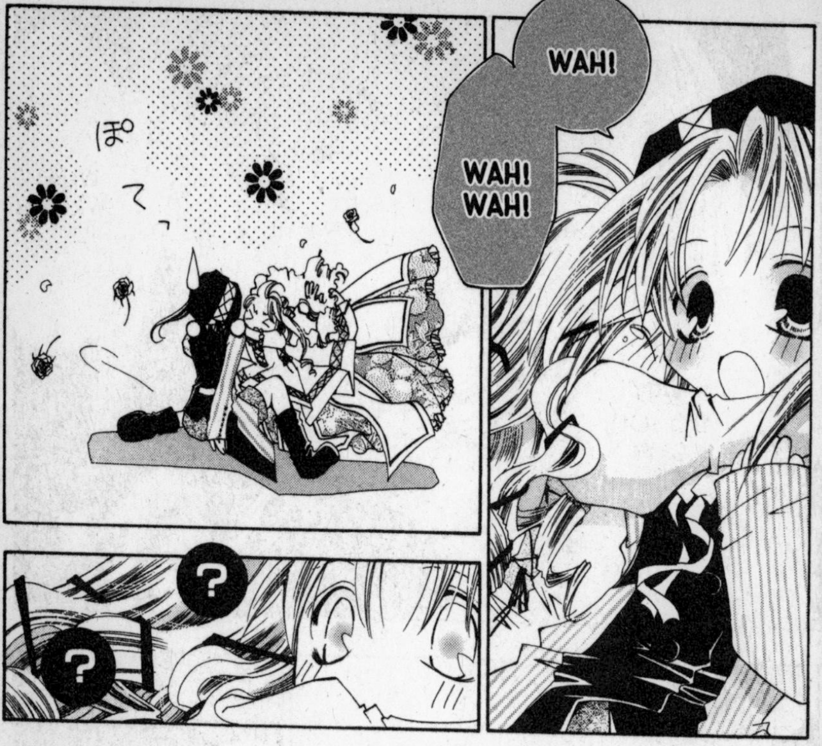
WAH!
WAH! WAH!
ぽてっ
?
?

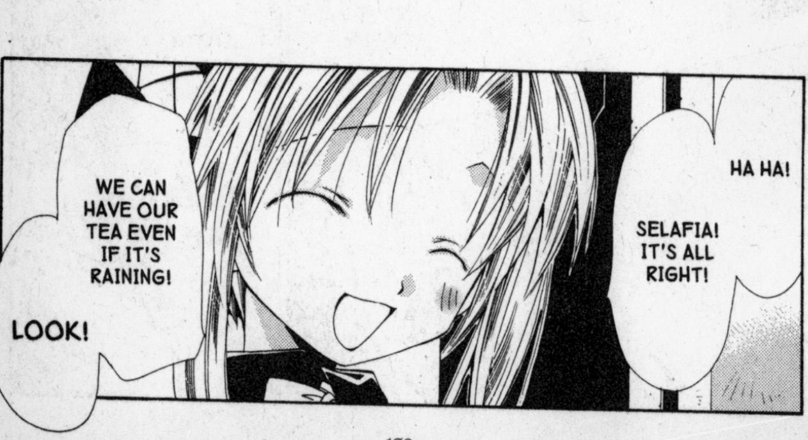
HA HA!
SELAFIA! IT'S ALL RIGHT!
WE CAN HAVE OUR TEA EVEN IF IT'S RAINING!
LOOK!

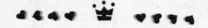

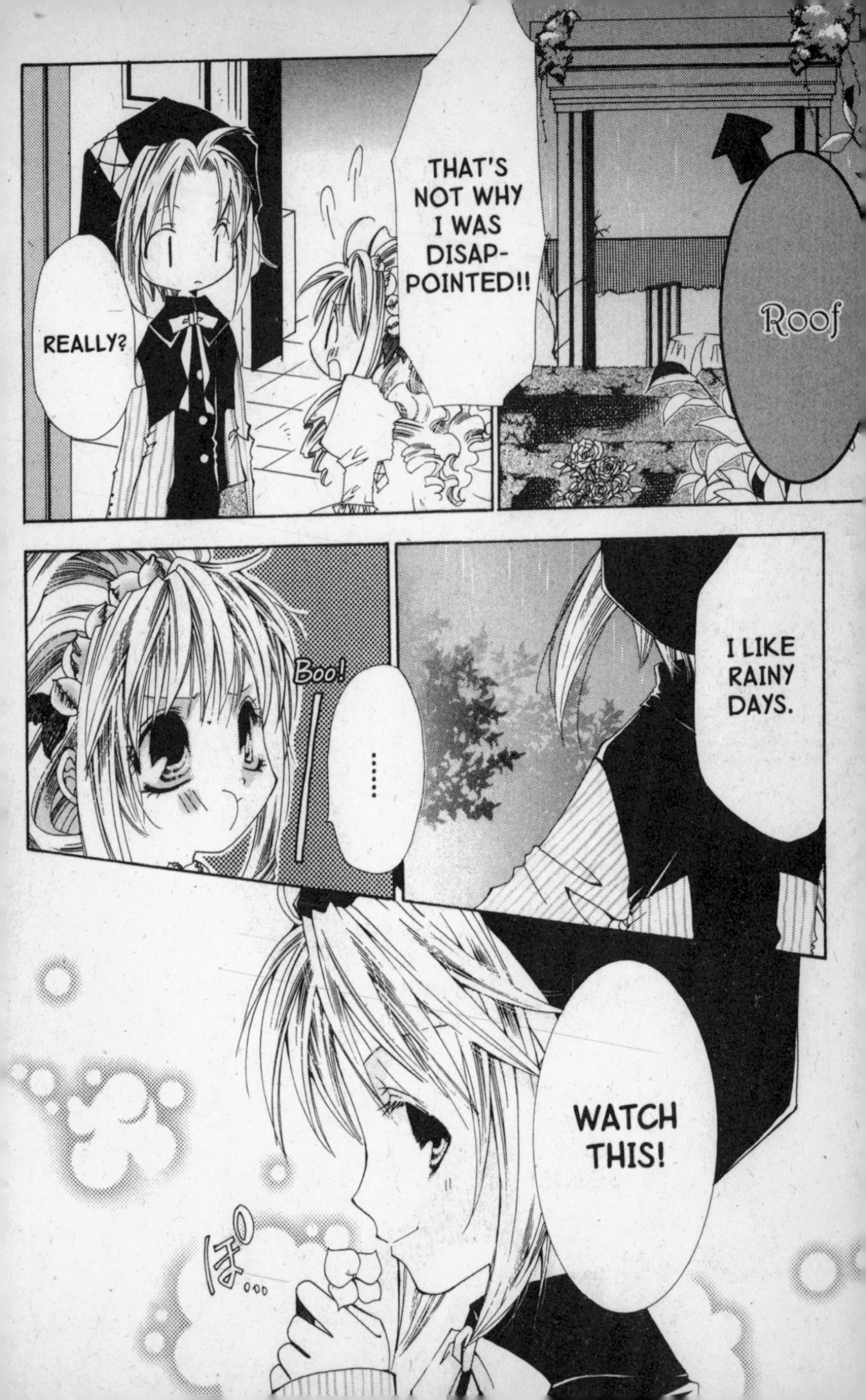
Roof
THAT'S NOT WHY I WAS DISAP- POINTED!!
REALLY?
I LIKE RAINY DAYS.
Boo!
......
WATCH THIS!

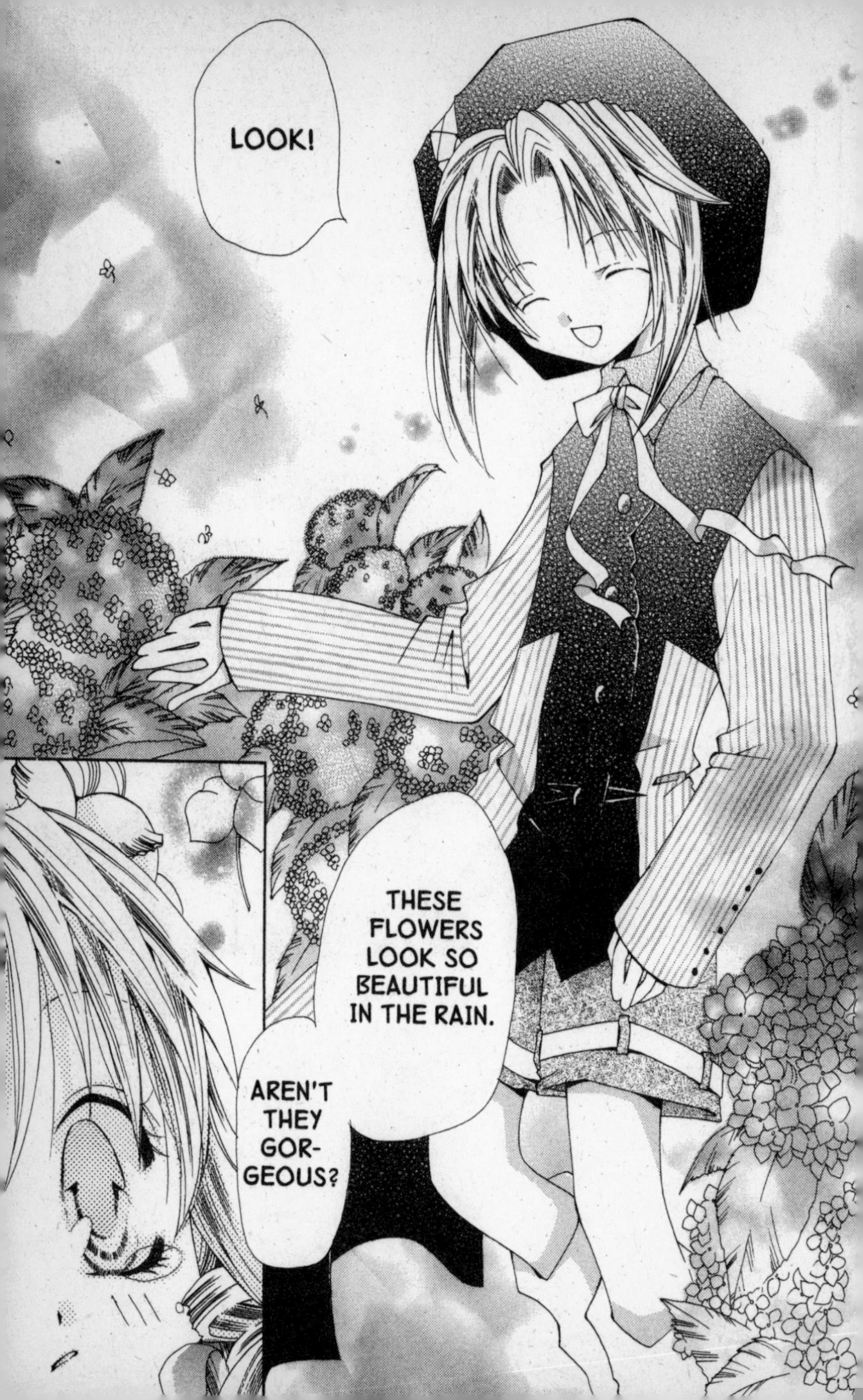
LOOK!
THESE FLOWERS LOOK SO BEAUTIFUL IN THE RAIN.
AREN'T THEY GOR-GEOUS?

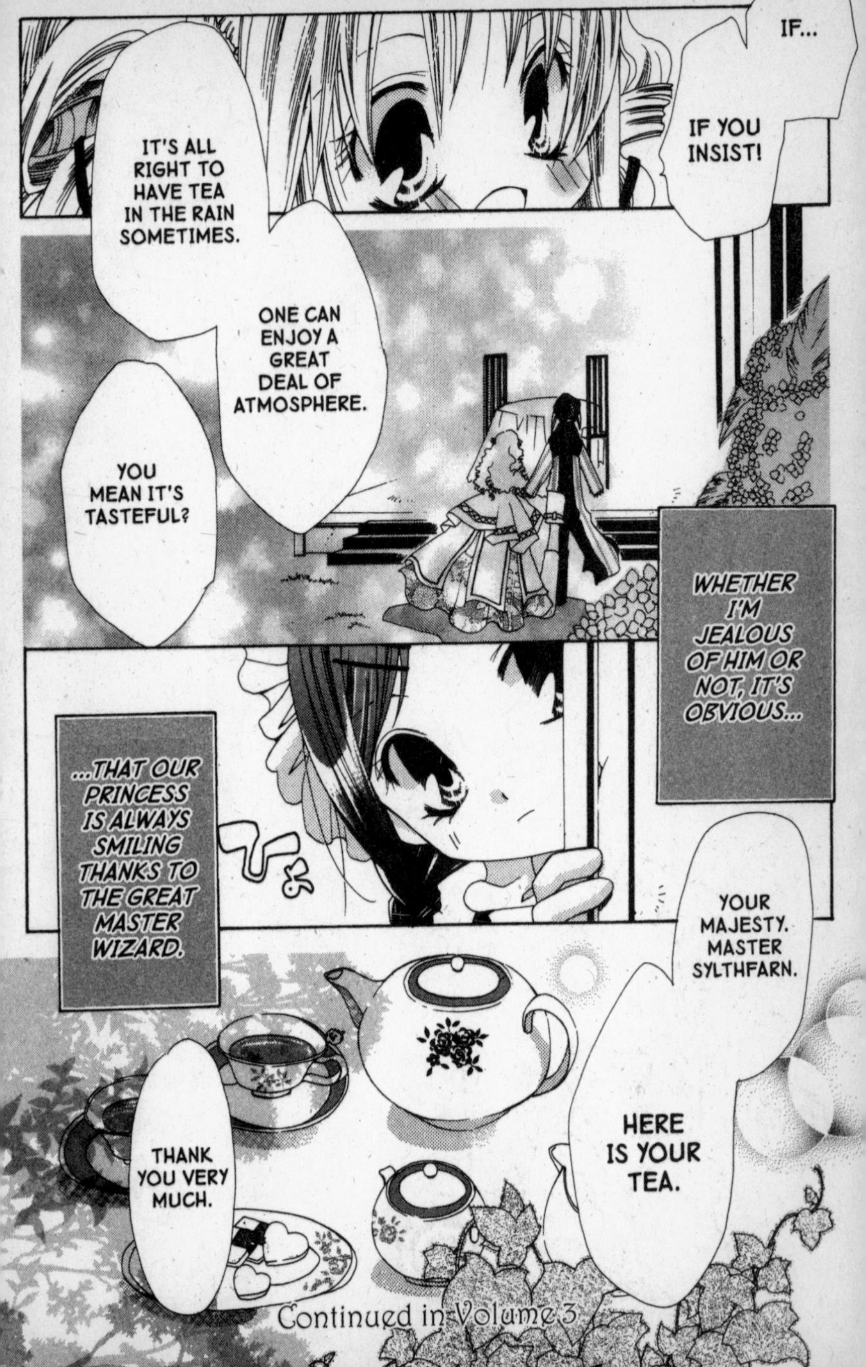
IF...
IF YOU INSIST!
IT'S ALL RIGHT TO HAVE TEA IN THE RAIN SOMETIMES.
WHETHER I'M JEALOUS OF HIM OR NOT, IT'S OBVIOUS...
ONE CAN ENJOY A GREAT DEAL OF ATMOSPHERE.
YOU MEAN IT'S TASTEFUL?
...THAT OUR PRINCESS IS ALWAYS SMILING THANKS TO THE GREAT MASTER WIZARD.
YOUR MAJESTY. MASTER SYLTHFARN.
HERE IS YOUR TEA.
THANK YOU VERY MUCH.
Continued in Volume 3

ほ

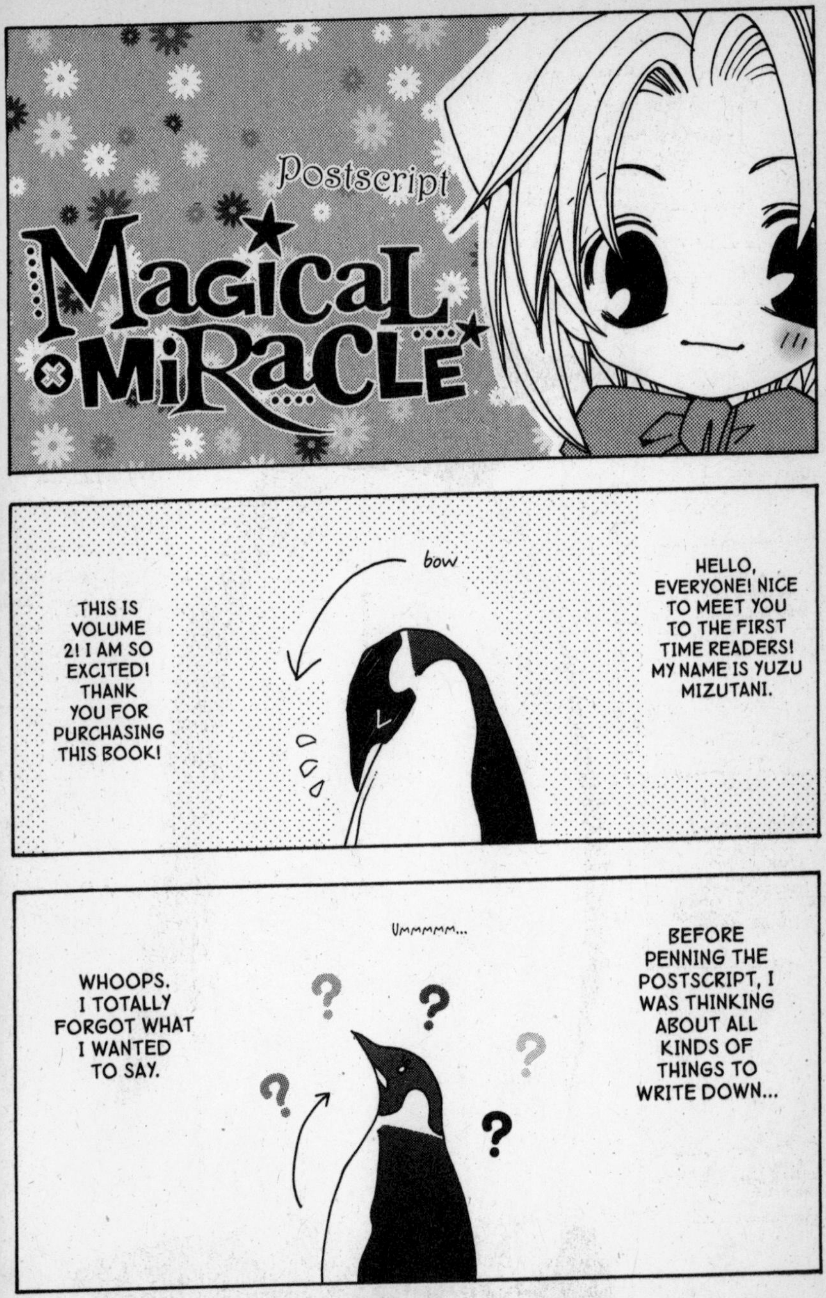
Postscript
MAGICAL MIRACLE
HELLO, EVERYONE! NICE TO MEET YOU TO THE FIRST TIME READERS! MY NAME IS YUZU MIZUTANI.
bow
THIS IS VOLUME 2! I AM SO EXCITED! THANK YOU FOR PURCHASING THIS BOOK!
BEFORE PENNING THE POSTSCRIPT, I WAS THINKING ABOUT ALL KINDS OF THINGS TO WRITE DOWN...
Ummmmm...
WHOOPS. I TOTALLY FORGOT WHAT I WANTED TO SAY.

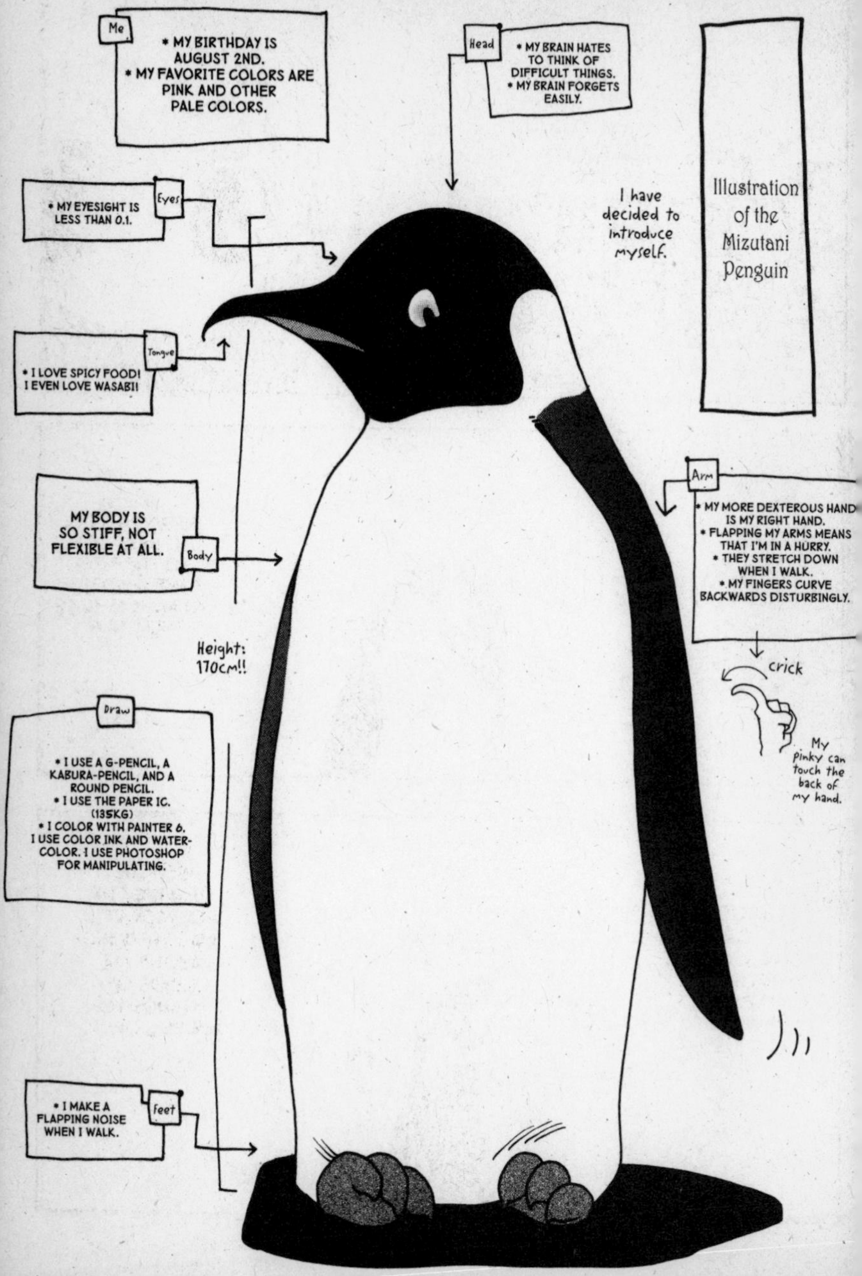

Illustration of the Mizutani Penguin
I have decided to introduce myself.
Head
* MY BRAIN HATES TO THINK OF DIFFICULT THINGS.
* MY BRAIN FORGETS EASILY.
Me
* MY BIRTHDAY IS AUGUST 2ND.
* MY FAVORITE COLORS ARE PINK AND OTHER PALE COLORS.
Eyes
* MY EYESIGHT IS LESS THAN 0.1.
Tongue
* I LOVE SPICY FOOD! I EVEN LOVE WASABI!
Arm
* MY MORE DEXTEROUS HAND IS MY RIGHT HAND.
* FLAPPING MY ARMS MEANS THAT I'M IN A HURRY.
* THEY STRETCH DOWN WHEN I WALK.
* MY FINGERS CURVE BACKWARDS DISTURBINGLY.
crick
My pinky can touch the back of my hand.
Body
MY BODY IS SO STIFF, NOT FLEXIBLE AT ALL.
Height: 170CM!!
Draw
* I USE A G-PENCIL, A KABURA-PENCIL, AND A ROUND PENCIL.
* I USE THE PAPER IC. (135KG)
* I COLOR WITH PAINTER 6. I USE COLOR INK AND WATER-COLOR. I USE PHOTOSHOP FOR MANIPULATING.
Feet
* I MAKE A FLAPPING NOISE WHEN I WALK.

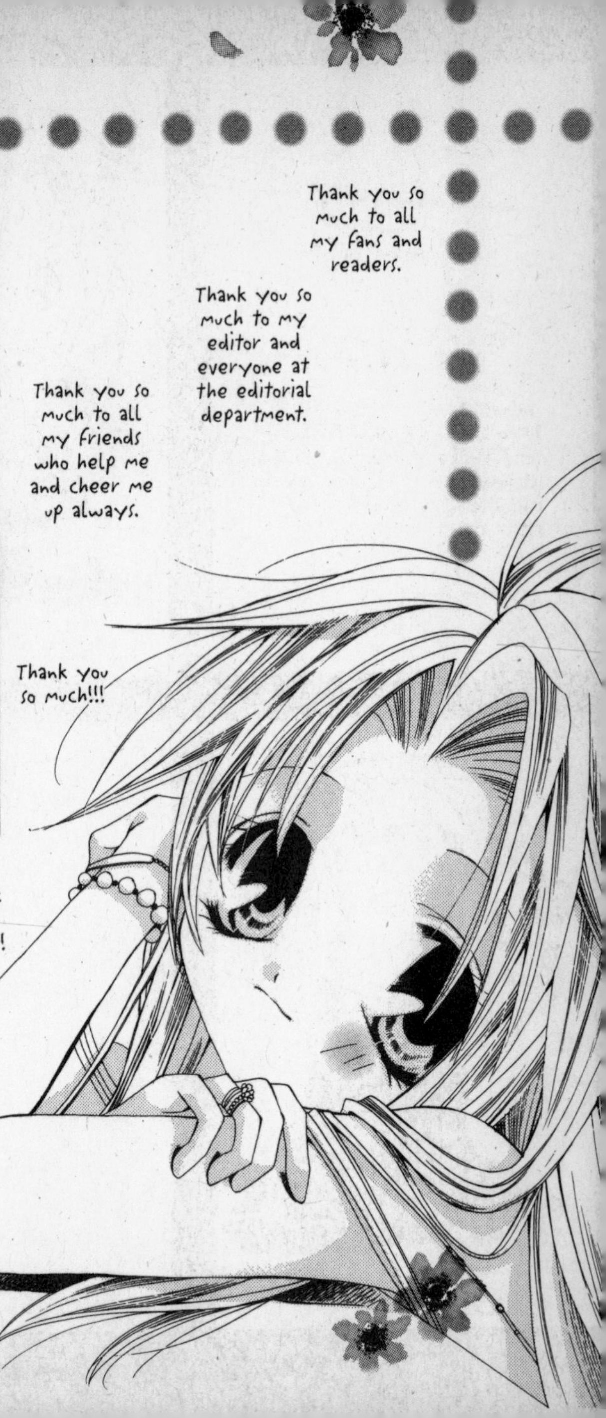
Thank you so much to all my fans and readers.
Thank you so much to my editor and everyone at the editorial department.
Thank you so much to all my friends who help me and cheer me up always.
Thank you so much!!!
I'll work hard! Seriously!

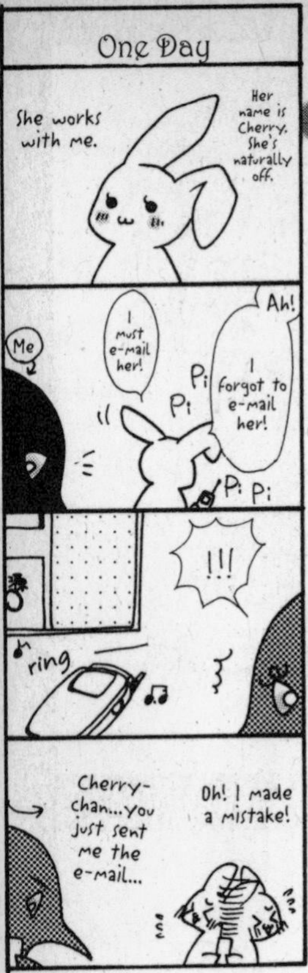
One Day
Her name is Cherry. She's naturally off.
She works with me.
Ah!
I forgot to e-mail her!
Pi Pi
I must e-mail her!
Me
Pi Pi
!!!
ring
Oh! I made a mistake!
Cherry-chan...you just sent me the e-mail...
This happens almost everyday.

I'll be glad to receive
any questions or ♡
opinions about
my work!

Please send a letter
to this address. ↓

160-0022
2-15-26 Shinjuku Shinjuku-ku,
Tokyo, Daisanntamaya Building 8F
Ichjinsha, Inc. Comic Zero Sum
Editorial department
Attn: Yuzu Mizutani

This is my website.

http://mizyuz.cool.ne.jp
"Moon Phobia"

Thank you so much,
everyone! ♡

Yuzu Mizutani

MAGICAL×MIRACLE

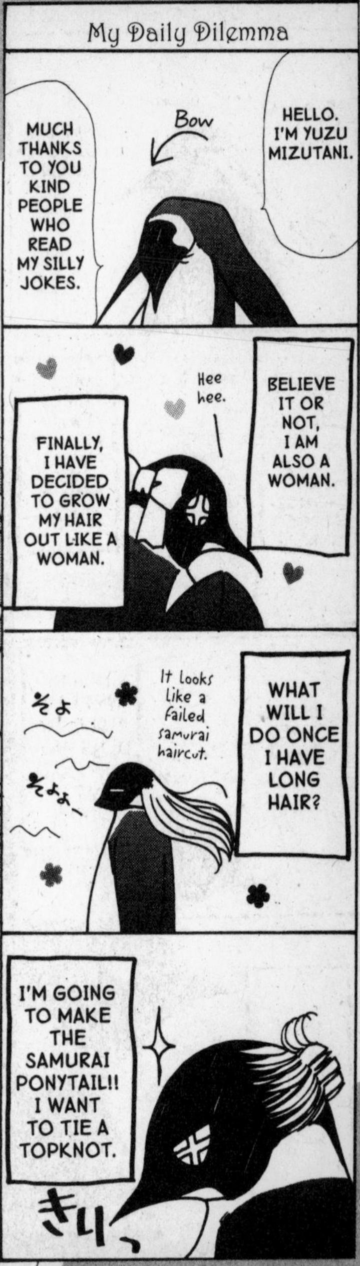

My Daily Dilemma
HELLO. I'M YUZU MIZUTANI.
Bow
MUCH THANKS TO YOU KIND PEOPLE WHO READ MY SILLY JOKES.
BELIEVE IT OR NOT, I AM ALSO A WOMAN.
Hee hee.
FINALLY, I HAVE DECIDED TO GROW MY HAIR OUT LIKE A WOMAN.
WHAT WILL I DO ONCE I HAVE LONG HAIR?
It looks like a failed samurai haircut.
そよ
そよそよ～
I'M GOING TO MAKE THE SAMURAI PONYTAIL!! I WANT TO TIE A TOPKNOT.
きりっ

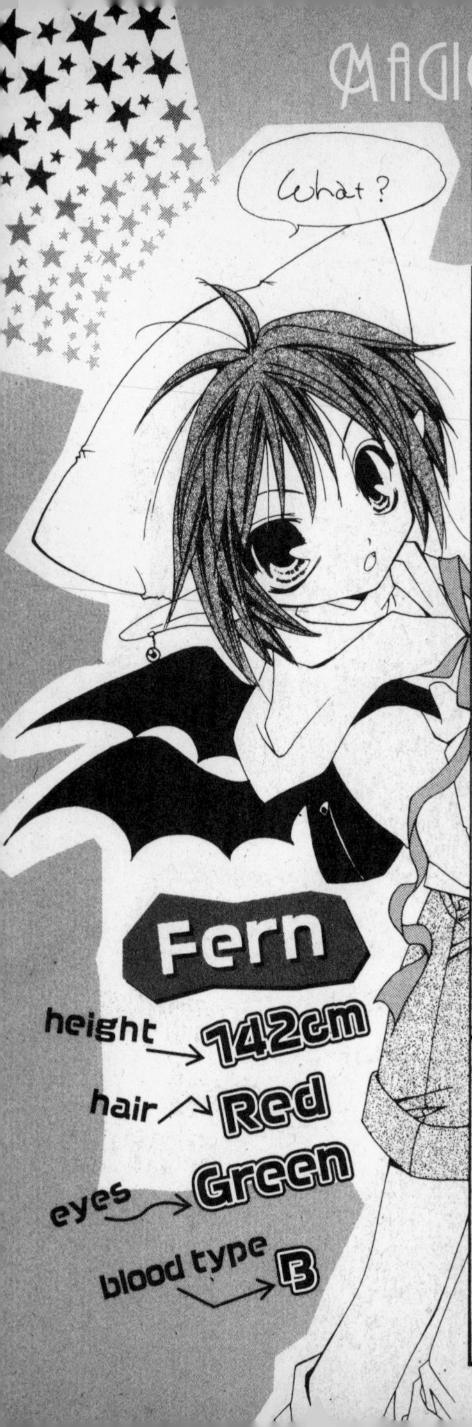

What?
Fern
height 142cm
hair Red
eyes Green
blood type B

YUZU MIZUTANI

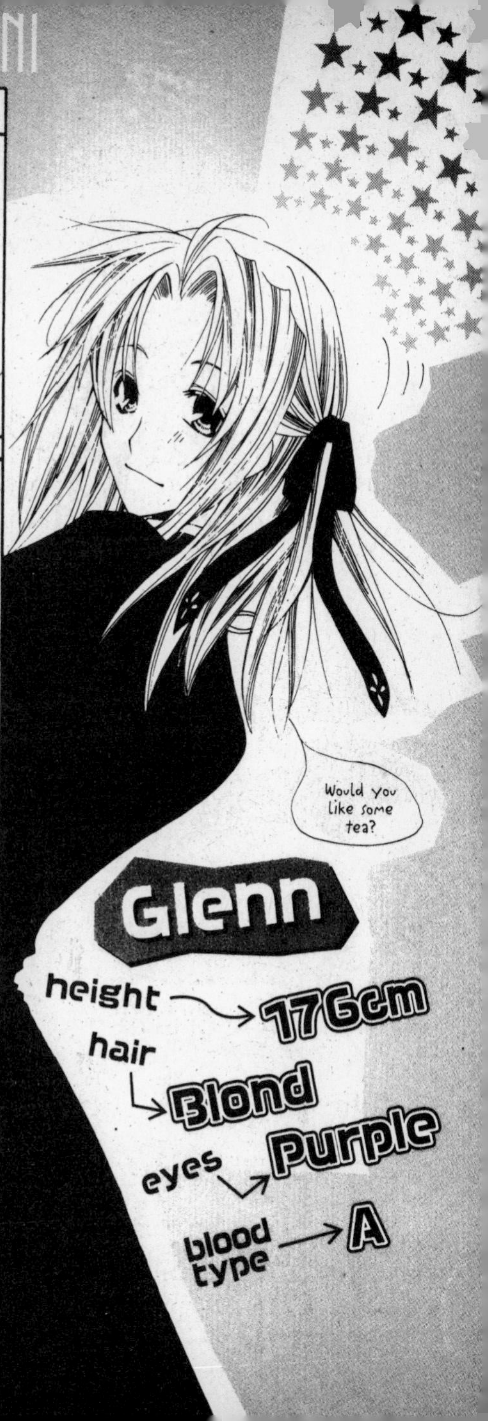
Would you like some tea?
Glenn
height → 176cm
hair → Blond
eyes → Purple
blood type → A

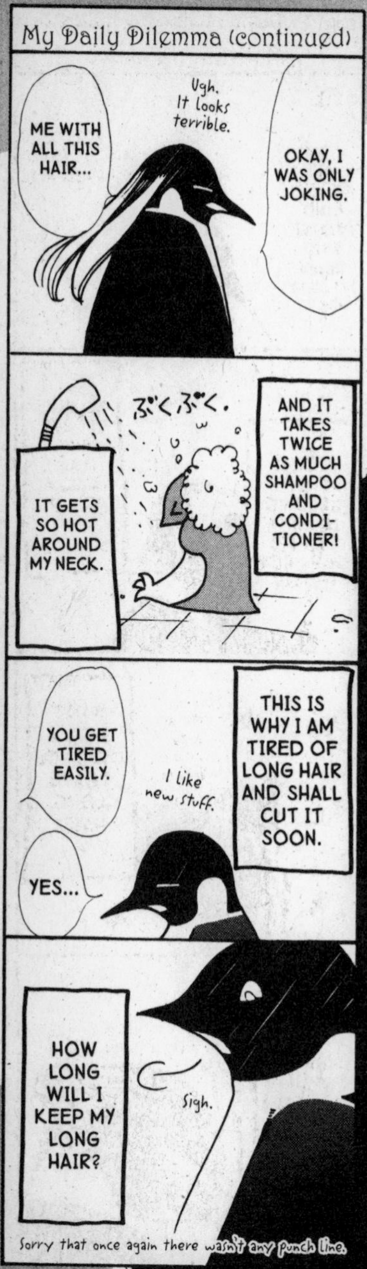
My Daily Dilemma (continued)
OKAY, I WAS ONLY JOKING.
Ugh. It looks terrible.
ME WITH ALL THIS HAIR...
AND IT TAKES TWICE AS MUCH SHAMPOO AND CONDITIONER!
ぷくぷく。
IT GETS SO HOT AROUND MY NECK.
THIS IS WHY I AM TIRED OF LONG HAIR AND SHALL CUT IT SOON.
I like new stuff.
YOU GET TIRED EASILY.
YES...
Sigh.
HOW LONG WILL I KEEP MY LONG HAIR?
Sorry that once again there wasn't any punch line.

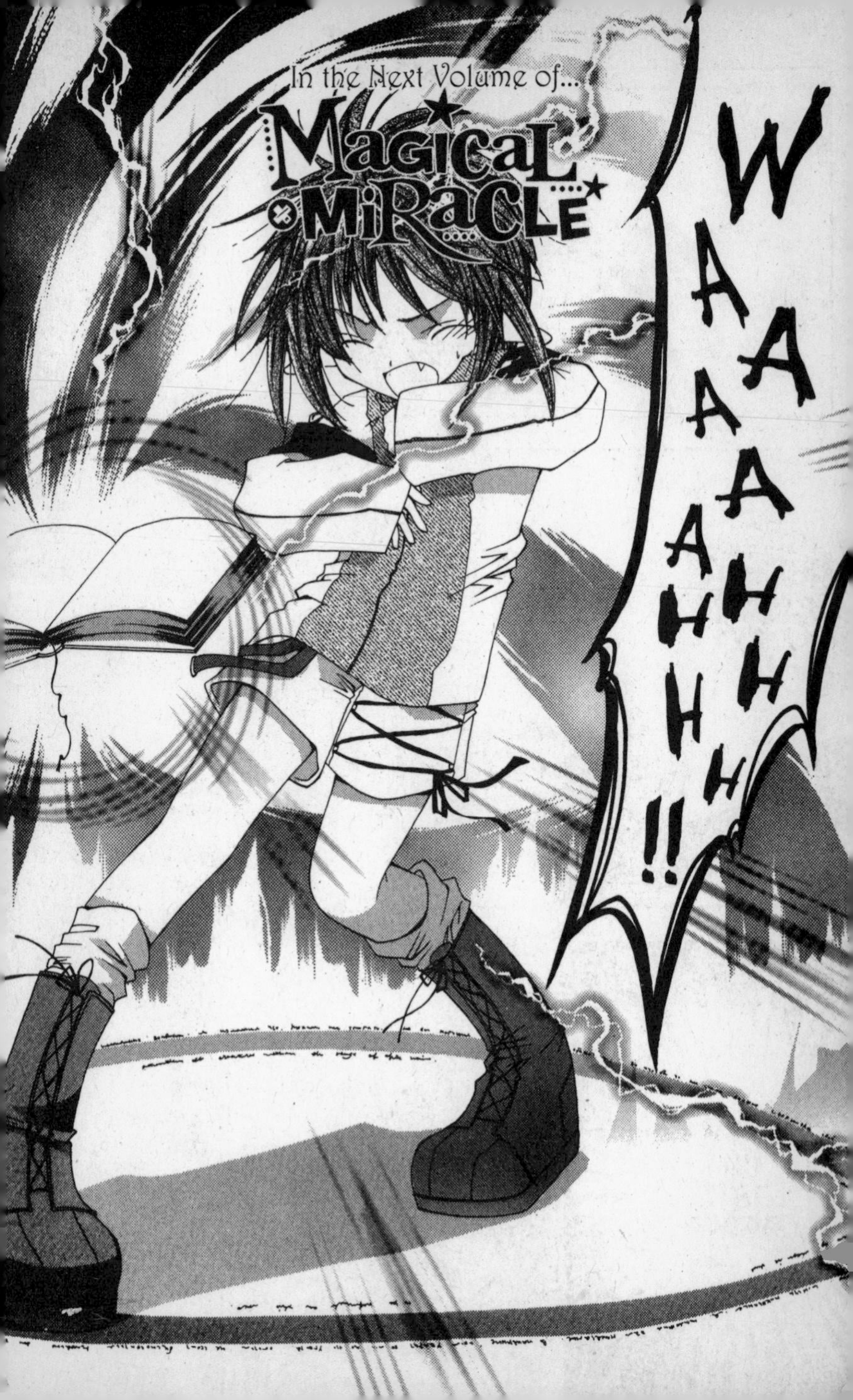
In the Next Volume of...
Magical Miracle
WAAAAAHHHHHHH!!

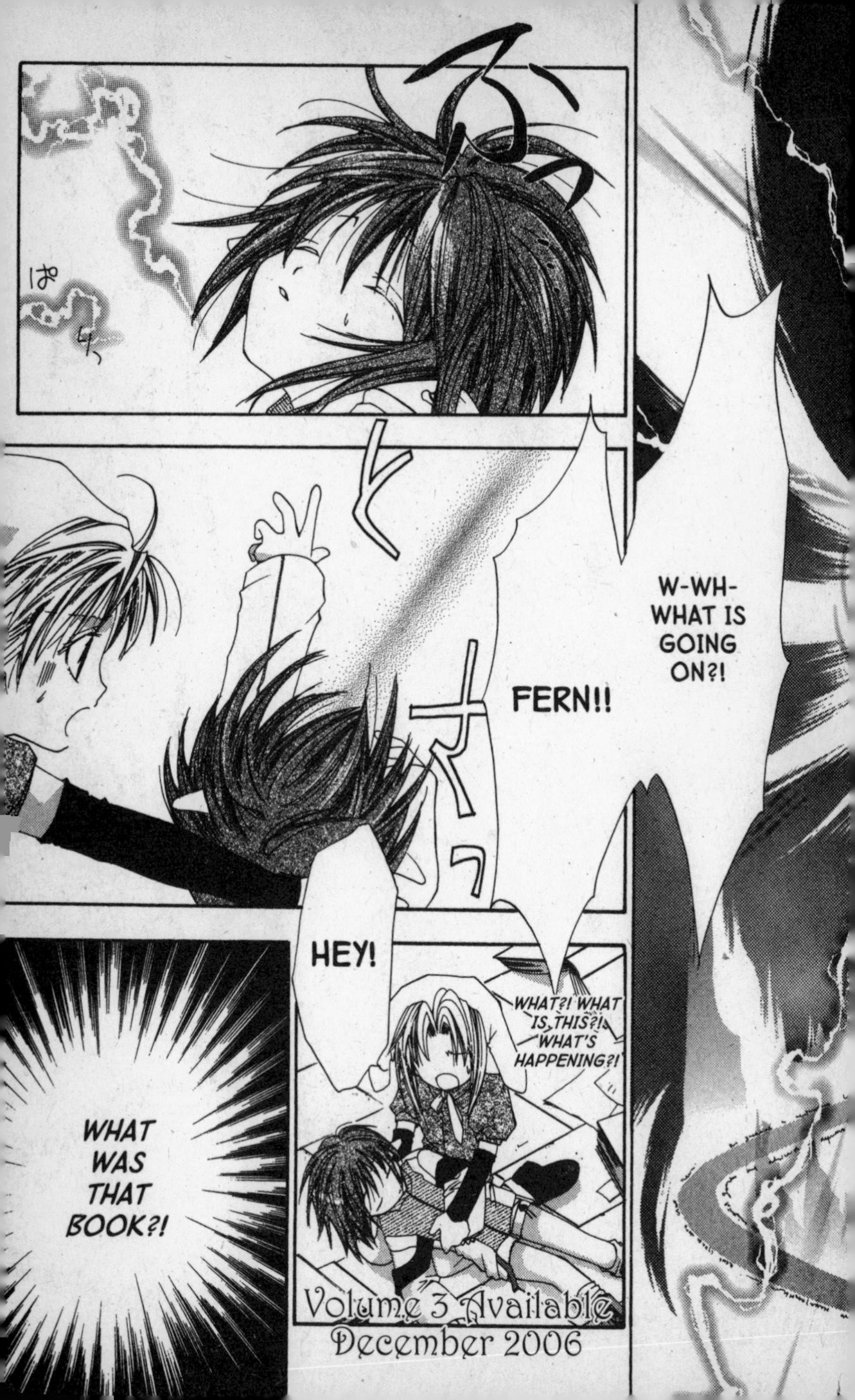
W-WH- WHAT IS GOING ON?!
FERN!!
HEY!
WHAT?! WHAT IS THIS?! WHAT'S HAPPENING?!
WHAT WAS THAT BOOK?!
Volume 3 Available December 2006

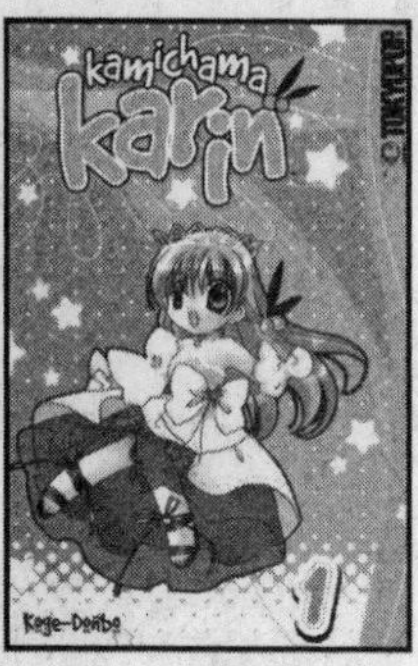
kamichama
karin
Koge-Donbo
1
TOKYOPOP

ROMANCE

Y YOUTH AGE 10+

KAMICHAMA KARIN

BY KOGE-DONBO

This one was a surprise. I mean, I knew Koge-Donbo drew insanely cute characters, but I had no idea a magical girl story could be so darn clever. *Kamichama Karin* manages to lampoon everything about the genre, from plushie-like mascots to character archetypes to weapons that appear from the blue! And you gotta love Karin, the airheaded heroine who takes guff from no one and screams "I AM GOD!" as her battle cry. In short, if you are looking for a shiny new manga with a knack for hilarity and a penchant for accessories, I say look no further.

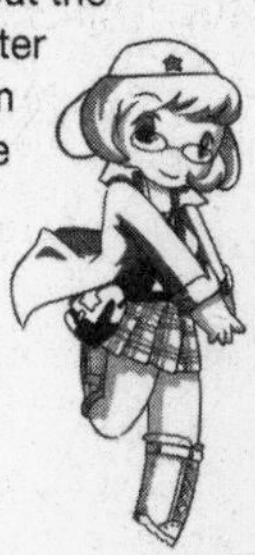

~Carol Fox, Editor

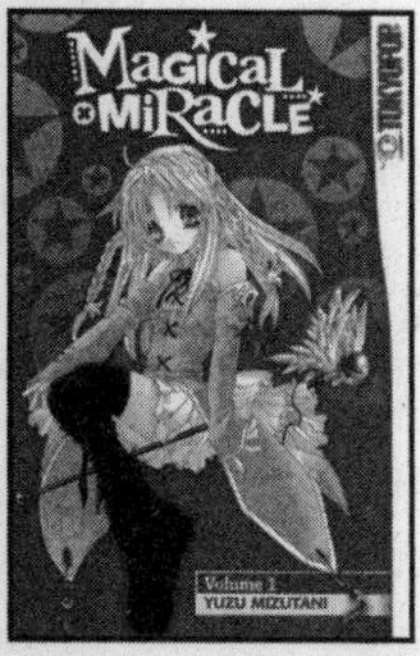
Magical
Miracle
Volume 1
YUZU MIZUTANI
TOKYOPOP

FANTASY

T TEEN AGE 13+

MAGICAL X MIRACLE

BY YUZU MIZUTANI

Magical X Miracle is a quirky—yet uplifting—tale of gender-bending mistaken identity! When a young girl must masquerade as a great wizard, she not only finds the strength to save an entire kingdom...but, ironically, she just might just find herself, too. Yuzu Mizutani's art is remarkably adorable, but it also has a dark, sophisticated edge.

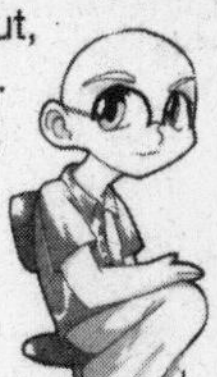

~Paul Morrissey, Editor

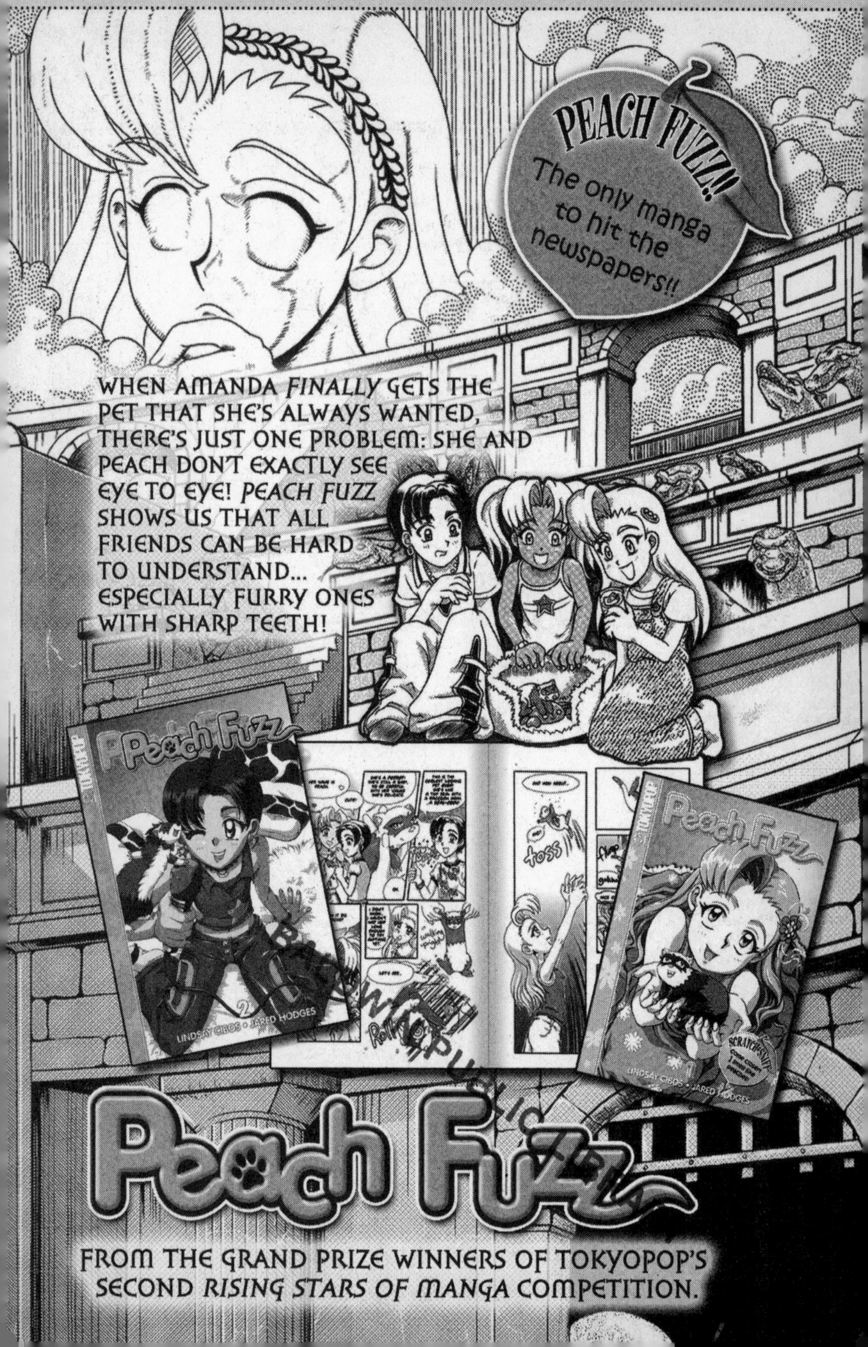
PEACH FUZZ!!
The only manga to hit the newspapers!!
WHEN AMANDA *FINALLY* GETS THE PET THAT SHE'S ALWAYS WANTED, THERE'S JUST ONE PROBLEM: SHE AND PEACH DON'T EXACTLY SEE EYE TO EYE! *PEACH FUZZ* SHOWS US THAT ALL FRIENDS CAN BE HARD TO UNDERSTAND... ESPECIALLY FURRY ONES WITH SHARP TEETH!
Peach Fuzz
LINDSAY CIBOS • JARED HODGES
toss
Peach Fuzz
LINDSAY CIBOS • JARED HODGES
Peach Fuzz
FROM THE GRAND PRIZE WINNERS OF TOKYOPOP'S SECOND *RISING STARS OF MANGA* COMPETITION.